HOLY MATTER

HOLY MATTER

CHANGING PERCEPTIONS OF THE MATERIAL WORLD IN LATE MEDIEVAL CHRISTIANITY

SARA RITCHEY

CORNELL UNIVERSITY PRESS
Ithaca and London

First published 2014 by Cornell University Press

Printed in the United States of America

Library of Congress Cataloging-in-Publication Data

Ritchey, Sara Margaret, author.
  Holy matter : changing perceptions of the material world in late medieval Christianity / Sara Ritchey.
    pages cm
  Includes bibliographical references and index.
  ISBN 978-0-8014-5253-6 (cloth : alk. paper)
  1. Nature—Religious aspects—Catholic Church—History of doctrines—Middle Ages, 600–1500. 2. Spiritual life—Christianity—History of doctrines—Middle Ages, 600–1500. 3. Natural theology—History of doctrines—Middle Ages, 600–1500. 4. Theology, Doctrinal—History—Middle Ages, 600–1500. I. Title.
  BX1795.N36R58   2014
  231.709'02—dc23   2013050341

Cornell University Press strives to use environmentally responsible suppliers and materials to the fullest extent possible in the publishing of its books. Such materials include vegetable-based, low-VOC inks and acid-free papers that are recycled, totally chlorine-free, or partly composed of nonwood fibers. For further information, visit our website at www.cornellpress.cornell.edu.

Cloth printing   10 9 8 7 6 5 4 3 2 1

Contents

Acknowledgments   *vii*

Introduction   1

1. The Mirror of Holy Virginity   24

2. *Viriditas* and *Virginitas*   55

3. Clare of Assisi and the Tree
   of Crucifixion   91

4. The Franciscan Bough   127

5. An Estranged Wilderness   159

Conclusion   196

Bibliography   *205*

Index   *227*

ACKNOWLEDGMENTS

While developing this book, I attended an annual conference on the history of medieval Catholic doctrine and practice. The thematic strain of the meeting that year was "Nature," making this conference an ideal opportunity to engage multidisciplinary approaches to the nebulous concept with which I had been grappling for some time. At the opening of the conference, all of the attendees—men and women, religious and secular, professors and graduate students—intermingled comfortably prior to the morning sessions, chattering over coffee and bagels, making introductions, renewing acquaintances. But once the panels commenced, a disturbing distinction emerged. We scattered into separate wings of the building along gendered lines. Down one hall, the majority of women attended the sessions on "spirituality," which featured female scholars and addressed medieval women's writings or women's lives. Down another, the sessions on "theology" were attended primarily by men and featured mostly male speakers who addressed the likes of Aquinas, Bonaventure, and Scotus. We were at an impasse before a single presider had introduced speakers.

During the afternoon's keynote, a mechanism of our division became apparent. In a lovely and thought-provoking lecture, our esteemed speaker addressed the subject of nature and grace in the theology of Aquinas. The audience responded eagerly, with many pressing questions that carried us well over the allotted time frame. One of those questions came from a woman involved in pastoral education. She reframed our speaker's presentation of Scholastic terminology and process through powerful images of a mother's love, asking if it might be appropriate to consider Aquinas's formulation of the relationship between nature and grace in maternal terms. "Yes," responded the speaker, to the collective relief of a fatigued audience who had struggled for the last two hours properly to grasp that tricky relationship and had finally, through this verbal picture, settled upon a stable framework. "But," he continued, "that's not theology." Next question.

That moment resonated with me. Maybe it wasn't theology. Not in the systematic sense, at least. But then what was it? I had long been conflicted about the images I repeatedly encountered in medieval monastic texts, images that I expected had something important to tell us about how women and men once comprehended God's relationship to the natural world; how, through the world's material, they achieved such intense love for and intimacy with this radical other they called God. But I stumbled over reconstructing and labeling this relationship, mixed up as it was in multiple modes of expression, blended between personal, experiential narratives and doctrinal assertions. And so I began to rethink how monastic communities committed to institutional restructuring communicated their ideas, their logic, about God's being in the world and how best to heed it.

This study began as a sustained meditation on a specific, pervasive image in medieval Christian art and prayer—trees. My fascination with nonreal trees, with arboreal metaphors and virtual forests, struck many as strange and unfashionable. Indeed it was. "Why trees?" I stumbled over responses, searched for an answer every time the question was posed: "They were everywhere in devotional literature." "They indicated spiritual filiation." "They guided the imagination from the material to the immaterial." All quite unsatisfactory, I admit. One senior scholar quipped that surely I was missing the forest. So I directed my gaze outward and retreated from the trees. I immersed myself in questions of environmentality, in object-oriented ontology, in natural theology. But the dense forest that was slowly emerging resisted this new approach and created tension in my readings. I found myself returning once more to the unrelenting presence of trees in medieval religious writing. The study that follows represents my long reckoning with them. I hope it accounts for some of the forest as well.

This book is the product of numerous conversations and friendships and many kinds of assistance—all of which have served to re-create its author. Alison Frazier and Martha Newman have been supremely generous scholars and devoted mentors to me. Together, they lit the torch that has since led my way. Alison's exquisite sensitivity to the activity of saints' cults awakened me to a whole new world for exploration and generated my first queries into premodern perceptions of materiality. Martha's command of the complex dynamic between individuals, ideals, and institutions pushed me to ground culture in community and provided me with the critical apparatus to appreciate the gendered construction of my sources. Alison and Martha each carefully read drafts of this book's various chapters, refining arguments and strengthening prose. For their continuing efforts to keep me afloat, even encouraged, in the often-anguishing business of academia I am exceedingly grateful.

At the University of Chicago, I was honored to learn from Rachel Fulton Brown, Amy Hollywood, James Ketelaar, Bernard McGinn, Lucy Pick, and William Sewell. I am grateful that Rachel supported my earliest interest in trees. My perception of Christian theology and devotion has been immensely enhanced by her instruction. Amy's questions and critiques brought a whole new level of interpretation to the texts I examine here, enabling me to think synthetically about their more poignant images and recurring themes. My experience at Chicago was enlivened by friendships with Daniel Gullo, Julian Hendrix, Anthony Perron, and the editorial crew at *Critical Inquiry*, especially Jay Williams. Thankfully, Alice Eckstein, Laura Scholl, Ellen Haskell, and Dominick Talvacchio victualed me daily, goading me to shut down the computer and connect with other humans, often in the delightful environs of our rooftop at sunset. Joshua Yumibe, in particular, endured my innumerable messes, supplied expert technical assistance, and provided a model of intellectual sophistication and serenity that I have ever admired.

I have had great fortune in the many colleagues and interlocutors who have helped me to navigate the scholar's world. For their attention, guidance, and support, I am especially grateful to Jane Chance, Bill Cook, Mary Dzon, Monica Green, Sarah McNamer, Jeff Rider, and Anna Taylor. For their kind assistance and advice on specific points in this book's images or arguments, I thank Winston Black, Gašper Cerkovnik, Glyn Coppack, Julian Luxford, Dennis Martin, Barbara Newman, Willemien Otten, and Jan Ziolkowski.

The support of the University of Louisiana at Lafayette has been critical to the completion of this project. I am grateful to the university for a research travel grant, publication subvention, and for the patience and friendship of my colleagues, especially Chad Parker, Emily Deal, Pearson and Lisa Cross, Rich Frankel, Mary Farmer-Kaiser, Robert Carriker, Arthur White, Michael Martin, and Jordan Kellman. I am extraordinarily thankful for my students, who have given my work a sense of purpose and have kept me anchored in the needs of the present. My life in southwest Louisiana has been significantly invigorated by the opportunity to work with my dear friend and feminist sage, Sarah Brabant, and with Billi Lacombe and the staff of Faith House of Acadiana.

Numerous institutions have funded research and travel without which this project would have been impossible. I thank the University of Chicago, the Mellon Foundation, the Hill Monastic Manuscript Library, the Huntington Library, the British Academy, the National Endowment for the Humanities, and the German Historical Institute. I am equally grateful to the many skilled librarians who have helped me along the way, especially those at the Joseph Regenstein Library, the British Library, the Bibliothèque Nationale de France, the Biblioteca del Sacro Convento in Assisi, the Getty Library, the Huntington Library, the Hill Monastic Manuscript Library, and the inde-fatigable staff of the interlibrary loan office at the Edith Garland Dupré Library, especially Yolanda Landry.

At Cornell University Press, Peter Potter's keen editorial care has trans-formed this book. I am enormously grateful that he saw in it a glimmer of possibility from the very beginning and that he patiently steered it through revision. At the end of that long process, Katherine Hue-Tsung Liu has been there with good cheer, greeting my anxious e-mails and phone calls. The two anonymous readers for the Press strengthened this book in countless ways, enabling me wholly to rethink its arguments and assumptions. I owe them a most sincere debt of gratitude.

In the Maraists and Ritcheys, I am grateful to have a supportive fam-ily, brimming with love and good humor. In particular, Gertrude Maraist, Kathryn and Jay Krachmer, Liz Maraist, Michael and Lori Maraist, Clare Maraist, Christine Weber, Lynne Bauersfeld, Clint Adcock, Carly Ingvalson, and William Jude Ritchey have been unceasing sources of strength, laugh-ter, and delight. Rebekah Troutman, Malisa Troutman Dorn, and John and Delores Vaughn welcomed me into their family like I was there from the start. Although Rebekah is painfully missed, her gentle attention to material need has radically altered this book, this life, indeed this world. My brother, Scot Ritchey, has my unreserved admiration. I thank him for being my most trusted adviser and best friend, and for all the crazy stories of our youth. I am grateful to my parents, Margaret Ritchey and Ronald Ritchey, for exposing us to a world of infinite possibility, for allowing us to question that world, and to revel in the questions. It would be impossible to overestimate my mother's degree of support. She is built of seemingly untapped reserves of joy and tenacity, and an unrivaled sense of adventure. I am astoundingly grateful for her love. My father—healer, painter, sailor, scholar—has believed in me. I could do nothing without that, and without his love.

This book is for John and Jack Florian, whose sustained presence sup-plies the matter and meaning of my world. Jack electrifies my days with startling energy. John is a genuine force of character, integrity, and wit, who has labored over every word of every draft of every piece of writing I have produced. But more: his love has snatched me from an anxious brink, for which I express long overdue thanks.

HOLY MATTER

Introduction

"The world and humankind became wild—
another world," beamed the voice of God to his eager pupil, Catherine of
Siena, offering her a brief symposium on the rationale and processes of the
creation and re-creation of the world.[1] In the first creation, he explained,
God fathered the heavens and the earth, ornamenting them with essential
light, water, and populace and balancing them in a harmonious providential
system. But, he continued, the sin of the first humans introduced disorder to
the whole of creation, a rebellion that passed from humans to plants and animals. The created world, then, was in need of re-creation. It was for the purpose of this second creation, God explained, that he became human, entering
material creation and subjecting himself to the suffering crucifixion:

> By sending into the world my Truth, the incarnate Word, I saw to it
> that he should take away the wildness and uproot the thorns of original
> sin. And I made it a garden watered by the blood of Christ crucified,
> and planted there the seven gifts of the Holy Spirit after rooting out

---

1. Catherine of Siena, *Il dialogo della divina provvidenza ovvero libro della divina dottrina,* ed. Giuliana Cavallini (Rome: Edizioni Cateriniane, 1968), 140, p. 387; *Catherine of Siena, The Dialogue,* trans.
Suzanne Noffke (Mahwah, NJ: Paulist Press, 1980), 288 (hereafter cited parenthetically in the text
in abbreviated form).

1

deadly sin. All this happened only after my only-begotten Son's death. (Catherine of Siena, *Il dialogo,* 140, p. 387; Noffke, 288)

Accordingly, he instructed in the candid voice of a seasoned tutor, it should be clear to Catherine and all the Christian devout, when gazing on the features of the well-ordered landscape, that it was God himself who was actively "feeding and nurturing the worm within the dry wood, pasturing the brute beasts, nourishing the fish in the sea, all the animals on the earth and the birds in the air, commanding the sun to shine on the plants and the dew to fertilize the soil" (*Il dialogo,* 141, p. 390; Noffke, 290).

Catherine's *Dialogue* reflects a perception, found at the heart of later medieval European Christian devotion, that the phenomenal world was the material matrix into which God entered when he became human via Mary, a world that he restructured and redeemed when he suffered and died on the cross.[2] The material into which God entered, that he chose to carry with him in his assumption into heaven, reasoned the progenitors of this conviction, must have been specially marked, rendering it capable of manifesting divinity. In this study I investigate medieval efforts to perceive such a potential manifestation. I examine how and why a perception of the material world as re-created emerged, and how it shaped Christian devotion in later medieval Europe as individuals and communities attempted to access God in their material surroundings.

This study, then, is my attempt to fathom the logic and language of later medieval Christianity. It is a history of ideas and of meditative teachings, a probing of the religious imagination, more than a chronicle of social practice or administrative maneuvering. As such, its purpose is not to bring to light new details documenting the rich reality of a distant social world, but to reevaluate our present understanding of that world, to offer a fresh interpretation of the details we have already amassed. Here I use the doctrine of re-creation, largely unrecognized and poorly understood by scholars, as a means to consider the complex relationships between women and men in professed religious life in the later Middle Ages, and to evaluate the gendered language and imagery of monastic instruction. At the same time, I argue for the absolutely pivotal importance of the doctrine of re-creation to the later medieval religious imagination, and demonstrate how a proper understanding of it allows us to rethink the meaning of key terms and concepts in the

---

2. On the occasions that I refer to beliefs about God by using the masculine pronoun, I am doing so in an effort to render the most appropriate medieval conceptualizations of God. On this problem of language, see Rosemary Radford Ruether, *Sexism and God-Talk: Toward a Feminist Theology* (Boston: Beacon Press, 1983).

scholarly literature of medieval Christianity, concepts like "nature," "incarnation," and "affective piety."

Such a project is necessary because, for various reasons having as much to do with our own contemporary preoccupations as with our analysis of the past, our explanations of these concepts have been insufficient and incorrect. It was neither the discovery of nature nor the creation of an eternally feminine virgin goddess of procreation nor even the invention of compassion for the suffering incarnate God that led medieval Christians to regard their phenomenal world as courier of the divine. What, then, was the cultural logic that would explain, for example, the behavior of the young Dominican nun Alheit of Trochau, who ambled about the garden of her community at Engelthal, embracing its foliage while exclaiming gleefully: "It seems to me that each tree is our lord Jesus Christ?"[3] It was the logic, I offer, of a world remade into holy matter, re-created through the incarnation of God in matter, and the promise of matter's ultimate and eternal redemption, which was accomplished by the crucifixion and resurrection of Christ. While Caroline Bynum has discussed holy matter in terms of "animated statues; bleeding hosts, walls, and images; holy dust or cloth that itself mediated further transformation," here I use the term to refer to the natural world as made holy by its re-creation in the incarnation and crucifixion.[4] In the elements of this world, God was visible, perceptible, to those trained to see and feel him.

This idea of the world remade into holy matter had major implications for the practices of Christian devotion. Later medieval Christians sought access to God by experiencing him in matter, in the phenomena of the re-created world. In their individual monastic and fraternal communities, spiritual directors designed liturgy, prayers, and images of a natural world refigured by the incarnation and crucifixion of Christ; and they offered explicit instructions for properly regarding that world. These efforts at remaking took place not only through liturgy, prayers, and images, but through artistic and architectural projects, new rules of regular life, and agricultural experiments. All were local efforts, meaning they were specific to each religious community; they were not attempts to remake the world writ large, but to remake *their* world. For this reason, the term "nature" does not properly characterize medieval perceptions of the material world. Shifting our own scholarly evaluation

---

3. Karl Schröder, ed., *Der Nonne von Engelthal Büchlein von der Genaden Überlast* (Tübingen: Litterarischer Verein, 1871), 14: "Da ist mir reht sam ieder baum unser herre Jesus Christi sei."

4. Bynum does not explicitly define "holy matter." I limit my use of the term "holy matter" to natural phenomena—grass, trees, fruit, flowers, bodies—that were believed to be re-created, and thus capable of mediating divine presence. See Caroline Walker Bynum, *Christian Materiality: An Essay on Religion in Late Medieval Europe* (New York: Zone Books, 2011), 20–21.

to accommodate the senses of creation and re-creation will help us better understand medieval concepts of the material world as they relate to evolving ideas of devotion in the later Middle Ages.

Natura and *Recreatura:* Medieval and Modern Approaches

As surprising as it may seem, nature has very little presence in the pious expressions of the later Middle Ages. Nature was not a religious concern, and for this reason one tends not to find appeals to nature in prayers, liturgy, or treatises on spiritual formation.

And yet, nature matters to this study because it is only by reference to our current, twenty-first-century web of concepts and confusions about nature and the natural that we can grasp the significance, for the twelfth century and beyond, of a re-created world. Marie-Dominique Chenu rightly sensed a grand, holistic scheme of salvation in the material concerns of twelfth-century poets and theologians such as William of Conches, Bernard Silvestris, and Alan of Lille.[5] He detected a profound, changing perception of the material world, an emerging concern with its status vis-à-vis the divine. The capitals at Reims cathedral, the bridge at Avignon, the florid language of canonical reform, the poetic lament of a procreative virgin goddess—each of these cultural expressions indeed signaled a discovery, or rather a sighting. They were gestures of desire, of a need for assurance about the place of the material world in the grand scheme of redemption. They signal an anxiety, and a simultaneous hope, about the possibility of accessing God in the material of the world. But they were formulated, expressed, felt, not as the fleeting semidivine powers of a cosmic force, "Nature," but as fragmented, local objects of a divinely created world that was re-created for their reassembly and redemption.

To people living in the twelfth century, therefore, the foremost meaning of the word "nature" was distinctly immaterial, and yet we have sought to fathom the material experience of the medieval world by weighing significations of this term. Natura, for example, has for many decades been an object of literary investigation as the allegorical trope that often appears in twelfth-century poetics.[6] More recently, however, literary scholars attuned to current interest in the body and sexuality have looked to nature's role as a guardian

---

5. M.-D. Chenu, "Nature and Man—The Renaissance of the Twelfth Century," in *Nature, Man, and Society in the Twelfth Century: Essays on New Theological Perspectives in the Latin West,* ed. and trans. Jerome Taylor and Lester Little (Chicago: University of Chicago Press, 1968), 1–48.

6. On Natura in twelfth-century poetry, see George Economou, *The Goddess Natura in Medieval Literature* (1972; repr., Notre Dame, IN: University of Notre Dame Press, 2002); and Brian Stock,

of heteronormativity, composing a model of sexual conduct applicable to all good Christians and against which one might easily identify the proclivities of heathen and heretic alike.[7] In related investigations of medieval medical theories and practices, scholars have sought to demonstrate medieval correlations between nature and female reproductive anatomy, and corresponding expectations for gender performance.[8] Students of scholastic philosophy and natural law have examined how theologians employed precepts from natural observation in order to establish a taxonomy and hierarchy of human and animal activity and productivity.[9] And medievalists working under the banner of ecocriticism have sought to examine all manner of individual flora and fauna as exemplifications of nature.[10] Hence, the editors of one ecocritically inspired volume aim to investigate nature by way of an examination of animal husbandry, agriculture, medicine, patterns of human settlement, among other seemingly unrelated activities, while at the same time professing that, "in spite of the ubiquity of nature's continual presence in the physical surroundings and the artistic and literary cultures of these periods, overt discussion of nature is hard to find."[11] Precisely. So what, exactly, are we looking for in our efforts to uncover nature by way of these categories?

Everything, apparently. Much of the scholarship on medieval concepts of nature tends to explain it as an all-encompassing force over humanity that, while exclusive of humanity, nevertheless holds dramatic sway over behaviors and psyches. For example, George Economou asserts that nature in the Middle Ages

---

Myth and Science in the Twelfth Century: A Study of Bernard Silvester (Princeton, NJ: Princeton University Press, 1972).

7. On the carnal regulations of nature, see Helmut Puff, "Nature on Trial: Acts 'Against Nature' in the Law Courts of Early Modern Germany and Switzerland," in *The Moral Authority of Nature,* ed. Lorraine Daston and Fernando Vidal (Chicago: University of Chicago Press, 2004), 232–53.

8. Katherine Park, "Dissecting the Female Body: From Women's Secrets to the Secrets of Nature," in *Attending to Early Modern Women,* ed. Adele Seeff and Jane Donawerth (Newark: University of Delaware Press; London/Toronto: Associated University Presses, 2000), 29–47.

9. Joan Cadden, "Trouble in the Earthly Paradise: The Regime of Nature in Late Medieval Christian Culture," in Daston and Vidal, *The Moral Authority of Nature,* 207–31.

10. See Gillian Rudd, *Greenery: Ecocritical Readings of Late Medieval English Literature* (Manchester: Manchester University Press, 2007); Alfred Siewers, *Strange Beauty: Ecocritical Approaches to Early Medieval Landscape* (New York: Palgrave, 2009). Ellen F. Arnold surveys five hundred years of legal and hagiographic documents from the monastic community of Stavelot-Malmedy, performing an "environmental exegesis" through which she seeks the "traces of nature" in every mention of a forest, tree, or flower. See Arnold, *Negotiating the Landscape: Environment and Monastic Identity in the Medieval Ardennes* (Philadelphia: University of Pennsylvania Press, 2013).

11. Lisa Kiser and Barbara Hanawalt, eds., *Engaging with Nature: Essays on the Natural World in Medieval and Early Modern Europe* (Notre Dame, IN: University of Notre Dame Press, 2008), 2.

could stand for the general order of all creation as a single, harmonious whole, whose study might lead to an understanding of the model on which this created world is formed. It could stand for the Platonic intermediary between the intelligible and material worlds; or for the divinely ordained power that presides over the continuity and preservation of whatever lives in the sublunary world; or for a creative principle directly subordinated to the mind and will of God.[12]

Here, nature hovers ethereally throughout the world, and yet is immaterial, nowhere *in* the world. An all-encompassing perspective of nature such as this one conveys the sense that individuals truly organized their lives, their loves, their communities, according to a distinct impression of a universal and abstract nature that clearly informed human normativity. In the words of Hugh White, "How people conceive of Nature is intimately and ineluctably bound up with their opinions on all sorts of important matters—on the existential predicament of human beings, on the possibilities for moral behavior, on God. If we are wrong about what people think about Nature, we will be hopelessly wrong about what they think—and feel—full stop."[13]

Perhaps. And yet the authors discussed in the present study make it resoundingly clear that any concept of an abstract, holistic nature was seldom an abiding daily concern or anxiety. If nature's great importance truly derived from its capacity to assuage "a deep longing for a reconciliation" of polarities such as matter and spirit, carnality and divinity, earth and heaven, then surely we would find it in places of prayer, in liturgy, in devotion; we would find it in the media through which later medieval Christians sought to allay their anxieties about such matters. But it is not found there. Rather than a conscientious regard for general, abstract nature, what the later medieval texts express is a concern for the local, for the immediate context, for the individual community and its capacity to remake itself in the image of its creator. It was a concern to establish correspondence, a relationship of creator to creation. While scholars have been focused on a totalizing concept of nature, medieval Christians themselves expressed their hopes and anxieties about reconciliation of humanity and divinity, time and eternity, through particular material forms. And they would not have recognized these particular forms as belonging to a whole abstract category, "natura," but to the redeemed material order, the *ordo recreationis*.[14] They were most concerned

---

12. Economou, *The Goddess Natura,* 2–3.

13. Hugh White, *Nature, Sex, and Goodness in the Medieval Literary Tradition* (New York: Oxford University Press, 2000), 2.

14. For the phrase *ordo recreationis,* see Albertus Magnus, *Commentarii in II Sententiarum,* in *Opera omnia,* vol. 27, ed. Stephen Borgnet (Paris: Ludovicum Vivès, 1894), Dist. Xxii; art. 1, p. 373: "Ordo

with the possibilities unleashed by a world re-created to yield divine presence and, ultimately, to be materially redeemed. This study seeks to resituate our comprehension of objects and matter in later medieval devotion away from discussions of nature and into the context in which medieval Christians would have experienced, theorized, and considered them—as the problem and promise of re-creation.[15]

To understand the reframing work that I seek to accomplish, let's take a look at how material nature has quietly formed a backdrop to the most important scholarship on female devotion. Feminist scholarship has attended variously to medieval personifications of nature as organic, holistic, and divine feminine abundance and to the simultaneous construction of an often misogynistic and totalizing dichotomy pitting blunt nature against human-cultivated art, rhetoric, and learning.[16] So, for example, Caroline Bynum's splendid *Holy Feast and Holy Fast* established a paradigm for interpreting later medieval female devotion by suggesting that women creatively seized on their own cultural association with an underappreciated nature and its base, material, bodily elements, vehemently opposed to culture, soul, and divine wisdom, in order to identify their own bodies with the body of Christ.[17] In subsequent scholarly refining of this paradigm, *body*, rather than material nature, became the key category of analysis, understood as the central site for female religious experience. For example, Amy Hollywood amended Bynum's paradigm to demonstrate that, by and large, it was male hagiographers and spiritual directors who imputed a materially oriented, corporeal identification to female religious practices, describing their religious behaviors and reported experiences according to externalized, physicalist models associated with the body

---

recreationis secundum ordinem primae perditionis fuit: sed in recreatione in gloriosa Virgine prima via vitae fuit fides."

15. While I acknowledge the important work of medieval literary scholars who have incorporated actor-network perspectives in order to produce a powerful sense of materiality's agency in the Middle Ages, I assert that the resulting picture is incomplete without a reckoning of matter as potentially holy, as capable of providing access to God. Alfred Siewers succeeds in demonstrating medieval concepts of matter's receptivity to the divine in his readings of early Irish Sea narratives; see his *Strange Beauty*, 10–20. On medieval ecomaterialism, see Jeffrey Jerome Cohen, ed., *Animal, Vegetable, Mineral: Ethics and Objects* (Washington, DC: Oliphaunt Books, 2012). On actor-network theory, see Bruno Latour, *Reassembling the Social: An Introduction to Actor-Network Theory* (Oxford: Oxford University Press, 2005); and Jane Bennett, *Vibrant Matter: A Political Ecology of Things* (Durham, NC: Duke University Press, 2010).

16. Sherry Ortner, "Is Female to Male as Nature Is to Culture?," in *Woman, Culture, and Society*, ed. Michelle Rosaldo and Louise Lamphere (Stanford, CA: Stanford University Press, 1974), 67–87; Carol MacCormack, "Nature, Culture, and Gender: A Critique," in *Nature, Culture, and Gender*, ed. Carol MacCormack and Marilyn Strathern (Cambridge: Cambridge University Press, 1980), 1–24.

17. Caroline Bynum, *Holy Feast and Holy Fast: The Religious Significance of Food to Medieval Women* (Berkeley: University of California Press, 1988), 245–93.

of Christ.[18] While scholars largely heeded the nuance of Hollywood's thesis, nevertheless body remained the site for fathoming medieval religious practice, the explanatory key to women's apprehension of the divine and men's depiction of it.

Sarah McNamer, in turn, has offered a fresh interpretation of female "affective piety" as an expressive performance regulated by a new genre of meditation, one generated in women's communities, that sought to prove their worthiness as brides of Christ by means of feeling compassion for his suffering.[19] While McNamer's focus is affectivity and demonstrable compassion, it is important to recognize that her study has grown out of this scholarly focus on the body to foreground, through affectivity, empathetic response to Christ's bodily suffering. What we have, then, is a movement from nature as material to the body of Christ and its replication or commemoration in the bodies of women. The result of this scholarship is our present sense of affective piety, spurred by meditation on or imitation of Christ's suffering, as the dominant mode of devotion in the later Middle Ages. Contrary to the current academic assessment of later medieval religiosity as oriented around the suffering body of Christ and empathetic efforts to experience that suffering in praxis and prayer, I argue that the physical and embodied thrust of later medieval devotion is more appropriately explained through an imaginative theology that centered on access to God within the material of the world, a theology that posited the world's total re-creation to offer God's presence in it.[20]

Therefore, I wish to draw the focus outward once again, to place medieval concerns and conversations about materiality, of which the body is entirely a part, at the analytical center.[21] Here, I show that women were critical agents

---

18. Amy Hollywood, *The Soul as Virgin Wife: Mechtild of Magdeburg, Marguerite Porete, and Meister Eckhart* (South Bend, IN: University of Notre Dame Press, 2001).

19. Sarah McNamer, *Affective Meditation and the Invention of Medieval Compassion* (Philadelphia: University of Pennsylvania Press, 2010).

20. As Barbara Newman proposes it, the defining feature of imaginative theology is that "it 'thinks with' images, rather than propositions or scriptural texts or rarefied inner experience—though none of these need be excluded." Imaginative theology relies on metaphor, narrative, and poetry to shape a vision—the *imago dei*—that ultimately leads to the ineffable experience of the *deus*. Its very unofficial quality contributed to its toleration by religious authorities and offers an alternative, perhaps even more broadly shared, glimpse into medieval theological thinking than "a chronicle of purely professional theologians would allow." See Newman, *God and the Goddesses: Vision, Poetry, and Belief in the Middle Ages* (Philadelphia: University of Pennsylvania Press, 2003), 298–304.

21. Caroline Bynum is now engaging in this very shift. She has recognized the presence of holy matter at the center of late medieval "Christian materiality," or the Christian emphasis on God's potential manifestation in matter. While Bynum focuses largely on Christians' reverence for specific holy objects, and the Scholastic theology that questioned and sustained the orthodoxy of

promulgating the doctrine of re-creation. Rather than a singular identification with Christ's body in his passion, I show that some women's communities in the twelfth-century Rhineland regarded their work in the cloister as an act of incarnation, making matter holy by incarnating divinity in the world. The doctrine of re-creation emerged as part of a larger cultural reimagining of the value of religious place, of the religious community and its liturgical worship as a site of concentrated divine presence, making God visible, sensible. To the Christian devout explored in this study, God's act of creating the world a second time opened up the possibility that the elements could mediate divine presence. Exploring the doctrine of re-creation, we can see that attention to the body, to the natural world, to the Eucharist, as well as meditation on the life of Christ, and other affective forms of imitating Christ's suffering, were all devotions oriented to accessing God in a world that was re-created for that very purpose.

An uneasy vocabulary accompanies discussions of the place of the material, phenomenal world in later medieval Christian devotion. Attempts to label properly the phenomenal, the "natural," world exhibit a cumbersome rhetoric. The meanings that we most commonly intend when we use the word "nature" today—meanings that connote objects and creatures and landscapes, the materially real plants and animals "out there"—are quite antithetical to the meaning that the word *natura* held in the period under investigation. In the High and later Middle Ages, *natura* most often referred to an immaterial process or being, the very act of becoming and the actor, or the goddess who directed the generation of earthly material.[22] Trees, plants, mountains, animals, landscapes—these diverse phenomena would not have been collectively gathered under the term *natura*. Rather, they would have been grouped together as elements of the created world, the *ordo creationis*. The daily anxieties of medieval religious were particularly geared to the role of matter in the course of salvation history. The place of material phenomena and the ability to access Christ among them generated great anxiety, as well as great rejoicing. But to glean any information about medieval perceptions of material phenomena we cannot look to nature. Medieval texts discussing nature tell us about rather the opposite perception—that of an immaterial, abstract sense of universal order, about which there appears to have been very little daily consternation or concern. Therefore, at the very least, we should

such reverence, in this study I am interested in spiritual instruction, in guidance, for communities of religious to see the world itself, or their immediate world, as potentially God-bearing.

22. The invention of the personified goddess Natura is attributed to the poet Bernard Silvester and his 1147 *Cosmographia*.

exercise extreme caution when speaking of nature in reference to medieval experiences or perceptions of the phenomenal, material world.[23] "Nature" is wholly inadequate for describing the contemplative charms recommended by one such as Henry Suso, or the appeal of the cloister garden to the nuns of Engelthal. What Alheit was searching for in her arboreal embrace was not nature but the presence of God. Francis of Assisi did not see in worms, wolves, trees, and mountains the presence of "nature"; rather, he saw God's creation, and in it he firmly believed that he could see God.

In the chapters that follow I offer an alternative way of thinking about the so-called discovery of nature that scholars have come to associate with the twelfth century—one that I believe better reflects contemporary understandings. At its heart is the concept of re-creation—a view of the world as having been re-created by God's incarnation through the body of Mary, the mother of Jesus. This notion of re-creation would have profound implications for Christian devotion in the later Middle Ages. Indeed, it would unlock the creative imaginations of men and women fascinated by the sheer possibilities of what it meant to live in a re-created world. Vegetal sculpture, trees of Jesse, and monastic wilderness retreats, I show, belonged not to a prolonged twelfth-century conversation about nature, but to a developing imaginative theology of re-creation, an abiding concern with holy matter. Women assume an important role in this development. I argue that it was the close interactions between women and men in reformed monastic houses that inspired some of the most poetic, most potentially transforming, descriptions of the world as God-bearing. In the female cloisters of the twelfth century, new conceptions of Christ's incarnation were taking hold, conceptions that attached to the embodiment of God a whole re-making of the world, with new rules and new means of divine access; conceptions that also grew to have lives beyond the cloister, to have meaning for men as well as women.

Rather than cataloging every instance of natural profusion that I encounter in a religious text, I have chosen a series of instructional treatises, guidebooks for how to imagine and to encounter God in the world. These texts suggest that engagement in concrete reality enabled meditants to enhance their perceptions of God, not just interiorly, as Mary Carruthers has shown, but actually to see the phenomenal world, exteriorly, as manifesting God's presence. At the same time, it should be noted that because these texts are prescriptive they often engage in spiritual ideals that did not necessarily conform to social

---

23. Although I avoid using the term "nature" in this study to describe the physical world, I do often employ "natural" in a similar fashion to "material" or "created," as an adjective describing objects in the *ordo creationis,* including plants, animals, and features of the landscape.

reality. They were above all instructional, attempts to elicit a certain sacred reading of the material world, to engage the reader or auditor to enter into a sanctified relationship with it. Nevertheless, with proper caution these texts are useful for what they tell us about the motivations behind behaviors that undergirded communal life. The texts under review here worked on their readers' imaginations, shaping meditation and prayer as well as perceptions of the world and the self within it. For the most part these texts are prayers and meditations, guides intended to reconfigure the religious imagination. They include the *Speculum virginum,* Hildegard of Bingen's *Symphonia,* the letters of Clare of Assisi, Bonaventure's *Lignum vitae,* Ubertino of Casale's *Arbor vitae,* Marguerite d'Oingt's *Page of Meditations* and *Mirror,* Ludolph of Saxony's *Vita Christi,* and the *Desert of Religion.*

Whatever their specific genre, I have chosen these texts because they were meant to direct their users in how they should regard the world around them and what their specific role should be—as individuals—in constituting this world. Viewed alongside more descriptive and circumstantial evidence, these texts suggest new possibilities, new explanations, for understanding devotional behavior and institutional change in later medieval religious communities. As I will argue, what we see happening during this period is the emergence of a new way of thinking about the material world—its flowers and spices and mountains and agriculture and animals, and even its people and their God. Everything was to be understood as holy matter—matter made sacred by the world's re-creation. And, as we shall see, this new understanding was significant in inspiring a great variety of religious behaviors.

A Deep History of Natural Awe

To illustrate why this argument matters, it is important to remember the long tradition of scholarship on the so-called Renaissance of the twelfth century. One of the many innovations associated with this period of renewal and revitalization in Europe is theological: Christian theologians began to reevaluate the role and significance of the human God in salvation history, with ever-greater emphasis on the incarnation of the suffering Christ.[24] The shift has been characterized, variously, as having gently carried western European society from "epic to romance," or as having redirected Christ's

---

24. The seminal work on this shift toward the incarnated and suffering Christ is Richard Southern, *The Making of the Middle Ages* (New Haven, CT: Yale University Press, 1953); for more recent treatments, see Herbert Kessler, *Spiritual Seeing: Picturing God's Invisibility in Medieval Art* (Philadelphia: University of Pennsylvania Press, 2000); and Rachel Fulton, *From Judgment to Passion: Devotion to Christ and the Virgin Mary, 800–1200* (New York: Columbia University Press, 2005).

role "from judgment to passion." It was accompanied by dramatic changes in devotional practices focused on the affective imitation of Christ's life— his birth, his childhood, his experiences with his disciples, and of course his passion and death on the cross. Along with this came an intense devotion to Christ's human mother, the Virgin Mary, as well as the emergence of cults and miracles surrounding the Eucharist, and liturgical innovations, including the proliferation of passion drama.[25] This renewed attention to Christ's incarnation (the embodiment of God in the person of Jesus Christ) had profound implications for Christian understanding of "the incarnate" in general—all the material objects of the created world, including, but not limited to, human bodies.

Perhaps no consequence was more profound than the emergence of the doctrine of re-creation. According to the doctrine of re-creation, when God became human and entered the created world, died there and resurrected its very stuff, he actually re-made the world so that the matter of creation, tainted since the fall of Adam in the garden, could once again reflect and provide contact with the Creator. This sense of a re-created world expanded the theater of Christian devotional practice, providing those who truly grasped its significance with innumerable points of contact with the divine. The re-created world was one in which God and the promise of salvation were manifest everywhere.

Acknowledging how *religiosi* came to evaluate Christ's incarnation and crucifixion as a re-creation in the later Middle Ages allows us to rethink some of the most sensitive and sophisticated examples of monastic and clerical devotion of the period. For instance, while Christian theologians had for centuries acknowledged Christ's presence in the Eucharist, it wasn't until the Fourth Lateran Council of 1215 that the church officially adopted the doctrine of transubstantiation. It was then that Rome affirmed Christ's real, material presence at the moment of consecration on the altar, asserting that the figure was identical to the true presence that it signified.[26] *Hoc est corpus meum*: the elements—bread made from wheat, wine from grapes—really contained the substance of the body of God.

---

25. A brief sampling of scholarship charting these devotional responses to the turn to Christ's incarnation includes Sarah Beckwith, *Christ's Body: Identity, Culture, and Society in Late Medieval Writings* (New York: Routledge, 1993); Caroline Bynum, *Fragmentation and Redemption: Essays on Gender and the Human Body in Medieval Religion* (New York: Zone Books, 1991); Thomas Bestul, *Texts of the Passion: Latin Devotional Literature and Medieval Society* (Philadelphia: University of Pennsylvania Press, 1996).

26. Miri Rubin, *Corpus Christi: The Eucharist in Late Medieval Culture* (Cambridge: Cambridge University Press, 1991), 12–34. See also Bynum, *Holy Feast and Holy Fast,* 49–50.

While clerics and Schoolmen sorted out the physics and theology of Christ's presence in the bread and wine, religious communities were developing new devotional practices around the Eucharist and pondering the implications and meanings of God's presence in such earthly material. What might it mean, asked Peter the Chanter, that the substance of God could be rendered from the elements of the earth? "If we concede," he continued, "without reservation, that the body of Christ is eaten, as Augustine says, why not say absolutely that one sees God?"[27] Peter was vexed by the possibility that if God's substance was summoned through consecration, the incarnation of God bore a distinct repeatability. That is, God's substance, over and over again, was made visible, accessible, present. What might it mean that the elements of the created world acted as conveyances for, as thin veils of, the Christian God? If the hands and voices of ordained ministers of the church could at once summon God's real presence in mere bread and wine, then God's incarnation was ever in act, recapitulating itself. And if God was perpetually reentering the matter of creation, was he also continuously recreating the created world, radically revising it to make it reflect his will and image? If God might indeed be seen in the elements, then the physical senses required training in order to detect the vestiges of God's presence. These are the kinds of questions posed, the implications drawn and tested, by the authors and visionaries, meditants and artists, explored in this study.

As important as these questions were, however, the origins of the doctrine of re-creation did not begin with the Eucharist but with Mary. Writing as early as 1073, Anselm of Canterbury praised Mary for her work in bringing forth the re-creation of the world:

> All nature is created by God and God is born of Mary./ God created all things, and Mary gave birth to God./ God who made all things made himself of Mary,/ and thus he refashioned (*reficit*) everything he made./ He who was able to make all things out of nothing/ refused to remake it by force,/ but first became the Son of Mary./ God therefore is the father of the created nature, but Mary is the mother of re-created nature (*rerum recreatarum*).[28]

---

27. Édouard Dumoutet, *Corpus Domini: Aux sources de la piété eucharistique médiévale par l'abbé Édouard Dumoutet* (Paris: Beauchesne, 1942), 109–10; quoted in Bynum, *Holy Feast and Holy Fast,* 51.

28. Anselm, *Oratio* 7, 3.97–100, in *Orationes sive meditationes,* in *S. Anselmi Cantuariensis archepiscopi opera omnia,* ed. F. S. Schmitt (Edinburgh: Thomas Nelson and Sons, 1946–61), p. 22; Anselm of Canterbury, *The Prayers and Meditations of Saint Anselm, with the Proslogion,* trans. Benedicta Ward, (Harmondsworth, UK: Penguin, 1973), 120–21 (hereafter cited parenthetically in the text in abbreviated form).

All was dead, useless, and contrary to its original destiny, proclaimed Anselm's third *Prayer to St. Mary,* until she renewed the elements by making "all creatures green again" (Anselm, *Oratio* 7, 3.85, p. 21: "revirescit omnis creatura"; Ward, 120). Mary animated a regreening of the world, rebirthing through her body "heaven, stars, earth, waters, day and night" in order to show forth the Creator "to the sight of all the world" (Anselm, *Oratio* 7, 3.64, p. 20; Ward, 118). From Anselm's third prayer in her honor, Mary emerged not only as the pitiful mother who looked on with outsized compassion as her son was "bound, beaten, and hurt," but also as the mediatrix of heaven and earth, the vessel of incarnation, and the mother of the re-created world.[29]

Not surprisingly, Mary as mother of re-creation became closely associated with the liturgy of Advent, the four-week season culminating in Christmas during which the church celebrates the world's re-creation in the incarnation.[30] The sermons of Bernard of Clairvaux, Guerric of Igny, and Amadeus of Lausanne emphasized the season as a temporal remaking wherein Christ's birth reshaped time, so that the past was endlessly repeatable and accessible to the present. Advent prepared *religiosi* to read the signs of Christ's presence in the world around them, the sun, the moon, the stars, clouds, and the sea. Mary played a critical role in the Advent liturgy as agent of the cosmic changes celebrated during the season. In particular during Ember week, at the close of the Advent season, she received praise as the Theotokos as well as the branch of Isaiah (11:1–2) from whose lineage the Messiah would spring.[31]

The Advent celebration of Mary's part in re-creating the world through her facilitation of the incarnation was replayed in the Feast of Mary's Nativity (September 8). Because Mary's birth was not described in the Bible, liturgists like Fulbert of Chartres had to draw creatively on scriptural texts and apocryphal legends in order to establish her lineage and the historical events of her infancy. The liturgy for her birth emphasized Mary *paritura,* her flesh as the flesh of Christ about to bear him, her lineage as the lineage of Christ, which had been foreordained by God and foreshadowed by the prophets. In *Approbate consuetudinis,* his popular sermon for the occasion, Fulbert blended imagery from Numbers 17, which tells of the flowering rod of Aaron, with Isaiah 11, the *stirps Jesse.* The combination of these fertile natural images in the body of Mary impending Christ's birth would have powerful results in

29. Rachel Fulton, "Mary," in *Christianity in Western Europe, c. 1000–c. 1500,* ed. Miri Rubin and Walter Simons (Cambridge: Cambridge University Press, 2009), 283–96.

30. Margot Fassler, *The Virgin of Chartres: Making History through Liturgy and the Arts* (New Haven, CT: Yale University Press, 2010), 59.

31. Ibid., 61.

the development of devotional art and meditational literature. The Mary that emerged from the liturgical creativity of the eleventh and twelfth centuries was a blossoming, ripe Mary of incarnation, the vessel of God's material becoming. To complete the celebration of her birth, Mary acquired a life story, a round of miracles in Latin and the vernacular, magnificent reliquaries to house her (noncorporeal) material remains (such as the sacred tunic at Chartres, her breast milk at the Shrine of Saint Oda, her girdle at Westminster, her slipper at Soissons), and a bevy of sermons and songs that spread throughout Europe.[32] Some of the most magnificent cathedrals in all of Europe were built in her honor, and every Cistercian monastery was dedicated to Mary, the Mother of God.[33] The body of Mary provided powerful images of material generation and redemption that held attraction for both male and female communities. As images of the human work of incarnation and re-creation, they enlarged devotional spaces for pondering the divine in relation to the material earth.

At precisely the same time that Anselm was crafting prayers in honor of the Virgin Mother as the "re-newer of the elements" (Anselm, *Oratio 7*, 3.82–83, p. 21: "per quam elementa renovantur"; Ward, 119), other monastic innovators sought to emulate the work of re-creation by directing their attention to the *actual* elements, to experiments in sacred land tenure. Robert of Molesme and his disciples were said to have departed from their monastery in search of lands "for their own use," and Stephen Harding celebrated the monastic foundation at Cîteaux as part of God's ongoing work of re-creating his original creation.[34] Later Cistercian authors such as Bernard of Clairvaux, Aelred of Rievaulx, Isaac of Stella, and Gilbert of Holland extolled the natural beauty of their estates, encouraged their brothers to cultivate a relationship with the natural world, and crafted a spiritual ideal celebrating the labor of the land. Changes in monastic land tenure were cast in large part as attempts to develop a spiritual hermeneutics for interpreting God's presence in the material world. Such movements gave providential significance to the material world, claiming a role for it in salvation history. Monastic ideals commonly exalted the European "wilderness" as the appropriate

---

32. See, in general, Gabriela Signori, *Maria zwischen Kathedrale, Kloster und Welt: Hagiographische und historiographische Annäherungen an eine hochmittelalterliche Wunderpredigt* (Sigmaringen: Thorbecke, 1995).

33. Alison Binns, *Dedications of Monastic Houses in England and Wales, 1066–1216* (Woodbridge, UK: Boydell, 1989), 18–32.

34. Jean de la Croix Bouton and Jean Baptiste Van Damme, eds., *Les plus anciens textes de Cîteaux,* vol. 2 of *Cîteaux-Commentarii Cistercienses: Studia et documenta* (Achel: Abbaye Cistercienne, 1974), 78. On Stephen Harding's use of *recreare,* see Giles Constable, *The Reformation of the Twelfth Century* (Cambridge: Cambridge University Press, 1998), 143–45.

environment for imitating the work of the re-creation.[35] Reformist ideals sought to remake the wilderness of the fallen earth into a sacred image for monastic contemplation. Cistercian methods of land acquisition, for example, aspired to subvert the secular attachments of charters and aristocratic endowments, removing all customary layers of land tenure and claims.[36] Such an effort, it was believed, would remake the land, demarcating it as sacred space. Cistercians designed their labor as a conversion process, transforming the land through their own cultivation and techniques, remaking it into a physical space endowed with God's presence.[37] Other monastic reformers pursued spiritual refinement by engaging in new relationships with their landed environments. They sought to remake their spiritual selves by means of wilderness jaunts, solitary retreats into semicultivated space, through which they meditated on God's presence in the elements. Even when, as often was the case, their so-called wilderness monastic foundations, "far removed from human habitation," were cultivated by lay brothers and shared borders with a town or manor, the evocation of environmental solitude, of the imaginary wilderness, was critical to their spiritual sense of self. The template of green space—real or imagined—was key to the recommended approach to God. Thus the Carthusian Bruno of Cologne insisted that it was only by toiling in the remote wilderness that men "can acquire the eye that with its clear look wounds the divine spouse with love, and that, because of its purity, is granted the sight of God."[38] The natural world, he would claim, was re-created in order to enable the sight of God's presence within it.

The ability to see God in the natural features of the European landscape was a singularly touted quality of the emerging devotion to the human Christ as the God of re-created matter. Medieval Christians were beginning to perceive the natural world in a changed manner, resulting in a proliferating dialogue on the importance of speculation as natural discernment. Certainly the act of regarding the natural world as a mirror of the divine was

---

35. In actuality, there was scarcely a wilderness to be found in western Europe by the twelfth century. See Michael Williams, *Deforesting the Earth: From Prehistory to Global Crisis* (Chicago: University of Chicago Press, 2006), 108.

36. On the language of natural renewal in twelfth-century monastic reform, see Giles Constable, "Renewal and Reform in Religious Life," in *Renaissance and Renewal in the Twelfth Century,* ed. Robert Benson, Giles Constable, and Dana Lanham (Toronto: PIMS, 1982), 37–67, as well as Constable, *The Reformation of the Twelfth Century.* On Cistercian utopian experimentation, see Martha Newman, *The Boundaries of Charity: Cistercian Culture and Ecclesiastical Reform* (Stanford, CA: Stanford University Press, 1996). On the subject of monastic foundation legends and the re-creation of the physical environment, see Constance Berman, *The Cistercian Evolution: The Invention of a Religious Order in Twelfth-Century Europe* (Philadelphia: University of Pennsylvania Press, 2000).

37. Newman, *The Boundaries of Charity,* 95–96.

38. Bruno of Cologne, *Lettres des premiers chartreux* (Paris: Éditions du Cerf), 1:70.

not original to the High or later Middle Ages. There are scriptural origins for the principle that the created world was a book, "the book of nature," which must be read in order to see the visage and values of God. Take, for instance, Paul's insistence that God's *invisibilia* are manifested in the created world (Rom. 1:20). Theologians and exegetes in the earlier Middle Ages interpreted this passage to mean that humanity was uniquely gifted with the reflection of God's image. The soul was restored to its original image by relinquishing sin, Augustine argued, and not through natural observation. For Augustine, human intellectual perception—reason, will, memory—must be restored and refined in order to enable it to discern the reflection of the Creator in the beauty of created things. The created beauty of nature, if properly "read," might signify the Creator. But neither words nor nature could deliver the experience of God.[39] Augustine's perception of "the book of nature" was one in which the created world reflected God's beauty in signs available to the intellectual senses rather than manifesting it in the material miscellanea of creation.

By the twelfth century, however, as a result of attention to the effects of God's incarnation as a re-creation of humanity and the world, many influential theologians and spiritual directors began to see in the natural created world more than mere resemblance to the Creator. The Victorines especially began to promulgate a view of the natural world not conceived in terms of its original hexaemeral creation, but in terms of its later incarnational re-creation. God and nature were no longer inseparable, but reconciled. Vestiges of the Trinity were not located in soul or mind, but in the material world known by the senses.[40] The natural order thus came to mediate rather than merely to represent or reflect God's presence. Whereas the patristic authors were concerned to show that the book of nature reflected divinity, later medieval theologians, mystics, poets, and spiritual writers scrutinized the book of nature incarnationally, seeing it as a manifestation of divinity, as a means of access to Christ. For this reason, when searching for medieval peregrinations into natural theology, the hexaemeral literature is often quite unhelpful. It required not the original divine act of creation but of incarnation and crucifixion—that is, of re-creation—to bring together the created and uncreated orders. All that remained, then, was for the human imagination to

---

39. For Augustine's role in the transformation of the doctrine of speculation, see Jeffrey Hamburger, "Speculations on Speculation: Vision and Perception in the Theory and Practice of Mystical Devotion," in *Deutsche Mystik im abendländischen Zusammenhang: Neu erschlossene Texte, neue methodische Ansätze, neue theoretische Konzepte,* ed. Walter Haug and Wolfram Schneider-Lastin (Tübingen: Max Niemeyer Verlag, 2000), 353–408.

40. Hamburger, "Speculations on Speculation," 374.

seize on the divine significances of the material world.[41] To be sure, Scholastic theologians like Peter Lombard and Thomas Aquinas considered God's work of re-creation (*opus recreationis*) an act directed toward the human person through an infusion of grace that enhanced human discernment.[42] But in devotional expressions, what mattered most was that humans could indeed expect to perceive God in the material of the world. The world itself was part of the process of re-creation, available to human intellectual and sensual apprehension of God. The instructional literature that I examine here offered its readers able guides to such speculative endeavors and suggested to its users the myriad ways in which God's presence might be discerned among the material of their surroundings.

Why Trees?

Trees occupy a special place in this study, beyond that of other natural matter. The reason for this is that trees became in the later Middle Ages emblematic of the work of re-creation, of the changes to be expected in the natural world as a result of God's remaking it in the incarnation, crucifixion, and resurrection of Christ. Tree imagery was pervasive, more so than that of any other flora. Hermits and ascetic monks sought solace and spiritual testing among the uncultivated trees of the dwindling thirteenth-century wilderness. Instructional manuscripts were filled with schematic arboreal flourishes that diagrammed for mnemonic ease the long lists of virtues and vices, the Beatitudes, the books of the Bible, and other such useful information that preachers and penitents were prudent to remember.[43] The use of trees for meditative model-making appears in medieval texts ranging from Hildegard of Bingen's *Scivias* to the elaborately designed folios of the Carthusian-transcribed *Desert of Religion*.

The importance of trees is not difficult to explain. A tree lay at the heart of God's original act of making, and of creation's slipping away from its ideal

---

41. Here, Peter Lombard is particularly important for his contributions to speculative theory. Peter argued that the *imago Dei* referred to the perceptual faculties of the human soul, that humans were made to discern God intellectually, corporeally, and imaginatively. While they shared intellectual perception with the angels, and sensory perception with animals, Peter insisted that the imaginative faculty belonged to humans alone. Therefore, according to Peter, it was the human imaginative faculty that brought together the material and immaterial. See Hamburger, "Speculations on Speculation," 378–79.

42. See Aquinas's *Commentary on the Sentences* 3.4, Quaestio 1, art. 1, quaestiuncula 2; and 4.46, Quaestio 2, art. 1, quaestiuncula 3.

43. Adolph Katzenellenbogen, *Allegories of the Virtues and Vices in Medieval Art: From Early Christian Times to the Thirteenth Century* (Toronto: University of Toronto Press, 1989); Jennifer O'Reilly, *Studies in the Iconography of the Virtues and Vices in the Middle Ages* (New York: Garland, 1988).

original image. It was the foundation of the world's great unmaking, first in the gospel narrative of Christ's crucifixion on a wooden cross, then in Revelations, where a tree of continuing life gave hope that creation might transcend into God. In between these books, all manner of trees stood as witnesses to the unfolding of salvation history. But among twelfth-century exegetes and liturgists, trees bore profound cosmic meaning and explanation in their twinned association with the virgin birth of Christ and the eternal effects of his crucifixion.

A long exegetical tradition, beginning in the third century with Tertullian's *Treatise on the Incarnation,* had interpreted the prophecy of Isaiah 11:1–2 as foretelling the birth of Christ from the Virgin Mary. Referred to as the *stirps Jesse,* the prophecy held that "a shoot shall come out from the stem of Jesse and a branch shall grow out of his roots and the spirit of the Lord shall rest on him." By the year 1000, exegetes like the anonymous compiler of the *Libellus de Nativitate Sanctae Mariae* and, later, Fulbert of Chartres, reveled in the similarities between *virgo* and *virga* and saw resonances between the miraculous flesh of the Virgin Mother and the flowering branch.[44] The artistic rendering of the *stirps Jesse* typically featured a reclining Jesse with a branch sprouting royal descendants from his belly, at the pinnacle of which was usually some rendition of the bust of Mary in the calyx of a flower, either cradling Christ or giving support to another flower that bore his visage.[45] The iconography of the *stirps Jesse* was often featured as the opening initial to Matthew's gospel, the introductory genealogy of which served as the reading for the Feast of Mary's Nativity.[46] The *stirps Jesse* was also frequently placed at the transition from the Old to the New Testament, reflecting the medieval interpretation of the tree as an image of renewal or re-creation.[47] It was a celebratory image, one of fulfillment, marking the coming of Christ into the world via the branches of a great tree.

The tree of the cross was represented in medieval arboreal legends of salvation as the instrument that reversed original sin. Thus just as the fall of humanity was occasioned by a tree, so human redemption was secured by

---

44. Fassler, *The Virgin of Chartres,* 80. On the literary life of the image in medieval French art and romance, see Zrinka Stahuljak, "The Graft of the Woman (the Tree of Jesse)," in *Bloodless Genealogies of the French Middle Ages: Translatio, Kinship, and Metaphor* (Gainesville: University of Florida Press, 2005), 112–41.

45. Arthur Watson, *Early Iconography of the Tree of Jesse* (Oxford: Oxford University Press, 1934).

46. Margot Fassler, "Mary's Nativity, Fulbert of Chartres, and the *Stirps Jesse:* Liturgical Innovation circa 1000 and Its Afterlife," *Speculum* 75 (2000): 389–434.

47. George Henderson, "*Abraham Genuit Isaac:* Transitions from the Old Testament to the New Testament in the Prefatory Illustrations of Some Twelfth-Century English Psalters," *Gesta* 26 (1987): 127–39.

a tree, the tree of cross.[48] Already in the second century, Irenaeus had connected the Edenic tree to the wood of the cross on which Christ died, so that
the latter would redeem the suffering and sin unleashed by the consumed
fruit of the forbidden tree.[49] Shortly thereafter, Ambrose of Milan could
identify the body of Christ with the wood of his cross: "By wood we began
to hunger until wood took his own flesh for food. The same Lord joined
flesh and wood in Christ that the old hunger might pass away and the grace
of life might be restored."[50] In the seventh century, the feast of the Exaltation of the Cross was introduced into the Roman liturgy; it centered around
a relic in the Constantinian basilica that Pope Sergius I (687–701) invited
the public to kiss.[51] By the tenth-century, we see in the Anglo-Saxon poem
The Dream of the Rood that Christ's body was fully fused into and identified
with the tree so that when the tree is felled and hacked, it experienced the
passion. The tree itself was pierced with nails, "bedewed with blood," so that
wood shared the experience of Christ's flesh, wood and flesh being the two
materials receptive of the nails of torment.[52]

By the later Middle Ages, devotional practices often centered on the material wood of the cross. These practices (including reverence of wooded relics
of the cross; narrative fascination with the type, origin, and uses of the wood;
portrayals of its fashioning, rediscovery, and elevation), maintains Barbara
Baert, "ascribed to the cross a biological ancestry in the Old Testament from
a twig from the Tree of Life to the trunk from which the Cross was made."[53]
Although this ancestry, which is characterized by a lack of uniformity among
legends of the wood of the cross, or the "holy rood-tree," was commemorated through a long oral history, Honorius of Augustodunensis was one of

---

48. According to legends of the "tree of the fall," a dying Adam sent his son Seth to the gates
of Eden to seek the oil of mercy. At the gates, Seth observed a single withered tree with a serpent
coiled at its base; at the top of the tree sat a tiny child—the savior that would come. An angel then
gave Seth three seeds from the fruit that his parents had eaten. From these seeds would grow the
tree of the cross that would take Christ's life and thereby reverse the woe brought by the tree of the
fall. See Simon Schama, *Landscape and Memory* (New York: Knopf, 1996); Romuald Bauerreiss, *Arbor
vitae: Der "Lebensbaum" und seine Verwendung in Liturgie, Kunst und Brauchtum des Abendlandes* (Munich:
Neuer Filser Verlag, 1938).

49. Irenaeus of Lyon, *Adversus haereses* 5.17.3, in *Contre les hérésies,* ed. Adelain Rousseau (Paris:
Éditions du Cerf, 1969).

50. Ambrose, *Explanatio psalmi* 35, PL 14:954 C-D.

51. Louis Van Tongeren, *Exaltation of the Cross: Toward the Origins of the Feast of the Cross and the
Meaning of the Cross in Early Medieval Liturgy* (Leuven: Peeters, 2000), 41.

52. *Dream of the Rood,* ed. Michael Swanton (Exeter: University of Exeter Press, 1996).

53. Barbara Baert, *A Heritage of Holy Wood: The Legend of the True Cross in Text and Image* (Boston:
Brill, 2004), 288. On the development and typology of the wood of the cross, see Wilhelm Meyer,
Die Geschichte des Kreuzholzes vor Christus (Munich: Verlag der k. Akademie, 1881); and Angélique
Prangsma-Hajenius, *Le légende du Bois de la Croix dans la littérature française médiévale* (Assen: Van
Gorcum, 1995).

the first Latin authors to commit parts of the legend to writing. In his formulation in the *Speculum ecclesiae,* the wood of the cross was essential to a prefigural typology such that the wood itself originated as a seed from the tree of knowledge of good and evil placed into the mouth of the dying Adam. After Adam's burial, that seed then sprouted into a tree at Calvary, where, before becoming the wood of the cross, it advanced Christian providential history by first serving as a panel in Noah's ark, the rod of Moses, a beam in Solomon's temple, and a plank in Joseph's workshop.[54] Through the legends of the wood of the cross, the whole history of salvation implanted itself in the natural history of the created world. The effects of Christ's crucifixion were thus ensured throughout all time, all creation. Attention to and elaboration of the legend of the wood of the cross were multiplied in illuminations in books for private use as well as in monumental art, and invariably in sermons, especially those preached by the friars. In addition to being praised in word and image, relics of the true cross were revered as precious and fertile material and were reported to emit luxuriant fragrances, drive out demons, and cure illnesses. Splinters of the true cross connected the entirety of salvation history, conflating the distant past with the spiritual potential to be unlocked and unleashed in the present. They promised to envelop the present in eternity.

Both trees, the *stirps Jesse* and the cross, suggested that salvation history and natural history must be bound up together, that the one must include the other. When medieval Christians sought to explain the phenomena of matter, of a God that entered the material world and died wholly in order to redeem it, they turned most often to trees. To be sure, flowers, fruits, vines, gardens, and meadows all spoke of the possibilities of re-creation and made God's work more graphically present to the imagination, but trees guaranteed it. In a very literal sense, trees *were* material, and God's choice to enter and redeem material via a tree only underscored matter's holiness. In a section on wood and its products, *De lignariis,* the Spanish encyclopedist Isidore of Seville, writing in the seventh century, had linked matter to the wood of trees and forests because of their propensity for change, for becoming: "All wood is called matter because from it something is made, so if you refer to a door or a statue, it will be matter. Material is always accepting with regard to something, just as the elements are said to be the matter of things that are made from them, and from this fact we see that matter is named from mother."[55] Although writing several centuries earlier than the authors

---

54. Honorius Augustodunensis, "De inventione Sacre Crucis," in *Speculum ecclesiae,* PL 172:941C–948. On the proliferation of legends of the true cross, see Esther Quinn, *The Quest of Seth for the Oil of Life* (Chicago: University of Chicago Press, 1962).

55. Isidore of Seville, *Etymologia,* PL 82:681A.

I discuss, Isidore had bequeathed to the generations that would follow him an abiding concept of matter as mothering, giving birth to, enabling, acts of becoming.[56] Around the twelfth century, Christian theologians, poets, and liturgists would firmly attach to this concept a God who became matter itself through the wood of a tree, and who promised while dying on a tree that matter would become God. The tree that glorified the incarnation in the jeweled glass of western European cathedrals, and the fragments of wood that were scattered across the continent as a testament to the crucifixion, were locked into a concept of *lignum* as material, and material as a conveyance for the substance of divinity, promising a great becoming.

The doctrine of re-creation originated in the twelfth century as a by-product of attempts by Christian thinkers to fathom the repercussions of an incarnate and materially transcendent God. In the process, they established new hermeneutics, new ways of reading, of seeing, the natural world. This process commenced as an effort to visualize God's body in images of the natural world. The chapters that follow reflect this movement from medieval tendencies to seek, and to find, the presence of God through metaphorical and imagistic flora to discovering explicitly more literal manifestations in the natural world. Each of chapters 1–5 discusses a "moment" in this rich history of Christian devotion, opening up space for new interpretations of devotional language, behavior, and imagery. In each chapter I attempt to explain the insistent presence of the material—the refusal to look beyond, the persistent desire to be caught up in, and the flurry of material trappings of devotion. The development I narrate is gradual and, because my analysis turns from images to texts to agricultural experiments to architecture, occasionally shifts backward and forward in time, indicating that there were multiple, amphibious ways of practicing Christian meditation, and that the doctrine of re-creation had many tributaries. But from start to finish, this study narrates a devotional turn from metaphor to material—from gazing upon images of a God made visible in the splendor of natural beauty to looking at the natural world itself, and the real, physical elements of the material world, and finding there God's presence and God's promise of salvation.

I begin in chapter 1 with the reform context of the *Speculum virginum,* suggesting that the author of this twelfth-century treatise proposed the twinned spiritual ideals of virginity and enclosure as a means for women to engage in a speculative hermeneutics of their own bodies and their own communities. In chapter 2, I turn to thematic ideals of virginity and enclosure in the liturgical performances scripted by Hildegard of Bingen, showing

---

56. Bynum, *Christian Materiality,* 231.

how she forged a powerful interpretation of consecrated women as vessels of the divine and, what is more, as capable of achieving material transcendence. Chapter 3 tracks the shift in emphasis from incarnation to crucifixion, acknowledging that communities dedicated to apostolic imitation and poverty read Christ's death as the fundamental event that sanctified the material world. I examine the struggle of Clare of Assisi to adopt a life of poverty as a means of sharing the material conditions of Christ, and compare Clare's meditations on natural imagery to those of Bonaventure in his *Lignum vitae.* In chapter 4, I consider the legacy of Clare in the meditational and visionary writings of Franciscans who, like her, sought to transform themselves and the whole created world into an image of the poor Christ. Chapter 5 investigates the ontological status of the wilderness—real and imagined, literal and metaphorical—in Carthusian meditations.

The narrative arc of this study moves from the emergence of spiritual ideals to the literal practices they inspired, tracing an ever-growing confidence in the possibility of remaking the local, the communal, and the self into sites for divine apprehension. Although the analysis tends to group texts within their origins in religious orders, it often moves across orders to discuss shared spiritual ideals, and to reflect on what their differences might reveal. Because cultural poetics have permeable borders, the geographic framework shifts from the Rhine valley to Italian city-states to the fabricated English forest. The real focus, however, is always on the authors' instructions to *see,* to look beyond the text into an imagined space that always bore the potentiality of becoming real in the locus of the cell and of the self.

This book therefore engages a fairly familiar narrative of the spiritual history of the later Middle Ages, moving from Hildegard of Bingen to Bonaventure to Henry Suso, but it asserts an essential remapping, an alternative perspective to this narrative, through an emphasis on the re-creation of the natural world and its resulting speculative hermeneutics. Later medieval imaginative theology asserted that natural phenomena existed to arrest human attention and to draw the spectator toward a vision and experience of God. The doctrine of re-creation demanded a committed engagement with the natural world, to regard it as having the capacity to manifest God and to find perfection in redemption. The resulting narrative should reframe our discussions of later medieval devotional practices. We must acknowledge the centrality of the re-created world and what medieval Christians may have come to expect of such a world. The re-created world offered itself—its trees, flowers, and vines, its worms and wolves—as a locus, a place for divine encounter. A God that entered matter, died in order to promise the salvation of matter, and continually reentered matter in the celebration of his promise was a God that could be discovered in matter, in holy matter.

CHAPTER 1

The Mirror of Holy Virginity

The *Speculum virginum* is one of the most important documents we have for understanding the lives of religious women in the twelfth century. Written around the year 1140, most likely in the Rhineland region of what is today Germany, this text can be seen as part of a long and rich tradition of medieval *speculum* texts. The word *speculum* means "mirror" or "reflection," and a *speculum* text was intended to encourage readers to engage in self-reflection for the purpose of edification.[1] The *Speculum virginum* (Mirror of Virgins) was aimed at the growing number of women in the twelfth century who were entering religious life and in need of pastoral care. More specifically, it was designed for male pastors to use in the care of the women affiliated with their monastic communities. It taught these men how to train religious women in Scripture, virtue, elements of theology, and monastic life. By means of the *Speculum virginum,* men learned how to interact with the women in their care, and women learned how to act and pray appropriately to their monastic life. In doing so, both men and women were learning through this text how to perceive God in the world.

---

1. On the medieval genre of mirror literature, see Margot Schmidt, "Miroir," in *Dictionnaire de spiritualité: Ascétique et mystique, doctrine et histoire,* ed. Marcel Viller et al. (Paris: Beauchesne, 1980), 10:1290–1303; Ritamary Bradley, "Backgrounds of the Title *Speculum* in Medieval Literature," *Speculum* 29 (1954): 100–115; Einar Már Jónsson, *Le miroir: Naissance d'un genre littéraire* (Paris: Belles Lettres, 1989).

I offer the *Speculum virginum* as a starting point for a discussion of the twelfth-century development of devotion and theology centered on the world's re-creation. As I will show, the *Speculum virginum* introduced into women's communities a reformed sense of positive affirmation in speculation, training religious eyes to see the divine imprint in the material world. Adopting language that was typical of monastic reformers in German lands at the time, the *Speculum virginum* described the monastic estate as a place of natural splendor where God could be found, a veritable prelapsarian Eden. Although male monastic reformers reveled in the transformation of the physical world through the ideal of manual labor that they praised, if not actualized, on their estates, for women they endorsed not agricultural labor but virginity and enclosure. And just as labor was a spiritual ideal for reforming men, one not always realized in practice, virginity and enclosure acted as spiritual ideals that informed but did not always define practice. The *Speculum virginum* thus exalts the natural world within the confines of the cloister and insists that the presence of God could be found in the material it enclosed—in virgin bodies. In this chapter I situate the *Speculum virginum* within twelfth-century monastic reform efforts in the Rhineland, a process characterized by the collaboration of men and women. The *Speculum virginum* reflects this atmosphere of enthusiasm, anxiety, and self-conscious emergence. After examining the context of twelfth-century monastic reform in which the treatise was composed, I turn to the *Speculum* itself to examine how the author fashions his own ideals of enclosure, virginity, and speculation. At the heart of the *Speculum virginum,* I show, is an exploration of, puzzlement over, and an embrace of paradox—that virgins can give birth, that enclosure breeds freedom, that a body can contain the world.

The *Cura monialium* in the Twelfth Century

The years between 1000 and 1300 saw a dramatic increase in women's participation in the monastic life. Scholars estimate that the number of religious houses for women increased by a factor of ten during this period, with the greatest number of foundations occurring between 1100 and 1250.[2] In German lands alone, the number of women's religious houses increased from an

---

2. On the growth of female monasticism in the twelfth century, see Brenda Bolton, "Mulieres Sanctae," in *Women in Medieval Society,* ed. Susan Mosher Stuard (Philadelphia: University of Pennsylvania Press, 1976), 141–58; Jane Tibbets Schulenburg, "Women's Monastic Communities, 500–1100: Patterns of Expansion and Decline," *Signs* 14 (1989): 261–92; Bruce Vernarde, *Women's Monasticism and Medieval Society: Nunneries in France and England, 890–1215* (Ithaca, NY: Cornell University Press, 1997).

estimated 150 to 500, housing anywhere from 25,000 to 30,000 women.[3] This upsurge was part of a larger revival of spiritual enthusiasm at the time, one shared by both women and men, whose monastic participation expanded at similar rates.[4] Women and men were encouraged by the powerful rhetoric of reform, leaving the secular world for the pursuit of religious life regulated by monastic vows. Some converts joined traditional Benedictine houses that were undergoing a process of renewal by recommitting to the spirit of the Rule. Others flocked to new orders, including the Cistercians, Premonstratensians, Carthusians, Augustinians, and Gilbertines.[5]

The increasing number of women entering religious life meant an increased need for oversight. Although female monasteries would have been run by women (usually women of high social rank), it was still necessary that religious women receive pastoral care from men, including sacramental services provided by priests. The Latin term for this pastoral care was *cura monialium* (care of nuns). Indeed, the care of women constituted a key duty of the active life of men associated with German reformed monasticism.[6] In order to provide this care, some reformed monastic orders established double houses consisting of two gender-segregated communities that observed the same rule and formed a single legal entity under the authority of a male abbot or canon as provost.[7]

---

3. Matthäus Bernards, *Speculum virginum: Geistigkeit und Seelenleben der Frau im Hochmittelalter*, 2nd ed. (1955; Cologne: Böhlau, 1982), 1. See also Franz J. Felten, "Frauenklöster und -stifte im Rheinland 12. Jahrhundert: Ein Beitrag zur Geschichte der Frauen in der religiösen Bewegung des hohen Mittelalters," in *Reformidee und Reformpolitik im Spätsalisch-Frühstaufischen Reich: Vorträge der Tagung der Gesellschaft für Mittelrheinische Kirchengeschichte vom 11. bis 13. September 1991 in Trier*, ed. Stefan Weinfurter (Mainz: Selbstverlag, 1992), 189–300.

4. Giles Constable, *The Reformation of the Twelfth Century* (Cambridge: Cambridge University Press, 1998), 47.

5. For many scholars this spiritual enthusiasm is part of the larger reform movement associated with the twelfth century. Its eloquent expressions of praise and persuasion are seen as the "rhetoric of reform." "Reform," however, is a contested term—as Gerd Tellenbach and others have shown. Here I use the term "reform" specifically in reference to instructional ideals expressed in rhetoric, very roughly in the period from 1100 to 1160.

6. Reformed Augustinian communities in German lands seem to have developed reputations for their willingness to care for women. See Constable, *The Reformation of the Twelfth Century*, 65; Fiona Griffiths, *The Garden of Delights: Reform and Renaissance for Religious Women in the Twelfth Century* (Philadelphia: University of Pennsylvania Press, 2007), 40–47.

7. I follow Sally Thompson's definition of "double monastery" in *Women Religious: The Founding of English Nunneries after the Norman Conquest* (Oxford: Oxford University Press, 1991), 55. Scholars have criticized the term "double monastery" because it encompasses too many variants of mixed religious life that deserve separate and distinct consideration, and suggests greater organization and regulation than may have actually existed. See, for example, Sharon Elkins, *Holy Women of Twelfth-Century England* (Chapel Hill: University of North Carolina Press, 1988), xviii.

In German lands, the Benedictine abbey of Hirsau played a critical role in establishing the customs around the regulation of religious women.[8] William of Hirsau (d. 1091) introduced the *Constitutiones Hirsaugienses* to the southern German abbey in the late eleventh century, making it into a reform center for the region.[9] The reform of houses according to the Hirsau customs, in addition to the new Augustinian orders, created a monastic identity around service to women. The monks of Hirsau and those of the monasteries that followed the customs of Hirsau incorporated, enclosed, and regulated female communities within their monastic structures, including their female associates in their liturgical rhythms and prayers, so that the presence and service of women became part of their monastic self-perception.[10] The head of the female community was identified as a *magistra,* who owed obedience to an abbot or male provost.[11] This title reflects the emphasis on her role as a teacher, and the reformers' interest in providing education and instruction to women.[12] Men, meanwhile, acted as preachers, confessors, and teachers to the women who lived adjacent to their communities.[13]

Questions of space naturally emerged as a result of men and women sharing religious life in double houses.[14] Men's physical contact with women was infrequent and closely policed. Only the abbot or prior was allowed to enter the nuns' enclosure, and then only with two or three witnesses and for the sole purpose of administering the sacraments to a bedridden nun or to preside, only very occasionally, over chapter. The nuns observed silence with the exception of appropriate conversations with spiritual friends mediated through a grille and in the company of witnesses.[15]

But while segregating the sexes was an important spiritual concern, we should not overstate the degree of female immobility. Although in theory all necessary resources for female houses were to be found within their walls, in

---

8. Urban Küsters, "Formen unde Modelle religiöser Frauengemeinschaften im Umkreis der Hirsauer Reform des 11. und 12. Jahrhunderts," in *Hirsau, St. Peter und Paul, 1091–1991,* ed. Klaus Schreiner (Stuttgart: Forschungen und Berichte der Archäologie des Mittelalters in Baden-Württemberg, 1991), 195–220.

9. For a general introduction, see Hermann Jakobs, *Die Hirsauer: Ihre Ausbreitung und Rechtsstellung im Zeitalter des Investiturstreites* (Cologne: Böhlau, 1961).

10. Julie Hotchin, "Female Religious Life and the *cura monialium* in Hirsau Monasticism, 1080–1150," in *Listen, Daughter: The "Speculum virginum" and the Formation of Religious Women in the Middle Ages,* ed. Constant Mews (New York: Palgrave, 2001), 66, 70.

11. Hotchin, "Female Religious Life," 71.

12. Alison Beach, *Women as Scribes: Book Production and Monastic Reform in Twelfth-Century Bavaria* (Cambridge: Cambridge University Press, 2004), 27.

13. Ibid., 132.

14. Hotchin, "Female Religious Life," 69.

15. Ibid.

practice absolute enclosure was often not the case.[16] The realities of pastoral care and the practical needs of business dealings, illnesses, and basic errands inevitably meant that women (especially those of high nobility) had occasion to leave the cloister, as well as to entertain guests from the outside.[17] We know, for example, that certain convents in German-speaking regions, shared space with parish church congregations. When the nun's choir, or "basilica," was located in the parish church in this manner, it often featured a raised gallery at the center or to one side of the nave, with stairs from the altar in the nave providing priests access to the nuns.[18] We also know that some nuns frequently visited the granges outside their walls. Under such circumstances, regulating the activities of cloistered women could prove challenging.[19]

It was largely under the pressure to structure and police shared monastic space that the notion of enclosure became yoked with sexual purity as the key to female virtue in religious life. In an environment of reform, it is not surprising that the general practice of segregating the sexes in monastic life would become an interminably detailed ideal involving the regulation not simply of physical circumstances but of the spiritual formation of the whole person.[20] The physical basis for enclosure—the gates, grilles, and high walls—created effects beyond the immediate purpose of separation. At the same time, as we will see, the discourse on enclosure gave shape to a concept of inhabiting a counterworld or other-space in which the enclosed individual gained a new identity separate from family, society, and even the male spiritual directors who sought to condition and control her behavior.[21]

The *Speculum virginum* was the product of this environment—an environment in which men and women, engaged in the reform of religious life,

---

16. Penelope Johnson, *Equal in Monastic Profession: Religious Women in Medieval France* (Chicago: University of Chicago Press, 1991), 150–63.

17. On the limits of claustration, see Elkins, *Holy Women,* 105–17; and Schulenburg, "Women's Monastic Communities," 274–85.

18. Roberta Gilchrist, "Unsexing the Body," in *Archaeologies of Sexuality,* ed. Robert Schmidt and Barbara Voss (New York: Routledge: 2000), 95. For a detailed discussion of the raised choir at St. Peter's in Salzburg, see Jeffrey Hamburger, *The Visual and the Visionary: Art and Female Spirituality in Late Medieval Germany* (New York: Zone Books, 1998), 47.

19. Jeffrey Hamburger, *The Visual and the Visionary,* 43. Hamburger quotes at length from Hermann von Minden's letter to the nuns of St. Lambert's, demonstrating that the pastoral care of women often inspired priors' frustration.

20. Marie-Luise Ehrenschwendtner, "Creating the Sacred Space Within: Enclosure as a Defining Feature in the Convent Life of Medieval Dominican Sisters (13th–15th c.)," *Viator* 41 (2010): 304–6. See also Roberta Gilchrist, *Gender and Material Culture* (New York: Routledge, 1994), 167–70.

21. Ehrenschwendtner, "Creating the Sacred Space," 309; see also Philip Sheldrake, *Spaces for the Sacred: Place, Memory, and Identity* (Baltimore: Johns Hopkins University Press, 2001), 90–118; Henri Lefebvre, *The Production of Space,* trans. Donald Nicholson-Smith (Oxford: Oxford University Press, 1991), 26–39.

shared a spiritual and liturgical identity and monastic space.[22] The paradise of the cloister that it determined to foster was the place where women fashioned and performed new identities. The treatise itself projects an imagined ideal representation of enclosure, not its lived reality. It conjured for the imaginations of both women and men that converted counterworld, a theater of spiritual ideals in which, protected from the dangerous wiles of outsiders, women might assume new identities and enact daring roles.

The *Speculum virginum:* Nature Comes Home

As far as we can tell, the *Speculum virginum* was composed in the mid-twelfth century. The manuscript transmission confirms that it was created in the context of German monastic reform, most likely by a male author for the purposes of the *cura monialium.*[23] The author's name and affiliation, however, are murky. One of the oldest manuscripts, London, British Library Arundel 44 (L), dated between 1140 and 1155, was in possession of the library of the Cistercian abbey of Eberbach, whence it was transmitted to many other Cistercian houses, including Clairvaux, Igny, Himmerod, Zwettl, and Ebrach.[24] Seven of the ten manuscripts that survive from the first century after the composition of the *Speculum virginum* come from Cistercian houses, though this detail may be indicative of later use rather than Cistercian authorship.[25] The other text of the *Speculum* from this earliest period, Cologne, Historisches Archiv W 276a (K), came from St. Mary in Andernach, an Augustinian abbey founded by Richard of Springiersbach for his sister Tenxwind (d. ca. 1152).[26]

Additional information about the authorship of the *Speculum virginum* derives from a twelfth-century catalog from the library at Hirsau, which

---

22. Hotchin, "Female Religious Life," 72.

23. Jutta Seyfarth, "The Testimony of the Manuscripts," in Mews, *Listen, Daughter,* 44. Seyfarth shows that the manuscript tradition of the *Speculum virginum* corroborates male authorship and usage, with twenty-seven extant Latin manuscripts and seven other fragments, excerpts, and references.

24. Seyfarth, "The Testimony of the Manuscripts," relies on the reconstruction of Eberbach's library holdings published by Nigel Palmer, *Zisterzienser und ihre Bücher: Die mittelalterliche Bibliotheksgeschichte von Kloster Eberbach im Rheingau unter besonderer Berücksichtigung der in Oxford und London aufbewahrten Handschriften* (Regensburg: Schnell & Steiner, 1998), 77–78.

25. Constant Mews, "Hildegard, the Speculum virginum, and Religious Reform," in *Hildegard von Bingen in ihrem historischen Umfeld: Internationaler wissenschaftlicher Kongress zum 900. Jährigen Jubiläum, 13–19. September 1998 Bingen am Rhein,* ed. Alfred Haverkamp and Alexander Reverchon (Mainz: P. von Zabern, 2000), 242–43; Seyfarth, "Die Handschriften," 56*–123*, in *Speculum virginum,* ed. Seyfarth, CCCM 5 (Turnhout: Brepols, 1995).

26. Seyfarth, "The Testimony of the Manuscripts," 45–46.

included a volume composed by "a monk of Hirsau known as Peregrinus."[27] The association of the *Speculum* author with Hirsau was later corroborated by Johannes Trithemius, the abbot of Sponheim, who published a catalog of Benedictine writers in 1492, identifying the author as a monk of Hirsau.[28] An additional comment linking the manuscript to Hirsau comes from Johannes Parsimonius, the abbot of Hirsau from 1559 to 1588, who mentioned in a personal notebook that the dormitory balconies at Hirsau were inscribed with passages from the *Speculum virginum*.[29]

Although the authorship and the precise provenance of the treatise remain uncertain, the *Speculum virginum* is best understood as the product of monastic reform in the Rhineland at a time when the number of women entering cloistered life was growing exponentially, as was the demand for male pastors to provide *cura monialium*.[30] The product of the close association of men and women in pastoral care, the *Speculum virginum* was preoccupied with the duty, incumbent on both men and women, of protecting the modesty of women, what it styled as their "virginity." The *Speculum virginum* unfolds as a series of exemplary dialogues on the virtues of virginity and the communal life. Featuring an exemplary pair, Peregrinus and Theodora, as a male pastor and his female disciple engaged in religious instruction, each of the twelve dialogues opens with an introductory illustration that orients the discussion.[31] The antiphons located at the beginning and end of the text suggest that the author intended its performance within a paraliturgical context.[32]

After a prefatory letter, the *Speculum* addresses the life of the cloister in twelve parts. In the first part, Peregrinus introduces Theodora to the leadership of *natura,* who can direct her from the visible world to the invisible one.

---

27. Mews, "Hildegard, the *Speculum virginum,* and Religious Reform," 245. See also Gustavus Becker, *Catalogi bibliothecarum antiqui* (Bonn: Cohen et filium, 1885), 220.

28. Mews, "Hildegard, the *Speculum virginum,* and Religious Reform," 246.

29. Seyfarth, "Die Einleitung," 38*–39*; Mews, "Hildegard, the *Speculum virginum,* and Religious Reform," 245.

30. Seyfarth, "Die Einleitung," 43*, concludes that the author of the *Speculum* had sympathies with reformed monasticism in general. See also Felix Heinzer, "Buchkultur und Bibliotheksgeschichte Hirsaus," in Schreiner, *Hirsau, St. Peter und Paul,* 259–96; Morgan Powell, "The Mirror and the Woman: Instruction for Religious Women and the Emergence of Vernacular Poetics" (PhD diss., Princeton University, 1997), 101. The houses of Hirsau and Springiersbach are the two likely candidates for the origin of the *Speculum virginum*. On the Hirsau reform, see Klaus Schreiner, "Hirsau und die Hirsauer Reform: Spiritualität, Lebensform und Sozialprofil einer benediktinischen Erneuerungsbewegung im 11. und 12. Jahrhundert," in Schreiner, *Hirsau, St. Peter und Paul,* 59–84; and Küsters, "Formen und Modelle religiöser Frauengemeinschaften," 195–220.

31. In enumerating the pictures and parts of the work, I follow Seyfarth, "Einleitung," 26*, in *Speculum virginum*.

32. Constant Mews makes this suggestion in "Hildegard, the *Speculum virginum,* and Religious Reform," 248.

"Because nature is a certain guide to the invisible," he explains, drawing on the words of Paul, "the intellect discerns the invisible things of God through it."[33] Key to this direction, he insists, is the cultivation of virtue, which is the primary activity of consecrated virgins. In part 2, Peregrinus upholds the cloister as the most appropriate site for the cultivation of virgins' virtue. He then proceeds, in part 3, to elaborate on the eponymous mirror of virgins, which he describes as a tool for self-evaluation, for determining one's progress in cultivating the virtues. Part 4 offers a narrative description of humility and pride, elaborating on how all other virtues and vices derive from these two foundations. Part 5 is a paean to Mary, whom the virgins must strive to emulate not only in her embodiment of virtue, but also in her act of making God visible in material forms. After distinguishing wise from foolish virgins in part 6, Peregrinus moves in parts 7 and 8 to present various arguments for the superiority of virginity to marriage and to encourage virginity as an interior virtue. Part 9 features a dramatic performance of the personified virtues of the virgin soul battling the worldly temptations of the devil. Part 10 returns to the theme of God's visibility in the material of creation, praising him for his manifestation in the created world. Peregrinus then reintroduces the descriptions of the virtues as flowers and fruits in part 11, and in part 12, he anchors these images in Christ, whose incarnation made human knowledge of God possible in the world. The tome ends with an epithalamium bursting with natural, fecund imagery.

The *Speculum virginum* was therefore preoccupied with updating the rules of cloistered life and the spiritual ideals governing the consecrated nun. It stands as evidence of a new moment in the history of devotion, one oriented around the body of the enclosed virgin. Body here was significant for its materiality. While virginity was the central concern of the treatise, it was a virtue that reproduced Mary's work of incarnating the divine.[34] Like Mary, the virgins who scrutinized their inner virtue in the mirror of the book

---

33. Seyfarth, *Speculum virginum,* 18; 1.386–89.

34. The *Speculum virginum* thus provides one "version" of virginity. Sarah Salih has argued that medieval virginities were always multiple—secular virginity, religious virginity, male virginity, female virginity, temporary virginity, and permanent virginity—possessing a variety of practices and meanings dependent on context. She has drawn on the work of Judith Butler, theorizing the discursive production of the body in order to foreground a notion of medieval virginity as a performance that one could move into and out of. While I do not agree with her reading of Butler, I do wish to emphasize the importance of the emerging variety in options for virgin identity in the twelfth century. See Sarah Salih, "Performing Virginity: Sex and Violence in the Katherine Group," in *Constructions of Widowhood and Virginity in the Middle Ages,* ed. Cindy L. Carson and Angela Jane Weisl (Basingstoke, UK: Macmillan, 1999), 95–112; and Salih, *Versions of Virginity in Late Medieval England* (Cambridge: Brewer, 2001). See also Kathleen Coyne Kelly, *Performing Virginity and Testing Chastity in the Middle Ages* (London: Routledge, 2000).

would incarnate the transcendent, they would re-create their world. The *Speculum virginum* therefore represents a point of origin for new devotional roles and a new theology of the incarnation that celebrated God's becoming human as a re-creation of the world.[35]

The ideal of virginity informed female emotional and psychic states as much as physical ones. Spiritual authorities generally acknowledged that definitions of virginity according to a physical and technical state of intact-ness, an imperforate hymen, were imperfect. One medical test, for example, directed physicians to cover a supposed virgin with a cloth, and then to fumigate underneath with coal, requesting that she attempt to whiff the resulting scent.[36] Her inability to detect the odor, the test advised, confirmed her virginity. The point here is that female virginity was based on an impos-sible ideal of bodily closure. It was an invention, a metaphor. The very impossibility of virginity—a body sealed so tightly as to exude or absorb nothing—made it such that the real test of virginity was a woman's modesty as detected in her gait, her speech, her behavior, her downcast eyes, but not her genitalia.[37] By and large, spiritual and theological treatises on virginity were unconcerned with medical tests or physical definitions. Instead, virgin-ity was inferred from, as well as performed through, outward signs of mod-esty. For this reason, the ideal of virginity emerged in the twelfth century as one open to women of various ages, even wives and widows.[38]

With virginity defined theologically as a quality of the soul, rather than a condition of the body, male pastors and female abbesses and *magistrae* praised virginity through complex language rooted in seeming paradox. Osbert of Clare, writing to Adelidis, the abbess of Barking, ca. 1156 extolled her virgin

---

35. Like Sarah McNamer, I read women's devotion in this period as constituting a "regime change" and a spiritual revolution; however, I see a greater variety of roles for women. McNamer has shown that religious women in the twelfth and thirteenth centuries considered themselves legally and literally betrothed to Christ, and viewed their lives in the cloister as a training ground through which they might demonstrate their merit for marriage in heaven. As a result, the performance of love and compassion for Christ gained importance. The *Speculum virginum* provides a different kind of script, the performance of which was an act of re-creation. On betrothal to Christ, see Sarah McNamer, *Affective Devotion and the Origins of Medieval Compassion* (Philadelphia: University of Pennsylvania Press, 2010), esp. 25–57.

36. Esther Lastique and Helen Rodnite, "A Medieval Physician's Guide to Virginity," in *Sex in the Middle Ages: A Book of Essays,* ed. Joyce Salisbury (New York: Garland, 1991), 56–82.

37. Salih, *Versions of Virginity,* 21.

38. Nicole Rice, "Temples to Christ's Indwelling: Forms of Chastity in a Barking Abbey Manuscript," *Journal of the History of Sexuality* 19 (2010): 115–32. Although child oblation was increasingly discouraged, young women from the ages of twelve to fifteen were frequently admitted to religious communities; see Jocelyn Wogan-Browne, "Convents and Women's Lives," in *Guidance for Women in Twelfth-Century Convents,* ed. Jocelyn Wogan-Browne and trans. Vera Morton (Cambridge: D. S. Brewer, 2003), 6.

childbearing by evoking the primordial parents to demonstrate how the practice of virginity reversed the effects of the first sin:

> Oh how lovely, how chaste, how joyful, how spotless is this childbear-ing when the woman in labor does not bring forth in sorrow like the daughters of Eve, and the offspring which she bears among the sons of Adam do not gain bread by sweat, nor does that mother plough or sow that cursed land which brings forth thorns and thistles, but Jesus tends the field of virginity with the mother and brings forth a hundredfold.[39]

Their bodies were fertile fields, capable of restoring Eden. The sinless child-bearing of the virgins of Barking thus aligned them, in Osbert's assessment, with the labor of the Virgin Mary, mother of this verdant world:

> Other women give birth without the blessing of virginity; from cor-ruptible flesh they give birth to mortal flesh; they give birth, I say, to what they conceive; sin from sin.... But indeed virgins are in no way put in danger in childbirth of that kind when they bear spiritual off-spring to God; when the creator of virginity, the virgin bridegroom, is he who begets and bears the virgin heart and as a father makes the flesh fruitful with that grace and heavenly seed. These women are imita-tors of her who, unstained in flesh, bore the Son of God, the son who has consecrated you for himself as bride and Virgin. For you conceive offspring from him in such a way that you give birth but do not expe-rience corruption from the flesh.[40]

That Barking was a Benedictine house of aristocratic nuns—indeed, one desperately in need of reform, if we are to trust Theobald, archbishop of Canterbury, who wrote a scathing letter criticizing the abbess Adelidis's inat-tention to the rules of enclosure—only emphasized the nature of virgin-ity as a shared spiritual ideal.[41] What is important to discern is how this spiritual ideal served to animate new perspectives on and relationships with the material world. Here, Osbert cast the virgin body as a contested terrain for negotiating relationships between Mary, Christ, and the community. He reckoned her body as a perfectly cultivated landscape, a garden that stood in stark contrast to the thistles and brambles of the fallen earth, which men must labor and sweat to make productive. Her body was distinct from other

---

39. Osbert of Clare, "Osbert of Clare, Prior of Westminster, to Adelidis, Abbess of Barking" in Wogan-Browne and Morton, *Guidance for Women,* 22; *The Letters of Osbert of Clare,* ed. E. W. Williamson (London: Oxford, 1929), epistle 42, p. 22.

40. "Osbert of Clare," 23; *The Letters of Osbert of Clare,* epistle 42, p. 23.

41. On this controversy, see Elkins, *Holy Women,* 147–50.

bodies that reproduced sexually, that experienced labor pain. The labor of the consecrated virgin, by comparison, was to give birth to virtue in the world.[42] She embodied Christ's virtue, materialized it. These were the ideals that the *Speculum* author, writing just a few years prior, celebrated and prescribed.

The World as *Speculatorium*

The texts under exploration in this and the following chapter—texts used for the instruction of women in the twelfth century—consistently invited cloistered readers and auditors to indulge their spiritual senses by seeking the invisible God in the visible world. They incited *sanctimoniali* to enjoy material images of God, to enter into them imaginatively, and to interact with them. Mary Carruthers has chronicled this aptitude of the trained imagination in monastic memory work from late antiquity through the twelfth century.[43] She has shown how monks used biblical and liturgical tropes and figures as the basis for imagined pictures that they sustained in their minds and built on for further thinking. Carruthers argues that the medieval craft of thinking about God was largely relational. Contemplative monks imbued images and objects of the real world with emotion and ornament in order to invigorate their presence in the imagination. Their ontological reality, their "truth," therefore, was not as important as their ability to ignite and propel thought. As Carruthers explains, "What is 'truthful' about them is not their content, that is *what* they remember, but rather their form and especially their ability to find out things, that is *how* they cue memories."[44] Monastic memory work was a means to see and experience things otherwise inaccessible to human sensoria, things like God, heaven, and charity. The mental image was the place in which one encountered unseen divinity. The goal of monastic meditation practices, then, was to find this place, and to dwell in it, discovering in its habitation that it led via *ducti* to further, deeper places.

My investigation of the craft of prayer turns specifically to how it was designed for women, that is, for "virgins"—a terrain of meditational practice largely overlooked by Carruthers. The *Speculum virginum* recommended a

---

42. The male necessity for agricultural work, *labor,* in order to reverse the effects of sin might be compared here to the female work of *dolor,* the painful birth labor women must endure in order to bring forth an understanding of that verdant world. My thanks to Martha Newman for calling my attention to this symmetry. See Newman, "Labor: Insights from a Medieval Monastery," in *Why the Middle Ages Matter,* ed. Celia Chazelle, Simon Doubleday, Felice Lifshitz, and Amy Remensnyder (New York: Routledge, 2012), 106–20.

43. Mary Carruthers, *The Craft of Thought: Meditation, Rhetoric, and the Making of Images, 400–1200* (Cambridge: Cambridge University Press, 2000).

44. Ibid., 35.

unique role for women contemplating the presence of God. It urged the act of speculation as a form of meditation. It emphasized the often illiterate or unadvanced quality of women's knowledge of the divine, a conceit remarked on repeatedly in the treatise, although one that did not reflect the reality of the literate and scribal women in a number of German communities.[45] It instructed cloistered women to use the natural world to perceive God's presence; in so doing, it suggested that, like Mary, in their conception they might bring forth the material presence of the divine, the very *imago dei*.[46]

Both male- and female-authored texts of religious instruction and spiritual biographies of the period often depicted women as straining to penetrate beyond the literal meaning of words, and falling back on the use of images to comprehend the divine.[47] The *Speculum virginum* is certainly an example of this portrayal of female instruction. But the *Speculum* also offers an alternative perspective on women's apprehension of images in meditation, one that proposes the physical world itself as an apt image for speculation. Peregrinus repeatedly denounces Theodora's inability to grasp the mystical meaning of the images and scriptural references he presents. The tense interactions between Peregrinus and Theodora forge an awareness of the text's own curious constitution as a composite of text and image, spiritual significance and literal referent. Peregrinus repeatedly comments on the need for images to pull their viewers toward the divine, while Theodora suggests a very different possibility, that the images' material basis reveals a God that created it and continued to act in it. One would suppose that the author who composed this dialogue intended Peregrinus's words to be authoritative. And yet his statements are undercut, indeed the whole treatise is unmade, by Theodora's dense interjections.

The ideal of imageless devotion, so often associated with the most stringent reforming ideals of the Cistercian order, was never exceptionally

---

45. Alison Beach has shown that many women were indeed exceedingly well educated and proficient in both reading and writing Latin. See Beach, *Women as Scribes.*

46. On images as the *imago Dei,* see Jeffrey Hamburger, "'In the Image and Likeness of God': Pictorial Reflections on Images and the 'Imago Dei,'" in *Femmes, art et religion au Moyen Age: Colloque international, Colmar, Museé d'Unterlinden, 3–5 mai,* ed. Jean-Claude Schmitt (Strasbourg: Presses Universitaires Strasbourg, 2004); and Hamburger, *Saint John the Divine: Deified Evangelist in Medieval Art and Theology* (Berkeley: University of California Press, 2002).

47. Contemporary scholars have posited increasingly complex arguments about the status of images in medieval devotion. Until somewhat recently, the scholarly assumption had been that images were not considered suitable for monastic contemplation, premised on Gregory the Great's epistolary remark that images were appropriate for the illiterate. Recently scholars have begun to update this position, seeing literate men as equal consumers of religious imagery; see Herbert L. Kessler, *Neither God nor Man: Words, Images, and the Medieval Anxiety about Art* (Freiburg im Breisgau: Rombach, 2007). Scholars have also turned to ocular theory and optical anatomy, which suggested that women were considered more physiologically apt to apprehend God through images; see Suzannah Biernoff, *Sight and Embodiment in the Middle Ages* (New York: Palgrave, 2002).

imageless.[48] While scholars have looked to Bernard of Clairvaux for his admonitions against the use of images in monastic contemplation, a more nuanced understanding of material images in reformed monastic life might be found in the "rhetoric of reform," which conveys a perception of the natural world as renewed through strict monastic observance, and the belief in its potential to lead humanity to the sight of God. Shared among many orders that espoused reforming ideals in the twelfth century was the sense that the world itself was an image of God, worthy of contemplation and devotional use.[49] Therefore, the monastic reformers' position on material images in devotion might more appropriately be considered according to their concern for *material,* a concern that pulsates throughout their rhetoric and approach to the monastic estate.

According to such authorities as Bruno of Cologne, Gilbert of Swineshead, Gilbert of Foliot, Adam of Dryburgh, Aelred of Rievaulx, and even Bernard of Clairvaux, the whole world should be a reflection, a material image, of paradise.[50] It should make God visible. These men proposed a mission to make the material world more perfectly reflect the prelapsarian Edenic splendor that God originally created, in which God could be seen. Twelfth-century founders and reformers of religious houses labored on the land in order to consider their monastic houses as direct reflections of paradise.[51] In the words of the historian of Selby, the abbey was "a most pleasant place, both planted with many trees and surrounded by several abundant rivers, as if it were an earthly paradise."[52] Gilbert of Holland considered the wooded valley of his abbey at Swineshead as a place that might "refashion (*recreare*) the dead spirit," a material image with the power to inspire and

---

48. Georges Duby, *Saint Bernard: L'art cistercien* (Paris: Arts et métiers graphiques, 1994); see also Hamburger's discussion of imageless devotion in *The Visual and the Visionary,* 161–82.

49. Throughout this section I have tried to find a more appropriate term than "monastic reformers." Recent scholarship has alerted us, when thinking about institutional reform, to the critical importance of local circumstances and long-term processes. Unfortunately, at this time, there is no agreed-on replacement for the term "monastic reformer," or a way to signal the ideals often associated with reformed monasticism and reformist identities. On refining and controlling our understanding of reform, see Steven Vanderputten, *Monastic Reform as Process: Realities and Representations in Medieval Flanders, 900–1100* (Ithaca, NY: Cornell University Press, 2013).

50. On the monastic landscape as a reflection of paradise in Cistercian thought, see Martha Newman, *The Boundaries of Charity: Cistercian Culture and Ecclesiastical Reform, 1098–1180* (Stanford, CA: Stanford University Press, 1996), esp. chap. 3; and Giles Constable, "Renewal and Reform in Religious Life," in *Renaissance and Renewal in the Twelfth Century,* ed. Robert Benson, Giles Constable, and Dana Lanham (Toronto: PIMS, 1982), 37–67.

51. Constable, "Renewal and Reform in Religious Life," 48–51.

52. *Historia monasterii Selebiensis in Anglia* 11, ed. Joseph T. Fowler, in *The Coucher Book of Selby* (Durham, UK: Yorkshire Archaeological and Topographical Association, 1891–93); quoted in Constable, "Renewal and Reform in Religious Life," 49.

convert.[53] Otloh of St. Emmeram insisted that, owing to the incarnation, nature could be read spiritually as revealing the secrets of heaven.[54] "Indeed, the cloister predicts Paradise, truly the monastery is a more secure place of Paradise than Eden," wrote Honorius Augustodunensis as he proceeded to interpret the physical, natural features of the monastery—its fruit, fountain, and trees—as bearing analogies to the celestial paradise.[55] The author of *On the Fruits of the Flesh and of the Spirit,* who has been identified as Conrad of Hirsau, discussed the virtuous life appropriate to reformed Benedictine monasticism, as well as the vices to be avoided, in terms of the fruits growing from trees rooted in humility and pride.[56] And Herrad of Hohenbourg chose a garden as the central thematic principle of her theological treatise and promoted it to the women of her community as a place where they could know God.[57]

The direct sensual experience of the physical world was essential to the twelfth-century monastic reformers' perception of the religious life, which sought to apprehend sensually and intellectually God's presence in the world.[58] Their monastic estates were for them the ideal image through which to imagine God, a means to discover God through material images in the world. The Cistercians were particularly savvy at promoting their estates as God-bearing. Their land acquisition records reveal a new sense of the spiritual capacity to engage in the material world. Although their original foundations were located in the settled regions of Champagne and Burgundy, the Cistercians nevertheless insisted that their first monasteries had been sited in wilderness areas, "inhabited only by wild beasts, and unaccustomed to the arrival of men at that time on account of the woods and thorns."[59] Early Cistercians removed from their charters any customary layers of land tenures and claims, and in so doing sought to manufacture an image of the transformation of the estate under their own cultivation, techniques, and labor. They believed that their labor altered the secular character of the physical world, endowing

---

53. Gilbert of Hoyland, *Tractatus VII ad Rogerum abbatem,* PL 184:283A (hereafter cited parenthetically in the text in abbreviated form).

54. On Otloh's interpretation of "the book of nature," see Irven Resnick, "Literatti, Spirituales, and Lay Christians according to Otloh of St. Emmeram," *Church History* 55 (1996): 165–78; see also Otloh of St. Emmeram, *Dialogus de tribus quaestionibus,* PL 146:77D–78C.

55. *Gemma animae* 3.149, PL 172:590B.

56. *De fructibus carnis et spiritus,* PL 176:997–1006. On the authorship of the text, see Robert Bultot, "L'auteur et la fonction littéraire du 'De fructibus carnis et spiritus,'" *Recherches de Théologie Ancienne et Médiévale* 30 (1963): 148–54.

57. Griffiths, *The Garden of Delights,* 135.

58. Constable, "Renewal and Reform in Religious Life," 50.

59. *Exordium magnum ordinis Cisterciensis,* PL 185:1009A: "et pro nemoris spinarumque densitate tunc temporis accessui hominum insolitus, a solis inhabitabatur feris."

it with divine presence, and that God would reward their labor by providing them with the ability to see the divine harmonies in the created world around them.[60] They were engaged in a process of land transformation in which their property was rendered into a religious domain, one in which the very manipulation of the physical world re-created it as sacred space. Once it was re-created through their labor and isolation, the twelfth-century Cistercians understood the material world as capable of yielding the presence of God.[61] Their estates became, through this process, a normative and appropriate image for devotional use.

Owing to their intimate involvement in the cultivation and maintenance of their landed property, the late eleventh- and twelfth-century monastic founders and reformers drew heavily on images of the natural world in order to convey their perception of God. They described their estates as physical locations in which it was possible to access God. For example, Bruno of Cologne, writing to his friend Raoul, provost of Reims, lauded the spiritual effect of the "flourishing meadows and flowery fields" of his Calabrian hermitage, which granted him "sight of God."[62] Gilbert of Holland similarly recommended to the abbot Roger the spiritual refreshment offered by the environs of his abbey, which was "a secluded place, cultivated, irrigated, and fertile," and thus offered to its inhabitants the experience of the first, sinless humans and their ability to discern God in the garden (*Tractatus VII,* PL 184:283A). In the same letter, Gilbert proceeded to praise the agricultural work conducted by the monks under Roger's care, comparing their landed labor to the remaking of their souls:

> Why should I presently place on record the farmlands, the property, the equipment, the clothing, the buildings, the men, a record of all that arose and sprung from your hands, of all that existed of the exterior

---

60. Newman, *The Boundaries of Charity,* 95.

61. On Cistercian labor, see Constance Bouchard, *Holy Entrepreneurs: Cistercians, Knights, and Economic Exchange in Twelfth-Century Burgundy* (Ithaca, NY: Cornell University Press, 1991); Christopher Holdsworth, "The Blessing of Work: The Cistercian View," in *Sanctity and Secularity,* ed. D. Baker (Oxford: Oxford University Press, 1973), 59–76; and Lisa Sullivan, "Workers, Policy-Makers, and Labor Ideals in Cistercian Legislation, 1134–1237," *Cîteaux: Commentarii Cisterciensis* 40 (1989): 175–99.

62. Bruno of Cologne, *Lettres des premiers chartreux* (Paris: Éditions du Cerf), 1:70. It should be noted that many monks tended to use the term "desert" to refer to a wilderness, intentionally evoking the solitary and sparse surroundings of the original desert ascetics. Clearly, there were no deserts in France or Italy at the time of Bruno's writing. Wilderness imagery is a formative theme in scholarship on the history of Christian literature; on the language of the desert and wilderness in medieval Christian spiritual writing, see Jacques Le Goff, "The Wilderness in the Medieval West," in *The Medieval Imagination,* trans. Arthur Goldhammer (Chicago: University of Chicago Press, 1988); George H. Williams, *Wilderness and Paradise in Christian Thought* (New York: Harper, 1962).

things of the religious life? From the time the lord bound you to cultivate this place and to align the soil of the valleys after him, how great
a crop of devoted souls has arisen! How abundant in grain are your
valleys! (*Tractatus VII,* PL 184:284D)

Frequently alluding to the lush fruits and vegetation described in the garden
of the Song of Songs, William of Malmesbury declared that the Abbey of
Thorney was itself an "image of paradise, which in its pleasantness already
resembles heaven."[63] Bernard of Clairvaux apparently passed a lily around
his chapter house, pointing to its coroneted stamens and white petals, and
instructing that they signified Jesus's crown of divinity and pure humanity.[64]

Of course, not all choir monks were engaged in land clearing and har-
vesting. Not, at least, in reality, as the necessity for the introduction of a lay
brotherhood makes clear. But they celebrated such engagement in the material world through labor as a method of personal and communal reform, a
spiritual ideal; and that ideal certainly shaped their reality, fashioned their
self-image. It may be that those communities that relied most heavily on the
agricultural labor of the lay brotherhood conveyed all the more resolutely
their spiritual ideals through the language of natural renewal, celebrating the
ideal of labor to re-create the monastic estate. Their ability, after all, to present themselves as living independently from secular servants, incomes, and
interference was often entirely contingent on the labor of the *conversi*. Particularly in German territories, fractured by twisted alliances between royal
and ecclesiastical authorities, monastic reformers played on their claim to
sacralized land, land that God had intended specifically for monastic cultivation and enjoyment. William of Hirsau's biographer, for example, described
William's reforming activity as reparative of a sullied world, and William
himself as an "architect" who built new monasteries and reformed old ones
from spiritual stones.[65] William was adamant about asserting the boundaries of the monastic estate at Hirsau and rejected all outside interference.[66]
For assistance in segregating monastic property from secular infringement,
he relied on the ministry of lay converts. For all of the twelfth-century
monastic orders, allusions to the cultivation of lilies, flowering fields, fruits,
gardens, and grains spoke of both a reality and an ideal. The manual labor

---

63. William of Malmesbury, *Gesta pontificum* IV, 186, ed. N. E. S. A. Hamilton, RS 52 (London, 1870), 326.

64. Newman, *Boundaries of Charity,* 91; Bernard of Clairvaux, *Sermones super Cantica Canticorum* 70.5, in *S. Bernardi opera omnia,* ed. Jean Leclercq (Rome: Editiones Cistercienses, 1957–77), 2:210.

65. Haimo of Hirsau, *Vita Willihelmi abbatis Hirsaugiensis,* ed. Wilhelm Wattenbach, MGH SS 12:209–25.

66. On Hirsau, see Schreiner, *Hirsau, St. Peter und St. Paul.*

that transformed thorns and brambles into fruitful gardens was a rhetorical necessity, an enactment of a biblical trope that began in Genesis, and a means of asserting distinctions in spiritual space.

Where does the *Speculum virginum* fit into this rhetorical eruption? How are we to account for the rich, lush, verdant imagery of the *Speculum virginum,* for its repeated request to see, taste, touch, and smell the earthly abundance of expansive fields, gardens, and orchards, particularly when it simultaneously insists on the strict enclosure of virgins? If we heed texts written by and for women, then we must revise our entire understanding of the meaning of the natural and material world as it was conceived by religious persons in the twelfth century. My reading of the *Speculum virginum* contends that it is only when considering the rhetoric of reform as applied within the ideal of female enclosure that the full range of meaning intended by this language becomes clear. The female body of the virgin acted as the material image through which to picture God. The same flowers and fields that seemed to have conveyed earthly speculation for male reformers, came to signify, when directed to religious women, a world re-created by the incarnation of God in Mary. The perspective on natural language offered from within the female monastery is necessary to fully comprehend the twelfth century's so-called discovery of nature.

As the product of the close association of men and women in pastoral care, the *Speculum virginum* was preoccupied with the duty, incumbent on both men and women, of protecting the modesty of women, what it styled as their "virginity." Men and women were closely affiliated in reformed circles, and their interaction was the subject of anxiety. What emerged from this self-consciously gendered dynamic as the most important theme in the *Speculum virginum* was a remaking of women's enclosed space, including their own bodies, as sites housing spiritual virtue. To this end, natural imagery came to characterize a rethinking of religious women's roles as virgins who enact and reflect the world's re-creation. As the ideal *magister* and *discipula,* Peregrinus holds up the book, the words and images that constitute the *Speculum virginum,* as a mirror into which Theodora must gaze. But as Theodora stares into the book, Peregrinus must fix his eyes on the woman before him; as a result, Theodora imitates Mary's virtuous incarnation of God, while Peregrinus meditates on the virgin presence of his disciple. The entire dialogue is a lesson on looking and looking beyond, as the author explains in his prologue: "The title indicates the usefulness of the following material, so that by a kind of analogy, you may learn how to seek what is invisible."[67] As

---

67. Seyfarth, 2; *Speculum virginum,* Epistula 38–40; Newman, "*Speculum virginum:* Selected Excerpts," in Mews, *Listen, Daughter,* 270 (hereafter cited parenthetically in the text in abbreviated form).

a self-proclaimed *speculatorium* that insisted, on every one of its nearly two hundred folios, that the reader "look" into its pages, its pictures, its songs, and text, the *Speculum* called attention to its own construction, to its function as a "paradise seeing aid."[68] In doing so, it suggested that the material world played a critical role in seeing, and thus knowing, God.

Mirror of Re-creation

As stated in its preface, the goal of the *Speculum virginum* was to materialize the image of God in the body of the enclosed woman. Like the titular mirror, it should provide reflection, "so that God's image in you may shine the more brightly and what is now hidden from mortals, being divine, may appear more radiant than the noonday sun" (Seyfarth, 3; Epistula 55–68; Newman, 270). The author explained that through the course of their instruction in this treatise, something previously hidden should become visible. Divinity would be seen in the cloistered women who benefited from his text.

The treatise began with a prolix Christian Platonism. "When you hear analogies that compare the rational creature or the Creator himself to sense-less or irrational things, this is the reason"; so Peregrinus begins to explain the principles of his lesson in earthly interpretation. "The human mind may be aroused by the beauties flashing forth from the native splendor of God's unity to seek things even more beautiful, and may advance from the lesser to the greater" (Seyfarth, 6; *SV* 1.54–58; Newman, 272). Peregrinus thus commences from the assumption that divine knowledge is gained through refinement or advancement from material things. That is, he began by sug-gesting that material objects lead humans to see, and thus to know, what is beyond them—the invisible God. But through the course of the instruction, the conversation transitions from pointing nuns upward to God from the material things of the earth, to bringing God downward, incarnating God, as a material presence *within* the female cloister, not beyond it. According to the author of the *Speculum,* the incarnation of Christ rewrote both Scripture and the world. In terms of Scripture, Christ's incarnation necessitated new ways of reading, proper ways of understanding the meaning of Scripture, via analogy, figuration, and fulfillment. In terms of the created world, Christ's incarnation meant much the same thing—that the material world might contain more than what the eye first glimpsed.

---

68. Powell translates *paradisum speculatorium* as "paradise seeing aid." Powell, "The *Speculum virginum* and the Audio-Visual Poetics of Women's Religious Instruction," in Mews, *Listen, Daughter,* 122.

The central image of the text through which the *Speculum* author sought to train women to see God was the *flos campi* of the Song of Songs. The titular mirror of the text, he insisted, reflected a field. Peregrinus thus directed Theodora's imagination to splendid scenes of agricultural cultivation not of monastic estates, but of the body of Mary: "The field of the wilderness is uncultivated earth—the virginal integrity of Mary. Fertile without a cultivator, from that shoot she brought forth in human sight a flower and its fragrance" (Seyfarth, 7–8; *SV* 1.85–87; Newman, 273). In its chaste styling by the *Speculum,* the body of the virgin became the material site requiring labor, the overgrown wilderness necessitating cultivation in order to show forth the presence of God.

Why would the *Speculum* author choose the sensual, lush imagery of the Song of Songs as the central image of his treatise? Why the Song—a text that was not used for the instruction of novices—as the means for exposition on the meaning and rules of female religious life? The lover of the Song praises his beloved's luxuriant physical appearance according to her likeness to the elements of creation—to fields, fruits, flowers, spices, gardens. Peregrinus likewise evokes these images in order to praise the body of the virgin with whom he is conversing.

It was at precisely the same time as the composition of the *Speculum virginum* that men of diverse religious affiliation, including Rupert of Deutz, Alan of Lille, Honorius Augustodunensis, Philip of Harvengt, and William of Newburgh, began crafting Marian commentaries on the Song of Songs.[69] Twelfth-century Marian commentaries on the Song derived from its use in the liturgy of the Assumption and the Nativity of Mary. These commentaries considered the Song a literal or historical account of the love and experiences shared between Mary and her son. According to the commentary tradition, the historical reading of the Song praised Mary's role as the vessel for the incarnation of God; it was through this tradition that she became the virgin bride of Christ. But more than that, the historical interpretation of the Song provided the transcript of a conversation, a dialogue, between Christ and Mary.[70] In this transcript, Mary was a seer, a prophetess. While

69. On the Marian commentaries on the Song of Songs, see E. Ann Matter, *The Voice of My Beloved: The Song of Songs in Western Medieval Christianity* (Philadelphia: University of Pennsylvania Press, 1990), 151–77; and Ann Astell, *The Song of Songs in the Middle Ages* (Ithaca, NY: Cornell University Press, 1990), 42–72; Denys Turner, *Eros and Allegory: Medieval Exegesis of the Song of Songs* (Kalamazoo, MI: Cistercian Publications, 1995); Rachel Fulton, *From Judgment to Passion: Devotion to Christ and the Virgin Mary, 800–1200* (New York: Columbia University Press, 2005), pt. 2.

70. Rachel Fulton, "Mimetic Devotion, Marian Exegesis, and the Historical Sense of the Song of Songs," *Viator* 27 (1996): 103–8.

the historical reading of the Song described the life of Mary, insofar as she spoke the words of the pre-Christian Song of Songs, she was also a prophet who saw the events of sacred history in anticipation of them.[71] As a result, the Marian commentary tradition fostered a devotional desire to experience sacred history in a mystical fashion, meditating, imagining, and reenacting the incarnation and crucifixion as if really present, involving all of the senses and emotion in the re-creation of gospel history. The Song of Songs therefore provided apt imagery for the *Speculum* author because he, too, envisioned himself, and the women and men for whom he wrote, as engaged in a process of witnessing the incarnation. Moreover, his treatise was an "intimate script," a dialogue between a virgin and her male instructor in the Word.[72] Together, through use of this text, men and women dedicated to reformed religious life in Germany forged a new religious temperament. These women and men negotiated the terms and conditions for perceiving the act of God's incarnation in the body of Mary as parallel to a second creation of the world, a recapitulation of the creation through the body of a woman.

The dialogue between *magister* and *discipula* commences in book 1, when Peregrinus describes the significance of monastic life in terms of the sensual experience of objects in the natural world. He initiates the conversation, stating: "I will converse with you, Theodora, about the flowers of paradise and the fruit of the virgin's crop" (Seyfarth, 5; *SV* 1.1–2; Newman, 271). The treatise thus describes the virgin and her community with the same natural imagery as found in the Song—trees, fruits, gardens, fields, and flowers. Peregrinus taught that each of these images retained tremendous religious importance, and pointed to lofty spiritual truths that were realized only through religious observance. Theodora therefore required only an allegorical understanding of their meaning.

But as Peregrinus continues to lecture, it becomes evident that each image bore a multiplicity of meanings, with ever-changing referents, so that Peregrinus eventually divulges his frustration with the task of importing such overdetermined language into the cloister. Barraged by an array of references to the natural world, the young virgin Theodora continually asks her instructor what these natural metaphors refer to, what they mean. And he continually

---

71. Ibid., 109.

72. On "intimate scripts" in the making of the identity of a virgin or *sponsa Christi,* see McNamer, *Affective Devotion,* 12. She defines the term as "scripts for the performance of feeling—scripts that often explicitly aspire to performative efficacy." Although this tradition of the virgin is very different, in terms of emotional orientation, from McNamer's focus on the making of *sponsa Christi,* the scripted character of the texts suggests that both understood virginity as a performance, and thus a means to produce a particular sense of selfhood.

changes his response, shifting their referents. They both appear confused, caught up, unable properly to transpose imagery of cultivation from fields outside to those within the cloister, inside the virgin body. Although he indicates that these metaphors signify "the holiness of the virginal life and the consummation of chastity in Christ's members," nevertheless at any point in the dialogue, the flower he holds up for Theodora to observe, whether as an artistic rendering or a verbal picture, might refer to Christ, Scripture, virtue, enclosure, the treatise itself, or Theodora's virgin body (Seyfarth, 5; *SV* 1.3–5; Newman, 271). His poetic efforts to analogize God through the earth's flora are repeatedly stifled by Theodora's verbal intrusions, which plead with him to "explain this more clearly" (Seyfarth, 55; *SV* 2.395; Newman, 279).

Her puzzlement is understandable, as the natural exploration and experience he encourages does not fit so neatly within the tightly enclosed space in which he limits her virginal activity. The *Speculum* author implored his virgin audience to delve into the *hortus deliciarum,* to delight her senses there:

> When the virgin of Christ, eager for the divine word, browses in these sections [chapters of the *Speculum virginum*] as if in adjoining meadows, delighting in the different flowers—that is, in the mystical senses—she may boast that she has woven a multicolored crown for her head from the word of God. (Seyfarth, 3; Epistula 60–64; Newman, 270)

Her male colleagues had recently come to appreciate the spiritual knowledge gleaned from "woods and stones," but the enclosed nun who used the *Speculum virginum* had no such forest or crag to enjoy.[73] Not, at least, according to the spiritual ideals this text sought to espouse. Instead of the fertile valleys of the monastic estate, Theodora had the instruction of this book, an illustrated guide for seeing God. The treatise acted as the floriated garden in which she had to find the otherwise invisible God. But the treatise was also a mirror, reflecting her own image, her very self. Continually directing Theodora's attention to the florid language of the Song, Peregrinus declares that her chaste body was its referent. Ultimately, she was the paradise garden. She was the field in which divinity was made incarnate. As a picture of a blossoming tree sprouted the visage of Christ, the audience was told that *they* were the virgins germinating the Son; as they sang an *epithalamium* praising the rose of creation that stands by eternally, hand in hand with the Creator, *they* became that rose, and their cloister, its garden. In the cultivation of herself, the virgin would know the "mystical senses"; she would see, taste, hear, smell,

---

73. Bernard of Clairvaux, *Epistola 106,* PL 182:242B.

and touch the presence of God in this garden. In doing so, her body became the cultivated field.

In its rapturous exposition on earthly flora, the treatise aimed to accommodate an experience of paradise on earth, the presence of God for the nun. The author sought to import into the female cloister the "rhetoric of reform" extolled by his contemporaries. And thus he communicated the experience of the cloister in extraordinarily earthly terms. He glorified natural, material pleasure:

> This garden, blossoming with delicious increase, bears the shoots of varied spices, the teeming fruits of peace and justice; in it grow flowers of different kinds, diverse in color and fragrance. There the white lily of chastity shines, the crocus of charity burns, the violet of humility glows; there the rose of modesty blushes, the spikenard breathes a fragrance of spiritual discipline; there the slender stalks exude balsam, there thousands of virgins multiply the hues of ardent love in the sight of God; and in short, this garden bears as many delightful perfumes as there are virtuous practices in the religious life. Whenever the bridegroom strolls in this spiritual garden, like a flower more charming than the rest, and rambles among the flowers, enhancing each by his grace, receiving from them no increase of his own native glory, he says, "I have gone down to the nut garden to see the fruits of the valleys." The soul plants a nut garden for God, with delicious fruits of the valleys, when it desires to please God in humility of mind with the unshakable holiness of chaste morals. (Seyfarth, 5–6; *SV* 1.21–35; Newman, 272)

Although the imagery—white lily, crocus, spikenard, shoots, perfumes, nut gardens—referred directly to the Song of Songs, nevertheless in the voice of Peregrinus it is unstable, saturated with multiple referents. On the one hand, his garden indicates the flowers of virtue, so that each virtue is a different flower to be gazed upon, smelled, plucked, and admired; each flower's fruit is to be savored. But he also insisted that Theodora herself was the garden enclosed. Admittedly confused, Theodora responds to Peregrinus's floriated monologue by requesting further training to unpack its metaphors: "But why did the Father and Creator of all flowering and fruit-bearing plants, and of everything that is born, call himself a flower of the field?" (Seyfarth, 6; *SV* 1.48–50; Newman, 272). Why would the Creator equate himself with creation, she puzzled momentarily, only to demand, impatiently: "Say then what this flower is!" (Seyfarth, 7; *SV* 1.59: "Dic igitur, quis sit iste flos"; Newman, 273). Peregrinus responds only by pulling Theodora deeper into his analogical abyss:

> This is the flower born of a flower, the virgin Christ of a virgin
> mother...the flower fairer than its root, more charming than its stalk;
> forever alluring beholders' eyes with its radiance and delighting their
> taste with its marvelous savor; sweet to the smell, pleasing to the touch,
> delightful to the ear, and always desirable to maidenly disciplines. (Sey-
> farth, 7; *SV* 1.61–66; Newman, 273)

Peregrinus's litany of praise, gesturing through all of the elements of the
natural world, seems finally to be anchored in Christ. But his botanical
instruction has only just begun.

By book 4, Peregrinus has returned to the flowers that were to be found
in the cloister, made present as virtues cultivated within the bodies of virgins
living under a monastic rule. He explained that, disciplined through enclosure, the virgin body received God's grace in the virtues:

> To be sure, I speak of not only the aforementioned flowers, that is, the
> virtues, but also the studious cultivators of the virtues in this garden
> of delights where every planting that the father in heaven sowed is
> watered with the showers of spiritual grace and is not easily capable
> of drying up, since that root is revealed by the flow that was emitted.
> Accordingly, this paradise that I place before you is the rule of monas-
> tic life, this garden is the harmonious community of holy virgins in
> Christ. (Seyfarth, 98; *SV* 4.401–6)

The taut and spirited rule of reformed monastic life was a means of strengthening the enclosure of the body, the will to cultivate virtue. But it was a
collective body. Together in community they produced a collective virginity. The materialization of virtues among the congregated virgins made the
cloister into a paradise, affirming the significant spiritual activity provided
by the men who oversaw their care, learning, and progress. In this process,
the men who shared their space and served their spiritual needs became the
"teachers of sacred virgins," guardians of virtue, and fathers in Christ (Seyfarth, 149; *SV* 5.1032: "magister Christi virginum").

What these fathers taught, specifically, were lessons in virtue and vice
that catered to the life of consecrated virgins living in religious communities most likely adjoining or otherwise affiliated with a male monastery.
They taught that, by attending to their bodies, protecting them against vice,
enclosed women participated in furthering the incarnation. Cultivation of
the virgins' virtues was an exercise in making God visible, in giving God
material form:

> Virgins hold mirrors before their eyes to see whether their beauty has
> increased or diminished. For the beholder's image is reflected in the

mirror, and even though the gaze and its reflection are distinct, the beholder's mind is informed about what it wishes to know. We read that Moses, God's confidant, "made a laver from the mirrors of the women who watched at the door of the tabernacle" [Exod. 38.8] in which "Aaron and his sons might wash" [Exod. 40.29]. Now the mirrors of the women are divine words set before the eyes of holy souls, in which they may see at all times how they either please the eternal bridegroom with the beauty of a holy conscience or displease him with the ugliness of sin. The women are said to "watch at the door of the tabernacle" because, as long as they remain in this flesh, they do not enter the holy of holies of our celestial mother Jerusalem. When the "enigma and mirror" by which we know God in part has passed away, what is now sought invisibly in Scriptures will be seen "face to face" [1 Cor. 13.12]. So, blessed virgins of Christ, wash your conscience in this laver constructed from the divine law, so that God's image in you may shine the more brightly and what is now hidden from mortals, being divine, may appear more radiant than the noonday sun. (Seyfarth, 2–3; Epistula 40–58; Newman, 270)

The author recommends two simultaneous practices in this passage. First, he instructs the virgins to gaze upon the ideal beauty in the mirror so that they may see how to progress in their own beauty, that is, in virtue. "The gaze and the reflection are distinct," but through such practice they were brought into greater conformity. That is, the ideal and reality might come together in the practice of virtue within the monastic enclosure. Looking into the *Speculum,* the virgins would find the words of Scripture, divine words. And what should be reflected back at them upon viewing was the earthly image of the divine utterance, that is, the Word. Therefore, through the proper living of monastic life as instructed in the *Speculum virginum,* the virgins would come to reflect the Word in their bodies. They would come to incarnate God. The treatise taught them to do so through cultivation of the virtues. It drew attention to their virgin bodies as potential conduits of the divine.

Second, through these words the virgins received instruction in allegorical reading, both of Scripture and of the material world. Just as the excerpted passage from Exodus had an allegorical, christological interpretation likening it to New Testament fulfillment in Corinthians, so also, according to the *Speculum,* the world itself could be read according to a christological hermeneutics. Within the virgins' bodies, waiting to be uncovered through a refining of the virtues, lay the image of God. The *Speculum* affirmed that the whole created world carried within it the likeness of the Creator. The cultivation of virtue thus fueled the imaginative process, enabled the virgin to see God, indeed to become an engine of the incarnation.

How could an ordinary virgin do such a thing? The opening image of the treatise, a tree of Jesse, provided assistance for appreciating the significance of the virgin's life (fig. 1.1).[74] Among the visages on the tree is that of the Virgin Mary immersed in tendrils connecting her to David, and through Jesse to Boaz. The word "virga" surrounds her. She was the branch connecting the prophets to Jesus Christ. Above her is the flower, Christ, with "flos" and "filius" etched beside his countenance. In the bottom left- and right-hand corners are busts of Peregrinus and Theodora, respectively, engrossed in conversation. They point at the blossoming foliage before them—the subject of their conversation, "the sacred virgins of Christ nourishing their flower and fruit in Christ's love" (Seyfarth, 3; Epistula 65–66; Newman, 270). The other virgins of the community also have a place among the branches, bringing Christ's members into being. Six of them congregate in various calyxes under Mary, while Christ pours out wine over them in a eucharistic gesture. A blossoming flower indicating the seven gifts of the Holy Spirit in seven perfect petals blooms over the entirety of the tree. The effort required of the virgins, I suggest, was to read the image, to learn to see Christ among them, and to make themselves ready for his presence. Their bodies were necessary to make Christ present; their prayers brought him forth. This was their shared identity, engines of re-creation, making the divine presence visible in the material world.

But the image does not stand alone. It was dependent on the multiple texts that accompanied it, texts that enlarged the networks presupposed in the composition of the *Speculum virginum*. Enclosed women would have used this image in discussion together with a male advisor, who was actively engaged in instructing them to think analogically. The meaning conveyed through the visual and verbal texts of the *Speculum virginum* was not anchored in either the text or the accompanying pictures.[75] Instead, its significance lay in the process of reading the world that it advocated. For example, the text

---

74. Morgan Powell has argued that the original version of the *Speculum virginum* opened not with the image of the tree of Jesse but with the trees of virtue and vice. He points to Johannes Trithemius's comment that the *Speculum* contained eight, rather than twelve, books. Examining the manuscript history of the *Speculum,* Powell corroborates other scholarship, such as that of Eleanor Greenhill and Matthäus Bernards, that has suggested that the early manuscripts have explicits at book 10 and that books 11 and 12 were later additions. But he adds that parts 1 and 2 were also later additions, concluding that "the author's original formulation of his project in text and image occurred at the beginning of what is now part three, in its *audi et vide* address." Powell, "The Audio-Visual Poetics," 117–19. Because I am interested in how the book was used to teach analogical reading, I will examine it according to the structure in which it most widely circulated, in twelve books with the *Flos campi,* which is announced at the beginning of book 1, as the subject of the entirety of the conversation.

75. Powell, "The Mirror and the Woman," 158.

FIGURE. 1.1. Tree of Jesse. *Speculum virginum*. Codex Zwettlensis 180, fol. 3r. Zwettl, Austria. Zisterzienserstift. Courtesy Zisterzienserstift Zwettl. Reproduction courtesy of the Hill Monastic Manuscript Library.

scribbled within the ornament of the Tree of Jesse explains, via a book in the virgin's hands, "like a terebinth tree I extend my branches" (Eccl. 24:22). The book was a means to see the invisible, just as the flower of Mary on the tree that she extended through her branches was a means to see the invisible God in Christ. In Zachary's book, in the upper right hand corner, it is written that, "new wine shall make the women flourish" (Zach. 9:17), a reference to the liquid that Christ pours over the heads of the virgins. Just as Christ ensured his presence on earth in perpetuity after his death by means of his blood in consecrated wine, so also, then, did the virgins provide material access to God by incarnating him through the exercise of virtue. In addition to the text inscribed throughout the image, the image was embedded in text. Peregrinus repeats the words of Zachary in his own dialogue, when he urges the nuns to taste the wine he offers. Throughout the text, Peregrinus issues injunctions to his readers to engage their senses in this manner—to hear, see, touch, taste the garden that the *Speculum* offered.

At the center of this garden, holding up the textual mirror, was Mary. Like a mirror, Mary made God visible. Peregrinus explains that she "brought forth in human sight a flower and its fragrance" (Seyfarth, 7–8; *SV* 1.86–88; Newman, 273). Not just Christ, but the whole world was born again through Mary. Mary was the key to the seemingly endless chain of natural referents. By incarnating Christ, Mary infused divine beauty into all creation, acting as a vessel to unite creation with the creator.

Peregrinus instructed the virgins to imitate Mary, to remake the cloister in the image of an earthly paradise. As Peregrinus insisted,

> Consider the Lord's mother—the ornament of sacred beauty, the mirror of holy virginity. By her distinction in the twin virtues of humility and virginity, she deserved to conceive him whom the heaven and earth do not contain, enclosing in the shrine of her womb the Word begotten without beginning by the Father, who came forth for the salvation of all. (Seyfarth, 114; *SV* 5.1–7; Newman, 283)

Mary was the mirror and guide for the virgins. They should emulate her work in continuing creation, in obliging God to re-create creation. Like Mary, they should reflect Christ. The cloister in which they dwelt should become the vessel itself, the site or container for the uncontainable. Their presence together in prayer, in community was to be an imitation of the Virgin's skill for containing the divine. They too were creatures who sought to bear the Creator (Seyfarth, 118; *SV* 5.123: "creantem creata portabat"). "Imitate this chief of virgins as far as possible," Peregrinus demands of Theodora, "and you too, with Mary, will seem to give birth spiritually to the son of God" (Seyfarth, 114; *SV* 5.11–12; Newman, 284). The virgins took direction from Mary, imitating her effort to cast visibility on divinity. They could do so by cultivating their most sacred virtue, chastity. Mary was more than the mother of God, Peregrinus instructed, she was

the mother of virginity itself. Certainly there had been virgins prior to the
birth of Christ in Mary. These individuals, however, were pure in body, a
strictly physical virginity. By bearing Christ, Mary produced the spiritual
virtue of virginity, the means of making God present in the world. This was
the true work of virgins, their exclusive virtue. Although certain prophets,
like Elijah, were virgins, nevertheless "the grace of virginity proceeded in
the first age of grace from the virgin mother Mary" (Seyfarth, 54; *SV*
2.379–80; Newman, 279). By giving birth to Christ, averred Peregrinus,
Mary clothed virtue in her own flesh. Through their labor to cultivate the
virtues, therefore, divinity was once again made incarnate in the bodies of
women, and heavenly paradise was re-created on earth. They signaled the
glories of a re-created world. It is no wonder that Peregrinus troubled to
limit his profusion of natural imagery—like Mary's labor to mother the
re-creation, these virgins in their cloister must contain the uncontainable.

Peregrinus praised enclosure as the site of the virgins' safekeeping and
the locus of daily incarnation. Their virgin bodies, regulated by the ideal
of enclosure, were sites for divine manifestation and its speculation. Rather
than a place of seclusion, restraint, and dark withdrawal, the enclosure that
Peregrinus praised, and in which he emplaced Theodora's experience of
the world, was a celebration of possibility premised on an alternate mode of
being.[76] Only through enclosure could Theodora become a true virgin and
thus experience the world as re-created. Indeed, according to the *Speculum,*
her enclosure paradoxically intensified her experience of the world because
it was not walls alone that enclosed her, but her impenetrable body itself,
which acted as a wall blocking outsiders and building her virtue. Owing to
her enclosure, and policed by proper decorum, the virgin could reenact with
her male pastor the scripts outlined in the *Speculum virginum,* a dialogue in
praise of the incarnation, a performance in which she was cast as *the* Virgin,
witness to evangelical history, indeed engine of it.[77]

With piqued excitement, Theodora requests that Peregrinus further
describe the Virgin Mother, so that her disciples might better imagine a

---

76. Ehrenschwendtner, "Creating Sacred Space," 310. On enclosure as seclusion, see Jane Tibbets
Schulenberg, "Strict Active Enclosure and Its Effect on Female Monastic Experience," in *Medieval
Religious Women: Distant Echoes,* ed. John Nichols and Lillian Shank (Kalamazoo, MI: Cistercian
Friends, 1984), 51–86. On more literary readings of enclosure, see Shari Horner, *The Discourse of
Enclosure: Representing Women in Old English Literature* (Albany: SUNY Press, 2001), esp. chap. 3; for
a more theoretical reading of the meaning, and pleasure, of enclosure, see Cary Howie, *Claustrophilia:
The Erotics of Enclosure in Medieval Literature* (New York: Palgrave, 2007).

77. Janice Pinder also reads the enclosure as the space necessary for a conversion and thus for the
virgin to merit the bride's kiss. See Janice Pinder, "The Cloister and the Garden: Gendered Images
of Religious Life from the Twelfth and Thirteenth Centuries," in Mews, *Listen, Daughter,* 159–79.

picture of her to emulate. Peregrinus, for once, is stumped. Suddenly he takes the role of the one humbled, unable to grasp Mary's grace, a failure to capture verbally her perfection. He resorts to Scripture, each word of which could bear her name:

> In paradise she is the flower and fruit of trees that exude the finest balsam, and the green shoot of all spices. Among the patriarchs, she is that stock and root from whom the seed and flower of eternal blessing burst forth for all who are foreordained to life. She is mother and virgin, she is revealed by a mystic figure in the bush that burned and was not consumed [Exod. 3.2]. In the tabernacle of Moses, fashioned with such variety of materials, and such marvelous art, she is supremely figured in the branch of Aaron and the golden urn. She is the dry branch that flowered among the other dry branches [Num. 17.2–8], bearing flower and fruit before the whole mass of humankind which had withered in sin, and yielding the sweetness of nuts with no root or moisture of human coupling, i.e. giving birth to Christ, the power of God and wisdom of God [1 Cor. 1.24]. (Seyfarth, 115; *SV* 5.48–58; Newman, 284–85)

Offering Theodora this biblical compendium of natural imagery, Peregrinus once again provides a lesson in analogical reading of the books of Scripture and nature. "If you seek Mary with a subtle understanding," he explains, one can find Mary in any part of the Scriptures or in the world itself (Seyfarth, 117; *SV* 5.98; Newman, 285). She is the *reconciliatrix mundi,* meaning that in her body, humanity and divinity, earth and heaven, matter and spirit, were reconciled (Seyfarth, 126; *SV* 5.369–70).[78] The created world was reconciled with God. More than that, Mary was conceived before time, "since all things existed in the wisdom of the Word of God, waiting to be unfolded as and when God willed, according to their nature, manner, order and species, how could the Mother not preexist with the Son?" (Seyfarth, 118–19; *SV* 5.135–37; Newman, 286). The author of the *Speculum,* through the voice of Peregrinus, articulated a bold place for Mary, though not one that was entirely uncommon for his time. Mary's eternal predestination was an ideal that emerged in the twelfth century and was shared among the likes of Rupert of Deutz, Bernard of Clairvaux, Godfrey of Admont, and, as I will

---

78. Additionally, *SV* 5.359–68: "Posuit ergo deus inimicicias inter virginem et hostem, dissolvens amicicias crudelis pacti, quod ausu temerario pepigerat malicia vel presumptio ad radicem ligni interdicti. Sic Maria repperitur in caelo, sic in paradiso. Maria itaque lucis aeternae . . . orta virga de radice Iesse in terris, ante tempora cuncta presignata Christi mater in caelis Syon et Ierusalem filia regali stirpe progenita."

explore in greater detail in the following chapter, Hildegard of Bingen.[79] What was unique to the *Speculum* author was his investigation of the implications of the world's re-creation and Mary's co-operation in it. He gave shape to an emerging devotional position, one in which women and men participated in the re-creation of the world, saw God in its material forms.

Peregrinus taught a worldly and scriptural hermeneutics adapted for the restrictions of enclosed women. Their access to the world may have been confined, but consecrated virgins, he supposed, might discover God within their own bodies. Men such as himself could thereby see God in the world in the material bodies of these women. The consecrated virgins, Peregrinus asserts, were an example of God's mediation of and materialization in the world. Practicing their virtuous chastity, the virgins enacted a sacrament: "Nothing more certain, nothing more holy than this degree of unity could be uttered or heard or even imagined, because the author of creation created all things that this sacrament [of unity] might be eternally consummated" (Seyfarth, 120; *SV* 5.176–79; Newman, 287). Their chaste virtue continued the sanctification of the material world, united creator and creation. Their bodies were a guarantee that access to the divine was possible on earth and that material bodies might reasonably hope for divine transcendence. As Peregrinus concluded one of his dialogues on enclosure, "It appears that the virginal life is a proof of the angelic life, and a pledge of the future resurrection" (Seyfarth, 10; *SV* 1.169–71: "Unde apparet vitam virginalem angelicae vitae testimonium et quoddam futurae resurrectionis insigne"; Newman, 275). Here the value of the *Speculum*'s instruction to men in particular is evident. In their relationships with and care for women in adjacent or nearby religious communities, male pastors shaped an ideal image, an ideal virtue for women, that necessarily included themselves and their work in a process of worldly sanctification.

As a lesson in analogical interpretation of creation, the *Speculum virginum* offered its users an experience, a means of interpreting the material world and their place in it. The author shaped a new religious way of being, a new identity for women through his particular brand of modeling of the virgin life based on Mary, the "creature who bore the Creator" (Seyfarth, 118; *SV* 5.123: "creantem creata portabat"; Newman, 286). By fashioning the virtues of virginity appropriate for observation in monastic space shared between the sexes, the author imported the naturalistic language of monastic reform into the female enclosure. There, rather than the sprawling, demarcated

---

79. Barbara Newman, *God and the Goddesses: Vision, Poetry, and Belief in the Middle Ages* (Philadelphia: University of Pennsylvania Press, 2003), 199.

monastic estate providing the material image through which to speculate the visible vestiges of an invisible God, the virgin body of the enclosed woman was the medium for speculation, the material image through which to see God. While "body" remains a key concept for interpreting female religious instruction, here its importance derives from the context of material concern, a concern articulated in the *Speculum* through Mary's role in re-creating the elements of the created world. The *Speculum virginum* demonstrates the real depths and implications of the language of natural renewal. Renewal and reform was of the whole created world; it was a celebration of the world's re-creation.

Chapter 2

Viriditas and *Virginitas*

The image of Hildegard of Bingen's merry band of virgins, attired in silken garments and embroidered crowns during tony feast day celebrations, has captured the imagination of scholars, filmmakers, and medieval enthusiasts alike.[1] These "blithe noble virgins" donned gold jewelry and allowed their hair to flow freely beneath floor-length veils to receive communion as true brides of Christ, free from the subjugation of an earthly marriage.[2] Hildegard's insistence on such fanfare was the source of tension between her and Tenxwind, the *magistra* of the reformed Augustinian house at Andernach, who criticized her luxury and her practice of admitting only the daughters of nobility into her community. Hildegard's love of opulent accessorizing has been considered more recently as a point of contrast with the reformed simplicity and modesty commanded of the virgins of the *Speculum virginum*. For example, Constant Mews has remarked

---

1. Pamela Sheingorn, "The Virtues of Hildegard's *Ordo virtutum:* or, It Was a Woman's World," in *The Ordo virtutum of Hildegard of Bingen: Critical Studies,* ed. Audrey Davidson (Kalamazoo, MI: Medieval Institute Publications, 1992); *Vision: Aus dem Leben der Hildegard von Bingen,* dir. Margarethe von Trotta (Munich: Celluloid Dreams, 2009).

2. For a criticism of Hildegard's "strange and irregular practices," see Letter 52, "Mistress Tengswich to Hildegard," in *The Letters of Hildegard of Bingen,* trans. Joseph Baird and Radd Ehrman (New York: Oxford University Press, 1994), 1:127–28; *Hildegardis Bingensis epistolarium,* ed. Lieven Van Acker, CCCM 91 (Turnhout: Brepols, 1991, 1993), 126.

that "the *Speculum virginum* offers a vision of the religious life so different from that provided by Hildegard of Bingen that it seems difficult to imagine that she was profoundly influenced by [the *Speculum* author's] perspective."[3] Whereas the author of the *Speculum* warned virgins against the lure of material extravagance, Hildegard actively encouraged vestmental grandeur and took into her care only nuns of aristocratic lineage. But an examination of the instructive texts that Hildegard designed for communal use demonstrates some important similarities with the *Speculum*. A new interpretation of Hildegard's devotion might emerge if we examine not what she saw—that is, her visionary tracts—but the performances she created to be seen.

Hildegard's famed fondness for sartorial luxury was no mere concession to the comforts of a noble upbringing. It made a devotional and theological point about the divine materiality of re-creation, and the role that the consecrated virgin played in it. Defending her sumptuousness, Hildegard's letter of response to Tenxwind, composed ca. 1148–50, championed *viriditas* as a speculatory means of identifying God's presence in the material world. "[The virgin] stands in the unsullied purity of paradise," she wrote, "lovely and unwithering, and she always remains in the full vitality of the budding rod."[4] Hildegard believed that the earth's canopy of green grass was proof of God's creative energy, or *viriditas,* at work in the material world of creation. In the same way, she taught, within the world of the cloister, the virgins' long flowing hair was the external manifestation of their virtues, their work through *viriditas* to render God present to the material world. For Hildegard, *viriditas* and *virginitas* were inextricably yoked; the practice of virginity compelled the world's viridity, making God materially present. Hildegard fashioned a theology of virginity in which her community might command a pivotal role in making God accessible in the world, even claiming for that community a participation in divinization itself.

It is possible that Hildegard knew the *Speculum virginum* and imbibed from it the notion that consecrated virgins retained a special task to continue the world's re-creation. Along with two or three other women, she lived until 1147 in a stone cell attached to the monastery of Disibodenberg, which was affiliated with the Hirsau reform. The *Speculum virginum* circulated during Hildegard's lifetime among the monasteries under the influence of Hirsau.

---

3. Constant Mews, "Hildegard of Bingen, the *Speculum virginum* and Religious Reform," in *Hildegard von Bingen in ihrem historischen Umfeld,* ed. Alfred Haverkamp and Alexander Reverchon (Mainz: P. Von Zabern), 250.

4. Hildegard, *Epistolarium,* 52.24–26, p. 128: "ipsa stat in simplicitate et in integritate pulchri paradisi, qui numquam aridus apparebit, sed semper permanet in plena viriditate floris virge"; *The Letters,* 129.

Additionally, a manuscript leaf depicting a tree of Jesse from a twelfth-century *Speculum virginum* belonged to the church of Rheinbrohl, which was proximate to Bingen, so that the text was likely known in her region.[5] But even if Hildegard did not know the *Speculum virginum* directly, it is clear that she deployed natural language and imagery to convey the same sense of possibility for divine access in the re-created world. For her, virgins were uniquely capable of incarnating God and, moreover, of achieving divinization. Although a public figure with frequent contact with the outside world, Hildegard nevertheless fashioned the female cloister as an enclosed space where re-creation was daily recapitulated by virgins practicing virtue while intoning the divine office.

The pervasive concerns of the texts that I examine in this chapter and chapter 1—the *Speculum virginum,* Hildegard's liturgical compositions, and, briefly, Herrad of Hohenbourg's *Hortus deliciarum*—stem from their context in serving the needs of women in religious houses in the twelfth-century Rhineland. Each of these texts relies on visual and verbal imagery rooted in trees and gardens, often explicitly modeled on the Song of Songs, to encourage and educate virgins. As I argued in chapter 1, the natural language and verdant imagery typically associated with the "rhetoric of reform" indicated an emerging sense of the world as having been re-created by God's incarnation in matter, remaking matter as potentially transcendent and a conveyor of the divine. Consecrated virgins, as brides of Christ and impersonators of his mother, held a special duty and devotional capacity in such a world. They continually incarnated Christ through their practice of virtue. The textual constellation of virgin audience, virtuous practice, and natural imagery, however, did not always align to project the same meaning. Hildegard's interpretation and use of the natural world and its re-creation in the liturgical performances she composed for her virgins held a very different meaning and purpose from those of the *Speculum virginum* and conveyed differences still from the textual garden that Herrad constructed for the virgins of Hohenbourg. But the varied treatment of this constellation of themes indicates their importance as shared spiritual ideals among communities of women in twelfth-century German reformed monasticism.

---

5. Margot Fassler has argued for a connection between the *Speculum virginum* and Hildegard's liturgical interpretation of the *stirps Jesse;* see Fassler, "Composer and Dramatist: Melodious Singing and the Freshness of Remorse," in *Voice of the Living Light,* ed. Barbara Newman (Berkeley: University of California Press, 1998), 158. See also Fassler, "History and Practice: The Opening of Hildegard's *Scivias* in a Liturgical Framework," *Religion and Literature* 42 (2010): 211–27.

The monastery of Disibodenberg, where Hildegard lived from 1112 to 1147, was a reformed Benedictine house in the Hirsau family.[6] Hildegard and her spiritual teacher, Jutta, lived in an enclosed cell opposite the monks' cloister.[7] Despite her presence in an anchor-hold, however, Hildegard was not socially isolated.[8] Jutta had developed a local reputation for prophecy and healing, and thus the women often found themselves in the company of visiting pilgrims and attracted the presence of additional daughters from nearby noble families.[9] When Hildegard assumed the position of *magistra* after Jutta's death, the community grew steadily, and she began to elaborate on their observance by composing songs and rituals to expand on the Psalter and the Divine Office. As her community continued to grow, along with her reputation for religious observance and prophecy, Hildegard began to cast about for a new location to found an enlarged house. Although the monks of Disibodenberg at first protested, Hildegard eventually managed, with grand theatrics, to secure the sisters' freedom from them as well as from lay interference.[10] By 1155, she had officially founded the new monastic community of the Rupertsberg. In addition to negotiating the right to maintain their property, including that which the sisters had brought with them upon entry into Disibodenberg, Hildegard also managed by 1158 to elicit the monks' consent to provide pastoral care and their pledge not to interfere with the appointment of her successor.[11] Hildegard's community therefore was remarkably independent. Moreover, as "abbess to the world," she cultivated a public persona, engaging in preaching missions in the Main, Moselle, and Rhine River valleys, and entertaining visitors to the Rupertsberg monastery as an acclaimed prophet and visionary.[12]

---

6. Julie Hotchin, "Images and Their Places: Hildegard of Bingen and Her Communities," *Tjurunga* 49 (1996): 23–38; Wolfgang Seibrich, "Geschichte des Klosters Disibodenberg," in *Hildegard von Bingen, 1179–1979: Festschrift zum 800. Todestag der Heiligen,* ed. Anton Brück (Mainz: Selbstverlag der Gesellschaft für Mittelrheinische Kirchengeschichte, 1979), 55–76.

7. John Van Engen, "Abess: Mother and Teacher," in Newman, *Voice of the Living Light,* 34.

8. On Hildegard and Jutta's life in the anchor-hold, and their relationship, see Julie Hotchin, "Enclosure and Containment: Jutta and Hildegard at the Abbey of St. Disibod," *Magistra* 2 (1996): 103–23.

9. At least seven more women joined the original community by the time of Jutta's death in 1136.

10. *Vita Sanctae Hildegardis,* ed. Monika Klaes, CCCM 126 (Turnhout: Brepols, 1993), 2.7, p. 31; trans. Hugh Feiss as *The Life of the Saintly Hildegard* (Toronto: University of Toronto Press, 1996).

11. The original documents confirming the properties and privileges of the Rupertsberg cloister are preserved in the *Mainzer Urkundenbuch,* vol. 2, pt. 1, ed. Peter Acht (Darmstadt: Verlag, 1968), nos. 230 and 231; trans. Anna Silvas in *Jutta & Hildegard: The Biographical Sources* (University Park: Pennsylvania State University Press, 1999), 240–45.

12. On Hildegard as "abbess to the world," see Joan Ferrante, "Correspondent: Blessed Is the Speech of Your Mouth," in Newman, *Voice of the Living Light,* 91–109.

Although Hildegard sought a public audience for her visions and letters, when she composed her liturgical pieces for the community in her care, she wrote as the head of a monastic community, the director of its liturgy, and with a specific set of spiritual ideals in mind, ideals that she believed were realized through the performance of the Divine Office. These ideals, affirming virginity and the monastic enclosure that protected it, might appear at odds with her pursuit of a public audience, preaching missions, epistolary activity, and exhortations to reform. But situated within the context of the community for whom they were composed, Hildegard's praise of enclosure takes on new meaning. Enclosure was not for her a policy of strict seclusion, apart from the world. For her it was tantamount to the conveyance of an experience, an alternate world that the community created. In twelfth-century reformed monasticism, particularly in German-speaking regions where men and women often lived communally, treatises on spiritual formation and pastoral care routinely employed an impassioned rhetoric of enclosure that had little bearing on reality.[13] For example, a report from Irimbert, abbot of Admont from 1172 to 1176 and spiritual tutor to its nuns, describes the nuns' quarters as enclosed by a triple-bolted gate and only accessible when a dying sister required last rites. Given the economic, educational, and scriptorial needs of reform, which necessitated contact with ordained men as well as with persons outside the cloister, however, this description could not have represented an accurate reflection of reality.[14] Irimbert's commentary, therefore, must represent a theoretical allegiance to enclosure, which served as a reassurance for women and an apology against potential detractors.[15] Hildegard's liturgical commentaries built on an ideal of enclosure that hardly reflected the lived reality of the Rupertsberg community. For her, the rhetoric of enclosure provided an imaginative space for living out virgin ideals and performing the Divine Office. It created an imagined community wherein, at least for the period of the liturgical performance, the virgins were impermeable to the world, and in which the monastery became an alternate space

---

13. Christina Lutter, "Christ's Educated Brides: Literacy, Spirituality, and Gender in Twelfth-Century Admont," in *Manuscripts and Monastic Culture: Reform and Renewal in Germany*, ed. Alison Beach (Turnhout: Brepols, 2007), 191–213.

14. Lutter, "Christ's Educated Brides," 198–201; for Iribert's report on the fire that destroyed parts of Admont, see *Ven. Irimberti abbatis Admontensis de incendio monasterii sui, ac de vita moribus virginum sanctimonialium parthenonis Admuntensis Ord. S. Ben. Narratio*, in Christina Lutter, *Geschlecht & Wissen, Norm & Praxis, Lesen & Schreiben: Monastische Reformgemeinschaften im 12. Jahrhundert* (Vienna: Oldenbourg, 2005), 222–26.

15. Lutter, "Christ's Educated Brides," 211.

where Christ was truly present.[16] Like Mary's womb, the monastic enclosure acted as a container, a vessel. For Hildegard, it was the site where God's presence was made manifest.

Hildegard's liturgical program contained an essential component of her instruction.[17] As she stated in her famous letter of 1178 to the prelates at Mainz, she intended in the Rupertsberg liturgy to reconstruct the conditions of heaven in the place of the cloister. When the nuns in her convent acted out their liturgical dramas and sang antiphons in the Divine Office, according to Hildegard, they re-created paradise, an enclosed, albeit imagined, monastic space. As Margot Fassler has argued, Hildegard "defined the rendering of communal song as an incarnational act, basic to the creative regeneration of life that takes place within the monastic community."[18] Music, as she understood it, brought humanity into conformity with God, harmonizing God and humanity in the community; song incarnated divinity. Hildegard viewed liturgy as incarnational in the sense that it made Christ present in the community; it reenacted the incarnation of Christ. When they merely read or recited the liturgy, humans failed to animate it with the spirit of the singing voice. Only through a fully embodied performance, Hildegard asserted, could the literal words deliver their due spiritual meaning.[19] Hildegard thus crafted liturgical songs with the intention that music give spirit to words, fusing them together as an indistinguishable composite, just as humanity and divinity were indistinguishable in the person of Christ. Perfect prayer was for her a reenactment of the incarnation, a complete fusion of humanity with God.[20]

Hildegard's theology of music developed from her interpretation of salvation history.[21] According to Hildegard, the Edenic Adam possessed the true

---

16. On the poetics of space created by the theoretical enclosure of the female monastic house, see Marie-Luise Ehrenschwendtner, "Creating the Sacred Space Within: Enclosure as a Defining Feature in the Convent Life of Medieval Dominican Sisters (13th–15th c.)," *Viator* 41 (2010): 308–10.

17. Beverly Mayne Kienzle has shown how Hildegard combined liturgy, drama, and exegesis in her teaching of the nuns at Rupertsberg. See Kienzle, "Hildegard of Bingen's Teaching in Her *Expositiones evangeliorum* and *Ordo virtutum,*" in *Medieval Monastic Education,* ed. George Ferzoco and Carolyn Meussig (New York: Leicester University Press, 2000), 72–86; see also Kienzle, *Hildegard of Bingen and Her Gospel Homilies* (Turnhout: Brepols, 2009).

18. Fassler, "Composer and Dramatist," 149.

19. Hildegard, "Epistola XXIII," in *Epistolarium,* 61–66; *The Letters,* 1:76–80.

20. For Hildegard, the union of harmony and word *is* the incarnation. See Bruce Holsinger, *Music, Body, and Desire in Medieval Culture: Hildegard of Bingen to Chaucer* (Stanford, CA: Stanford University Press, 2001), 93.

21. On Hildegard's musical thought, see, in addition to Barbara Newman's introduction to Hildegard of Bingen, *Symphonia: A Critical Edition of the "Symphonia armoniae celestium revelationum,"* ed. and trans. Barbara Newman, 2nd ed. (Ithaca, NY: Cornell University Press, 1998), 12–26; Holsinger, *Music, Body, and Desire,* 87–136; M. Immaculata Ritscher, "Zur Musik der hl. Hildegard von Bingen," in Brück, *Hildegard von Bingen 1179–1979,* 189–210; Fassler, "Composer and Dramatist," 149–75.

voice of prayer. Adam communicated with God perfectly, immediately: "For while he was still innocent, before his transgression, his voice blended fully with the voices of the angels in their praise of God."[22] Adam's voice, according to Hildegard, was pure music. His harmonious words perfectly communicated their meaning. They were immediate. In the postlapsarian world, however, unsung words faltered; "man needed the voice of the living spirit, but Adam lost this voice through disobedience."[23] Sung liturgy therefore mimicked the voice of Adam in paradise. To Hildegard, liturgy was a form of immediate prayer, the union of human with the divine. Liturgical song was the perfect communication, conveying the practitioner to an immediate, wordless union with God.

According to Hildegard, Adam's estrangement from perfect communication with God caused the stifling of an additional human faculty. Just as Adam's song was muted, his vision of paradise also began to fade, and he "fell asleep to that knowledge which he possessed before his sin, just as a person on waking up only dimly remembers what he had seen in his dreams."[24] No longer could he see God in the created world, as he had in paradise. Adam and his progeny were impaired, their senses dulled and misled by separation from paradise. Hildegard taught that the incarnation had been necessary in order to heal human sight, in order to see God in the world.

Just as Mary's womb was key to the incarnation of Christ, so it would be key to the restoration of the human capacity to perceive God. Mary enabled prayer to accomplish the reunion of humanity and divinity: "For heaven flooded you like unbodied speech/ and you gave it a tongue."[25] Hildegard likened the incarnation to a renewed speech capacity that enabled humans to access divinity. The sin that dulled the senses when Adam ate the fruit of the tree of knowledge, cutting him off from his vision of God, was reversed when Mary incarnated divinity in her womb. The liturgical and paraliturgical songs that Hildegard composed for the nuns of Rupertsberg clarify her understanding of the role of virgins in the human perception of God. Her *Ordo virtutum* (Play of the Virtues), a morality play set to music,

---

22. Hildegard, *Epistolarium,* p. 63, no. XXIII, lines 67–71: "qui ante transgressionem, adhuc innocens, non minimam societatem cum angelicarum laudum vocibus habebat, quas ipsi ex spiritali natura sua possident, qui a Spiritu qui Deus est spiritus vocantur"; *The Letters,* 77.

23. Hildegard, *Epistolarium,* p. 63, no. XXIII, lines 66–67: "recolimus qualiter homo vocem viventis Spiritus requisiuit"; *The Letters,* 77.

24. Hildegard, *Epistolarium,* p. 63, no. XXIII, lines 71–77: "Similitudinem ergo vocis angelicae, quam in paradiso habebat, Adam perdidit, et in scientia qua ante peccatum preditus erat, ita obdormiuit, sicut homo a somno evigilans de his, que in somnis viderat, inscius et incertus redditur"; *The Letters,* 78.

25. Hildegard, *Symphonia,* 122–23: "Nam hec superna infusio/ in te fuit/ quod supernum Verbum/ in te carnem induit."

and *Symphonia armoniae celestium revelationum* (Symphony of the Harmony of Celestial Revelations), a lyrical cycle consisting of sequences, hymns, antiphons, and responsories, illustrate how Hildegard believed that, within the sacred enclosure created by the cloister, the nuns' voices could serve to reverse Adam's sin and to recapitulate the incarnation. Through liturgical song, she believed, the nuns made God present in the world.

Enacting the Incarnation

Hildegard designed her liturgical compositions for the women of her community as sung performances intended to reenact for the imaginations of the assembled women the act of God's incarnation. This performative re-creation is captured in her *Ordo virtutum de patriarchis et prophetis.*[26] Hildegard's liturgical drama featured an almost entirely allegorical cast. Hildegard likely composed the *Ordo* as a liturgical celebration performed for the formal consecration of virgins, the service during which the bishop conferred on the virgins the special garb that Hildegard had devised for her nuns. The *Ordo* emphasizes repeatedly the presence of robes, perhaps referencing the act of taking the veil at the consecration ceremony, which signified the changing of robes that the virgins perform when they take their vow of chastity.[27] But the robes also called attention to themselves as made objects, as material fragments of creation. In their colors, they represented flowers that performed the majority of acting in the play as virtuous blossoms budding forth God. As she conceived it, the play was entirely allegorical, a means to draw out the cosmic significance of the liturgical work performed by the women of Rupertsberg. Hildegard designed the cloister as a heavenly garden where her nuns held unfettered sight of and conversation with God, just like the prelapsarian Adam. Performing the *Ordo,* the virgins of Rupertsberg would have acted out roles as personified virtues, battling the devil for a tempted soul (Anima). The only spoken words in the play are uttered, or shouted rather, by the devil.

The opening scene of the *Ordo virtutum* presents the sixteen personified virtues, cloaked in dazzling robes of bright colors, assembled on a dais, and

---

26. The lengthier *Ordo virtutum de patriarchis et prophetis* is the title given in British Library Additional MS 15102, a fifteenth-century copy of Hildegard's corpus undertaken by John Trittenheim, abbot of Spanheim, who claims that it was copied from a volume housed in the Rupertsberg cloister that was said to have been written by Hildegard.

27. On the special bridal vestments Hildegard used to dress her nuns in, with rings, veils, and tiaras, see Sheingorn, "The Virtues of Hildegard's *Ordo virtutum,*" 52.

staggered upward in the form of a tree. A chorus of virtues sings the first lines of the play:

> The Word of God grows bright in the shape of man
> And thus we shine with him
> Building up the limbs of his beautiful body.[28]

For Hildegard, much like the author of the *Speculum,* the virtues mediated Christ's manifestation on earth, delivering to humanity the presence of the divine body. As the nun exercised true virtue, she incarnated Christ, built his limbs on earth.

Similar to the imagery weaved throughout the *Speculum virginum,* Hildegard's vision of the incarnational work of the assembled women functioned as a liturgical exegesis of the "flowering branch" of Isaiah 11:1. When the virtues sing, "I will lead you/ into the radiant light of the flower of the rod," Hildegard alluded to the *virga* that medieval exegetes had identified as the *stirps Jesse,* the flowering branch of Christ's lineage based on Matthew's genealogy.[29] By the twelfth century, the exemplary *stirps Jesse* iconography could be found, for example, in the window commissioned by Abbot Suger for St. Denis in 1144, which was reproduced, most notably at Chartres, throughout the second half of the twelfth century and into the thirteenth.[30] This exemplar portrayed a reclining Jesse with a branch growing from his loins into buds of David, Mary, and the floral Christ. Madeline Caviness has argued that the *stirps Jesse* imagery, which is particularly pervasive in books of hours, appealed to women who identified with its subversive "claim to matriliny and even matriarchy."[31] Hildegard, however, adapted the Isaiahan branch imagery further to embolden even matriarchal claims. In her hands, Jesse and David are unimportant—it is Mary's work of incarnating God that gave the branch its generative life. For Hildegard, the image recognized the analogous role of the consecrated virgins in incarnating God, "building his limbs" in the cloister. It was their duty to preserve the "noble

---

28. Peter Dronke, *Nine Medieval Latin Plays* (Cambridge: Cambridge University Press, 2008), 180: "Verbum dei clarescit in forma hominis,/ et ideo fulgemus cum illo,/ edificantes membra sui pulcri corporis."

29. Dronke, *Nine Medieval Latin Plays,* 166: "et perducam vos in candidam lucem floris virge."

30. Arthur Watson, *Early Iconography of the Tree of Jesse* (London: Oxford University Press, 1934).

31. Madeline Caviness, "Anchoress, Abbess, and Queen: Donor and Patrons or Intercessors and Matrons?," in *The Cultural Patronage of Medieval Women* (Athens: University of Georgia Press, 1996), 129–30.

flower" by mediating the light of divinity into the created world.[32] They performed this work liturgically, by exercising their chaste virtue. The roots of
Hildegard's tree therefore were composed not of members of the lineage of
Israel, Jesse and David, but of the patriarchs and prophets who first believed
in and foretold the incarnation of God in the womb of a virgin.

Building this allegorical flower, the limbs of Christ, Hildegard aimed in
the *Ordo virtutum* to create a garden within the cloister. Her stage directions
compelled the women to align in descending order, wearing colorful robes,
as a stunning floriated tree in the sanctuary. Their role in the play, intoning
the parts of personified virtues, was to bear fruit at the top of the tree. In the
rafters, more nuns, dressed as prophets, played the part of the tree's roots. In
Hildegard's replica of this verdant landscape, God was represented by light,
and the job of the virtues was to disseminate God's light by casting shadows
from their branches. The tree of the *Ordo* grew from earth to heaven, from
the created world to eternity, from the Old Testament prophets to their fulfillment in the incarnation and salvation accomplished through Christ and
his mother.

The virgins' work in this performance was to restore human memory
of the garden paradise, of the created world as God originally intended it.
Therefore the performance re-created the garden visually and aurally, as an
experience. Hildegard used the materials at her disposal—bodies, robes, and
voices—to promote the restoration of memory, harking back to the earliest
time of creation, when humans enjoyed unmediated access to God:

> Daughters of Israel, God raised you from beneath the tree, so now remem-
> ber how it was planted.
> Therefore rejoice, daughters of Jerusalem.[33]

The virgins would "remember" by re-creating a garden in the cloister,
endowing it with material presence through their performance of song. Hildegard's liturgical and paraliturgical compositions were an extension of her
theological teaching. The *Ordo virtutum* thus offered a natural theology for
virgins, a means to procreate chastely. But Hildegard's play was no crude substitute for the life of mothering and childbirth the women had forsaken—it
rendered them anew into proud builders of the body of Christ.

Drama ensues in the *Ordo* when Felix Anima, catching sight of the tree,
wishes to take her place among the virtues on the highest branches. She

---

32. Dronke, *Nine Medieval Latin Plays,* 166–69: "venite ad me, Virtutes, et perducam vos in
candidam lucem floris virge" and "cum te sol perfulgit ita quod nobilis flos tuus numquam cadet."
33. Dronke, *Nine Medieval Latin Plays,* 172–73; scene 2, lines 156–58.

yearns to return to the bliss of Eden: "Oh sweet divinity, oh gentle life, in which I shall wear a radiant robe, receiving that which I lost in my first manifestation. I sigh for you and invoke the virtues."[34] Felix Anima must rely on the virtues for guidance in recovering the lost robe of her body, the perfect garments in which she would have been clothed when soul and body were in harmony before Adam's fall. When Anima protests that exercising virtue is too grueling a task, that she lacks the strength "to fight against the flesh," the virtues reply that the incarnation of Christ remade the world in order more simply to render access to God in the garden.[35]

> You instrument of bliss, why are you so tearful
> In the face of an evil God crushed in a maidenly being?[36]

The problem against which the felicitous soul struggles is already resolved, they explain. When Christ came in the incarnation, he perfected the created world and enabled humans to know and love God. Virgin bodies participated in remaking the world by their practice of virtue.

The exchange between the optimistic virtues and the sheepish soul is interrupted by a lengthy musical interlude in which each virtue intones a self-referential song in chorus. The interlude is the dominant piece of the entire *Ordo virtutum,* occupying about half of the published score.[37] In terms of action forwarding the narrative, however, nothing occurs other than perhaps some light dancing performed by the virtues. At the immediate center of the *Ordo,* during the musical interlude, the virgins intone their most lavish and musically florid verses, each word imbued with extended melismata:

> The flower in the meadow falls in the wind, the rain splashes it,
> But you, Maidenhood, remain in the symphonies of heavenly habitants:
> You are the tender flower that will never grow dry.[38]

The play once again unfolds in order to re-create a resplendent springtime garden blooming within the walls of the cloister. Here in this verdant, blossoming spell of garden song, Hildegard directed the nuns of Rupertsberg to remake the world. For Hildegard, the life of the nuns in the cloister was the life of prelapsarian bliss in the garden of paradise, the world as originally

---

34. Ibid., 160–61; scene 1, lines 16–19.
35. Ibid., 162–63; scene 1, line 28.
36. Ibid., lines 30–31.
37. Robert Potter, "The *Ordo virtutum:* Ancestor of the English Moralities?" *Comparative Drama* 20 (1986): 207.
38. Dronke, *Nine Medieval Latin Plays,* 167–68; scene 2, lines 108–11.

designed. The women who entered the cloister, Hildegard's play asserted, should know that they are re-creating heaven on earth, and continuing the incarnation in the created world. With their voices as mediators, the virgins restored sight of God to their community.

When the action resumes, it is at the hands of Anima, who casts off her robes and thus rouses Diabolus. Screeching inharmoniously in spoken word, he tempts Anima to pleasure herself with worldly delight. His reason is supreme—God's deputy, Natura, goads abundance and fertility whereas chastity

> Know[s] not what you bring forth
> because your womb is empty of any fair form taken from man.[39]

Diabolus reasoned that, in observing virginity, the nuns acted unjustly, against God's order to procreate. It went against Nature to slough off sexual procreation, thwarting her orderly governance of the created world.

It is unlikely that Hildegard knew directly the *Cosmographia,* composed in faraway French lands in the 1140s. The imaginative theology of virginity that she constructed in the *Ordo* nevertheless presupposes an exposure to Natura's function as continuator of God's creation.[40] She must have encountered— and, moreover, transformed—the interest in the philosophy of nature so prevalent in the twelfth-century schools. Hildegard adapted the contemporary interest in the theology of the natural world better to accommodate the needs of the women of Rupertsberg. The arguments placed in the mouths of the personified virtues indicate that Hildegard worked through her theology of virginity with Natura's behest in mind. Indeed, Natura's post as supervisor of earthly fecundity presented a problem for all those who wished to observe sexual abstinence, women and men. Bernard of Silvestris and Alan of Lille, the great poets of the twelfth century who personified, praised, and delineated Natura's powers, themselves churchmen obliged to vows of chastity, responded squeamishly to the goddess's procreative bidding. Bernard failed to remark on the conundrum.[41] Alan, with covert subtlety, suggested that in

---

39. Ibid., 178–79; scene 4, lines 235–37.

40. Laurence Moulinier has examined the botanical references in both Hildegard and Bernard Silvestris to conclude that Hildegard was more interested in crafting a theology of creation that included the human and natural order. Laurence Moulinier, "Abbesse et agronome: Hildegarde et le savoir botanique de son temps," in *Hildegard of Bingen: The Context of Her Thought and Art,* ed. Charles Burnett and Peter Dronke (London: Warburg Institute, 1998), 141.

41. Bernard Silvestris, *Cosmographia,* ed. Peter Dronke (Leiden: Brill, 1978); *The Cosmographia of Bernard Silvestris,* trans. Winthrop Wetherbee (New York: Columbia University Press, 1990). Bernard's "Microcosmos" ends with Physis crafting the "wanton loins" of man, which are the only means to fight Lachesis and mortality.

matters sexual, Natura was an inferior guide to Theology.[42] Hildegard was far more daring. Although she acknowledged Natura's function of ensuring the proliferation of creation, she both accepted and moved far beyond the fulfillment of this command. For Hildegard, chastity was not hostile to the requirements of Natura because the incarnation of Christ rewrote the rules of the created world. Through the virtues of the *Ordo,* Hildegard argued that the virgin birth of Christ through Mary ultimately transformed nature, re-created the world so that it could contain the presence of divinity. By attributing to virginity the fecund characteristics of fruits and flowers, she naturalized the virgin birth as a process now to be expected, ordinary.

Hildegard's natural theology of virginity endowed consecrated virgins with a formidable role. Their labor reestablished the world as a paradise garden, renewed its former greenness, its *viriditas.* The final procession of the play acted as Hildegard's *commentaria* on Genesis, on how the incarnation continued to remake creation:

> In the beginning all creation was verdant,
> Flowers blossomed in the midst of it;
> Later, greenness sank away.
> And the champion saw this and said:
> "I know it, but the golden number is not yet full.
> You then behold me, mirror of your fatherhood:
> In my body I am suffering exhaustion,
> Even my little ones faint.
> Now remember that the fullness which was made in the beginning
> need not have grown dry,
> and that then you resolved
> that your eye would never fail
> until you saw my body full of jewels.
> For it wearies me that all my limbs are exposed to mockery:
> Father, behold, I am showing you my wounds."[43]

This final processional song might be considered a tableau vivant, a living tree of Jesse.[44] Hildegard sought to materialize the renewed creation, which

---

42. Alan of Lille, *Complaint of Nature,* ed. and trans. James Sheridan (Toronto: Pontifical Institute of Medieval Studies, 1980); his Natura pawns off the work of overseeing human sexual relations to the distracted, philandering Venus, who grows easily bored of heterosexual procreative sex and thus allows other forms of sexuality into the created realm.

43. Dronke, *Nine Medieval Latin Plays,* 180–81; finale, lines 252–66.

44. Audrey Davidson has called it "early word painting." Audrey Davidson, "Music and Performance: Hildegard of Bingen's *Ordo virtutum,*" in Davidson, *The Ordo virtutum of Hildegard of Bingen,* 21.

she imagined was accomplished by the incarnation *in act* as the virgins performed in the sanctuary. In this processional piece, the florid virtues would have descended from on high in the branches of the tree, climbing down to the ground as they "stretch[ed] out" their limbs and spread their viridity. As the virgins extended their arms, the audience received cues to remember Christ's own arms stretched across the wood of the cross.[45] Although it was the virtues who intoned, "Father, see, I show my wounds to you," they truly were, as actors, Christ's incarnate body, and it was his wounds to which they referred. Here, Christ was literally crucified by the virtues. The image had sacramental bearing for the community at Rupertsberg—the virtues made Christ's body and blood present on earth. According to the play, they incarnated him just as his sacrifice made possible human, material transcendence in resurrection. Hildegard selected the word *gemmae* to describe the appearance of Christ's flesh. Meaning both "jewels" and "buds," the word implied here that Christ's body is a living tree that forever buds new branches through the work of the virgins/virtues on earth, though in heaven he was festooned with jewels rather than leaves. Christ's words in the play are urgent, goading the final fruition of the branches, his "limbs." Through song, Hildegard argued that the incarnation occurred continuously in creation only through the action of the virgins. Their virtuous daily prayer built the body of God on earth.

At the close of the play, the virgins were prompted to implore: "So now, all you people, bend your knees to the Father that he may reach you his hand."[46] As the audience would have bent down on their knees so that Christ could stretch out his arms to them, audience and performers would come together hand in hand. This gesture, enacted as one final, emphatic incarnation, sought to connect humanity with divinity, audience with actors. Such was the *viridatas* established by Christ and the virtues.[47] "Curre

45. Davidson, "Music and Performance," 30.

46. Dronke, *Nine Medieval Latin Plays*, 180–81; finale, lines 267–69: "Ergo nunc omnes homines, genua vestra ad patrem vestrum flectite, ut vobis manum suam porrigat."

47. On Hildegard's concept of *viriditas*, see Victoria Sweet, who surveys the Latin fathers for their use of the term. Victoria Sweet, *Rooted in the Earth, Rooted in the Sky: Hildegard of Bingen and Premodern Medicine* (New York: Routledge, 2006). Before Hildegard, theologians and botanists restricted the term to the life of plants, but Hildegard changed its meaning by using it as a characteristic of the re-created world. Heinrich Schipperges was the first scholar to comment on the primacy of *viriditas* as "greening power" in Hildegard's oeuvre; Schipperges, *Healing Nature of the Cosmos*, trans. John Broadwin (Princeton, NJ: Markus Weiner, 1997), 84. See also Gabrielle Lautenschläger, "*Viriditas*: Ein Begriff und seine Bedeutung," in *Hildegard von Bingen: Prophetin durch die Zeiten*, ed. Edeltraud Forster (Freiburg: Herder, 1997), 224–37; Miriam Schmitt, "Hildegard of Bingen: *Viriditas*, Web of Greening Life-Energy I," *American Benedictine Review* 50 (1999): 253–76; and Schmitt, "Hildegard of Bingen: *Viriditas*, Web of Greening Life-Energy II," *American Benedictine Review* 50 (1999): 353–80.

ad nos," the virtues entreat. Following them, with the audience reaching their arms up to the virgins on the tree, earth was joined to heaven in the music of the *Ordo*.

It is difficult to characterize Hildegard's imaginative theology by means of our present scholarly terminology. While the incarnation of God in Christ was surely fundamental to Hildegard's purpose and to the meaning of life in the cloister, I hesitate to limit the description of her liturgy and devotion with the term "incarnational."[48] Although the spirituality of her monastic contemporaries is also characterized as incarnation-centered, nevertheless their understanding of how properly to express devotion to the incarnation is strikingly different from hers. Rachel Fulton has charted the devotional transformation of Christ from fearsome judge and warlord to weeping sufferer.[49] She attributes this transformation to the eleventh-century monastic meditations of Anselm, John of Fécamp, and Bernard of Clairvaux, which sought to incite empathy, establish identity, and express the loss of selfhood. Sarah McNamer has challenged male authorship of this transformation in Christian devotion. Women's communities, she has argued, requested from male advisers impassioned prompts as "intimate scripts" and fueled new modes of pious and devotional expression, modes that included longing, literal imitation, and spousal love.[50] While all of these modes overlapped with and affirmed one another, they have all come to be considered under the category of "affective devotion," an umbrella term for compassion for a suffering, wounded Christ and the abject sorrow of his mother. Hildegard does not fit so neatly into this characterization of twelfth-century devotional expression. Without detracting from the importance of compassion for the suffering Christ and his sorrowful mother in twelfth-century devotion, I call attention to an alternate mode of devotional expression in this period, one centered on the world's re-creation.

The tradition of meditative assimilation into Christ through the material elements of the world originated in women's communities at the same time that Fulton's narrative of devotional empathy tapers off, in the middle of the twelfth century. This tradition represents another developing strain of devotion to the incarnation, one that just as powerfully insisted on identity

---

48. "Incarnational" is the description provided in Barbara Newman, *Sister of Wisdom: St. Hildegard of Bingen's Theology of the Feminine* (Berkeley: University of California Press, 1987); Kienzle, *Hildegard of Bingen and Her Gospel Homilies,* esp. 170–87; and Fassler, "Composer and Dramatist."

49. Rachel Fulton, *From Judgment to Passion: Devotion to Christ and the Virgin Mary, 800–1200* (New York: Columbia University Press, 2005), 142–92.

50. McNamer, *Affective Meditation and the Origins of Medieval Compassion* (Philadelphia: University of Pennsylvania Press, 2010), 58–85.

with, transformation into, Christ. Against the chorus of male monastic writers who constructed elaborate commentaries on Christ's vulnerability and Mary's sorrow, Hildegard's voice stands out as distinct in its conception of the proper work of women in the cloister, as well as in its influence on her later contemporaries' efforts to reimagine their world as incarnation-centered. Hildegard's liturgical compositions suggest that "affective meditation" took many forms.[51] While the songs and drama that Hildegard composed for the women of Rupertsberg were certainly "affective," they remain distinct from the compassionate suffering and longing typically associated with the devotional movement tracked by McNamer and Fulton. Like the spiritual hermeneutics outlined in the *Speculum virginum*, I argue, Hildegard considered consecrated virgins as distinctive in their ability to incarnate Christ in their virtuous bodies, to conceive of God and enflesh his limbs within the walls of the cloister. In Hildegard's theology, the meaning of the incarnation had a different valence from that ascribed by many of her early male contemporaries and associates, like Rupert of Deutz and Bernard of Clairvaux. For Hildegard, the incarnation signaled a re-creation of the world, one that she interpreted personally, as a continuing process that resonated even on the local level, within her cloister, within her own body. For Hildegard, the incarnation re-created even the Rupertsberg cloister, all the women who inhabited it, and the men who assisted them. Everything within her environment thus responded to the internal logic of the re-created world, each element offered a means through which to know God.

Hildegard's theology of the re-creation of the world and her vision of women's work in the cloister are even more explicit in the liturgical cycle she composed for the women of Rupertsberg. The liturgical song cycle *Symphonia armoniae celestium revelationum,* which Hildegard compiled intermittently throughout her tenure as *magistra,* included themes that are similar to those found in her *Ordo virtutum,* particularly the concern with how the incarnation altered and re-created the material world. Hildegard composed the songs of the *Symphonia* as occasional pieces, at various times; they were not intended as a programmatic whole or a conceptual cycle.[52] The recurring themes and imagery found in the songs—trees, flowers, fruits, birthing, blossoming, imbibing—were therefore not part of a narrative whole, as they were in the plot of the *Ordo* with its construction of a great tree of virtue that

---

51. Particularly as these affective responses to the humanity of Christ have been shown to have a much longer history. See Celia Chazelle, *The Crucified God in the Carolingian Era: Theology and Art of Christ's Passion* (Cambridge: Cambridge University Press, 2001).

52. Peter Dronke, "The Composition of Hildegard of Bingen's *Symphonia," Sacris Erudiri* 19 (1969–70): 389.

incarnated Christ and vanquished sin. The images found in the *Symphonia* were those that pervaded Hildegard's consciousness throughout her lifetime at Rupertsberg, constantly supplying her mind with a form when it strove to sustain a picture of God's presence in the world.

The most concrete and persistent of these naturalistic images of God's presence is that of Mary embodying Christ as the flower crowning her virgin *virga*. Once again, Hildegard turned away from the standard *stirps Jesse* iconography that accentuated lineage and instead chose to shape her *virga* and *flos* to emphasize the act of re-creation in the incarnation. Hildegard portrayed Mary's body as a pleasure garden in which God took ample delight. As she imagined it, God impregnated Mary by singing into her grassy womb a seed that would forever flower in a tree. In *Ave Generosa,* Mary's body rings with sound and flourish:

> And your womb held joy when heaven's
> harmonies rang from you,
> a maiden with child by God,
> for in God your chastity blazed.
> Yes your flesh held joy like the grass
> when the dew falls, when heaven
> freshens its green.[53]

For Hildegard, *viriditas* was the act of God's re-creation of the world, an act that the women of Rupertsberg perpetually recapitulated through their practice of the liturgy. *Viriditas* conveyed for her the power of the re-created world. And this re-created world issued new orders, new laws, especially for devout women to follow. She put forth in song a theology of re-creation in which creation was renewed with the incarnation of Christ, so that humans could discover God in *viriditas.*

According to Hildegard's liturgical theology, Adam's lost musicality was restored through the new creation, and with it, humanity's ability to communicate effectively with God. In the act of performing these songs, Hildegard considered herself and the nuns of Rupertsberg as inhabiting the garden before the fall. Chanting, they were *in act.* Their sung voices conjured an alternate world. The songs are exceedingly self-referential, playing on the continuities between the content of the words and the persons vocalizing them. For example, in a sung dialogue between Mary and Christ, mother

---

53. *Symphonia,* ed. and trans. Newman, 122–23 (parenthetical citations in the text hereafter refer to pages in Newman's edition/translation of Hildegard's *Symphonia*).

and son discuss the odd mechanics of virgin procreation. Mary explains how conception occurred in her fertile womb:

> God who created me
> and formed all my limbs
> and laid in my womb
> all manner of music
> in all the flowers of sound. (*Symphonia*, 260–61)

This curious hybrid form, flowers of sound, was likely a self-referential comment to be crooned by the nuns in choir.[54] Hildegard wished for her nuns to understand that their duty was to incarnate God. Harmonizing daily, *they* were the flowers of sound, decked in robes of rose, violet, and marigold.

Just as in the *Ordo,* Hildegard visualized the virgins' bodies as both floral and musical, analogous to Mary's *virga.* The project in which they were all engaged was incarnational. For example, Hildegard interrupted the poetic flow of her "Hymn to the Virgin" in order to excite the virgins to sing more passionately: "Sing for Mary's sake, sing, for the maiden, sing for God's mother. Sing!" (*Symphonia*, 122–23). In harmonizing, their job was to re-create the musicality of Mary's womb that mingled humanity and divinity in its harmonies. Through song they constituted within the choir the greenness of a re-created world. Just as in the *Ordo,* here Hildegard sought to import *viriditas* within the walls of the cloister. As Bruce Holsinger has suggested, the cloister that the women of Rupertsberg inhabited was seen by them as Mary's enclosed womb.[55] Hildegard designed the cloister as an idealized site where women worked to incarnate the transcendent God. By raising their voices in song, the virgins "filled" Mary's womb, impregnating it with their harmonies.

The consecrated virgins held the premier role in the liturgical life of Rupertsberg. Hildegard's hymns for the virgins outlined their unique duties. Six of Hildegard's liturgical compositions are dedicated to the praise of Saint Ursula and her virgins, whom Hildegard lauded as "a fruit-bearing orchard, a garden in bloom" (*Symphonia*, 234–35). Through liturgical song, Hildegard believed that the virgins were re-creating the verdant garden in which their voices and bodies were restored to innocence. She encouraged them in their extensive round of liturgical songs by insisting on their critical role in the postincarnational world. They constituted a verdant paradise in the cloister:

---

54. On the performance of the songs, see Newman, introduction to *Symphonia,* 27–32.
55. Holsinger, *Music, Body, and Desire,* 104.

the king saw his image
in your faces
when he made you mirrors of
all heaven's graces,
a garden of surpassing
sweetness, a fragrance
wafting all graciousness. (*Symphonia,* 218–19)

Expressing sentiments strikingly similar to those in the *Speculum virginum,*
Hildegard imagined that virgin bodies were mirrors through which the face
of the invisible God was made apparent. They made God's body visible:

Exquisite
eyes fixed on God,
blithe noble virgins,
beholding him and building
at dawn. (*Symphonia,* 218–19)

Their liturgical work built Christ's body and enabled the whole cloister to
behold him, to see God among them. Here Hildegard issued the bold assertion that God's members were made visible to creation through the work of
virgins. Through them, he marked the world. Their liturgical gesticulations
animated God's limbs like so many marionettes:

Loving your son you loved
us all into being; let us
all be his limbs. (*Symphonia,* 106–7)

Through virtuous song, they recapitulated God's act of entering the material
of the world. In these songs, it was not God becoming *body* that Hildegard
celebrated. Her songs rejoiced in God's accessibility, his being, in the world.

Hildegard's liturgical compositions provide insight into her understanding of the relationship of God and creation. In them, she linked re-creation,
incarnation, and *viriditas* to the work of the cloister through the practice of
virginity. The result was an imaginative theology, which is most clear in the
collection of songs celebrating the imagery of the *virga.* To Hildegard, the
incarnation introduced a new creation. It unfurled *viriditas,* "thus the tender
shoot that is her son opened paradise through the cloister of her womb"
(*Symphonia,* 134–35). Mary opened her womb to bring forth the body of
God, and in so doing ushered forth a second creation, a verdant paradise in
which Christ was ever present in the world. In O *quam preciosa,* one can
sense Hildegard working out the implications of her nascent theology of the

re-creation, of what it might mean for the consecrated virgins of Rupertsberg to bear capacities truly analogous to the Virgin's powers of re-creation.
She equated the birth of Christ with the first light of creation:

> But the Holy One
> flooded [Mary] with warmth
> until a flower sprang in her womb
> and the Son of God came forth
> from her secret chamber like the dawn.
>
> Sweet as the buds of spring, her
> son opened paradise
> from the cloister of her womb.
> And the Son of God came forth
> from her secret chamber like the dawn. (*Symphonia,* 134–35)

Christ's birth here "opens paradise," not returning to, but renewing the first
creation wherein humans had direct access to God. Hildegard's attention to
light expressed her concern for the role of sight in visually deciphering the
presence of God in the material world.

Hildegard's use of *virga* imagery diverted the significance of the *stirps Jesse*
from royal ancestry to cloistered women's peculiar vigor. Although during
her lifetime *stirps Jesse* iconography was pervasive for expressing Christ's
genealogy, Hildegard here preferred the Isaiahan *virga* to convey the incarnational power of virginity. According to her visualization of the tree, prophets
and patriarchs composed branches and roots, casting a light that connected
heaven to earth:

> In a luminous shade you proclaim
> a sharp living brightness
> that buds from a branch
> that blossomed alone
> when the radical light took root. (*Symphonia,* 158–59)

Even though they lived in darkness after the fall, the prophets were gifted
with luminous sight to perceive the forthcoming lucidity of the incarnation:

> O you happy roots
> with whom the work of miracles
> was planted—
> and not the work of crimes—
> in a rushing course
> of translucent shadow. (*Symphonia,* 160–61)

Although replete with Jesse-like imagery—roots and buds and shoots that bring forth the great flower—Hildegard was concerned here not with Jesse and his progeny but with the unique capacity of the patriarchs and prophets to intuit the "radical light" of the incarnation. A handful of twelfth-century exegetes focused on this more Marian reading of Christ's lineage. An early twelfth-century sermon, for example, likely written by Hugh of St. Victor and composed for the Feast of the Nativity of the Virgin, praised Abraham as the root, Isaac and Jacob as the trunk, the boughs of patriarchs, and the most vivid red flower of Mary.[56] But Hildegard did not bother to name the prophets and patriarchs. Her eyes were fixed on the work of Mary, and she extolled these ancestral figures only for their ability to see Mary's forthcoming labor.

Mary's body composed the flowering branch of Hildegard's vision of the *stirps Jesse*. Her *virga* song cluster celebrated Mary not for her lineage but for her merits as *virgo:*

> O sweetest branch
> budding from the stock of Jesse,
> what a mighty work is this! (*Symphonia,* 132–33)

The "work" that Hildegard mentions here is Mary's role as a mediatrix, fusing humanity and divinity, in order to provide the necessary sight of God. With these words, Hildegard celebrated not Mary's passive acceptance of God's seed, but the active labor that Mary performed in order to warrant it. Mary's radiant beauty, like the sun, attracted God's attention and affection to her. She was the proactive agent who induced and inspired God to enter the material of the world through her womb: "The supernal father saw a maiden's splendor/ and her mortal flesh spoke his word" (*Symphonia,* 132–33). Because Mary spoke God's word for the benefit of humanity, humans should rejoice by exercising their voice, singing God's materiality continually into being. Mary accomplished this "work" through the incarnation, providing the "sweetest branch" of the tree that remade the created world.

Bruce Holsinger has noted the musical double entendres evoked by Hildegard in her songs in the "*virga* cluster." *Virga* and *virgo,* he shows, also carry meanings that refer them to the staff of the musical note. The term *virga* was self-referential, addressing Hildegard's own music. In this way, the musical connotation of the term *virga* was interchangeable with the generative stem of the virgin, *virgo:*[57]

---

56. Charles Scillia, "Abbess Herrad of Landsberg and the Arbor Patriarcharum," *Proceedings of the Patristic, Medieval, and Renaissance Conference* 8 (1984): 38.

57. Holsinger, *Music, Body, and Desire,* 123–24.

Alleluia! light
burst from your untouched
womb like a flower
on the farther side
of death. The world-tree
is blossoming. Two
realms become one. (*Symphonia,* 124–25)

Like music itself, this song celebrated the fusion of humanity and divinity. Riffing on the similarities between *virga* and *virgo,* Hildegard insisted that the Word is made incarnate in the virgins' sung words of the liturgy.[58] For Hildegard, the *virgo* was the *virga*. The one replaced the other—Mary's virgin body fulfilled Isaiah's prophecy and sprouted the tree of life:

O branch and diadem
of royal purple,
you stand fast in your cloister
like a breastplate.

Unfolding your leaves, you blossomed
in another way
than Adam brought forth
the whole human race. (*Symphonia,* 128–29)

In the same way, the virgins performing these songs in the cloister generated a new progeny. Mary's labor was the tree in the center of the cloister—the tree on the stage during the performance of the *Ordo* and the branch generated into being through the chanting of these songs.

Hildegard employed the second person in musical address to Mary—she did not beseech Mary but redescribed her, rewriting the work of Mary in a manner suitable to her theology of re-creation. So she pleaded with Mary to continue the incarnational work she began, bringing Christ into being as the nuns of Rupertsberg sang:

O saving lady,
you who bore the new light
for humankind:
gather the members of your Son
into celestial harmony. (*Symphonia,* 129–31)

---

58. *Symphonia,* 276. As Barbara Newman has shown, the words were virtually interchangeable.

The effect of the liturgy was to sing Christ's presence into the womb of the cloister. At the very instant that the virgins of the Rupertsberg would sing, "Hail," in remembrance of the annunciation—"When the time came/For you to blossom in your branches/ "hail" was the word to you"—Hildegard hoped to recapture that act of conception.[59] "Hail," uttered through the womb of the cloister, impregnated it with the divine seed, recapitulating Mary's conception with that very word. Hildegard's rhetorical play with *virga/virgo* demonstrates the unique incarnational thrust of her devotional program. While her peers often responded to the incarnation through affective compassion or bridal longing, Hildegard's response was to encompass the incarnation, to recapitulate it. She sought to participate in the world's ongoing re-creation by offering a spiritual ideal of virginity that made God present, accessible in the material of the world.

The work of the virgins in community, specifically in the Divine Office, was thus to recapitulate the incarnation. As they did so, Mary was the exemplar for their work. She conceived not sexually, like Adam and his progeny, but by unfurling leaves from her womb. Her fertility was *viriditas*, which restored human life as the image of God:

> From your womb
> came another life,
> the life that Adam
> stripped from his children. (*Symphonia*, 128–31)

Mary's labor generated a new breed of humans, freshly restored to God's image. Mary herself was thus a great mirror, reflecting the image of God through the world as the progenitor of this reformed species:

> Oh how great
> in its strength is the side of man,
> from which God produced the form of woman.
> He made her the mirror
> of all his beauty
> and the embrace
> of his whole creation. (*Symphonia*, 128–31)

Mary was the "embrace," the gatherer, of the whole created world, the link that bound creator with creation. Through her, God was made present on earth in *viriditas*. And the nuns of Rupertsberg were responsible for maintaining *viriditas*, for making their cloister verdant through liturgical performance:

---

59. Holsinger, *Music, Body, and Desire*, 124.

for the heat of the sun distilled in you
a fragrance like balsam.
For in you bloomed the beautiful flower.
that gave fragrance
to all the spices
that had grown dry.
And they all appeared
in full verdure. (*Symphonia,* 126–27)

Hildegard understood Christ's incarnation as acting as a renewal of material creation that restored the human sensory capacity to apprehend God in the viridity of creation. To her, the incarnation served to recalibrate creation so that enclosed women would better perceive God in creation. For Hildegard, the true creation began with the incarnation. The paradise garden of creation was not in the past, nor was it in the heavenly future. Through song, it was made present in the virgin *virga* of the cloister.

Like the author of the *Speculum virginum,* Hildegard seized on natural imagery, particularly the *viriditas* of the *virga,* as a vehicle for capturing, for the collective imagination of the cloister, the potentialities unleashed by the re-creation. Hildegard was even more resolute than the *Speculum* author on how virgins participated in divinity. She augmented their power, employing them to craft an imaginative theology in which virgins were charged with the task of materializing God, and through which they became divine. Through liturgical performance, they made their cloister into a garden where, like Mary, they attracted God's descent and bestowed his presence on the world.

Performing Salvation: Another Look at the *Virga*

Hildegard's conception of the re-creation as *viriditas,* as enabling access to divinity in the material of the world, was not a prevalent theological inter-pretation of God's action in the world. As a counterpoint, I wish to turn briefly to another twelfth-century treatise composed for a female commu-nity in the Rhineland. Like Hildegard's liturgical compositions and the *Spec-ulum virginum,* the *Hortus deliciarum* of the abbess Herrad of Hohenbourg was written for the instruction of women's communities in the twelfth century. It is a compendium of scriptural exegesis, music, poetry, and images; and, in a most striking similarity to Hildegard's composition and the *Speculum,* it presents itself as a metaphorical garden of flowers and trees for virgins to enjoy. One would thus expect at least the natural imagery and overall agenda of the texts to be similar. And yet the *Hortus deliciarum* represents a very different theological interpretation of the incarnation and of the particular role of virgins in the female monastery. Most noticeable here is the absence of attention to the re-creation of the world and to the specialized role of virgins in accessing divinity on earth. In particular, a comparison of the *virga* imagery in the *Hortus* to that found in the *Speculum virginum* and in Hildegard's *Ordo virtutum* and *Symphonia* demonstrates that these images do not always convey the same meaning or function in like manner. This comparison emphasizes why it is thus critical not to read every example of natural imagery as expressing a feeling for nature, evidence of its discovery, or of how it once "led men to God." More important, it demonstrates how some women—Hildegard and her flock and perhaps some of the readers and users of the *Speculum virginum*—interpreted the theological and rhetorical currents of their time in radically different ways that would enable surprising claims for subsequent generations.

The *Hortus* is an instructional text supervised by Herrad, the abbess of Hohenbourg, around 1175. It is a compendium of Scripture and theology that served to provide the basis of a theological education for the women in Herrad's care.[60] Text and images in the *Hortus* are mutually dependent means of narrating salvation history and of prescribing proper virtuous behavior for enclosed virgins. Herrad announced her intentions in a poem on the first folio: "[Herrad] salutes the Hohenbourg virgins and with good wishes invites them to faith and love of the true bridegroom."[61] Though certainly not all of the canonesses in her care were physical virgins, Herrad addressed the women of her community as such in order to portray them as formidable spouses of Christ.

The *Hortus* had no circulation outside the community of Hohenbourg. It was never copied during the medieval period, which suggests that Herrad intended it solely for the instruction of the women of Hohenbourg, selecting her images, music, subjects, and excerpted texts and composing her poems according to their specific needs. Herrad wished to help the women of Hohenbourg to better understand the theological messages conveyed to them

---

60. The manuscript no longer survives. The standard edition of the *Hortus* (see note 61) is a facsimile published in 1979 and generated from copies, notes, and transcriptions made by scholars prior to its destruction in the 1870 Prussian bombing in Strasbourg, in the library where the manuscript was housed.

61. Herrad, *Hortus deliciarum,* ed. Rosalie Green, Michael Evans, Christine Bischoff, and Michael Curschmann (London: Warburg Institute, 1979), no. 1 (hereafter cited parenthetically in the text in abbreviated form); "Latin Texts and Translations," in Fiona Griffiths, *The Garden of Delights: Reform and Renaissance for Religious Women in the Twelfth Century* (Philadelphia: University of Pennsylvania Press, 2007), 226 (hereafter cited in the notes and parenthetically in the text as Griffiths).

by visiting priests and to supplement their theological education when suitable priests were unavailable.[62] She therefore chose to include in the *Hortus* a number of texts from which priests themselves would have learned, notably the *Speculum ecclesiae* of Honorius Augustodunensis and the *Liber de divinis officiis* of Rupert of Deutz.[63] Herrad may well have been inspired to create such an elaborate visual agenda in the *Hortus* by Honorius's instructions to priests on sermon delivery, which exhorted them to evoke word images or narrative illustrations.[64] The visual reception of the images was clearly a crucial consideration in Herrad's construction of the *Hortus*. She took special care to design each and every image in the *Hortus* to satisfy the specific needs and interests of the women of Hohenbourg.

The *Hortus* is distinct from many of the male-authored compilations of the later twelfth century in its organizational structure. Unlike later compilations, the *Hortus* does not include chapter headings, indexes, or other navigational tools for the user.[65] If a user of the *Hortus* wished to learn about a particular subject, she would need to know where that material fit chronologically in the grand scheme of salvation history. The salvation history recorded by Herrad began with creation, interpreting Old Testament history typologically until the time of the incarnation; it then proceeded to a narrative of the life of Christ, which occupies a third of the pictorial scheme of the treatise; next it examined the church allegorically as the *sponsa Christi,* conveyed a picture of the Last Things, and mused on the individual's struggle against vice.

Throughout this narrative of salvation history, a pleasure garden acted as Herrad's central organizing image. She selected the garden to mark the beginning of salvation history in the creation of the world in Eden, and to denote its final culmination in the heavenly garden of eternal paradise. While the content of the treatise was a garden, a description of the route from Edenic creation to final heavenly delivery, Herrad also considered the text itself, its form, as a garden. She begins the book by explaining: "Here begins the *Hortus deliciarum,* in which the little young maidens are constantly delighted by the collected flowers of Scripture."[66] The flowers of the *Hortus* are decidedly textual. Unlike those of the *Speculum virginum*

---

62. Griffiths, 68.

63. Herrad draws most commonly from Honorius Augustodunesis, Rupert of Deutz, Ivo of Chartres, and Walter of Chatillon. See Griffiths, 49–81.

64. Griffiths, 67.

65. Danielle Joyner, "A Timely History: Images and Texts in the *Hortus Deliciarum*" (PhD diss., Harvard University, 2007).

66. Herrad, *Hortus deliciarum,* no. 3: "Incipit Ortus deliciarum, in quo collectis floribus scripturarum assidue jocundetur turmula adolescentularum"; my trans.

or of Hildegard's liturgical songs, the flowers of the *Hortus deliciarum* do not invite the listener/viewer into a relationship of identity, occasioning an experience of the images portrayed within the text. Instead, the *Hortus* was a compendium of knowledge designed for the salvation of the women of Hohenbourg. The *Hortus* enabled the individual member of Hohenbourg to find her place in salvation history and facilitated her understanding of how to combat vice en route to the garden paradise.[67]

Unlike the gardens and trees of both the *Speculum virginum* and the Hildegardian corpus of songs, which convey a great confidence in the potential of the material world to contain the presence of God, those of the *Hortus deliciarum* suggest a more skeptical response to the prospect of material access to the divine. The opening garden of the *Hortus* presents two trees, one of knowledge and one of life. In this image, Adam is sleeping, unaware, under the tree of life while God labors to create Eve. Adam's slumber served as a warning to those who exhausted themselves in the pleasures of the garden without being prudent, cautious of their excess, of the burgeoning of temptation to sin.[68] The serpent, representing temptation, is denoted as the "father of death," the creator of sin and suffering. He entices Eve to "eat of the fruit prohibited to you/ So that, without doubt, you will be like the Lord./ You will know all" (*Hortus deliciarum*, no. 69; my trans.). According to Herrad, their desire for knowledge, to be like God, led the first humans to sin. While Hildegard saw in consecrated virgins the potential for a return to the angelic life of prelapsarian humans, Herrad considered redemption an ontological state reserved for the afterlife. Access to God on earth was only ever partial for Herrad because sin isolated humanity from divinity until death's deliverance. Toil in this world was devoted to combating vice, the rewards of which would be enjoyed in the heavenly afterlife.

Herrad's interpretation of the meaning of Christ's life for the overall scheme of salvation in the created world serves as an interesting point of comparison with Hildegard's understanding of the incarnation. For Herrad, the coming of Christ did not inextricably reverse all of the sins committed by the first humans, as Hildegard had celebrated the occasion. Rather, the incarnation appeared in Herrad's version of events as a continuation of salvation history, a new chapter offering the hope of human redemption in heaven, but not a reversal suggesting a fresh start, a new creation, or the possibility for human fulfillment in God's presence on earth. This second

---

67. Joyner, "A Timely History," 27–36.

68. Rosalie Green, "The Adam and Eve Cycle in the *Hortus deliciarum*," in *Late Classical and Medieval Studies in Honor of Albert Mathias Friend, Jr.*, ed. Kurt Weitzmann (Princeton, NJ: Princeton University Press, 1995), 340–47.

section of Herrad's text, spanning the incarnation to the ascension, opens with a full-page frontispiece at fol. 80v that displays a tree of prophets culminating in the person of Christ (fig. 2.1). Here, God the Father—God as Creator—stands at the bottom of the illustration where he plants a tiny branch in the earth. The accompanying text explains that God had planted the root of this tree in his land and now tends it until it grows to perfection. Gérard Cames has connected this statement to a passage from Honorius of Augustodunensis's *Speculum ecclesiae,* where, in a section on the discovery of the cross (*De inventione sanctae crucis*), it is said that God planted the garden of delight at the beginning.[69] Abraham stands in a seed-like pod in the interior base of the tree, gazing up to the stars just out of his reach, above his head. The stars recall God's promise to Abraham in Genesis 15:5 that his seed shall number the stars in heaven. This land is heaven, so the tree is not earthly. The busts of Jesus's ancestors according to their names in Matthew 1:1–16 line the interior of the tree, capped at the top by the figure of Joseph, who was Mary's husband but not, of course, the genetic father of Christ. Above Joseph is a prominent figural representation of Mary, and above her, a bearded Christ and a dove representing the Holy Spirit. The tree is a spiritual genealogy of Christ, rather than his blood genealogy.[70] Jesse, for example, is wholly absent. The message is strictly spiritual, not material. Above the lineage, on the branches, are tendrils holding the portraits of important biblical figures—patriarchs, prophets, kings, Jews, and bishops—and, at the very top of the tree, where it flowers, an array of Christian worthies including apostles, martyrs, popes, bishops, hermits, nuns, and virgins.

Herrad's tree is hopeful in that it posits women in heaven as the spiritual progeny of Christ. The women of Hohenbourg were meant to identify with the veiled woman and two unveiled virgins among the figures in the heavenly garden. But Herrad's branches exclude any wine poured out to sprout virgins, and any musicality suggesting human intimacy with the divine. Herrad does not present the incarnation as the reversal of sin, the opportunity for human apprehension of the divine. The tree is scarcely incarnational; it belongs more to a theological curriculum than a visionary one. It is not a means of participating in a process of divine encounter with the material world. Its purpose, placed at the beginning of Herrad's textual foray into postincarnational history, was to link the events of the past with those of the present and future. It was an instructional image meant for the women of

---

69. Gérard Cames, *Allégories et symboles dans l'Hortus deliciarum* (Leiden: Brill, 1971), 37: "Deus ab initio paradisum plantavit voluptatis."

70. Joyner, "A Timely History," 320; Christiane Klapisch-Zuber, *Ombre des ancêtres: Essai sur l'imaginaire médiéval de la parenté* (Paris: Fayard, 2000).

FIGURE 2.1. "Genealogical Tree of Christ." *Hortus deliciarum*, ed. Aristide D. Caratzas (New Rochelle, NY: Caratzas Bros., 1977), plate 25 bis. Courtesy of Aristide D. Caratzas.

Hohenbourg to study and better recall the spiritual genealogy of Christ, the lineage of Abraham.

The texts surrounding the image further convey Herrad's message of the necessity of scriptural and theological learning to salvation. She cites a passage from Daniel 12:3 in which the learned are commended for their brightness and are promised that they will shine as stars in eternity. Another passage, from 1 Corinthians 15:41, praises virgins as shining most brightly in the heavens. Herrad's verses couple Abraham and Sarah's sterility, which was made abundant through God's intervention and Abraham's covenant, with the nonprocreative practices of the women of Hohenbourg. The glory of this branch, she insists, lay in its sterile root, which bent to God's will. Through it, virginity endures in perpetuity (*Hortus deliciarum,* no. 300). In these words and image, Herrad's poem explained to the women of Hohenbourg that their guarded virginity would bear fruit in heaven.

Although Herrad's *virga* portrays Christ's ancestry through Mary, the image is not one that emphasizes Mary's role of incarnation. Mary as Virgin Mother of God was less significant than her role as virtuous, impenetrable stronghold. To Herrad, Mary displayed a *contemptrix mundi,* and it was her rejection of the world that suggested her as the vehicle for Christ's delivery. Mary's place was outside the world, in heaven. She was "the sea's shining star," where the sea was the world (*Hortus deliciarum,* no. 1; Griffiths, 232).[71] Herrad instructed that Mary would "join you to her son" *after* the human journey in this world. "Navigate through this sea," Herrad wrote to her community. "When you leave this mortal vessel may you attain holy Sion" (*Hortus deliciarum,* no. 1; Griffiths, 231). Although Mary was the virgin's beacon in the sea of this world, her work of incarnation was completed in the past. It was not ongoing in the cloistered life of the virgins. The work of the virgins and canonesses was to "suffer bitterness now/ despising the fortunes of the world/ Be now a partner in Christ's cross/ And thereafter a sharer in his kingdom" (*Hortus deliciarum,* no. 1; Griffiths, 231). For Herrad and the women of Hohenbourg, the experience of God was in the future.

The penultimate folios of the *Hortus* reflected the women's place at Hohenbourg. A full facing-page miniature depicts the monastery of Hohenbourg at its foundation and at the time of Herrad's writing (ca. 1175–91) (fig. 2.2). In the left-hand image Christ occupies the central position, standing atop the mountain at the front of the convent church. He is in heaven in the company of Mary, Saint Odile, John the Evangelist, and Peter. The presence of Saint Odile, the monastery's first abbess, worked to guarantee that the women of Hohenbourg would also have their place there, in the

---

71. Elsewhere, *mare* is glossed as *mundum.* On the glosses in the *Hortus,* see Griffiths, 119–22.

future. A band of illustration under the heavenly feet reflects the foundation of Hohenbourg. Odile, Duke Adalric, the monastery's founder, and Relinde, its luminary reformer and Herrad's mentor, are all present. In a final band of illustration below, a profusion of trees signifies the monastic setting. On the facing recto, the assembled community, consisting of forty-eight canonesses and twelve novices, is shown gazing at their future and their past.

Herrad appears in the bottom right-hand corner of this image, the sole full figure represented. She displays for view a page from her manuscript that offers a message to her community:

> O snow-white flowers giving forth the scent of virtue,
> Always resting in divine contemplation,
> Hasten to heaven, after despising earthly dust
> That you may be able to see the Bridegroom, who is now hidden. (*Hortus deliciarum,* fol. 323r; cat. no. 346; Griffiths, 235–36)

Similar to the vocative addresses to women in the *Speculum* and those uttered by Hildegard, with these words Herrad speaks to the canonesses as flowers of virtue. But for Herrad, Christ remained hidden from these virginal flowers. The women of Hohenbourg were alienated from Sion, "confined" (*Hortus deliciarum,* fol. 322v; cat. no. 345). The cloister was an enclosed garden where women learned theological truths and preserved their virginity so that they would one day see Christ.

Herrad's whole scheme of salvation history unfolded in a manner that instructed her canonesses to believe in a Christ that could not be seen because he was in another world. Perhaps her distrust of the world stemmed from Hohenbourg's immersion in it—the canonesses were deeply involved in administrative dealings with the emperor Frederick Barbarossa, with the Abbey of Marbach, with book borrowing from other monastic libraries, and through their admission of noble women.[72] Because of her labor to reform a convent that had once been corrupted by the world, Herrad remained skeptical about the presence of divinity there. But Hildegard had known the world and its corruption. She, too, although given to religious life at the age of eight, held audience with numerous authorities and petitioners from outside her monastery, conducted multiple preaching missions, and regularly journeyed across the Rhine to her daughter house at Ebingen. The marked differences in tone, then, may relate more to communal purpose. Herrad was an autonomous abbess of an independent community. She designed her book

---

72. On Hohenbourg's involvement in the world outside the cloister, see Griffiths, 24–48.

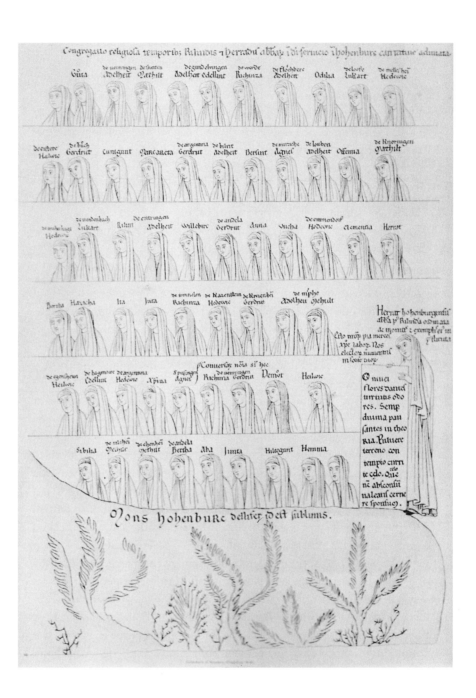

Congregatio religiosa temporibus Rælindis Herradis abbatissarum in seruicio Thohenburc cantatiue admirata

Gúta · Adelheit · Gerthilt · Adelheit · edellint · Rihenza · Adelheit · Odilia · Lukart · Hedewic

Halewic · Gerdrut · Lantgunt · Margareta · Gerdrut · Adelheit · Berlint · Agnes · Adelheit · Offemia · Gerthilt

Hedewic · Lukart · Judint · Adelheit · Willebirc · Gerdrut · Anna · Sucha · Hedewic · Clemencia · Hernst

Bertha · Hazecha · Ita · Jüta · Rihenza · Hedewic · Gerdrut · Adelheit · Gehilt

Herrat hohenburgensis abbatissa pro salute ordinata de monte exemplii in scriptura

Hedewic · Edellint · Hedewic · Xpina · Agnes · Richina · Gerdrut · Demot · Haluue

¶Converse nomina sunt hee

Sibilia · Gebur · Gerhilt · Bertha · Aba · Junta · Hiltegunt · Hemma

O nivei flores dantes nimius odores. Semp duuina pansantes in theoria. Putuere terreno contempto entre te celo. Que ne absconsii valeant cernere sponsum.

Mons hohenburc delhiec idest sublimis.

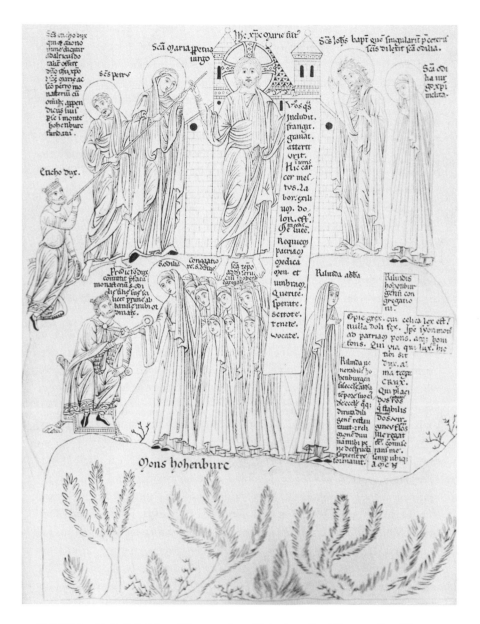

Figure 2.2. "Duke Eitchon founds the monastery of Hohenbourg" and "Congregation of the nuns of Hohenbourg." *Hortus deliciarum*, ed. Aristide D. Caratzas (New Rochelle, NY: Caratzas Bros., 1977), plates 74 and 80. Courtesy of Aristide D. Caratzas.

as a substitute for male religious instruction and pastoral service.[73] For her, salvation for women came by way of intellectual understanding of Scripture and theology. Her book fit into a theological curriculum, not a devotional one intended to animate personal religious experience.[74] Not so for Hildegard. For her, as a self-consciously (or, rather, self-constructedly) meek *magistra,* unlearned and subservient to the abbot of Disibodenberg, intellectual apprehension was not the heart of religious experience or the route to salvation. Her compositions were designed for performance, and performance was the means to salvation, to reparation. Through an active liturgical program, Hildegard directed her virgins to enjoy, on earth, in community, the company of God. Though with differing purposes, Herrad and Hildegard, as well as the author of the *Speculum virginum,* crafted texts for the religious instruction of women that greatly relied on natural imagery.[75] Indeed, they each constructed their lessons and significance directly from the features of the natural world, without which their texts could not operate. This dependence on natural imagery in order to instruct—theologically, spiritually, and morally—"virgins" on life in community, demonstrates the permeation of the rhetoric of reform in the shared spiritual context of twelfth-century German monastic reform.

For Herrad, therefore, salvation awaited in another garden, the garden of paradise. The garden of Herrad's book offered knowledge and instruction on how correctly to live and to understand God so that the consecrated woman could truly hope to reside in that heavenly garden, to guarantee her residence there. It was a text for upright living to demonstrate that monastic holiness was attainable for women. But the *Hortus* stopped short of promising the delivery of that garden for the present life of the canonesses. For Hildegard, by contrast, and for the women instructed in the *Speculum,* salvation was made possible by the incarnation and included the material of the natural world. Whereas Herrad was concerned with sin and the distance it introduced between God and humanity, Hildegard relished the possibility of overcoming sin, overcoming distance, and perfecting the self. For Herrad, the garden of the cloister was the best protection from "earthly peril" but was no escape from it (*Hortus deliciarum,* no. 1: "De terrenis eruar," glossed "de periculis"; Griffiths, 232). Herrad occasionally interjected hopefulness for heavenly splendor, praying that Christ will

---

73. Griffiths, 222.
74. Ibid., 185.
75. An excellent comparison of the image cycle in the *Hortus* and that of the *Speculum virginum* can be found in Griffiths, 184–88.

"count us in the number of [his] elect," or that he "adorn each face" (*Hortus deliciarum,* nos. 346, 1; Griffiths, 235, 230). But her hope for salvation was oriented toward the future.

I have attempted to create links between the language of monastic reform and the devotional possibilities unleashed by the doctrine of re-creation. Herrad demonstrates that this path was hardly straight, nor was it frequently tread. Despite the multiplicity and variability of devotional and theological patterns in the twelfth century, it is critical to connect reformist ideals that emphasized the material world with fresh interpretations of the incarnation as a re-creation. An examination of the interplay of images—particularly those of the *virga* and *virgo*—among the *Speculum virginum,* Hildegard's liturgical writings, and the *Hortus deliciarum* indicates a range of reception for the rhetoric of reform and the "discovery" of nature in the twelfth century. Hildegard used the language of reform, the allusions to the lush fields of the Song of Songs so frequently expressed by contemporary male monastic reformers, in a manner that offered possibilities for her community in the present. Images of green pastures, of laboring, of cultivation, spoke to her of the potential to incarnate, to bring forth God in the world. The *Speculum virginum* and Hildegard's liturgical corpus founded a devotional posture that celebrated the very stuff of their material environment—the cloister garden, the illuminated pages of texts, the bodies of the virgins, the smell of the liturgy, the sounds of music. These sensoria promised an encounter, and that their womanhood, their images, their flesh, were not an obstacle but rather a vehicle to God. Their bodies, their communities, were the green pastures in which God was made visible.

The finale of the *Ordo* is perhaps most indicative of this nascent devotional posture. The setting was sparse but for the magnificent robes of the assembled cast, staggered upward from the base of the stage to its rafters. It was an intimate affair, a ceremonious occasion intensified by the dramatic chanting of female voices. Under Hildegard's direction, the nuns exhorted their audience with song, literally pulling them onto the stage, hands gripping hands, up onto the incarnational *virga* erected before them, where they might reside with Christ and Mary. Audience and performers remade themselves through this liturgical drama into an image of *viriditas,* the very power that had remade the world itself. In performing on stage in this manner, the women of Rupertsberg enacted a process whereby they asserted their transformation into the divine while simultaneously relying on the guarantee of divinity within the material world. Hildegard's liturgical performances represented a new devotional strain characterized by a daring effort to see God in the material world, to celebrate God in the material of art, song, and performance and thus to share in God's creative powers, to bring incarnation into process. It suggests a world for which salvation was very much in process. Incarnation, too, was in process. Hildegard, and many who succeeded her among the monastic and mendicant elite, strove not to imitate Christ's humanity, but to imitate the process of incarnating the divine and transcending the incarnate.

CHAPTER 3

Clare of Assisi and the Tree of Crucifixion

Leaving behind the twelfth century and the female communities affiliated with German reformed monasticism, we move forward to thirteenth-century Italy, where a very different kind of female community struggled to identify with the memory of its charismatic founder, Francis of Assisi (d. 1226). Specifically, Clare of Assisi, the devoted follower of Francis and the founding abbess of the community of poor virgins at San Damiano in Assisi, survived Francis by more than a quarter century and spent the rest of her life seeking papal approval for the right of her flock to maintain its commitment to the "privilege of poverty." As we will see, Clare was also a key figure at a crucial moment of transition and innovation in ideas about the re-created world and how Christians might come into a relationship with the incarnate God. Some sense of Clare's influence can be gained through a comparison of her meditations on natural imagery with those of Bonaventure in his *Lignum vitae* (Tree of Life), which I briefly examine at the end of this chapter.

The "Clarian question," as Maria Pia Alberzoni has called it, presents some difficulties for interpreting the influence of Clare's authenticated writings on later female Franciscanism.[1] My concern here, however, is not

---

1. Maria Pia Alberzoni, "San Damiano nel 1228: Contributo alla 'questione clariana,'" *Collectanea Franciscana* 67 (1997): 459–76; on the state of the question, see Lezlie Knox, *Creating Clare of Assisi: Female*

with Clare's influence on women associated with the Franciscan order but
with her devotional persuasion over the men in that order, the Friars Minor.
I argue that Clare's prayer life, developed during her struggle to observe
poverty, influenced later meditations written by and for Franciscan men of
the First Order. Clare was a creative agent in Franciscan meditation and
theology of the re-created world. In her meditations, she articulated an
enduring Franciscan assumption about the potential of poverty to transform
the self. Clare associated with several members of the early brotherhood
including Elias, Ruffino, Juniper, and Leo, who likely found the same inspiration in her spiritual life that Francis had.[2] After Francis's death, Brother Elias,
then minister general of the order (1232–39), acted as a secretary for Clare,
facilitating her communication with a certain princess from the kingdom
of Bohemia named Agnes, who had embraced the Franciscan lifestyle and
founded a community of poor women in Prague. Over the ensuing years
Clare and Agnes would become close spiritual friends, exchanging letters
and mutual support as Clare strove to preserve evangelical poverty at San
Damiano and to associate the female followers of Francis juridically with
the Friars Minor. Clare, of course, understood that women could not preach
and practice mendicancy as men in the First Order did, so their only option
was to have their own Rule, one that enabled them to observe a life of strict
poverty. In 1253, drawing near her death, Clare wrote a final letter to Agnes,
urging her and the women under her guidance to continue to pursue her
vision of the proper communal and spiritual life. Toward this end she gave
them a new technique of prayer designed to bring them closer to a true
understanding of God's presence in the material world. She instructed them
to contemplate the events of Christ's incarnation and crucifixion as if gazing
into a mirror suspended on a tree. In that mirror they could see reflected
the face of the poor virgin. Little did Clare know that she was providing a
metaphor—the tree as the narrative structure for and instrument of Christ's
crucifixion and of human redemption—that would prove to have incredible

---

Franciscan Identities in Later Medieval Italy (Leiden: Brill, 2008), 8–14. The question came to the fore in
1995 when Werner Maleczek determined from diplomatic practices and canon law that San Damiano
would not have attracted the attention of the papal chancery in order for it to have truly received the
privilege of poverty. Werner Maleczek, "Das 'Privilegium Paupertatis' Innocenz III und das Testament
der Klara von Assisi: Überlegungen zur Frage ihrer Echtheit," *Collectanea Franciscana* 65 (1995): 5–82;
trans. Cyprien Rosen and Dawn Nothwehr as "Questions about the Authenticity of the Privilege
of Poverty of Innocent III and of the Testament of Clare of Assisi," *Greyfriars Review* 12 (1998): 1–80.

  2. Knox, *Creating Clare of Assisi,* 13. From 1212 to 1215, Francis's companions often lingered
intermittently at San Damiano as a resting place after long journeys. See Bert Roest, *Order and
Disorder: The Poor Clares between Foundation and Reform* (Leiden: Brill, 2013), 15.

longevity and adaptability in the spiritual life of the Franciscan order for decades to come.

By examining Clare's innovative meditation as described in her letters to Agnes, I hope to show that her struggle to achieve poverty and acceptance of the Rule shaped her spiritual direction and her goals for communal religious life. Clare's use of arboreal and natural imagery signals a devotional change—a shift from the *virga* of incarnation to the *ligna* of crucifixion. In the prayers she shared with her sisters in Prague, she focused on Christ's crucifixion—his "suffer[ing] on the tree of the cross"—as the one event that had utterly altered the rules of the material world. Through Christ's death God had re-created the world so that human beings could achieve material salvation. This understanding of death as renewal and possibility came to characterize Franciscan devotion more generally, especially the Franciscan penchant for meditation on narrative images of Christ's life and death as found, for example, in Bonaventure's *Lignum vitae*.

The Pursuit of Poverty

Clare of Assisi's four letters to Agnes of Prague, composed over the course of nearly twenty years, represent her methods of spiritual direction and instructions for communal life. The correspondence is colored by two separate influences that come together in her approach to prayer. First was the practice of poverty. Clare understood poverty to be Christ's formative characteristic and believed that Francis had perfected the imitation of that poverty, a practice she wished to emulate. The second shaping factor in Clare's spirituality was the natural language for virgin incarnation that had emerged from the context of twelfth-century monastic reform and the *cura monialium*. Like Peregrinus in the *Speculum virginum,* Clare continually appealed to her sisters as virgins with unique prerogatives for their spiritual lives. She exhorted them to envision their own lives by gazing into a mirror in order to gauge their spiritual progress, their advance in virtue. In Clare's mirror, however, the reflection staring back was not a bejeweled, budding flower, but the glum visage of the poor Christ. Visualizing Christ in their own person in this manner, she taught, earned them his "kiss." Combining the ideal of Franciscan poverty with naturalistic imagery, Clare created a fresh means of visualizing God through the material forms of creation. She forged her vision amid the drama of her personal struggle to secure for her sisters at San Damiano the formal legal status of true followers of Franciscan poverty, a context that gave urgency to her prayers.

Clare began her observance of Franciscan poverty on Palm Sunday of 1212, when she received the tonsure from Francis at the church of Santa Maria degli Angeli.[3] After her profession she lived just outside of Assisi with the Benedictine nuns of Sant'Angelo of Panzo, then moved to the church of San Damiano. Throughout her tenure as abbess of San Damiano, Clare embraced what she perceived to be Francis's dying wish for his foundation of women: "I ask you, my ladies, and I give you my advice that you live always in this most holy life and poverty. And keep careful that you never depart from this by reason of the teaching or advice of anyone."[4] In accordance with his interpretation of poverty as the key to inculcating Christlike humility, Francis provided Clare with a *forma vitae* (form of life) that emphasized dedication to poverty and filiation with the Franciscan friars.[5] In addition, he pledged, at least initially, that he and his successors would provide pastoral care for the women of San Damiano.[6] But the legalities of thirteenth-century ecclesiology were not to allow Clare and her sisters to observe Francis's form of life with any degree of ease. Canon Thirteen of the Fourth Lateran Council forbade the creation of new orders, so that, in swearing her obedience to Francis and accepting the position as abbess of the community at San Damiano, Clare was forced to live within the basic strictures of the Rule of Benedict.[7] The Rule of Benedict, contrary to the spirit of Franciscan poverty, allowed for communal ownership of possessions in the form of land and material goods. Clare faced something of a challenge, therefore, in erecting the legal and ecclesiastical protections necessary for her desired way

---

3. *Legenda Sanctae Clarae Assisiensis,* in *Fontes Franciscani,* ed. Enrico Menestò, Stefano Brufani, and Giuseppe Cremascoli (Assisi: Edizioni Porziuncula, 1995), pp. 2401–50, pt. 1, chap. 3, para. 8, lines 8–9; Regis Armstrong, trans., *The Lady: Clare of Assisi: Early Documents,* rev. ed. (Hyde Park, NY: New City Press, 2005), 285–86 (unless otherwise indicated, I will use Armstrong's translation for Clare's letters, Rule, and Legend). Hereafter these two sources will be cited parenthetically in the text in abbreviated form as Menestò and Brufani, and Armstrong, respectively.

4. *Regula* [Rule of Clare], Menestò and Brufani, p. 2300, 6.8–9; Armstrong, *The Lady,* 118.

5. Clare mentions the form of life in her Testament, Menestò and Brufani, p. 2319, line 33.

6. Francis's promise to "bind himself" to the community is also mentioned in Clare's Testament, Menestò and Brufani, p. 2314, line 29; Armstrong, *The Lady,* 61. On Francis's inconsistency with regard to *cura monialium,* see Roest, *Order and Disorder,* 29–31.

7. On the repercussions of Lateran IV for religious communities, see Herbert Grundmann, *Religious Movements in the Middle Ages: The Historical Links between Heresy, the Mendicant Orders, and the Women's Religious Movements in the Twelfth and Thirteenth Century, with the Historical Foundations of German Mysticism,* trans. Steven Rowan (South Bend, IN: Notre Dame University Press, 1995). On the tensions between Francis and Clare regarding the Rule of Benedict and the title of abbess, see Optatus Van Asseldonk, "'Sorores Minores': Una nuova impostazione del problema," *Collectanea Franciscana* 62 (1992): 595–634. Clare would not have been fully enclosed at this point. Ugolino's 1218–19 redaction of the *Forma vitae* was attached to the Rule of Benedict but allowed for more stringent practices of poverty and asceticism, with occasional justifications for leaving the confines of the enclosure. See Roest, *Order and Disorder,* 25.

of life. Until she could manage to do so, the Rule by which her community lived was directly at odds with the spirit of its founder.[8]

The growing popularity of women's movements that embraced evangelical poverty and the uncertainty of their placement in diocesan jurisdictions caused papal concern for the stability of female religious communities based on the apostolic model.[9] Francis and the friars retreated from pastoral service to women in the face of unforeseeable expansion of his male and female followers. Ugolino, the future Pope Gregory IX and cardinal-legate to Pope Honorius III, had become in 1221 the official protector of the female pauperistic movement in central and northern Italy, seeking to protect, regulate, and enclose them. Ugolino's process of incorporating Clare and the women of San Damiano took place from 1220 to 1228. He exempted the women of San Damiano from episcopal jurisdiction, placing them directly under the care of the papacy and ordering them to follow the Rule of Benedict glossed with his own constitutions.[10] By 1227, Ugolino, now Pope Gregory IX, compelled the minister general of the Franciscan order, Giovanni Parenti, to provide pastoral care to the Order of Poor Ladies of San Damiano, which served to incorporate the Damianite houses into the Franciscan order.[11] In 1228, Gregory finally issued to Clare and the Poor Ladies of San Damiano the privilege of poverty, which theoretically guaranteed their practice of material poverty.[12] In exchange, Clare was compelled to accept the constitutions he had penned as cardinal-legate, constitutions that associated her community formally with the Rule of Benedict. Clare would spend her remaining years involved in a series of negotiations with various popes and

---

8. On Ugolino's constitutions and involvement in uniting the central and northern Italian women's convents dedicated to poverty, see Joan Mueller, *The Privilege of Poverty: Clare of Assisi, Agnes of Prague, and the Struggle for a Franciscan Rule for Women* (University Park: Pennsylvania State University Press, 2006), 18–21.

9. It is possible that Clare actually managed to convince Pope Innocent III to grant her a dispensation to practice poverty at San Damiano. However, as with so many early Franciscan documents, there are doubts as to the authenticity of Innocent's *privilegium paupertatis;* see the texts found in *Clare d'Assise: Écrits,* ed. Marie-France Becker, Jean-François Godet, and Thaddée Matura, SC 325 (Paris: Éditions du Cerf, 1985), 196–99; for arguments regarding its spurious authenticity, see Werner Maleczek, "Questions about the Authenticity of the Privilege of Poverty of Innocent III and the Testament of Clare of Assisi," *Greyfriars Review* 12 (1998), Supplement, 1–80.

10. For the complicated legislative background and regulatory diversity distinguishing the Order of Ugolino from the Order of the Ladies of Santa Maria of San Damiano, see Mueller, *The Privilege of Poverty,* 21–22.

11. Lezlie Knox, "Audacious Nuns: Institutionalizing the Franciscan Order of Saint Clare," *Church History* 69.1 (2000): 44.

12. Gregory IX was fairly lax and unfaithful in overseeing the implementation of the privilege, as evidenced by the succeeding dispensations he issued. See Englebert Grau, "St. Clare's *Privilegium Paupertatis:* Its History and Significance," *Greyfriars Review* 6 (1992): 327–36.

cardinal protectors in order to defend this privilege of poverty—that is, the legal exemptions supporting her community's wishes to remain completely bereft of income and property in excess of their church and housing—and to establish a Franciscan rule for women.[13]

Cardinal Ugolino's interest in regularizing the new communities of women professed to poverty had extended beyond providing for their material needs. He also sought to supply Clare and her sisters with regular spiritual advisers and priests to administer the sacraments at a time when the *cura animarum* for new female communities was reduced because of the suspicions and complications of mingled sexes. In order to provide regular care for the new women's foundations in Italy, Ugolino had personally assigned Cistercian advisers to the poor enclosed ladies.[14] He appointed the Cistercian Ambrogio as the first visitor general to the houses under his protection.[15]

Clare was in frequent contact with Cistercian and Cistercian-influenced visitors, preachers, and directors such as the cardinal protectors Rainaldo of Ostia and the bishops of Assisi, who presided over consecration ceremonies. These advisers would have employed typically Cistercian readings of the *Song of Songs* imagery in discussing with the community of poor ladies the value and rules of enclosure.[16] Perhaps it was from these advisers that Clare came to grasp the image of virgin bodies as springtime blossoms, branching trees, and flowering virtues. Certainly she emphasized the familiar ideal of virginity as an identity suited for female enclosure, and the necessity of speculating on a mirror in order to gauge virtuous progress.[17] Clare's letters of instruction appealed to Agnes and her sisters as virgins. By the time she initiated correspondence with Agnes, Clare had been living an enclosed life for at least fourteen years.[18] Her letters drew on nuptial imagery from the Song of

---

13. For more background on Clare and her relationship to other female houses dedicated to evangelical poverty, see Knox, *Creating Clare of Assisi,* 1–86; Maria Pia Alberzoni, *Chiara e il papato* (Milan: Edizioni Biblioteca Francescana, 1995).

14. Knox, "Audacious Nuns," 44.

15. Roest, *Order and Disorder,* 23. Roest claims that Ugolino was inspired by the Cistercian model of establishing female religious houses in previous decades.

16. As Constance Bouchard has argued, it was Cistercian commentators who were most responsible in the early thirteenth century for disseminating glossed interpretations of the Song of Songs; see Constance Bouchard, "The Cistercians and the *Glossa Ordinaria,*" *Catholic Historical Review* 86.2 (April 2006): 183–92. Frederic Raurell has argued that Clare was exposed to William of St. Thierry's commentary on the Song of Songs; see Frederic Raurell, "La Lettura del Cantico dei Cantici al tempo di Chiara e la IV Lettera ad Agnese di Praga," in *Chiara: Francescanesimo al femminile,* ed. Davide Covi and Dino Dozzi (Rome: Edizione Dehoniane, 1992), 250–75.

17. Additionally, Clare could have come into contact with Cistercian spirituality during her brief stay in the monastery of Sant'Angelo of Panzo or in the monastery of San Paolo of Bastia, both temporary residences before she entered San Damiano. On her Cistercian influences see Ingrid Peterson, *Clare of Assisi: A Biographical Study* (Quincy, IL: Franciscan Press, 1993).

18. See Roest, *Order and Disorder,* 32, on the ambiguities of dating Clare's enclosure.

Songs, with which she would have been familiar from her advisers and from the liturgical readings for the feasts of Mary, specifically the *historia* read for the Feast of the Assumption and the reading of the First Nocturne for the Feast of the Nativity of the Virgin.[19]

We might think of a typically Cistercian reading of the *Song of Songs* as a tropological interpretation of the soul's ascending journey into espousal union with God. Bernard of Clairvaux was of course the order's great exegete of the Song, composing eighty-six sermons on the book over a period of eighteen years.[20] Bernard's exegesis of the Song, in contrast to the Marian commentaries, was insistently christocentric, based explicitly on a desire to "know Jesus and him crucified."[21] To clutch the Song's "bundle of myrrh" was for him to embrace the humbled, denigrated, scorned, life and passion of Christ. Love of this debased God was the whole goal of Cistercian life, according to Bernard. That love was accomplished through a considerate remaking of the self, of the will.[22] Twelfth-century Cistercian exegesis of the Song had emphasized the possibility for transforming one's will through a preceding transformation in sexual appetite, one analogous to the transformation of land as sacred through the spiritual ideal of manual labor.[23] If the will was disciplined through faith, the Cistercian exegetical tradition held, then passionate desire of the flesh could be curtailed; and with desire harnessed, a new physical person emerged, one capable of perceiving the divine in present material reality. William of Saint Thierry thus speculated about the phrase "May he kiss me with the kiss of his mouth" that

---

19. This is the reading listed in the breviary promulgated by Haymo of Faversham (d. 1243); see Stephen J. P. Van Dijk, *Sources of the Modern Roman Liturgy* (Leiden: E. J. Brill, 1963), 2:2–195. On scriptural allusions in Clare's writing, see Engelbert Grau, "Die Schriften der heiligen Klara und die Werke ihrer Biographen," in *Movimento religioso femminile e francescanesimo nel secolo XIII*, ed. Roberto Rusconi, La Società Internazionale di Studi Francescani (Assisi: La Società, 1980), 195–238.

20. Ann Matter, *The Voice of My Beloved: The Song of Songs in Western Medieval Christianity* (Philadelphia: University of Pennsylvania Press, 1990), 124. Jean Leclercq has traced the diffusion of Bernard's sermons on the Song of Songs, which circulated under various titles, including *Sermones super Cantica Canticorum, Homiliae,* and *Tractatus, Expositio, Liber, Opus.* Jean Leclercq, "Histoire du texte," in the introduction to *Sermones super Cantica Canticorum,* 1–35, in *S. Bernardi opera omnia,* ed. Jean Leclerq, C. H. Talbot, and H. M. Rochais (Rome: Editiones Cistercienses, 1957), 1:xv.

21. Rachel Fulton, *From Judgment to Passion: Devotion to Christ and the Virgin Mary, 800–1200* (New York: Columbia University Press, 2005), 305.

22. Martha Newman, *The Boundaries of Charity: Cistercian Culture and Ecclesiastical Reform* (Stanford, CA: Stanford University Press, 1996), 67; on twelfth-century exegesis of the Song of Songs, see also Rachel Fulton, "Mimetic Devotion, Marian Exegesis, and the Historical Sense of the Song of Songs," *Viator* 27 (1996): 86–116; Ann Astell, *The Song of Songs in the Middle Ages* (Ithaca, NY: Cornell University Press, 1990), esp. chaps. 2 and 3, pp. 42–104; Denys Turner, *Eros and Allegory: Medieval Exegesis of the Song of Songs* (Kalamazoo, MI: Cistercian Publications, 1995), 159–74.

23. On these linked transformations, see Newman, *The Boundaries of Charity,* 67–96.

[the Bride] longs to be noticed and to be made one with her Bridegroom in knowledge and love and in some measure to be made privy to his secrets. This is the kiss of his mouth.... We must see what kind of kiss this is, what kind of mouth is his, what are the lips of the giver of this kiss, what are the lips of her who receives it.[24]

Investigating various interpretations for the mechanics of this kiss, William finally concluded: "The meeting together of Word and hearer, of divinity and humanity, is a kind of kiss of charity. Isaiah foresaw this in his spirit and said, 'There shall come forth a shoot from the root of Jesse and a flower will break forth from the root.'"[25] William's exegesis of the Song may have emerged from conversations he had with Bernard while at Clairvaux in the 1120s, and laid the foundation for Bernard's *Sermons on the Song of Songs*.[26] Both William and Bernard connected in this manner the sensuality of the Song with the restored soul's bliss at perceiving divine harmonies in the world, harmonies made possible through the incarnation. Gilbert of Holland, who continued Bernard's commentaries after his death, pushed the christological interpretation of the Song even further toward Christ's crucifixion when he described the union of Bride and Bridegroom in the bedchamber as an ecstasy made possible through the suffering of Christ: "To me, good Jesus, the softest pillow, is that crown of thorns from your head; a sweet little bed is that wood of your cross."[27]

While Clare used the affective intensity and nuptial imagery that often characterizes Cistercian exegesis, she fused it with her own dedication to evangelical poverty in order to create a specific vision of Christ as poor, hideous, and crucified. To Clare, this debased Christ reflected the proper image of the individual virgin in her community. A telling example of Clare's distinct use of nuptial imagery is found in Letter 4, where she draws on familiar references from the Song of Songs in order to coach her spiritual sisters on the exact phrases to utter and images to evoke in order properly to invite God's presence into their embodied selves. For example, she exhorted, "Cry out from the great desire and love of your heart," asking them to beseech of God:

Draw me after you,
let us run in the fragrance of your perfumes,

---

24. William of St. Thierry, *Cantici Canticorum priora duo capita brevis commentatio ex. S. Bernardi sermonibus contexta, ubi de triplici statu amoris*, PL 184:407–15; 412A; trans. Turner, *Eros and Allegory*, 283.

25. William of St. Thierry, *Brevis commentatio*, PL 184:413D; Turner, *Eros and Allegory*, 286.

26. Turner, *Eros and Allegory*, 275; Matter, *The Voice of My Beloved*, 132.

27. Gilbert of Hoyland, *Sermones in canticum II*, PL 184:17C–22B, 21D.

O heavenly spouse!
I will run and not tire,
until You bring me into the wine-cellar,
until your left hand is under my head
and Your right hand will embrace me happily,
You will kiss me with the happiest kiss of your mouth![28]

Clare's use of the Song sought to incite a desire that could be fulfilled only sensually by looking face to face, eye to eye, in a spousal gaze. Although she would have heard these verses recited every year in the liturgy for the Feast of the Virgin's Nativity, here Clare rearranged and supplemented them in order to achieve her own desired effect. The range of meaning of Clare's use of the Song here only becomes clear with an appreciation of its context. She made this injunction after a lengthy meditation on Christ's incarnation, his life of poverty, and the despondence of his crucifixion. The means for approaching sensual union with the Godhead, for Clare, was imitation of Christ's earthly, material lowliness. The reference to the beloved's "left hand" and "right hand" was incorporated in *Sicut manifestum est,* Pope Gregory IX's privilege of poverty, issued to Clare and her sisters at San Damiano in 1228.[29] It was a document that Clare was said to have cherished because although it did not guarantee her absolute freedom from possessions, it was a movement in the direction of asserting her poverty, acknowledging that she "could not be compelled by anyone to receive possessions."[30] Clare's imagined embrace of Christ, then, receiving the kiss in his arms, was her true privilege of poverty, the privilege to imitate and transform herself into the image of Christ, to mirror him as his spouse, by observing his earthly life of impoverishment. Remembering the suffering of Christ in the world, the destitute conditions that he took on in order to enter humanity, would draw the female meditant to Christ her spouse. She would "run and not tire" from her desire to pursue the poor conditions of the earthly life of Christ, and, accomplishing this, she would rest in his arms.

Clare's use of nuptial Song of Songs imagery therefore must be read in the context of her goal to live a life of poverty and to establish an explicitly Franciscan rule for women. It must be understood in terms of her foremost desire to create a specific form of life for herself and her sisters. The love

---

28. *Epistola ad Sanctam Agnetem de Praga* [IV], Menestò and Brufani, pp. 2279–84; Armstrong, *The Lady,* 57.

29. *Privilege of Poverty of Pope Gregory IX,* in Armstrong, *The Lady,* 87–88.

30. Bullarium Franciscanum I:771: "Ut recipere possessiones a nullo compelli possitis." Gregory's language permits Clare to refuse endowments but leaves room for her and her sisters also to accept them—i.e., they are not compelled to accept.

of the contemptible Christ was a theme dear to the heart of Francis as well; but unlike Clare, Francis never developed this theme in the context of nuptial language.[31] Clare understood the specific role of enclosed women as a spousal commitment to the downtrodden Christ.[32] Given the diffuse manuscript transmission of the *Speculum virginum,* the liturgical readings and artwork associated with the Marian feasts, and the pastoral care provided by Cistercian pastors to the Damianites, it is quite possible that Clare was at least somewhat familiar with the *virga* imagery of twelfth-century women's instruction. But instead of a tree of incarnation, she chose to imagine a tree of crucifixion in order to address the specific meditational goals of the women to whom she wrote. In doing so, she portrayed the world as re-created through Christ's crucifixion.

Poor Virgins

Corresponding with Agnes and the women of the Prague foundation, Clare sought to supply guidelines for women seeking to follow her example of poverty within enclosure. She employed a mirroring trope, which encouraged the act of speculation, of seeing Christ among their present surroundings. The *Speculum virginum* was distributed rather broadly in both its Latin and vernacular forms and could be found throughout religious houses in western Europe. The extensive circulation would make it more likely that Clare, through the pastoral care of the Cistercians and Friars, would have been exposed to the devotional speculation through naturalistic metaphors advocated in the *Speculum.*[33] Although there is no proof that Clare knew the *Speculum virginum,* her use of imagery for the instruction of enclosed virgins, we will see, places her within the same tradition and understanding of female spiritual life. Clare considered the mirror as an ideal means of encouraging enclosed women to identify as virgin brides of the poor Christ. Even if all of the women under her instruction were not physically virgins, it was Clare's spiritual ideal for them to return to that state of bodily helplessness,

---

31. Bernard McGinn discusses Clare in the context of Franciscan piety and mysticism in *The Flowering of Mysticism: Men and Women in the New Mysticism, 1200–1350* (New York: Crossroad, 1998), 64–69.

32. Sarah McNamer, *Affective Meditation and the Origins of Medieval Compassion* (Philadelphia: University of Pennsylvania Press, 2010), 25–57.

33. On the interactions between the sisters of San Damiano and the Franciscan friars, see Lazaro Iriarte, *Franciscan History,* trans. Patricia Ross (Chicago: Franciscan Herald Press, 1982), 441–45; Roberto Rusconi, "The Spread of Women's Franciscanism in the Thirteenth Century," *Greyfriars Review* 12.1 (1998): 35–75; and Maria Pia Alberzoni, "Clare of Assisi and Women's Franciscanism," *Greyfriars Review* 17.1 (2003): 5–38.

which could be achieved through the practice of poverty. Although Lezlie Knox has suggested that Clare's reputation for encouraging stoic virginity was a later interpolation of her hagiographers and papal bulls, I maintain that the ideal of virginity was vital to Clare's creation of a communal vision.[34] Virginity provided for Clare a spiritual identity for articulating the necessity for practicing poverty. Betrothed to Christ, the virgin must reflect her poor spouse's own humble material presence.

In the letters to Agnes and her sisters in Prague, Clare was clearly concerned with distinguishing her sisters as virgins and characterizing their spiritual work as unique to virgins.[35] Agnes, the daughter of King Premsyl Otokar I of Bohemia and Queen Constance of Hungary, had in 1233 rejected marriage to the emperor Frederick II and established a monastery for women based on the model of poverty of San Damiano.[36] Agnes entered the monastery in 1234 and shortly after began corresponding with Clare about the spiritual direction of the sisters.[37] In total, Clare wrote a series of four letters to Agnes and her sisters in Prague, to provide spiritual instruction and encouragement for the community to persevere in their attempts to practice a life of poverty. Clare, it seems, initiated the conversation in 1234 by writing to Agnes to congratulate her on her choice to observe the Franciscan life by taking the poor Christ as her spouse.[38] Clare repeatedly praised Agnes's decision to remain a virgin by marrying Christ, "whom in loving, You are chaste/ in touching, You become more pure/ in embracing, You are a virgin" (Menestò and Brufani, p. 2264; *Ep.* 1, line 8; Armstrong, 44). Through marriage to

---

34. Knox, *Creating Clare of Assisi*, 49–54.

35. Although Lezlie Knox has argued in *Creating Clare of Assisi* that the association of Clare with virginity is a result of hagiographical tradition, and not a real reflection of Clare's concerns, I think there is reason to continue to examine her exhortations to virgin brides, but to update our understanding of what this identity would have really meant to Clare. I argue that, for Clare, virginity was a material practice for conforming the self to holy matter. Note that Clare addresses her readers as *virgo* and *sponsa* twenty-two times throughout her letters.

36. Agnes was perhaps first exposed to Franciscan poverty when her cousin, Elizabeth of Hungary, began learning about it with the arrival of the Franciscans in Germany in 1220. Agnes emulated her saintly cousin in establishing a hospital in Prague dedicated to Francis of Assisi. She also acquired land on which she oversaw the building of a residence for "poor ladies." She wrote to Clare requesting permission to establish the Order of Saint Damian in Prague and asked that Clare send sisters from Italy to reside there. Agnes's *vita* can be found in Jan Kapistrán Vyskocil, *Legenda blahoslavené Anezky a ctyri listy sv. Kláry* (Prague: Nakladatelstvi Universum, 1932), 99–149.

37. Only Clare's side of the conversation survives. The manuscript history of the letters exchanged between Clare and Agnes can be found in Joan Mueller, *Clare of Assisi: The Letters to Agnes* (St. Bonaventure, NY: Michael Glazier, 2004). For the spiritual themes found in the letters, see Alfonso Marini, "'Ancilla Christi, plantula sancti Francisci': Gli scritti di santa Chiara e la Regola," in *Chiara d'Assisi, Atti del XX Convegno internazionale Assisi, 15–17 Ottobre 1992* (Spoleto: Centro italiano di studi sull'alto Medioevo, 1993), 127ff.

38. Armstrong, *The Lady*, 43.

Christ, Clare suggested, Agnes and her sisters were redeemed, they were restored to their true selves. She was most awed by God's humbling acts of reversal and paradox—that divinity entered humanity, that Christ became incarnate, that the richest majesty made himself poor, in order to reverse sin, to restore humanity to its true image. Clare praised virginity as a similar means of reconciling opposites and inverting order. She celebrated the royal woman's choice to remain unmarried and poor: "Oh blessed poverty, who bestows eternal riches on those who love and embrace her!" (Menestò and Brufani, p. 2264; *Ep.* 1, line 15; Armstrong, 45). By choosing to love Christ, she was truly a virgin; by choosing to live as a poor woman, she wedded a divine spouse, with all his riches and splendor.

In nuptial language, Clare described a mirroring process as a means of imitating the incarnate Christ. In her community, practicing poverty, Agnes and her sisters could see for the first time their true identities, the reflection of God in which they were originally created. In her portrayal of a spousal relationship between the poor women and the poor Christ, Clare's focus was not union with the divine, but union with the conditions of the incarnate Christ. She wished to encourage an identity of the virgins with the material conditions taken on by Christ, thereby forging an identity with Christ. "O holy poverty," "O blessed poverty," "O pious poverty"—Clare repeatedly promoted the means by which it was possible to become true brides. God chose to reveal himself to human sight as a poor man. Therefore, only through "holy service of the Poor Crucified," and commitment to the poor Christ "who endured the suffering of the cross," could Agnes and her sisters truly see their reflections in him in whose image they were created (Menestò and Brufani, p. 2264; *Ep.* 1, lines 13–14; Armstrong, 45). Clare's use of bridal imagery, then, was not otherworldly, not concerned primarily with consummation in heaven. It was this-worldly, and directed to the material conditions of the present.

In 1235, as part of his efforts to ensure the financial security of all female monasteries, Gregory IX issued constitutions for Agnes's monastery at Prague that effectively rendered it a heavily endowed papal institution.[39] In response to Gregory's constitutions, Clare wrote a second letter to Agnes encouraging her to persevere in her efforts to observe the Franciscan ideal of poverty and to reject the endowment for the monastery at Prague. She exhorted Agnes to trust no one, as even those whom she respected, like

---

39. Gregory gave Agnes and the Poor Enclosed Nuns the benefits of Agnes's dowry, which she had given to the hospital before her entry into the religious life. The possessions of the hospital would heretofore be legally tied to the Monastery of Prague. See Mueller, *The Privilege of Poverty,* 67.

Gregory, would try to persuade her of the need and merit of accepting endowments.[40] Reminding Agnes that poverty was her "founding purpose," Clare advised her to embrace the poor bridegroom, and to remain constant in her own poverty as his wife. Married to one who was poor, she must remain poor.[41] Despite Gregory's attempts to force her to maintain possessions, she and her sisters at Prague could remain true to their vows as spouses of Christ by adopting Christ's life of poverty.

By replicating the material conditions of Christ's life, Clare taught that poor virgins refashioned him and made him present among themselves. Clare's repeated order was that the women must "look" upon Christ in graphic detail, they must "gaze/ consider/ contemplate" (Menestò and Brufani, p. 2271; *Ep.* 2, line 20; Armstrong, 49). She explained that the way to share in the life of the spouse was to adopt his conditions, his manner of being: "Look upon him who became contemptible for you, and follow Him, making yourself contemptible in this world for Him" (Menestò and Brufani, p. 2270; *Ep.* 2, line 19; Armstrong, 49). And so the women of Prague must also embrace the marks of poverty in order to match their spouse's body internally and externally. When God chose to make himself visible to humanity, it was as a poor man, and therefore poverty was essential for visibility, to cultivate in oneself the image of God.

By 1238, when she wrote Letter 3 to Agnes, Clare was beginning to break free of the instructional modes she had inherited from those who first directed her at San Damiano. She wrote Letter 3 after Agnes had questioned her about fasting regulations. Clare's response to Agnes indicates that fasting regulations were far less important to her than the prayer life of the community, and she instructed them accordingly by once again reminding them of the importance of gazing at the image of their impoverished spouse. Clare urged the women to "follow in the footprints of the poor and humble Jesus Christ" (Menestò and Brufani, p. 2275; *Ep.* 3, line 4; Armstrong, 52). They were to conform their bodies and identities to his so that they might make him present among them. Through their efforts, the sisters would become "a support for the weak members of His ineffable body" (Menestò and Brufani, p. 2276; *Ep.* 3, line 8; Armstrong, 50).

Clare's instructions to women that they make Christ present in the cloister by fashioning his limbs differ from the exhortations issued by Hildegard to the women of Rupertsberg "to build his beautiful body." Whereas Hildegard

---

40. *Epistola ad Sanctam Agnetem de Praga* [II], Menestò and Brufani, pp. 2267–71.

41. See Clara Gennaro, "Chiara, Agnese e le prime consorelle: Dalle 'Pauperes dominae' di S. Damiano alle Clarisse," in Rusconi, *Movimento religioso femminile e francescanesimo,* 167–91.

considered the women's liturgical work as incarnational in that they imitated Mary in their virgin bodies, here Clare's analogy rested not on similarity to the body of Mary but to the body of Christ. Agnes and her sister made Christ present by replicating the material conditions of his body, that is, his poverty. Truly like Christ in their humble poverty, they were the material manifestation of the body of God on earth, "co-worker[s] of God Himself" (Menestò and Brufani, p. 2276; *Ep.* 3, line 8; Armstrong, 50). "Place your mind before the mirror of eternity," she instructed them. "Through contemplation transform yourself completely into the image of divinity itself" (Menestò and Brufani, p. 2276; *Ep.* 3, line 12; Armstrong, 51). The practice of poverty would erase their sense of self, rendering them spouses of the poor Christ and enabling them to identify entirely with the figure of the divine substance.

Mary has played an indeterminate role in interpretations of Clare's spirituality.[42] Although Clare routinely requested that the women of Prague consider themselves as following in Christ's footsteps, primarily by imitating his poverty, the model of Mary also informed her recommendations for cloistered life. Compelling her sisters to "cling to His most sweet mother," Clare looked to Mary for spiritual succor. What she found so satisfying about Mary, I would argue, was her affiliation with the material presence of God. Clare depicted Mary as a vessel for divinity, the one who provided a channel for God's overflowing into the world. She praised Mary for her role in facilitating this excess into creation: "[she] who gave birth to a Son whom the heavens could not contain" (Menestò and Brufani, p. 2276; *Ep.* 3, line 18; Armstrong, 51). In Clare's third letter to Agnes, the cloister was analogous to Mary's womb as the receptacle for God's overabundance; Mary "carried him in the little cloister of her holy womb and held him on her virginal lap" (Menestò and Brufani, p. 2276; *Ep.* 3, line 19; Armstrong, 51). For Clare, the life of the cloister must imitate Mary's work by enclosing God within. "As the glorious virgin of virgins carried him materially," Clare instructed, "so you too by following in her footprints, especially those of humility and poverty, can, without any doubt, always carry him spiritually in your chaste and virginal body" (Menestò and Brufani, p. 2277; *Ep.* 3, line 25; Armstrong, 51). Clare was struck by Mary's ability to materialize, to

---

42. Catherine Mooney, "Imitatio Christi or Imitatio Mariae: Clare of Assisi and Her Interpreters," in *Gendered Voices: Medieval Saints and Their Interpreters,* ed. Catherine Mooney, (Philadelphia: University of Pennsylvania Press, 1999), 52–77; Rosemary Hale, "Imitatio Mariae: Motherhood Motifs in Devotional Memoirs," *Mystics Quarterly* 16 (1990): 193–203; Clara Bruins, *Chiara d'Assisi come "altera Maria": Le miniature della vita di Santa Chiara nel Manoscritto Thennenbach-4 di Karlsruhe,* Iconographia Franciscana 12 (Rome: Instituto storico dei Cappuccini, 1999).

manifest, Christ, something only approximated in the cloister through the observation of poverty. Indeed it was poverty that made them true virgins and brides of Christ.

But while Mary was certainly important for Clare as a model for the work of the cloister, the imitation of Christ was also central to Clare's recommendations for her sisters. For Clare, the work of the cloister as a whole was to imitate Mary in making Christ present; but the work of the individual was to follow in Christ's footsteps by enacting his virtues of poverty and humility. When addressing not the community life of the women of Prague, but Agnes as an individual, Clare insisted that her zealous practice of poverty yoked her "to the footprints of him to whom you merited to be joined in marriage" (Menestò and Brufani, p. 2269; *Ep.* 2, line 7; Armstrong, 47). And she praised Agnes in Letter 3 for following in the footsteps of the poor Jesus more closely than her sisters. Therefore, we might consider Clare's references to Mary as guiding communal life, and her exhortations to imitation of Christ as an individual responsibility, one that each individual in the community must uphold for the collective. In the particular circumstances in which Clare was writing to Agnes in 1238 there was as yet no approved form of life affiliating the sisters definitively with Franciscan poverty. Corporately, the sisters' identity was attached to Gregory IX and his constitutions, and therefore corporately they did not imitate Christ's poverty or identify with Francis. But as individuals they could embrace poverty and thus imitate Christ himself. For Clare, imitating Mary through imaginatively re-creating the person of Christ was a method of making Christ present in the cloister. Christ was holy matter; Mary was the vessel that brought God into the world. Christ's material conditions were to be imitated; the vessel was the protection afforded by the cloister, the place in which they were enacted. Poverty was more important to Clare than any other religious observance. It was only through material poverty, she believed, that the Damianites could experience the real presence of God. Her community thus *had* to defend the privilege of poverty.

Seeing God

The three letters to Agnes and her sisters in Prague, dated 1234, 1235, and 1238, set the tone and provide explanatory context for Clare's final instructions on contemplation in Letter 4, dated 1253. Clare wrote Letter 4 immediately after Cardinal Rainaldo, at the request of Pope Innocent IV, had finally accepted Clare's form of life. The letter marks a change in Clare's tone, in the direction of her spiritual advice. It was in this letter that she first drew concretely on the natural world, turning in particular to the image of a tree in order to supply her imagination with a proper form for the material God. For Clare, the tree was a metaphor for Christ's crucifixion and revealed the true image of humanity. When Clare instructed her sisters to pray through the mirror, she directed them to demonstrate their commitment as the *sponsa Christi,* to conform themselves to his material conditions. When she used the image of the tree, in Letter 4, it was to encourage the sisters' transformation into Christ. But unlike the trees found in earlier instructional treatises for women, those associated as *virgae* with the incarnation, Clare's meditational image was focused on the crucifixion.

At the time that she wrote Letter 4, the communal identity of the sisters had fundamentally changed. Their immediate ability to enact Christ's virtues both communally and individually had changed. The formal identification of the sisters as followers of Francis had modified the needs and goals of Clare's devotional program. It was a remarkable victory, and Clare wrote to Agnes to encourage a new form of contemplation adapted to these changed circumstances. This final letter to Agnes and the sisters at Prague, composed on Clare's deathbed after a fifteen-year break in their correspondence, represents the most considered and mature example of Clare's devotion.

Clare described for Agnes a mirror that reflected an image of material being. Christ was the mirror. And it was not simply Christ's body that was reflected back in the imagined glass surface but a sequential narrative structured around his life and death to which the women could direct their attention and conform themselves. The process of visualizing, of imagining the physical presence of Christ, was at the heart of the practice she recommended. For Clare, Christ was the perfect human form to which meditants must aspire and conform themselves. In the mirror, according to Clare's instructions, one should see the events of Christ's earthly narrative passing before one's eyes.

Clare's final epistle must be read as a set of instructions for how to proceed in her absence. She was aware that this would be her final letter, and she sought to explain completely her vision of proper community. What remained crucial for Clare and consistent throughout the letters to Agnes was the virgins' work in replicating the material conditions of Christ's life. Clare described their daily pursuit as staring face-to-face with Christ, "the mirror without blemish" (Menestò and Brufani, p. 2282; *Ep.* 4, line 14; Armstrong, 55). Emphasizing the need for daily practice, Clare insisted that Agnes and the sisters at Prague "gaze upon that mirror each day, O Queen and Spouse of Jesus Christ, And continually study your face in it" (Menestò and Brufani, p. 2282; *Ep.* 4, line 15; Armstrong, 55). Reflecting back at them would be the Christic virtues, "blessed poverty, holy humility, and ineffable charity," available for their contemplation. "You will be able to contemplate them throughout the entire mirror," she instructed (Menestò and Brufani, p. 2282; *Ep.* 4, line 18; Armstrong, 55).

For Clare, Christ's death on the cross transformed his divinity into a mirror that reflected the poor Christ in creation. The mirror Clare described and urged her sisters to adopt was also a tree, a "mirror, suspended on the wood of the Cross" (Menestò and Brufani, p. 2283; *Ep.* 4, line 24: "unde ipsum speculum, in ligno crucis positum"; Armstrong, 56). By dying on the tree of the cross Christ reversed the effects of Adam's sin. Adam had defaced humanity though his disobedience, and Christ, through his death, restored humanity. Christ's death, then, marked a restoration, a means for human remaking, and a way to see God in the world as Adam once had. For Clare, Christ in his crucifixion provided a mirror of true, restored, original creation. Her vision of Christ's remaking of the world is subtle, but through the mirror she articulated her understanding that his death made possible a world in which humans could be restored to perfection because his death remade the material conditions of human embodiment and of the created world. Clare understood Christ's crucifixion on the tree of the cross as a transformation of the created world, one that opened up new possibilities for humanity. His death made him accessible to humanity. Poverty was for Clare the means to his access.

In her fourth letter to Agnes, Clare set forth the means for human transformation, outlining in great detail the facets of the mirror of the tree. By staring into the mirror, she directed the sisters to locate each facet and to remember the biblical details of Christ's birth, life, and death. Her meditation progressed as a narrative in which she trained the women to gaze upon this image to witness the movements, events, and story of Christ's life unfolding before them, as if they were spectators. Her injunctions to them were to visualize, to inhabit the narrative. "Look, I say, at the border of this mirror," she began, pointing first to Christ's incarnation and the poor conditions in which he came into material form. Examine "the poverty of him who was placed in a manger and wrapped in swaddling clothes" (Menestò and Brufani, p. 2282; *Ep.* 4, line 19; Armstrong, 56). She gave affective cues, eliciting and directing the readers' emotional response to the graphically imagined narrative. Their meditation would commence with a commemoration of the impoverishment of the incarnation. Her meditations cried out for attention to what she saw as Christ's jarring infant poverty, wailing: "Oh marvelous humility!" The women should be astounded as they imagined how God entered the world: "O astonishing poverty! The King of angels, the Lord of heaven and earth, is laid in a manger!" (Menestò and Brufani, p. 2282; *Ep.* 4, line 20; Armstrong, 56). The meditation thus began with a

consideration of the incarnation, the birth of a child and God who chose
not to express his majesty but to enter creation as a poor infant dependent
entirely on the charity of others. Whereas the *Speculum virginum* had used a
similar mirror-tree device in order to encourage women to visualize God's
incarnation on the branches of a tree, Clare used it in order to imagine a
God whose physicality was shocking not for its miraculous act of becoming
human but for its radical materiality, its visceral poverty. In Clare's hands,
the tree that mirrored God's presence had changed from a means of conveying the mystery of the incarnation to a means of delivering the bold reality
of the incarnate.

Clare's meditation then moved to account for the details of Christ's adult
life, where again his poverty was the central characteristic reflected in the
surface of the mirror:

> Then reflect upon, at the surface of the mirror,
> the holy humility, at least the blessed poverty,
> the untold labors and punishments,
> that he endured for the redemption of the whole
> human race. (Menestò and Brufani, p. 2283; *Ep.* 4, line 22; Armstrong, 56)

As her instruction here illustrates, Clare saw in Christ's life, just as she had
in his birth, a defining mark of poverty and toil. She urged the sisters to
recognize their own struggles in the reflection of Christ's. The purpose of
this mirror that she designed, therefore, was to project an exemplary image
of their own observation of poverty. The result of this toil, she taught, was
redemption, a re-created self.

Clare then turned to the final facet in the mirror. Deep in the mirror's
interior the women should gaze upon the virtue that Christ expressed in
his death:

> Finally, contemplate, in the depth of this same mirror,
> the ineffable charity that he chose
> to suffer on the tree of the cross
> and to die there the most shameful kind of death. (Menestò and Brufani,
> p. 2283; *Ep.* 4, line 23; Armstrong, 56)

With this sentence, Clare chose to conjure a wretched Christ. For her,
Christ's shameful death was a sign of God's willingness to be debased.
Throughout the letter she continues to return the meditant to the mirror.
Calling up mental images of Christ was for her a process of self-reflection.
She counseled the sisters' participation in the humility of his material exis-
tence, as spectators of his birth, life, and death:

Therefore,
that Mirror, suspended on the wood of the Cross,
warned those passing by that here are things to be
considered, saying:
"All who pass by the way, look and see if there
is any suffering like my suffering!"
"Let us respond to him," It says,
"crying out and lamenting, in one voice, in one spirit:
'Remembering this over and over
leaves my soul sinking within me!'" (Menestò and Brufani, p. 2283; *Ep.* 4,
lines 24–26; Armstrong, 56)

Here Clare imported a dialogue between the soul and Christ, a script
for this meditative encounter. She employed many of the stylistic attributes and emotional prompts of passion meditation, including a progressive
narrative, exhortations directing the reader regarding what emotions to feel,
the present tense, and feminized subject positions as spouses of Christ.[43]
In their meditations they were to be present with Christ as witnesses, not
just contemplating and imagining Christ but participating in his life and
death so that Christ was present to them. The urgency of Clare's meditation must be read within her own urgent historical context. How was it
possible, worried Clare, to practice the Franciscan apostolic life within the
limits of enclosure?

The limits of enclosure, I argue, spurred Clare to reimagine the significance
of their spiritual work as poor virgins. The meditation that Clare created
for Agnes and her "daughters in Christ" was a mechanism for promoting
personal transformation and identity in Christ. Through fierce dedication
to the practice of poverty, the virgins' bodies became worthy of Christ, their
spouse. Through meditation, she believed, they achieved identification with
him. Meditation on the tree of life that Clare created would allow the sisters
to see God in his material degradation. The meditation would lead them,
Clare declared, to "ineffable delight." Here was the marriage act, the consummation of their poverty:

Draw me after you,
let us run in the fragrance of your perfumes,
O heavenly spouse! (Menestò and Brufani, p. 2283; *Ep.* 4, line 30;
Armstrong, 56)

---

43. McNamer, *Affective Meditation,* 85.

Poverty for Clare was thus the means to achieve an experience of the bridegroom's "happiest kiss of [the] mouth," wherein she became a true spouse (Menestò and Brufani, p. 2283; *Ep.* 4, line 32; Armstrong, 57). Sarah McNamer has shown that the task of the *sponsa Christi* was to prove herself worthy of Christ as a spouse. Following this logic, we can see Clare's loving dedication to poverty as the pursuit of *maritalis affectio,* the emotional disposition required to contract a legal marriage.[44] But Clare's dedication to a life of poverty, I would urge, was not patently directed to the purpose of proving her worthiness of the bridegroom through demonstrable compassion for his suffering. The stimulation of compassion for his suffering was not her foremost goal. Truly she wished to share the experience of his body, the material being of God. For her, poverty was the means to attain this experience.

In her final letter to Agnes of Prague, Clare depicted the early phases of a method of contemplation that would resonate throughout Christian meditation for the next century. I have argued that, because of her dedication to a life of Franciscan poverty, the nuptial language of erotic union with Christ became significant for Clare less because of its ability to convey a sense of the soul's desire to submerge itself in divinity than because of the bonds of obligation and imitation it required for the community's present practice. The poor sister was wedded to the poverty of her spouse, bound to adopt his conditions, to live as he lived. Such a loving bond was, in Clare's understanding, utterly transformative. Clare adapted an image commonly associated with twelfth-century female communities, the tree of incarnation, so that it addressed more concretely not God becoming human, but God transforming humanity through the crucifixion. Clare's use of natural imagery did not emphasize God's becoming incarnate but the incarnate world's potential to transcend the immediate circumstances of its own body, to become a spouse of Christ in order to share the conditions of his materiality. In her use of arboreal imagery, Clare managed to transform the spiritual ideal of virginity as it had been handed down to her. Clare's own directions for the life of the virgins focused on adopting the material conditions of Christ, not only as an act of compassion for his suffering, but in an effort to emulate his material presence as a true virgin spouse.

Some may contest that this exclusive focus on a single image, that of the tree, as opposed to the whole range of natural options explored in a treatise like the *Speculum virginum*—the seeds and roots, fruits and flowers, of a verdant world—indicates that Clare was working from a very different tradition, regarding the world's material potential in a vastly different and

---

44. Ibid., 25–57.

unrelated manner. To this concern I would respond by noting the recombination of important and widely shared spiritual ideals among female religious communities. Clare willfully combined vivid arboreal imagery with traditions of female religious instruction, mirroring strategies, and espousal to Christ. These tropes, reworked in a letter to enclosed virgins, mark an important devotional shift. They demonstrate Clare's valuation of the world's radical materiality. She regarded the world as transformed by the presence of a poor, dying God, a God who chose to enter and live in the world in its most reduced, basic material forms. It was a far cry from *viriditas*. For her, the natural, material world was not something that virgins bodied forth. Rather, it was the condition of Christ's humble presence. As such, it reflected God's self.

Clare's letters of instruction for religious life scarcely outlasted her own lifetime. Her original writings—her letters to Agnes, her Form of Life, and her Testament—were preserved and her ideals practiced only by tiny bands of her spiritual progeny, such as the Neapolitan foundations of Santa Chiara and Santa Croce.[45] The vast network of female houses that bore her name, officially institutionalized as the Order of Saint Clare in 1262 by Pope Urban IV, subscribed to a much different brand of spiritual vocation than that advocated in Clare's letters.[46] The Order of Saint Clare followed a new monastic rule, one that provided for the use of property and possessions, and one whose adherents subscribed to the hagiographical version of Clare, that of an obedient virgin who was not terribly concerned with the issue of evangelical poverty. Clare's commitment to transforming poverty, however, had not disappeared entirely from her official re-presentation. The Spiritual Franciscans, I show in chapter 4, would champion Clare's interpretation of poverty as a sharing of the material conditions of Christ.

In placing Clare at the origin of a meditative tradition based on poor transformation I do not wish to suggest that women were the exclusive authors, audience, or even originators of a new brand of Christian devotion. I do not wish simply to claim a more active role for women's creative energy, although it is clear that her expressive devotion—the words and images through which Clare meditated—was extraordinarily dynamic and innovative in its claims for how women should properly enact their Franciscan identity and love of Christ. Rather, it seems obvious to me that our resulting picture is rather changed when we include female voices and texts in the context of their personal struggle with legislative limitations to express

---

45. Knox, *Creating Clare of Assisi,* 117–20.
46. Ibid., 4.

devotion. When examined from the perspective of Clare's efforts to secure the privilege of poverty and approval of her Rule, the explanation for the creation of this tradition becomes grounded in a signification of the world as God's material presence. The restrictions of the practice of poverty and the demand for female enclosure necessitated by Clare's gender required that she develop a novel explanation for her need to become truly poor like Christ. More than an act of imitation of Francis, or of compassion for Christ, the practice of poverty was for Clare a sharing of God's material being, her claim that such a shared being was indeed possible in this world. It is no mere coincidence that, in order to achieve that shared being, she instructed enclosed virgins to examine their virtuous progress in the mirror of a tree. It remains to be seen how that instruction developed outside the virgins' enclosure.

Clare and Bonaventure

In 1310 the artist Pacino di Bonaguida was commissioned to paint an altar panel for the Poor Clare convent of Santa Maria dei Monticelli in Florence. The panel was to depict a tree representing among its branches scenes from the life of Christ as they corresponded to the narrative reported in Bonaventure of Bagnoregio's *Tractatus qui lignum vitae dicitur* (ca. 1260) (fig. 3.1).[47] As a visual translation of Bonaventure's *meditationes,* Pacino's painting was the first in a long line of monumental devotional renditions of the *Lignum vitae,* all of which testify to the pervasive appeal and use of the *Lignum vitae* among fourteenth-century Franciscans. And yet Pacino's panel, as an image created for a specifically female community, is distinct from those that followed.[48] The panel makes the treatise visible by portraying forty-eight roundel scenes, constituted by twelve branches, with four "fruits" per branch, exactly as described in Bonaventure's work. But Pacino's *Lignum vitae* is unique in its emphatically narrative structure. Rather than scrolls of text or the portraits of prophets and patriarchs, the Monticelli altarpiece features scenes aligned

---

47. For a full description of the panel and its place at Monticelli, see Jeryldene Wood, *Women, Art, and Spirituality: The Poor Clares of Early Modern Italy* (Cambridge: Cambridge University Press, 1996), 179.

48. Other examples of visual renditions of Bonaventure's *Lignum vitae* can be found in Florence, Milan, Pistoia, Padua, Orvieto, Bergamo, Udine, and Sesto al Reghena. On the different uses of the other *Lignum vitae* paintings, see Alessandro Simbeni, "L'iconografia del *Lignum vitae* in Umbria nel XIV secolo e un'ipotesi su un perduto prototipo di Giotto ad Assisi," *Franciscana: Bollettino della Società internazionale di studi francescani* 9 (2007): 149–83.

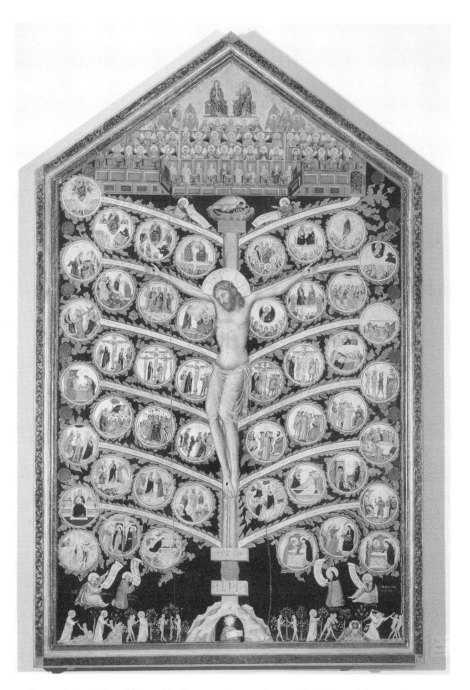

Figure 3.1. Pacino di Bonaguida (fl. 1302–after 1340), "Tree of Life (Tree of the Cross)." Tempera on panel, 248 x 151 cm. Ca. 1305–10. Accademia, Florence, Italy. Photo credit: Scala/ Art Resource, NY.

to help imaginatively and visually re-create a narrative.[49] These variations suggest different uses of *ligna* imagery among Franciscan women and men. Women's communities were less likely to have accessible copies of meditational and devotional treatises, so that a narrative depiction like Pacino's would have compensated for the lack of texts, allowing members of such communities to follow the scenes visually while Bonaventure's instructions were read aloud.[50]

The similarities between the *Lignum vitae* paintings intended for male and female communities, however, suggest further meanings that this imagery may have communicated in the fourteenth century. All such paintings uniformly depict twelve branches with four fruits per branch, which carry the weight of the crucified body of Christ. They all clearly represent Bonaventure's treatise, translating his meditation from a textual to a visual medium. They each include a portrait of Francis and Clare of Assisi at the base of the tree. Adjacent to Clare is Bonaventure, always clutching his open book. Like Francis's presence there, as well as Bonaventure's, Clare's appearance apparently lent authority, even in the predominantly male communities for which these later images were created. The question is why—why was Clare affiliated with this tree, this treatise? And what did her image at the base of the tree convey to its viewers?

During her lifetime, the papacy, under Gregory IX and Innocent IV, deliberately sought to institutionalize Clare and her followers, to compel them to accept property and other sources of income, while, at the same time, the majority of friars resisted pastoral responsibilities and deliberately thwarted efforts to incorporate women's houses into their order.[51] After Clare's death, these same entities struggled to control her sanctified, and thoroughly sanitized, image.[52] Furthermore, poverty had ceased to inform the spiritual and practical life of the Franciscan Second Order. The epistolary Clare was replaced with the hagiographical Clare, the docile and submissive virgin.

---

49. The one exception is on the right transept of the Basilica of Santa Maria Maggiore in Bergamo, where the *Lignum vitae* includes both textual scrolls from Bonaventure's treatise and accompanying narrative scenes. This particular wall painting, however, is badly damaged and fragmented, making it difficult to determine the uses it was originally designed to meet. On the *Lignum vitae* at Bergamo, see Sandro Angelini, *Santa Maria Maggiore in Bergamo* (Bergamo: Instituto italiano d'arti grafiche, 1968).

50. As Jeryldene Wood has argued in *Women, Art, and Spirituality,* the format and details of the painting are suggestive of a full-page illumination derived from manuscript painting. It is possible that if such an image existed, Pacino took his model directly from an illumination within an early version of Bonaventure's treatise. Wood argues that the panel served as a statement of the nuns' ideology rather than a meditative image.

51. Knox, *Creating Clare of Assisi,* 33–55; Maria Pia Alberzoni, *Clare of Assisi and the Poor Sisters in the Thirteenth Century* (St. Bonaventure, NY: Franciscan Institute Publications, 2004).

52. Knox, *Creating Clare of Assisi,* esp. 57–86.

Given the contested status of Clare's image, why should she, almost of necessity, be portrayed in the presence of the *Lignum vitae*? Which version of Clare was represented therein, and what was her function?

I would argue that Clare was one of the original creators of a profoundly influential method of Franciscan meditation. The lineage of the meditative devotional practice usually associated with the *Lignum vitae* runs through Clare and her sisters. In crafting her meditations on Christ's life through the branches of a tree, Clare surely recalled instructional advice designed to shape enclosed women's identities as virgins. But Clare interpreted the significance of the life of Christ in a rather different manner. She was particularly receptive to the nascent imaginative theology of the re-creation, but she considered not the incarnation but the crucifixion of Christ as the critical cosmic event that restructured the material world. The crucial devotional task of enclosed women, she believed, was to identify with the impoverished Christ, whose sacrifice offered hope for material redemption, for transformation into the image of divinity. She reinterpreted the role of brides of Christ as one of transformation rather than incarnation, not embodying the divine but sharing an identity with the divine body. Put another way, Clare took a largely Marian image of incarnation and gave it a more firmly sacerdotal meaning by emphasizing the work of the crucifixion.

Although Clare was an innovator in creating an arboreal meditation based on a shared identity with Christ, Bonaventure is more closely associated with it because he ordered the meditation in his *Lignum vitae*. Bonaventure provided a viable structure for the meditation that, as the numerous visual renditions of the *Lignum vitae* give testimony, was highly repeatable as a practice. He recognized the importance and appreciated many of the highly participatory forms of affective piety associated with the women's religious communities of his day, and he authorized them for male use by transforming them into a systematized method of prayer. Both Clare and Bonaventure, writing within just a few years of one another, seized on the image of a tree in order to describe the life, death, and resurrection of Christ and to imagine how, by picturing him and conforming the self to his image, one might come to see God.

Bonaventure, the esteemed Doctor Seraphicus, certainly appreciated the use of images in his own meditations. Bonaventure's epistemology held that mental images were critical for the cognitive process of knowing God.[53] He understood mental images as impressions of the natural, material world that,

---

53. Michelle Karnes, *Imagination, Meditation, and Cognition in the Middle Ages* (Chicago: University of Chicago Press, 2011), 63–92.

with the aid of illumination, helped to convert physical perceptions into spiritual knowledge.[54] In fact, for Bonaventure, Christ was the exemplary species, or physical means and reflection of spiritual truth. Christ enabled all true understanding by ensuring that images correctly represented their intended objects in the cognitive process.[55] Bonaventure thus constructed his meditations, highly visual mental itineraries, in order to promote knowledge of the divine through sensory apprehension. Imagination was key to this process of knowing God. It was in the active construction of mental images from sensory impressions in the imagination that the individual could proceed from material to spiritual understanding. Theorizing on how best to know and love God, then, Bonaventure located the most critical role in the act of the imagination to re-create the personhood of Christ. Meditation was for him the means to guide the imagination, and the meditational form he took, the mental image through which he chose to communicate the presence and knowledge of Christ, was a tree.

Like Clare's, Bonaventure's meditations, situated around the branching structure of a tree, sought to recapitulate Christ's life imaginatively through narrative. Although he may not have been directly exposed to Clare's letters of instruction, he certainly had knowledge of her spiritual life and of the development of her community. Tales of her spiritual acumen and special intimacy with Francis had spread throughout western Europe, and her *vita* was in circulation as early as 1255.[56] In 1259, while Bonaventure meditated on Mount Alverna, seeking to imagine Francis's own method of conjuring Christ in the imagination, Brother Leo perhaps relayed stories to him of Clare, her sisters, and their very public struggles to adopt a life of poverty.[57] After her death, Bonaventure memorialized Clare in a sermon he delivered to her sisters on the occasion of the dedication of the church of Saint Clare in Assisi.[58] In preparation for this address he must have procured a number of reports about her pious activity and devotional expression. Despite his knowledge of Clare's piety, however, it is unlikely that Bonaventure read

---

54. Ibid., 92.

55. Ibid.

56. On Clare's renown, see Marco Bartoli, *Clare of Assisi,* trans. Sister Frances Teresa (Quincy, IL: Franciscan Press, 1993).

57. "A Letter to the Abbess and Sisters of Saint Clare in Assisi," trans. Ilia Delio, in *Simply Bonaventure: An Introduction to His Life, Thought, and Writings* (Hyde Park, NY: New City Press, 2001), 185. Armstrong also makes the claim that Leo was delivering information to Bonaventure, reminding him of the responsibility to care for the enclosed women; *The Lady,* 340.

58. On the delivery of the sermon, see Armstrong, *The Lady,* 28.

Clare's correspondence.[59] Nevertheless, through their contacts with Brother Leo and other early followers of Francis, Clare's sisters must have communicated much of the spirit of her language, her commitment to poverty and to the conditions of the crucified Christ, her preferred metaphors, and her manner of devotion to the mirror suspended on the tree of the cross.[60]

Bonaventure was clearly aware of the distinct characteristics of Clare's expressive devotion. In writing to the Poor Ladies of San Damiano, he incorporated a number of the themes that had become closely associated with Clare's instructions to her sisters. In his 1259 "Letter to the Abbess and Sisters of Saint Clare in Assisi," he praised the women's service as spouses to the "poor crucified Christ."[61] He instructed the sisters to "boldly take hold of the mirror of poverty."[62] In doing so, he urged, they might merit the kiss of Christ so that, enkindled by love, they would enter marriage with him. Bonaventure's repetition of key themes from Clare's letters provides further evidence that he was cognizant of Clare's manner of instruction to her sisters and perhaps even admired it. Even if he was not immediately aware of her specific creation of the tree outlining Christ's birth, life, and death as a means of contemplation and self-reflection, Bonaventure and Clare clearly shared this poignant imagery for structuring meditation on the gospel life of Christ.

Bonaventure's instructions on imaginative devotion to the life of Christ contemplated through the branches of a tree, in his *Tractatus qui lignum vitae dicitur,* show distinct similarities to and dependence on earlier meditations on the life of Christ, such as Eckbert of Schönau's *Stimulus amoris* and Aelred of Rievaux's *De institutione inclusarum.*[63] It is no coincidence that these earlier meditations were written for female communities. Women's religious communities were fundamental to the generation of affective meditation on

---

59. Anton Rotzetter suggests that Bonaventure had exposure to Clare's letters. Anton Rotzetter, *Klara von Assisi: Die erste franziskanische Frau* (Freiburg: Herder, 1993), 337.

60. Jay Hammond has also noted similarities between Bonaventure and Clare's use of mirror imagery and teachings on the crucified Christ and has suggested the possibility of Clare's indirect influence on Bonaventure's theology. See Jay Hammond, "Clare's Influence on Bonaventure," *Franciscan Studies* 62 (2004): 101–18.

61. *Epistola* VIII, in *Opuscula varia ad theologiam mysticum et res ordinis Fratrum Minorum spectantia, Opera omnia* (Quaracchi: Collegio San Bonaventura, 1898), 8:473–74; trans. Delio, *Simply Bonaventure,* 185.

62. Delio, *Simply Bonaventure,* 185.

63. See Patrick O'Connell, "The *Lignum vitae* of Saint Bonaventure and the Medieval Devotional Tradition" (PhD Diss., Fordham University, 1985); and Thomas Bestul, *Texts of the Passion: Latin Devotional Literature and Medieval Society* (Philadelphia: University of Pennsylvania Press, 1996). *Aelredi Rievallensis opera omnia,* ed. C. H. Talbot, vol. 1, *Opera ascetica,* CCCM 1 (Turnhout: Brepols, 1971), 635–82. Ekbert of Schönau, *Stimulis dilectionis,* in *"Die Visionen" der hl. Elisabeth sowie die Schriften der Äbte Ekbert und Emecho von Schönau,* ed. Friedrich Wilhelm Erich Roth (Brünn: Verlag der Studien aus dem Benedictiner- und Cistercienser-Orden, 1884), 293–303.

Christ's gospel narrative.[64] Instructional treatises designed for the meditational needs of female communities thus act as the fundamental background of Bonaventure's *Lignum vitae*. Indeed, it is possible that he wrote the treatise for an audience of Franciscan-identifying women. The treatise does, after all, assume a contemplative setting rather than the active one that novice friars would have experienced.

Each of these three meditative treatises developed a phrase from Psalm 44:3, *speciosus forma prae filiis hominum*.[65] The authors juxtaposed the imagistic association of Christ as the most beautiful form of human life, God made flesh, with the atrocities of his beaten body as it hung from the cross. Clare, it should be noted, also used Psalm 44 and to the same effect, in her second letter to Agnes. Imitate your spouse, she ordered, "[who,] though more beautiful than the children of men became, for your salvation, the lowest of men, was despised, struck, scourged untold times throughout his entire body and then died amid the suffering of the cross" (*Ep.* 2, line 20; Armstrong, 49). Although Clare's correspondence has not received the same degree of attention as these more formal, lengthier meditations, nevertheless she worked from a similar interpretation of the passion, from the same textual community.[66] But Clare's point was not, or not only, one of compassion or empathy. Her interest was in a material God, a God who became human. The psalmic epithet of the beautiful turned wretched anchored this interest scripturally. For both Clare and Bonaventure, the tree brought beauty into the world in the infant Jesus and distorted that beauty in the crucifixion. The tree's beauty was tempting in Eden but brought decay as the source of sin and death. They each envisioned the suffering finality of the *virga* of incarnation as the *lignum* of crucifixion. Although Clare's brief letter to Agnes lacks the formal structure and scriptural grounding of Bonaventure's treatise, nevertheless Bonaventure and Clare shared a tradition of meditation and self-reflection through the structuring medium of a tree.

Bonaventure's Arboreal Meditation

Bonaventure took up writing the *Lignum vitae* in response to the specific circumstances and needs of the Franciscan order in the late thirteenth century. He became minister general of the order in 1257, after Pope Alexander IV

---

64. McNamer, *Affective Meditation,* 58–62.

65. Bestul, *Texts of the Passion,* 38.

66. Brian Stock, *The Implications of Literacy: Written Language and Models of Interpretation in the Eleventh and Twelfth Centuries* (Princeton, NJ: Princeton University Press, 1983), chap. 2.

forced John of Parma to resign because of his Joachite leanings.[67] Bonaventure managed to bring temporary peace and cohesion to the order when it was in such disagreement about the interpretation of Francis's *Testament* and the practice of *usus pauper,* or "poor use," of material goods.[68] His ability to referee the battles between the Spiritual and Conventual parties earned him credit as "the second founder of the order."[69]

Bonaventure's *Lignum vitae* offers the friars an example of contemplation that fit his vision of moderation for the order. If Francis was the perfect exemplar, who imitated the life of Christ with such perfection that he merited to be transformed into his very likeness as the *alter Christus,* then his followers, though perhaps unable to imitate his life literally, could imitate his contemplative practices. The *Lignum vitae* outlined those practices and served as a map for guiding meditants into the affective experience of Christ that Francis may have felt while praying on Mount Alverna. It sought to re-create Francis's own interior experience of meditating on the life and death of Christ.[70] For Bonaventure, Francis was the perfect meditant, so much so that he merited to be transformed into the likeness of that on which he so perfectly meditated.[71]

The tree became a cognitive map that outlined Francis's contemplative practices.[72] Bonaventure divided the meditation into three levels of branches, each bearing four "fruits" for the meditant to savor, so that there were "twelve branches bearing twelve fruits according to the mystery of the tree of life."[73] Through meditation on the tree, the individual

---

67. John Moorman, *A History of the Franciscan Order: From Its Origins to the Year 1517* (Oxford: Clarendon Press, 1968), 140–54; Rosalind Brooke, *Early Franciscan Government: Elias to Bonaventure* (Cambridge: Cambridge University Press, 1959), 270–85. On the thought of Joachim of Fiore, see Bernard McGinn, *The Calabrian Abbot: Joachim of Fiore in the History of Western Thought* (New York: Macmillan, 1985).

68. On questions of poverty and schism in the Franciscan order, see David Burr, *The Spiritual Franciscans: From Protest to Persecution in the Century after Francis* (University Park: Pennsylvania State University Press, 1999).

69. McGinn, *The Calabrian Abbot,* 74.

70. See John Fleming, *An Introduction to the Franciscan Literature of the Middle Ages* (Chicago: Franciscan Herald Press, 1977).

71. In chapter 4, I will discuss in more detail Bonaventure's consideration of Francis as the perfect exemplar. See the Prologue to the *Legenda maior,* where Bonaventure describes Francis as "positus est perfectis Christi sectatoribus in exemplum."

72. For a spiritual-theological reading of Bonaventure's *Lignum vitae,* see Richard Martignetti, *Saint Bonaventure's "Tree of Life": Theology of the Mystical Journey* (Rome: Frati Editori di Quaracchi, 2004); for an aesthetic interpretation, see Thomas Jefferson McKenna, "Delight in the Cross: The Beautiful, the Agreeable, and the Good in St. Bonaventura's Spiritual Treatises" (PhD diss., Yale University, 2004).

73. *Lignum vitae,* Prologue 2, p. 68; *Bonaventure: The Tree of Life,* trans. Ewert Cousins (Mahwah, NJ: Paulist Press, 1978), 120 (hereafter cited parenthetically in the text in abbreviated form).

sought to be perfectly conformed in habit of mind to the suffering Christ. More than a guide to imitation of Christ, the *Lignum vitae* was a means of imagining the world through Christ's sensory apparatus, a restored human nature. He connected the tree of life at the origin of the world's creation, in Genesis 2:9, to the tree at its extinction when material itself would share, like Christ, a divine nature (Rev. 22:2). According to Bonaventure, Christ bridged these two biblical trees, having died on a tree in order to provide a means for humanity to reach divinity. Bonaventure's goal in writing the *Lignum vitae* was to assist in bringing the meditant into conformed identity with the crucified Christ so that he or she might say: "With Christ I am nailed to the cross" (Gal. 2:19). Such conformity could be accomplished only through affective response, so that by emotionally reliving the events of Christ's life narrative, the meditant "shapes this understanding" (*LV,* p. 68: "formetur cogitatus"; Cousins, 119). Bonaventure insisted that the visual recollection of the specific gospel narrative of Christ's life would enable the imagination to grasp and thus know that life more vividly. For this reason, he proclaimed, he chose a tree as the organizing principle for the descriptive journey through Christ's life.[74] The tree, according to Bonaventure, was the material and mental image that made the events of Christ's life cognitively and affectively available: "Since imagination aids understanding, I have arranged in the form of an imaginary tree the few items I have collected" (*LV,* p. 68; Cousins, 120). Here we find a valuable distinction between the purposes of the arboreal meditations authored by Clare and Bonaventure. Whereas Bonaventure's meditation sought to stimulate conformity of mind between the meditant and Christ, Clare's had aimed to prepare the virgin as a worthy spouse of Christ, one who practiced poverty.

The tree was not only the subject of the treatise, but also its form. Its branches unfolded according to the meditant's process of visualization:

> In the first or lower branches the Savior's origin and life are described; in the middle, his passion; at the top, his glorification. In the first group of branches there are four stanzas placed opposite each other in alphabetical order. So also in the second and third group of branches. From each of these branches hangs a single fruit. So there are, as it were, twelve branches bearing twelve fruits according to the mystery of the tree of life. (*LV,* p. 68; Cousins, 120)

---

74. The original manuscript of the *Lignum vitae* may have included a drawing of the twelve-branched tree inscribed with lines from the treatise. The Quaracchi edition of the *Lignum vitae* includes a rendition of this drawing; see Bonaventure, *Lignum vitae,* in *Opera omnia,* 8:68–69.

Bonaventure suggested that visualizing the tree would "imprint this memory" of the events of Christ's life onto the individual meditant (*LV,* p. 68: "imprimatur memoria"; Cousins, 119). For Bonaventure, the visual recognition of Christ in his material form led to knowledge of his divinity. Christ truly existed as species in those mental impressions so that the mind's images of God in Christ provoked a transition from material to spiritual cognition.[75] Visually re-creating in the mind's eye the events of Christ's narrative according to this arboreal structure, he asserted, effected a real physical encounter with Christ, God and man.

Bonaventure selected the tree for meditation on Christ's life also because of its metonymic associations with the body of Christ. Not only did Christ die on a tree in order to reverse the sins occasioned by a tree, but he was also born through the branches of a tree, the *virga Jesse.* For Bonaventure, the fruit of his tree "took its origin from the Virgin's womb and reached its savory maturity on the tree of the cross" (*LV,* p. 69; Cousins, 21). Bonaventure portrayed Christ's arboreal biography as connecting the tree of incarnation to the tree of crucifixion, emphasizing the tree's capability of fusing divine and human, material and immaterial. For him, God had become human in the tree of Jesse, the Creator had become part of creation, through the incarnation, when God entered the material realm by blossoming from the branch of the Virgin Mary. Bonaventure sustained his meditation on the incarnation in order to further draw out the association of incarnation and crucifixion, their ties to the natural world, and how the events so altered material creation. He rhapsodized on Christ's body as the fruit of the incarnation that the meditant must taste, must incorporate into his or her own body in order truly to be nailed with Christ to the cross.[76] Although the fruits of the tree, Bonaventure explained, were varied in taste and experience from the sweetness of the incarnation to the bitterness of the crucifixion, nevertheless they were "one and undivided" (*LV,* p. 69; Cousins, 121).

According to Bonaventure, God condescended to enter humanity out of overflowing of love for creation. Statements of wonder, prompting sensual apprehension, appear throughout his description of the incarnation, adding to the emotional intensity of the meditation. "If you could see the sweet embrace" of the Virgin and her infant son, he swooned, "if you could hear the voice of his Word," then, the meditation implied, you could not help but be overwhelmed with affection (*LV,* p. 71; Cousins, 127–28). The senses

---

75. Karnes, *Imagination, Meditation, and Cognition,* 76.

76. For a eucharistic reading of the *Lignum vitae,* see Ann Astell, *Eating Beauty: The Eucharist and the Spiritual Arts of the Middle Ages* (Ithaca, NY: Cornell University Press, 2006), 38–40.

must be engaged in the meditation, must be alert to the apprehension of a God who entered the world. Like Clare, Bonaventure was most impressed by the humility of a God who would demean himself, impoverish himself, in the most decrepit conditions of human flesh:

> Although he was great and rich, he became small and poor for us. He chose to be born away from the home in a stable, to be wrapped in swaddling clothes, to be nourished by virginal milk and to lie in a manger between an ox and an ass. (*LV*, pp. 71–72; Cousins, 128)

Great and small, rich and poor, home and stable, virgin milk, human and animal: Bonaventure links these paradoxical images in a chain. The effect was to make the manger into a site of reckoning opposites, of complete remaking into a world that embraced paradox.

When Bonaventure transitioned to the crucifixion, he issued careful instructions to the reader on how to react to the vision of the events. He guided his readers on how to feel as they witnessed the events of Christ's torture and death:

> Who could hear without grief how the cruel executioners laid murderous hands upon the King of Glory and bound with chains the innocent hands of the gentle Jesus, as if he were a robber, and insultingly dragged as a victim to sacrifice that most meek Lamb who offered no objection? (*LV*, p. 76; Cousins, 143)

The debasement of the creator God was a particularly moving image to Bonaventure—how he was "defiled by the spittle of polluted lips, struck by impious and sacrilegious hands" (*LV*, p. 76; Cousins, 145). His words project marvel at the pollution of purity, the infection of divinity. Citing Psalm 44, Bonaventure lamented that he who was "fairer in beauty than the sons of men" (Psalm 44:3) in suffering "appeared ugly for the sons of men" (*LV*, p. 79; Cousins, 154). After describing the mockery and scourging of Christ, with particular attention to the blood streaming down his virginal white flesh, Bonaventure returned his attention to the reader:

> And you, lost man,
> the cause of all this confusion and sorrow
> how is it
> that you do not break down and weep? (*LV*, p. 77; Cousins, 147)

Just as Clare had done before him, Bonaventure staged the meditation, providing emotional cues for his audience, instructing them on how to feel at each moment in the narrative. He interrupted his narrative, just as Clare had, to address the reader/auditor, to ensure that the practitioner felt anguish. His descriptions aimed to elicit an affective response in the reader, to help the reader feel with Paul that "having been totally transpierced/ in both mind and flesh/ [you are] fixed/ with my beloved/ to the yoke of the cross" (*LV,* p. 78; Cousins, 149). Why did he so value this affective response? What was its purpose for the meditation? Again, Mary may have provided a provisional answer.

Here, Mary was important to Bonaventure's meditations less for her work of incarnation than for her work of compassion as she labored at the foot of the cross. Bonaventure instructed his audience to watch Mary in order to know how properly to respond to the crucifixion. Not only was Mary "present at all these events, standing close by and participating in them in every way," but her flesh was Christ's flesh, and thus she felt his pain and identified with him in the manner that Bonaventure wished for his readers. Again, here we have an important distinction from the role of Mary in Clare's meditation. Mary was absent from Clare's meditation on the crucifixion in Letter 4. When prompting the virgins of Prague to imagine their personae in meditation, Clare repeatedly referred to them as the spouses of Christ.[77] As his virgin spouses, they took Christ's material form by practicing poverty. But for Bonaventure's meditation on the crucifixion, Mary was paramount. According to Bonaventure, Mary witnessed hanging from the wood of the cross

> this blessed and most holy flesh,
> which [she] so chastely conceived,
> so sweetly nourished
> and fed with [her] milk,
> which [she] so often held on [her] lap,
> and kissed with [her] lips. (*LV,* p. 79; Cousins, 153)

Gazing upon this scene of suffering with her own bodily eyes, Mary was "more deeply pierced by a sword of compassion than if [she] had suffered in [her] own body" (*LV,* p. 79; Cousins, 153). She provided the exemplary affective response to the visualization of Christ's passion not only because she was a witness to the events, but because she bore Christ's flesh; she nourished, cradled, and kissed him. Her emotional intensity made real for her the bodily experience of Christ. It was this emotional intensity that Bonaventure sought to conjure:

---

77. Clare used the term *sponsa* six times in Letter 4, inciting Agnes and her sisters to regard themselves as Christ's poor spouse when gazing on the mirror she described.

O my God, good Jesus,
Although I am in every way without merit and unworthy,
grant to me,
who did not merit to be present at these events
in the body,
that I may ponder them faithfully
in my mind
and experience toward you,
my God crucified and put to death for me,
that feeling of compassion
which your innocent mother and the penitent Magdalene
experienced
at the very hour of your passion. (*LV,* p. 80; Cousins, 158)

In this little prayer, Bonaventure's exemplary meditant asked for a specialized kind of sight, one made available only through emotionally engaged meditation. Although owing to the passage of time he could not be present at the crucifixion, nevertheless he prayed that it might be recapitulated for him. He wished to experience Christ's death emotionally, just exactly as the Marys had experienced it, in the branches of this meditation.

At the ninth fruit, Bonaventure advanced to portray the body of the resurrected Christ. The tree remained critical to Bonaventure's efforts at guiding visualization, "the most beautiful flower of the root of Jesse, which had blossomed in the incarnation and withered in the passion, thus blossomed again in the resurrection so as to become the beauty of all" (*LV,* p. 81; Cousins, 160). The beauty reflected in his body on the tree of Jesse was an image—a mirror—of what the rest of humanity could expect of their own potentially resurrected bodies. Christ on the tree was a mirror to be gazed at—"Happy the eyes that have seen!" (*LV,* p. 81; Cousins, 161). The tree was a mirror through which to see God in the world. For the meditant succeeding in this task of visualization, the end point of the meditation was a glorious wedding feast. When the meditant completed Bonaventure's itinerary of contemplation, he would be "introduced into that sacred and secret bridal chamber and will be united to that heavenly lamb in so intense a covenant that bride and groom will become one in spirit" (*LV,* p. 84; Cousins, 168). They would become one, a new created being.

Although Bonaventure's meditation was based on a Scholastic underpinning in which imagination retained the power to impel the meditant from humanity to divinity, enveloping her in the very being of Christ's dual nature, still his conviction in meditation's transformative powers was equally informed by less academic sources.[78] He clearly regarded Francis as the exemplary meditant, himself transformed into Christ's very being. His *Legenda maior* makes this point clear—for Bonaventure, it was Francis's focused visualization of Christ on the cross that first converted him at San Damiano, and his contemplation of Christ crucified on Alverna that transformed him into the "seal of the likeness of the living God, namely of Christ crucified which was imprinted on his body."[79] The meditant who gazed at the tree of crucifixion, Bonaventure hoped, might undergo a similar physical transformation into the crucified image held before her eyes.

Both Clare and Bonaventure chose to turn to natural imagery, to a tree of crucifixion, in an attempt to conform the self to Christ. Meditation on imagery drawn from the material of the incarnation and crucifixion stimulated their love for Christ, forging an identification with him. But Clare and Bonaventure pursued their goals of meditative unity in quite distinct ways. Clare yearned for her sisters to identify with the material conditions of Christ, as his spouse, in poverty. Bonaventure aimed for affective identification. Considering Christ as the exemplary species, he instructed meditants on seeing, feeling, and thus becoming one with the image placed before them. The painted renditions of the *Lignum vitae* nevertheless depict Bonaventure as the author, and Clare the recipient, of this meditative guide to Christic assimilation. They often feature Clare kneeling with a scroll in her hands that reads: "A bundle of myrrh is my beloved to me." These are the same words that Bonaventure longed for the contemplative to utter, after successfully contemplating Christ's "labor, suffering, and love" in the *Lignum vitae*. In the Monticelli altarpiece, they are in the arms of Clare. Through her own *lignum vitae*, she had "enkindl[ed]" this affection."

But Clare was far more stringent in her pursuit of the ideal religious life than the series of *Ligna vitae* that portray her as a practitioner of this meditation might have wished to validate. Depicting her in this manner, as an obedient virgin kneeling in the company of Franciscan men of authority and their biblical exemplars, eclipsed the memory of her radical insistence on poverty, her efforts to outmaneuver Gregory IX, and her meditation on the transformative power of the crucifixion. As I will show in chapter 4, meditation on the tree of crucifixion became a contested site for defining the legacy of Francis and his early followers. The official hagiographical image of Clare,

---

78. Karnes, *Imagination, Meditation, and Cognition,* 130–34.

79. *Legenda maior,* in *Opera omnia,* 8:504–49; 505: "signaculum similitudinis Dei viventis, Christi videlicet crucifixi, quod in corpore ipsius fuit impressum"; *Bonaventure: The Life of Francis,* trans. Cousins, 181–82.

as attested by the *Ligna* paintings and her *Legenda,* may have been absorbed by the Franciscan establishment, which, like Bonaventure, had accepted papal modifications to Francis's Rule. But more radical interpreters of Franciscan life would cling to the oral tradition of Clare, which remembered her for her forthright insistence on emulation of Christ's poverty as a means of sharing his material being.[80]

---

80. Giovanna Casagrande argues that the repeated references to Clare in later Franciscan stories about the founder, particularly the Fioretti, represent her oral tradition; see Giovanna Casagrande, "Le Compagne di Chiara," in *Chiara d'Assisi,* 383–425; and Casagrande, "Presenza di Chiara in Umbria nei secoli XIII-XIV: Spunti e appunti," *Collectanea Franciscana* 62 (1992): 481–505. Her letters and Testament were preserved by Brother Leo, who copied them into the Messina codex; Knox, *Creating Clare of Assisi,* 13–14.

CHAPTER 4

The Franciscan Bough

Trees abound in Franciscan devotional expressions of the late thirteenth and fourteenth centuries. They appear as the singular subject of frescoes in monumental and private settings, in the illumination of liturgical and devotional manuscripts, and in Franciscan legends, poetry, prayers, and meditations. The popularity of Bonaventure's marvelous *Lignum vitae* (Tree of Life), which I examined briefly in chapter 3, was an early indication of the profound impact that arboreal imagery would have on Franciscan spirituality. Perhaps not surprisingly, later followers of Francis would adapt this contemplative process to the memory of their founder, imagining Francis's life story unfurling according to the branches of a tree, in perfect conformity with the life of Christ. Fourteenth-century Franciscan art and homiletics frequently linked the two men through figural trees decorated with branches illustrating biographical similarities. With the outbreak of the controversy between Spiritual and Conventual Franciscans, arboreal imagery would be used in a polemical fashion by both sides seeking to delineate the proper way of following their founder.

In this chapter I turn to the rich tradition of arboreal imagery in Franciscan spirituality as it emerged from the earlier meditational work of Clare and Bonaventure. As we will see, the first generations of Francis's followers drew on associations of the tree in fresh new ways. Contrary to what one might expect, they were less interested in the saint's love of nature, instead choosing to emphasize Francis's shared material being with Christ. Franciscan writers, poets, and artists repeatedly made use of the image of a tree in order to explain Francis's bodily transformation into Christ.[1] They reasoned that he had so replicated the material condition of God in Christ that he was in fact Christ's mirror image or copy, the *alter Christus*. Drawing on the imagery of a tree helped Franciscans to explicate how such a thing was possible: how humanity and divinity could inhere simultaneously in created matter, how Francis could be the *alter Christus,* the Word made flesh "come to earth again," and how his followers might also hope to be transformed in this way. Indeed, some friars began to consider themselves as so conformed to the will of Francis that they envisioned even themselves as growing from the branches of the tree he founded.

Although this interpretation of Francis as the *alter Christus*—as so perfectly conformed to Christ that he actually became a second Christ—did not emerge until the fourteenth century, the foundations for it were laid much earlier. Bonaventure sanctioned such an interpretation in his 1263 life of Saint Francis, *Legenda maior.* According to Bonaventure, Francis bore such similitude to Christ that his reception of the stigmata was a seal confirming his transformation into Christ.[2] By the following century a considerable number of friars had begun to regard Francis as a second Christ, as can be seen in a work such as *The Little Flowers of St. Francis,* written in the late fourteenth century.[3] For these men, Christ was once again perceptible, incarnate in the body of Francis. In what follows, I show how the seed planted by Clare and Bonaventure grew into this new Franciscan vision of a re-created world in which Francis was transformed into a second Christ. Reading these later Franciscan texts against the background of Clare and Bonaventure's arboreal meditations allows us to perceive new arguments that had emerged among the fourteenth-century Franciscans. It enables us to recognize how poverty was interpreted by the Spiritual Franciscans as a means of making the self into holy matter.

---

1. I am not concerned in this chapter with the "real" Francis, but with how he was remembered, celebrated, and politicized in posthumous texts. On the historically real Francis, and the most reliable sources for revealing him, see Augustine Thompson, *Francis of Assisi: A New Biography* (Ithaca, NY: Cornell University Press, 2012), esp. pt. 2, "Sources and Debates," 149–278.

2. On Francis as the second Christ (*alter Christus*), see Henk Van Os, "St. Francis of Assisi as a Second Christ in Early Italian Painting," *Simiolus: Netherlands Quarterly for the History of Art* 7.3 (1974): 115–32; and Stanislao da Campagnola, *L'angelo del sesto sigillo e l'"Alter Christus": Genesi e sviluppo di due temi francescani nei secoli XIII-XIV* (Rome: Laurentianum-Antonianum, 1971).

3. *Actus beati Francisci et sociorum eius,* ed. Pierre Béguin (Louvain: CETEDOC, 1987); "Franciscus alter Christus," 6.1, 18.27, in *Francis of Assisi: Early Documents,* ed. Regis J. Armstrong, Wayne Hellman, and William J. Short (Hyde Park, NY: New City Press, 1999–2002), 3:448, 473.

Incarnation, Re-creation, *Alter Christus*

It is a commonplace that Francis was a nature lover, that his reverence for the diverse objects and beings of creation indicated his love of "nature" and was evidence of his peculiar "nature spirituality."[4] I will not speculate here on what the historically "real" Francis, if such a singular subject exists, actually experienced in his multiform relations with the natural world and its creatures. But I will argue that his followers commemorated not his love of nature but his appreciation of the material world as holy matter, as capable of yielding the presence of God. For his followers, Francis's admiration for "flowing springs" and "blooming gardens," and his predilection for taming wolves, rescuing worms from human foot traffic, and preaching to birds, were indications of his perception of creation as capable of mediating an experience of the Creator.[5] Celano, for example, explained that Francis "used to embrace more warmly and to observe more gladly anything in which he found an allegorical likeness to the Son of God."[6] In Celano's depiction, nearly everything in the world seemed to reveal the face of God to Francis. Celano thus frequently depicted him as delighting in all of material creation:

> How great do you think was the delight the beauty of the flowers brought to his soul whenever he saw their lovely form and noticed their sweet fragrance? He would immediately turn his gaze to the beauty of that flower, brilliant in springtime, sprouting from the root of Jesse. (*Vita prima* 1.29.81; Armstrong, 251)

Celano hardly gave the impression that when Francis gazed upon "fields and vineyards, rocks and woods, and all the beauty of the fields," he was revering "nature" (*Vita prima* 1.29.81; Armstrong, 251). Nature was simply not part of his discussion; it had no role in the impression of Francis he wished to impart. Rather, Celano described a Francis who was intensely enthralled by

---

4. On Francis of Assisi and nature, see Alfonso Marini, *Sorores Alaudae: Francesco d'Assisi, il creato, gli animali* (Assisi: Edizioni Porziuncula, 1989); Edward A. Armstrong, *Saint Francis, Nature Mystic: The Derivation and Significance of the Nature Stories in the Franciscan Legend* (Berkeley: University of California Press, 1973); and Roger Sorrell, *Saint Francis of Assisi and Nature: Tradition and Innovation in Western Christian Attitudes toward the Environment* (New York: Oxford University, 1988).

5. Timothy Johnson has recently argued for a similar interpretation of Francis's followers, particularly Bonaventure, Angela of Foligno, and Duns Scotus, as recognizing his ability to perceive God in the elements of creation; see Timothy Johnson, "Francis and Creation," in *The Cambridge Companion to Francis of Assisi,* ed. Michael Robson (Cambridge: Cambridge University Press, 2012), 143–60.

6. Thomas of Celano, *Vita prima S. Francisci,* in *Analecta Franciscana* (Quaracchi: Collegium S. Bonaventurae, 1941), 10:3–115; 1.28.77; Thomas of Celano, "The Life of Saint Francis," trans. Regis Armstrong, in Armstrong, Hellman, and Short, *Francis of Assisi: Early Documents,* 1:248 (hereafter cited parenthetically in the text in abbreviated form).

the material world of creation. When gazing at the elements of the world, Celano reported, Francis saw the incarnation, the root of Jesse, the substance of God. The flowers and fields of creation placed before his mind the incarnation—God entering into matter. His love and reverence for vineyards, birds, and fields, then, was a reverence for the material of the world, because for him material creation embodied the Creator.

Bonaventure, continuing the theme established by Celano, praised Francis's ability to perceive links between a material God and material creation: "He embraced more affectionately and sweetly those [creatures] which display the pious meekness of Christ in a natural likeness."[7] This affectionate embrace spoke to Bonaventure of Francis's desire to see God in the material being of creation:

> he rejoiced in all the works of the Lord's hands
> and through their delightful display
> he rose into their life-giving reason and cause.
> In beautiful things he contuited Beauty itself
> And through the footprints impressed in things
> he followed his Beloved everywhere,
> out of them all making for himself a ladder
> through which he could climb and lay hold of him. (*Legenda maior* 9.1, p. 530; Armstrong, 596)

Like Celano, Bonaventure commemorated Francis's ability to see God in *things*. It is important to note here Bonaventure's fixation on things as a description of Francis's ardor (*per impressa rebus*). In his depiction of Francis's devotion, he gave a particular power to created objects to convey the experience of God.

From this perspective on Francis set by his official hagiographers, the founder's pioneering devotion to the Christ child at Greccio bears new meaning. Celano's narrative of Francis staging Christ's nativity at Greccio was a tale of perception, of Francis's wishing to *see* God's presence in the world, and to illustrate for his followers how the incarnation continued to inhere in the created world.[8] At Greccio, Celano reported that Francis wished, through this mimed scene, to "enact the memory of that babe

---

7. *Legenda maior S. Francisci Assisiensis,* ed. P.P. Collegii a Sancti Bonaventurae (editio minor) (Quaracchi: Collegii Sanctae Bonaventurae, 1941) 2–125; 8.6, p. 527; Bonaventure, *The Life of Saint Francis,* trans. Regis Armstrong, in *Francis of Assisi: Early Documents,* 2:590 (hereafter cited parenthetically in the text in abbreviated form).

8. On the significance of Greccio for Italian art, see Erwin Rosenthal, "The Crib of Greccio and Franciscan Realism," *Art Bulletin* 36 (1954): 57–60; more recently, Beth Mulvaney, "Standing on

who was born in Bethlehem" (*Vita prima* 1.30.84; Armstrong, 255). After gathering the hay, building the crib, and summoning oxen and sheep from nearby farmers, Francis reiterated the events he had just commemorated by celebrating Mass. In celebrating the Eucharist over the crib he wished to witness the physical elements of the created world bending to reflect the presence of God. "Greccio is made a new Bethlehem!" exclaimed Celano (*Vita prima* 1.30.85: "et quasi nova Bethlehem de Graecio facta est"; Armstrong, 255). In this small Italian town, Francis rejoiced that God had entered the elements. His celebration of the act of transubstantiation over the manger at Greccio—of goading God into matter—reinforced his desire to see God in matter.[9]

According to his biographers, the reverence Francis felt for the incarnation was a crucial component of his pursuit of poverty. The incarnation, they believed, was God's work of humble and loving self-emptying, an extension of himself into creation. They urged that it was this divine act that Francis wished to imitate. The practice of poverty was thus a means to imitate God's condescension, God's inhabitation of material. In their understanding of it, poverty made matter holy by reflecting God's being. According to Bonaventure, it was Francis's pious emulation, through the practice of poverty, of God's *condescensionem* that transformed him:

> This is what, through devotion, lifted him up into God; through compassion, transformed him into Christ; through self-emptying, turned him into his neighbor; through universal reconciliation (*per universalem conciliationem*) with each thing, refashioned him to the state of innocence. (*Legenda maior* 8.2, p. 526; Armstrong, 586)

Bonaventure's *Legenda maior* gave official license to the representation of Francis as transformed into Christ. Through piety he was "refashioned" into a new being, returned to a state of sinlessness. His humble service and attention to creation had emptied his selfhood. In this way, Bonaventure proposed, Francis was "conciliated" through all of creation.

Just as, according to his disciples, Francis had shown such reverence for God's act of entering the created world in the incarnation, and had sought

---

the Threshold: Beholder and Vision in the Assisi *Crib at Greccio*," in *Finding St. Francis in Literature and Art,* ed. Cynthia Ho, Beth Mulvaney, and John Downey (New York: Palgrave, 2009), 23–34.

9. The Franciscan order introduced the elevation of the Host into the Roman missal, an act that emphasizes their focus on *seeing,* visually deciphering the material of God in Christ in the elements of the earth. On the Eucharist among the Franciscans, see David Burr, "Eucharistic Presence and Conversion in Late Thirteenth-Century Franciscan Thought," *Transactions of the American Philosophical Society* 74 (1984): 1–113.

to honor that act in his practice of poverty, so they also emphasized his conformity to Christ in the crucifixion, by depicting his stigmata as a real bodily transformation. They portrayed his reception of the stigmata as a reward sent by God that served as a seal, confirming Francis's status as the *alter Christus.*[10] Because Francis had been conformed to Christ's incarnation, so also he should be transformed into the image of Christ in his suffering passion. As Bonaventure explained, "The man filled with God understood that, just as he had imitated Christ in the actions of his life, so he should be conformed to him in the affliction and sorrow of his passion" (*Legenda maior* 13.2, p. 542; Armstrong, 631). According to Bonaventure, Francis was "totally transformed into the likeness of the crucified," so that the stigmata were the imprint of Christ's likeness (*Legenda maior* 13.3, p. 543: "totum in Christi crucifixi similitudinem transformandum"; Armstrong, 632). He explained that Francis merited this transformation because he was "filled with God," through his ardent desire to imitate Christ in "carrying his cross" and "empty[ing] himself" (*Legenda maior* 13.1–2, p. 542; Armstrong, 630–31). Bonaventure's portrayal of Francis set a pattern for human transformation into the divine. The potential for human transformation became a devotional goal, particularly among the Spiritual Franciscans, who pursued it by practicing poverty.

According to his followers, love was the transforming agent, the catalyst that rendered Francis capable of sharing the material of his beloved Christ. God's love for his creation compelled him to enter it, to transform his divinity into materiality. Thus Bonaventure declared that "it was through love that the divine nature was united to flesh and through love that Christ humbled himself and underwent death."[11] According to Bonaventure, God's love of creation impelled him to enter it. Bonaventure depicted Francis's love as drawing God, once again, into matter and inducing God to transform that matter:

> After true love of Christ
> transformed the lover into his image,
> when the forty days were over that he spent in solitude...
> the angelic man

---

10. On Francis's reception of the stigmata, see Octavian Schmucki, *The Stigmata of Saint Francis of Assisi: A Critical Investigation in the Light of Thirteenth-Century Sources,* trans. Canisius Connors (St. Bonaventure, NY: The Franciscan Institute, 1991).

11. *Sermo* IV, in *S. Bonaventurae opera omnia,* ed. R. P. Bernardini et al. (Quaracchi: Collegium S. Bonaventurae, 1882–1902), 9:589; *The Disciple and the Master: St. Bonaventure's Sermons of St. Francis of Assisi,* ed. and trans. Eric Doyle (Chicago: Franciscan Herald Press, 1983), 91–92.

> Francis came down from the mountain
> bearing with him
> the likeness of the Crucified,
> depicted not on tablets of stone or panels of wood
> carved by hand, but engraved on parts of his flesh
> by the finger of the living God. (*Legenda maior* 13.5, p 543; Armstrong, 634)

In this passage, Bonaventure suggests that God had, once again, acted in matter through the person of Francis. God had altered the person of Francis, changing him into the crucified image of Christ upon which he gazed. According to his followers, Francis's meditative intimacy with the image of the crucified Christ was so strong, he so perfectly imagined the suffering of his body, that God, in turn, altered the material condition of Francis, marking him to reflect his assimilation.

"Do you desire to imprint Christ crucified on your heart?" Bonaventure continued, addressing his audience. "Do you long to be transformed into him to the point where your heart is aflame with love?" Those who wished to achieve the kind of transformation experienced by Francis learned that they must cultivate love, enflame their passion for the crucified Christ. So Bonaventure instructed:

> Just as iron when heated to the point where it becomes molten can take the imprint of any mark or sign, so a heart burning fervently with love of Christ crucified can receive the imprint of the Crucified Lord himself or his cross. Such a loving heart is carried over to the Crucified Lord or transformed into him. That is what happened to Saint Francis.[12]

Bonaventure represented Francis's stigmata as a sacramental act, a bursting forth of divinity into the material of creation (*Legenda maior* 13.4, p. 543; Armstrong, 633). Through Francis, God acted in the world. Bonaventure's devotional logic mirrored his philosophy of the imagination. That philosophy, outlined in his *Itinerarium mentis ad Deum,* suggested the possibility of the real presence of Christ within the person of the meditant. Christ truly inhered in the human insofar as Christ was, in Bonaventure's formulation, really present in the species that conveyed information to the individual. For him, Christ was the exemplar for how humans must apprehend all created objects so that, through its species, one might apprehend Christ. "Because

---

12. *Sermones de diuersis,* in *Opera omnia,* 9:589; Doyle, 92.

Christ is the exemplar of any object," Michelle Karnes has explained of Bonaventure's cognitive mysticism, "the species of an object leads one not only to apprehend the object but, to some degree, Christ. Species lead the individual to know the object that generated it, and so the impression of the divine species, or Christ, on the soul leads the individual back to God."[13] Francis's intense apprehension of Christ, according to Bonaventure, thus led to his transformation into him. It was a transformation that might also be available to others.

Even before Bonaventure, of course, Celano had interpreted the stigmata as an infusion of divinity in the body of Francis occasioned by love. For Celano, the sacrament that transformed Francis was accomplished through his love of Christ. "For this reason," Celano explained, he was "stamped with Christ's brilliant seal." (*Vita prima* 9.115; Armstrong, 284). At least as early as Celano's *Vita prima* (1229), Francis's followers were already associating his body with that of Christ. In the *Vita secunda* (1245–47), they were identical. Celano reported that one friar, while absorbed in prayer, saw a vision of Francis: "'Is this not Christ, brother?' a group of onlookers asked. And he replied, 'It is he.' Others asked him again, saying: 'Isn't this Saint Francis?' And the brother likewise replied that it was he. For it really seemed to that brother, and to the whole crowd, as if Christ and Saint Francis were one person."[14] According to his followers, Francis achieved complete bodily identity with Christ.

How could Francis, a human, be equated with Christ, God and man? How could any human, a created, material object, be made holy? Just as Francis had been converted by seeing the crucifix at San Damiano, just as he had been transformed into Christ by the sight of the seraph on Mount Alverna, so his followers believed that they might also undergo such a conversion process through their own skilled observation and imitation of Francis.[15] Francis's wish, as reported by Celano, to witness bodily God's incarnation in all things resembled his followers' wish to witness *his* incarnation bodily into Christ, his transformation into holy matter.[16] For example, Celano

---

13. Michelle Karnes, *Imagination, Meditation, and Cognition in the Middle Ages* (Chicago: University of Chicago Press, 2011), 102.

14. *Vita secunda sancti Francisci* 2.219.6; trans. as *The Remembrance of the Desire of a Soul*, in Armstrong, Hellman, and Short, *Francis of Assisi: Early Documents*, 2:389.

15. Lester Little refers to this phenomenon as *imitatio Francisci*. Lester Little, "*Imitatio Francisci*: The Influence of Saint Francis of Assisi on Late Medieval Religious Life," in *Defenders and Critics of Franciscan Life: Essays in Honor of John Fleming*, ed. John Fleming, Michael Cusato, and Guy Geltner (Leiden: Brill, 2009), 195–218.

16. Celano explained (*Vita prima* 1.30) that Francis erected the crèche at Greccio because he wished "to see as much as is possible with his own bodily eyes" God coming into matter in the birth

remarked that his followers also wished to see Francis's stigmata with their own bodily eyes. In the process of seeing Francis in this manner, perhaps they too might be transformed into his likeness.[17] Here, Celano indicated his contemporaries' hope to train their eyes to see the created world as mediating God's presence. The body of Francis was for Celano a site for instruction in this kind of discernment, for faith in seeing creation as potentially holy matter. By touching Francis's wounded body, his followers understood and perceived a new pattern of salvation, that matter could reveal God. Francis's transformation into Christ "[did not] require evidence of miracles for we have seen it with our eyes and touched it with our hands" (*Vita prima* 3.124; Armstrong, 203). Celano depicted the Franciscans' great pleasure at seeing their founder's wounds for the first time:

> they had never heard or read in Scripture
> about what their eyes could see:
> they could not have been persuaded to believe it
> if it were not demonstrated by such clear evidence.
> In fact,
> there appeared in him
> the form of the cross and passion
> of the spotless lamb. . . .
> It seemed
> he had just been taken down from the cross,
> his hands and feet pierced by nails
> and his right side
> wounded by a lance. (*Vita prima* 2.9.112; Armstrong, 280)

It is important that Celano places emphasis on sight. Actually seeing the marks of Christ on the body of Francis was a transformative experience for his followers.[18] Observing the wounds of Francis was an exercise in seeing

---

of Christ. He then repeated this coming into matter of God by choosing to celebrate Mass over the manger scene.

17. Beth Mulvaney has shown, examining three scenes from the upper church of the Basilica of Saint Francis in Assisi, that imagery commemorating the life of Francis sought to instruct devout viewers to perceive in new ways. She concludes that the paintings take on "the challenge of constructing the reality of the material world while also suggesting the higher truths are discernable above the surface of appearances. . . . The beholder is encouraged to imagine participating in the spiritual pilgrimage of Francis, the *alter Christus,* and is also beckoned to join him, now and forever." Mulvaney, "Standing on the Threshold," 32.

18. In Bonaventure's *Life,* seeing and touching the wounds strengthens faith: "Many of them kissed the stigmata out of devotion and touched them with their own hands to strengthen their testimony" (Armstrong, 636).

the presence of God in the material of creation. As Celano reported it, seeing and touching the body of Francis "raise[d] their hearts to the love of things unseen through wonderful works that are seen!" (*Vita prima* 2.9.114: "et ut per visibilium mirabile opus ipsorum corda amore invisibilium rapiantur!"; Armstrong, 282).

What was at issue for Celano was a process of perception—*seeing with bodily eyes*—that enabled a new idea to be made more real to the Franciscans. Seeing and touching the wounded body was for them a process of substantiation, of "making real" a new truth.[19] The new truth was that Francis was transformed into holy matter. His becoming holy, indeed becoming the *alter Christus,* was a process they each witnessed. In the body of Francis the mystery of the incarnation was recapitulated; touching and seeing his wounded and thereby transformed body affirmed for his followers that the transformation of matter into holy matter was a continuous process that all devotees must effect, in which they must all participate. The Franciscan disciple sensorially experienced the reality of divine matter *in* Francis. This became for the Franciscans the ultimate meaning of their founder's stigmata—that such a transformation was indeed possible. And more: that the whole created world required reframing, a new discernment, in order to make God visible through it. Francis—who had been praised for his ability to see God in matter—thus became a model for detecting the presence of God in created matter.

Francis and Christ: Arboreal Transformation

Thus far I have argued that Francis's devotion, as portrayed in the early official writings of Celano and Bonaventure, was intimately tied up with the material objects of the created world because in them he recognized the presence of a God who created that world and continually acted in it. According to the early hagiographical tradition, Francis's outstanding love for and emulation of Christ rendered him into Christ's exact replica. I turn now to the manner in which Francis's followers depended on the image of the tree as a model for imagining Francis's transformation into Christ, for commemorating and celebrating it. The fourteenth-century Franciscans promoted the idea of Francis's conformity to Christ by experimenting with the branches of the *Lignum vitae,* turning those gospel branches into structural episodes on which hung conclusive examples of Francis's biographical analogues to

---

19. Elaine Scarry, *The Body in Pain: The Making and Unmaking of the World* (New York: Oxford University Press, 1985), 215.

Christ, in the events of his life, his method of prayer, his perfection of virtue, and finally, in the very members of his body. They borrowed from Bonaventure's *Lignum vitae* the image of the tree, which illustrated events of Christ's life for the imagination. But they used the imagery from the *Lignum vitae* to demonstrate Francis's physical and psychological conformity to Christ and, through Francis, the ability of his poor followers to be transformed by literally observing his life and virtues. Bonaventure had suggested in the *Lignum vitae* that the meditant could be conformed interiorly to Christ by imagining events from his life and death arranged as fruits hanging from a tree, and he had advocated an image of Francis in the *Legenda maior* in which Francis himself had perfected this conformity, being sealed externally with the wounds of Christ. Many of these later authors who borrowed from Bonaventure, however, advocated the literal imitation of Francis's rigorous observation of poverty as a means to re-create his transformation, a position they may have associated with Clare's struggle to secure the privilege of poverty. With the eruption in the late thirteenth century of the great controversy between Spiritual and Conventual Franciscans over the interpretation of Francis's teachings, many Spiritual Franciscans adapted Bonaventure's *Lignum vitae* as a device for contemplating Christ and Francis the second Christ. To be sure, all Spiritual Franciscans did not believe precisely the same thing, nor did they strive to reform the order according to the same plan.[20] They did, however, share a basic vision of Francis as transformed through poverty and as ordaining poverty as the means, in turn, for transformation of the world. In this context, arboreal meditations outlined the means by which Francis was transformed into holy matter, and further, suggested that the friars could also reasonably hope to be so transformed. For them, trees came to naturalize the supernatural union of contraries.

The most explicit treatment of the correspondences between events in the life of Christ and of Francis, rendering the life of Francis into a typological fulfillment of the life of Christ, was that of Ubertino of Casale in his *Arbor vitae crucifixae Jesu Christi* (Tree of the Crucified Life of Jesus).[21] Ubertino composed the *Arbor vitae* in 1305 on Alverna, the site of Francis's reception

---

20. On the nuances among particular Franciscans, see David Burr, *The Spiritual Franciscans: From Protest to Persecution in the Century after Saint Francis* (University Park: Pennsylvania State University Press, 2001).

21. Ubertinus de Casali, *Arbor vitae crucifixae Jesu,* with an introduction and bibliography by Charles T. David, Monumenta Politica et Philosophica Rariora 1.4 (Turin: Bottega d'Erasmo, 1961) (hereafter cited parenthetically in the text in abbreviated form). For the dissemination of the *Arbor vitae,* see Frédégand Callaey, "L'influence et diffusion de l'*Arbor vitae* de Ubertin de Casale," *Revue d'Histoire Ecclésiastique* 17 (1921): 533–46.

of the stigmata. His treatise sought to instruct meditants on how to replicate Francis's transformation into Christ. In the prologue to his work, Ubertino described his own experience of transformation while rapt in contemplative ecstasy on Alverna:

> I became more and more sublimely and ineffably transformed into Jesus, and having piously undergone this new state, I remained almost continuously transformed. There, wholly ineffably, not only the glory, the passion, and the cross of Christ but at the same time the life of the God-man were inspired within me, and I shed inestimable tears over the destruction of the life of Christ. (*Arbor vitae,* second prologue, 5)

Ubertino claimed to have been, like Francis, transformed through contemplation of Christ's life and death on Alverna. He aimed in his treatise to instruct readers on how similarly to reproduce the process of such contemplative becoming.

Ubertino's presence on Mount Alverna was the result of his banishment from a teaching post at Santa Croce in Florence, on the charge that he preached critically against the excesses of the papacy. Ubertino began lecturing at Santa Croce in 1287, at the invitation of Peter Olivi.[22] He was greatly influenced by his mentor Olivi, particularly his Joachite historical perspective as espoused in the *Postilla in Apocalypsim.* Joachim of Fiore first introduced the tripartite division of world history that would so greatly influence Franciscan interpretation of their cosmic mission of reform. Joachim divided his chronological scheme into the age of the father, represented by the historic events of the Old Testament; the age of the son, which commenced with the nativity of Christ and his church; and the age of the Holy Spirit, a period of renewal and redemption.[23] According to many prominent Franciscans, including Bonaventure, Francis represented the dawn of the sixth stage of church history, the third age of world history, when the cosmic forces would align to usher in the final reform of Christianity. The nuances of Ubertino's apocalyptic interpretation of history should not detain us here. What is most important about his work for my argument is the manner in which

---

22. Burr, *Spiritual Franciscans,* 47.

23. Bernard McGinn, *The Flowering of Mysticism: Men and Women in the New Mysticism, 1200–1350* (New York: Crossroad, 1998); see also David Burr, *Olivi's Peaceable Kingdom: A Reading of the Apocalypse Commentary* (Philadelphia: University of Pennsylvania Press, 1993). Joachim also employed trees as *figurae,* specifically as apocalyptic symbols of growth and development. McGinn suggests that Joachim was attracted to the tree because of his "organic theory of the interrelation of ages (*initium* or *germinatio, fructificatio,* and *consummatio* are constant themes)"; McGinn, *The Calabrian Abbott: Joachim of Fiore in the History of Western Thought* (New York: Macmillan, 1985), 109.

he adapted Bonaventure's *lignum* of Christ's life into an *arbor* that clearly outlined how the world's history culminated with Francis's imitable transformation into Christ.[24]

Ubertino was indebted to the work of Bonaventure. He conceived of the fifth book of his *Arbor* as largely a supplement to Bonaventure's *Legenda maior,* which, he believed, had omitted some of the details of Francis's life and of his followers' abandonment of the Rule.[25] Like Bonaventure and Olivi before him, Ubertino identified Francis as the *alter Christus* and the apocalyptic angel of the sixth seal who was sent from heaven to usher in the third age of world history.[26] He cited Bonaventure as his authority on this matter, as the prologue to the *Legenda maior* had claimed that Francis was "the angel ascending from the rising of the sun bearing the seal of the living God. For at the opening of the sixth seal, John says in Apocalypse, I saw another Angel ascending from the rising sun having the sign of the living God" (*Legenda maior,* Prologue 1, p. 504; Armstrong, 527). Ubertino interspersed episodes from Francis's life in the *Legenda maior* among the branches he borrowed from the *Lignum vitae,* and thus adapted Bonaventure's arboreal structure of meditation on Christ's life in order to advance an image of Francis's life as so conformed to Christ that it, too, was worthy of its own meditation.[27] At the same time, it is possible that Ubertino was inspired to revise Bonaventure's meditative tree by the stories of Clare's radical refusal to accept property, which circulated among the Spiritual Franciscans orally along with her letters and *Testament.* The Spirituals fostered through oral tradition an image of Clare as a hero who passionately refused to accept property.[28] Angelo Clareno, for example, erroneously celebrated her excommunication by Pope Gregory IX on the grounds of such refusal.[29] This particular image

---

24. For a discussion of these nuances, see Malcolm Lambert, *Franciscan Poverty: The Doctrine of the Absolute Poverty of Christ and the Apostles in the Franciscan Order, 1210–1323* (St. Bonaventure, NY: Franciscan Institute Publications, 1998), 157–214.

25. According to Ubertino, Bonaventure neglected this information because he did not wish to prematurely disgrace the brothers; Ubertino, *Arbor vitae,* p. 199.

26. Ubertino cites Bonaventure as his authority on this matter.

27. The formal similarities between Ubertino and Bonaventure's trees can be seen in Ubertino's borrowing of a number of chapter titles from Bonaventure: "Jesus Begotten of God," "Jesus Bound with Chains," "Jesus Linked with Thieves." Ubertino chose to entitle his treatise with the living sense of "arbor," whereas Bonaventure relied on the dead wood of "lignum." The choice of title may suggest that Ubertino believed Francis had provided the antidote for death, a method of renewed life.

28. See Lezlie Knox, *Creating Clare of Assisi: Female Franciscan Identities in Later Medieval Italy* (Boston: Brill, 2008), 85–86; on the oral transmission of Clare stories, see Giovanna Casagrande, "Presenza di Chiara in Umbria nei secoli XIII–XIV: Spunti e appunti," *Collectanea Franciscana* 62 (1992): 485; Duncan Nimmo, *Reform and Division in the Medieval Franciscan Order: From St. Francis to the Foundation of the Capuchins* (Rome: Capuchin Historical Institute, 1987), 79.

29. Knox, *Creating Clare of Assisi,* 86.

of Clare as an activist for Franciscan poverty may have included an appreciation for her own meditation on the tree.

Regardless of his knowledge of or feelings for Clare, there is no doubt that
Ubertino's meditations are dedicated to a similar vision of poverty as necessary to the proper Franciscan life. He interpreted Christ's greatest suffering
as his poverty: "[He] was girded with poverty; for he was born the poorest
in confutation of worldly wealth. He began this in his birth, continued it in
his life, and consummated it in his death" (*Arbor vitae* 1.11, 63). Poverty was
the founding virtue of Ubertino's arboreal meditation, just as it had been for
Clare. He regarded Christ's death on the cross as a consummation (*consum-
mauit*) of poverty, making it a means to holy perfection.[30]

Ubertino organized his arguments for the literal imitation of Francis's life
and the transformative potential of the practice of poverty by outlining them
on the branches of a living and growing tree:

> Now I thought to name this book the *Arbor vitae crucifixae Jesu Christi,*
> which I have divided into five parts. The first book is the root of the
> tree beginning from Jesus' eternal generation by the Father up until
> His physical and, for us, happy birth by his mother. The second book
> raises the trunk of this sacred tree, beginning with the circumcision
> of Jesus up until his manifestation through the witness of the precur-
> sor. The third book extends the branches of this tree in Jesus' fruitful
> preaching and the elect college of disciples, beginning from John the
> Baptist up until Jesus' entry into the holy city of Jerusalem on Palm
> Sunday, where he offered Himself in Holocaust to God his father. The
> fourth book crowns the top of this blessed tree in that it deals with
> the powerful conflict of the Passion of Jesus and His most reverend
> Mother, beginning from his royal entry into Jerusalem up until the
> glorious assumption of the Queen of Heaven into the celestial Jeru-
> salem. The fifth and last book is about the numerous offspring from
> the Gentile church joined to Jesus by a new martyrdom extending up
> until the everlasting wedding banquet of a human nature universally
> beatified. (*Arbor vitae,* second prologue, 7)

Commencing with the meditation itself, Ubertino proceeded to narrate the
mysteries of the uncreated Word (*verbum increatum,* book 1) and the incarnate
Word (*verbum incarnatum,* books 2–4) before moving in his lengthy book 5 to
describe the history of the earthly church and its contemporary ongoing

---

30. Mariano Damiata, *Pietà e storia nell'"Arbor vitae" di Ubertino da Casale* (Florence: Edizioni
Studi Francescani, 1988), 87–89.

excesses and to provide instruction for hastening the arrival of the future church.

Ubertino followed the structure of the *Lignum vitae* in meticulous detail in the first four books of the *Arbor crucifixae,* with the chapter titles from each book corresponding to chapter titles in the fruits of Bonaventure's *Lignum vitae.* But his final book diverged from its exemplar considerably. Book 5 introduced new material that portrayed Francis as *alter Christus* and the harbinger of the third age. Book 5 of the *Arbor vitae* was often copied independently from the previous books and circulated separately from them, which is how most Franciscans would have encountered it.[31] It was critical to the treatise as a whole because it outlined Ubertino's understanding of Francis's transformation into Christ. Book 5 amplified the scope of Bonaventure's *Lignum vitae,* claiming the stigmata of Francis, just as Bonaventure had, as the sixth seal of the apocalypse. But Ubertino went beyond Bonaventure's interpretation to describe other earthly manifestations of the coming of the third age, such as the appearance of the mystical antichrist in popes Boniface VIII and Benedict XI. For Ubertino, the meaning of the Apocalypse ushered by Francis was bodily transformation. Entering the third age, all true followers of Christ's poverty, all true followers of Francis, would be transformed into holy matter.

Ubertino began his treatise with an explanation of its intent—to encourage and enflame ecstatic, transforming love of Christ. Grounding his meditation in authority, he referenced Dionysius's *Divine Names,* asserting that "ecstasy means 'making outside the self'" (*Arbor vitae,* second prologue, 8: "Extasis autem est dicta extra se faciens"). For Ubertino, the goal of contemplation of the lives of Francis and Christ was to make a self outside the self, to transform the self into another composite being through love: "There is nothing in this book that does not address the intimate knowing, loving, and imitating of the life of Jesus Christ. Here is the beautiful bundle of myrrh that, since the first days of my novitiate, I have sought to gather to my breast" (*Arbor vitae,* first prologue, 3). Like Bonaventure and Clare, Ubertino drew on the Song of Songs' image of myrrh against the breast, the image of unification that contemplation of Christ's passion on the tree promised in the *Lignum vitae.* Ubertino thus offered his meditation as a means of

---

31. Frédégand Callaey, *L'idéalisme franciscain spirituel au XIVe siècle: Étude sur Ubertin de Casale* (Louvain: Bureau du Recueil, 1911), 134–35. Furthermore, the popularity of Ubertino's treatise can be attributed to the fact that many versions had retracted some of the more incendiary claims, such as the condemnations of Brother Elias and the popes and prelates.

self-transformation, of becoming one with God. He reported his own experiences of such transformation in detail:

> I confess that he joined me so closely in union to himself that it seemed
> to me I was not merely recalling what had been but that I was seeing
> it as if present. And it seemed I was now the ass, now the ox, now the
> manger, now the straw upon which he lay, now his servant at hand, now
> his uterine brother, now Little Jesus himself; for by a wondrous trans-
> formation, I was one with him in all of his life's events. In a wondrous
> way I appeared with him there, he led me with him fleeing into Egypt,
> going up to the Temple, and returning to Nazareth with his Mother,
> living with him in baptism, in the desert, in his preaching—continually
> in danger, flight, injury, and insult. At last, he made me transform into
> himself, joined to him in his suffering passion, that it seemed to me
> I was now Magdalen the sinner, but also his chosen bride, now his
> brother and chosen disciple John, now his pious mother who bore him,
> lamenting, now the thief nailed on his right, now pure Jesus himself
> crying out on the wood of the Cross and dying in grief. (*Arbor vitae,*
> first prologue, 3)

Ideally, the ecstasy generated by contemplation of the *Arbor* was such that the meditant at once identified with the hay in the manger, at once with infant Jesus himself, at once with the criminal hanging beside him, at once with the suffering Christ. The meditant became the hay, the ass, a mourning Mary, a suffering Christ. Here was Ubertino's "conciliation" through all of creation. Each of these objects from the site of the birth of Christ were witnesses to God's entering into material creation. Ubertino imagined these objects of creation as possessing an eternal affinity, as containing God's essence so that, even from the vantage of his temporal distance from the birth and death of Christ, he too could witness this moment of God touching creation.

Ubertino suggested that Christ entered the world for the purpose of bring-ing hope for all humans to achieve this same conciliation and this identity with the incarnate God. He taught that God had entered material creation in order to shape its potential for conformity. For Ubertino, the hypostatic union of God and world in the body of Jesus was a model for the transformative effects of ecstatic love.[32] Christ had completely emptied out his personhood in kenotic love and sacrifice for humanity. Ubertino thus instructed the indi-vidual who wished to become one with God to imitate Christ's love through acts of humility and abnegation. According to Ubertino, the most efficient

---

32. See Kurt Ruh, *Geschichte der abendländischen Mystik* (Munich: Beck, 1990), 2:393–94.

route to such self-emptying, indeed the only true route, was poverty. He wrote that, at the moment of the incarnation, Christ was armed with poverty, humility, and austerity. Ubertino therefore insisted that the incarnation was recapitulated by the emulation of Christ's virtuous poverty in the manner that Francis had practiced it. In practicing poverty Francis reincarnated Christ in his own person. The followers of Francis, through the observation of holy poverty, therefore perpetuated the coming of God into the world by conforming themselves to him in this manner.

Book 5 of the *Arbor* introduced the apocalyptic portions of Ubertino's interpretation of evangelical poverty and Francis's role in ushering in a new age.[33] In this final book, he detoured significantly from Bonaventure by suggesting that Francis was an emissary sent to usher in the new age, a reformed manner of imitating Christ's life and effecting transformation into him. Ubertino construed Francis as an *alter Christus* with a distinctive historic mission—to inaugurate the third age of world history. His transformation into Christ enabled Francis to commence the renewal of the church. Comparing the life of Francis to the life of Christ, Ubertino enumerated their shared gifts of prophecy and authority, their lives of poverty and miracle working. All of these branches of resemblance proved for Ubertino that Francis was "beyond resemblances" to Christ. He was transformed into Christ, a reproduction or offshoot of Christ: "Who among the sons of God is like God? This man was, however, in an exceptional fashion a son of God and of the blessed Jesus."[34] Christ gave birth to Francis: "Jesu generans Franciscus." Ubertino read the reception of the stigmata by Francis as a sign of his rebirth into the body of Christ. Christ impressed the model of his body on Francis because "he was a most beloved son to Him, His other self!" (*Arbor vitae* 5.4, 434: "immo dilectissimo filio: immo alti se sue"; Armstrong et al., 188). In this remarkable assertion, Jesus was envisioned as the mother of Francis, the mother of a re-created human.

Such an assertion was not altogether uncommon among the early Franciscans.[35] In the upper church of the Basilica of Saint Francis in Assisi, for example, there was a visual rendering of this sentiment. Adjacent to a window

---

33. Callaey argues that book 5 was composed later than the four earlier books on the life of Christ. Callaey, *L'idéalisme franciscain spirituel,* 263–69.

34. *Arbor vitae* 5.3, 434; trans. as *Tree of the Crucified Life of Jesus,* in Armstrong, Hellman, and Short, *Francis of Assisi: Early Documents,* 3:186 (hereafter cited parenthetically in the text in abbreviated form).

35. For an exploration of Jesus specifically as the mother of Francis, see Jerome Poulenc, "Saint François dans le 'vitrail des anges' de l'église supériéreur de la basilique d'Assise," *Archivum Franciscanum Historicum* 76 (1983): 701–13.

depicting Mary embracing the child Jesus is an analogous portrayal of Jesus embracing a diminutive Francis.[36] Francis's followers could see in this image their own perception of him as the *alter Christus,* who was given a divine mission, charged by Christ to enter the world in order to reform it. Just as Mary gave material visibility to Christ, so Christ shared his holy matter with Francis, making him a son. According to Ubertino's logic, Christ was the mother of Francis. Since the twelfth century, the incarnation of Christ in the womb of the Virgin Mary had been depicted as a re-creation of the material world by reference to the *stirps Jesse.* With Ubertino, the arbor was made to depict the incarnation of Francis in the body of Christ. By imprinting Francis with his wounds, Ubertino explained, Christ gave birth to Francis, making him "a most beloved son" (*Arbor vitae* 5.4, 434; Armstrong et al., 188). And if Mary had mothered God in order to provide a vessel for God's entry into creation, to mother the re-created world, then why had Christ mothered Francis in the stigmatization? Christ generated Francis in order to "transform the whole world, furnish it with a seal to inflame it, and bring those willing to follow the perfect likeness of the crucified" (*Arbor vitae,* 5.3, 434; Armstrong et al., 186). The mothering of Francis would enable material conformity to Christ. Christ brought forth Francis in order to inaugurate yet another creation. According to Ubertino, it was only through the practice of poverty that the friars could hope for the initiation of this final age, the final re-creation and perfection of the world.

For Ubertino, the transition into the third age was *the* transformation into Christ, wherein Christ's true followers would assume his body, take on his likeness, and be restored to the unfallen image in him. The adoption of poverty was for Ubertino the key to hastening the third age. To observe poverty was to live as Christ and to effect bodily transformation into him, just as Francis had done:

> As [Francis] saw it, up to the manifestation of the Church's sixth *status* the guidance of souls was not to be conducted through prelacy, if it were to be beneficial, but rather to be committed to the spirit of poverty. It is then that those who are like new apostles will be described as the pillars of the future *status.* (*Arbor vitae* 5.3, 424; Armstrong et al., 156)

---

36. On the plan of windows in the upper church, see Rosalind Brooke, *The Image of St. Francis: Responses to Sainthood in the Thirteenth Century* (Cambridge: Cambridge University Press, 2006), 307; and on Jesus embracing Francis, see pp. 326–31.

The observation of poverty pushed time forward because it anticipated the heavenly kingdom. Poverty, according to Ubertino, was such a destitute state in terms of material comfort that those who practiced it must live solely off of the stuff of heaven:

> To [poverty] Jesus has consigned the undisturbed possession in this life of the kingdom of heaven; ... because those who imitate true poverty in fervor of spirit must, of necessity, live off celestial fare ... , those who yield to [poverty's] wishes she shapes to the likeness of Jesus, son of God, by a renewal in which the perfecting of every state consists. (*Arbor vitae* 5.3, 425; Armstrong et al., 159–60)

Poverty was unique among virtues, according to Ubertino, because it completely filled humans with the will of God, the "crumbs" that fell from the table of the angels. The practitioner of poverty, he argued, lived in the kingdom of heaven in this lifetime. Ubertino's paean to the virtue of poverty in book 5 is replete with the juridical language of *usus pauper,* and invective for those who obstructed efforts to fulfill literally Francis's Rule and Testament. The practice of poverty was for him an incarnational act, making matter holy, and to interfere with its practice was to deny God's action in creation.

Like the poverty through which he founded a "new religion," Francis, for Ubertino, was an example of God's incarnation in the material world, the presence of the kingdom of heaven on earth. Ubertino linked the stigmata to Christ's kenotic love and sacrifice, his salvation of humanity, by making Francis into a eucharistic figure. His wounds were not only reminders of Christ's sacrifice, but evidence that God's material presence remained within the realm of creation: "The outpouring of the blood of Jesus does not perish in forgetfulness, in the new wounds of Francis it grows warm again (*recalescit*)" (*Arbor vitae* 5.4, 435; Armstrong et al., 189). Christ's blood flowed in the present and could be accessed in the present. The stigmata were for Ubertino signs of Francis's transformation and of Christ's return. He envisioned Francis's "crucifixion" in Christ as a replication of Christ's presence, which brought forth the sixth stage of church history, the third age of world history. Resurrection was the promise for those who followed, "so they will be living their lives like 'little Christs,'" smaller figures of Jesus, as it were, perceiving themselves in their mortal flesh transformed into Christ" (*Arbor vitae* 5.4, 437: "christicole crucifixi iesumculi"; Armstrong et al., 191).

Just as Bonaventure's *Lignum vitae* sparked a flurry of visual transcriptions of Christ's life arranged as forty-eight fruits on the twelve branches of an arborescent cross, so Ubertino's treatise was accompanied by the creation of similar arboreal depictions of *Francis's* life. In Verona, for example,

FIGURE 4.1. *Lignum vitae Francisci.* Verona, San Fermo Maggiore. Photo by the author.

in the church of San Fermo Maggiore, the vestiges of a fresco on the east wall depict events from the life of Francis in the form of a tree (fig. 4.1). The style of the acanthus leaves suggests that the artist was borrowing from Taddeo Gaddi's *Tree of Life,* a fresco in the refectory at Santa Croce in Florence, though the medallions that contain images from Francis's life resemble the narrative display of Pacino di Bonaguida's tree made for the women of Monticelli. The Veronese artist may have intentionally called to mind both visual trees in order to emphasize his public announcement that Francis was the new Christ, both in the events punctuating his biography and in his practice of prayer.

The Franciscans of Verona commissioned the *Tree of Life of Saint Francis* between 1320 and 1330. Badly damaged and interrupted by the later addition of an archway leading to a side chapel, the remains of the fresco include scenes depicting the funeral of Francis, the investigation of his stigmata, a few of his posthumous miracles, the Franciscan martyrs at Thana, and numerous saintly visages, such as that of Bonaventure.[37] That support of the fresco came

---

37. On the formal qualities of the fresco, see Alessandro Simbeni, "Il *Lignum vitae Sancti Francisci* in due dipinti di primo trecento a Padova e Verona," *Il Santo* 46 (2006): 185–214.

from lay Franciscans affiliated with the reconstruction and artistic design of such property suggests that the idea of Francis as a Christlike tree of life, an image of the divine in the material world, was resonant with members of the community. If Francis was truly the *alter Christus,* then surely he too was the tree of life, and his life could also be plotted on branches for contemplative fodder and mimetic facility. After all, no more orthodox an institution than the Basilica of Saint Francis in Assisi portrayed Francis's life as a mirror reflection of Christ's.[38] The Franciscans of Verona simply sought to illustrate Francis's life for arboreal contemplation, bringing together in the image of the tree, as Ubertino had, Francis's life and that of Christ.

Although the monumental setting of the Verona *Tree of Life of Saint Francis,* located on the south wall of the upper church, suggests its public purpose to promote the idea of Francis as the *alter Christus,* a similar image in Padua indicates personal, contemplative uses for this unique iconography (fig. 4.2). In an enclosed chapel annexed to the chapter hall in the friary of Padua, the fragments of two badly damaged arboreal frescoes remain on the north and south walls, mirroring one another. Depicted on the south wall is a *lignum vitae* of Christ, bearing a strong resemblance to the Santa Croce *lignum vitae.* Twelve prophets ensconced in roundels flank the branches of the tree.[39] The central figure, making up the trunk, is Christ crucified. Scrawled along the length of the branches are *tituli* taken from the chapters of Bonaventure's *Lignum vitae.* The Franciscans of Padua most likely used this fresco, which was located in a private chapel adjacent to the chapter hall, for contemplative purposes, much as they did the one at Santa Croce. The fresco would have provided further visual context for the form of meditation advocated by Bonaventure in his *Lignum vitae.*

Directly across the room from the Paduan *Lignum vitae Christi* is a second, structurally similar *lignum vitae.* This one on the north wall, however, represents the body of Francis in the usual trunk position of Christ. Francis bears the stigmata, suggesting that he was crucified on this tree. The foliated roundels contain images from the life of the saint, similar to the *lignum vitae* of Christ executed by Pacino di Bonaguida and another at Bergamo. Those scenes that are decipherable include Francis on his deathbed,

---

38. On the official image of Francis, see Brooke, *The Image of St. Francis;* William Cook, *Images of Francis of Assisi in Painting, Stone, and Glass from the Earliest Images to circa 1320 in Italy* (Florence: Leo S. Olschki, 1999).

39. Alessandro Simbeni suggests that the image is from the workshop of Giotto, basing this connection on similar geometric frame patterns in the Scrovengi chapel as well as similarities in the formal properties of the prophets, who resemble those of the *lignum vitae* at Sesto al Regehena. Simbeni, "Il *Lignum vitae Sancti Francisci,*" 191.

FIGURE 4.2. *Lignum vitae Francisci.* Padua, Friary of St. Anthony. Photo by the author.

surrounded by his prayerful followers; Francis with arms uplifted to the sky, which possibly portrays his assumption into heaven; and his trip to the Holy Land. The most striking feature of the *Lignum vitae Francisci* is the central depiction of Francis himself. From his side wound sprout the branches of the very tree that displays scenes from his life.[40] The meditative function of the *lignum vitae* was dependent on his wounds, the seal of his transformation into Christ as the *alter Christus*. What sustained and supported the contemplative function of the *lignum* was Francis's transformation, and the possibility that this transformation held for others who followed him. His wounds bleed the limbs of this tree, markers of the promise of material transformation, of the possibility of holy matter.

How might these two images work together, as they must have worked together, two trees of life staring at one another from across the hall? The Franciscan author and legal scholar Bartholomew of Pisa offers an answer in his *Liber de conformitate vitae beati Francisci ad vitam domini Jesu* (Book of Conformities of the Life of Blessed Francis to the Life of Lord Jesus). The treatise examines forty conformities assimilating the life of Francis to that of Christ. This strategy of likening the saint to Christ through similar life events had been tested previously by Arnald of Sarrant, provincial minister of Aquitaine, whose 1365 *De conformitate B. Francisci ad Christum* (The Conformity of Blessed Francis to Christ) had outlined nine specific ways in which Francis's life was conformed to that of Jesus Christ:

> He appeared singularly conformed to Christ in calling together his friends, in the establishment of their conduct, in contemplation of the sublime, in revelation of the mysteries, in the instruction of peoples and the transformation of their members, in the gathering of merit, in the accumulation of rewards, in the operation of wonders.[41]

Arnald arranged the conformities thematically according to the virtue that each action represented rather than chronologically according to the sequence of their occurrence. For example, the first conformity was the calling together of his followers: "In the first place, then, the most perfect man Francis appeared conformed to our Lord Jesus Christ in the choice of his friends."[42] Here Arnald indicated that Francis, like Christ, chose twelve followers, one of whom was a traitor, one of whom was crucified like Peter, one

---

40. A poetic correlate to this visual image can be found in the lauds of the Spiritual Franciscan poet Jacopone da Todi, who wrote that "the precious balsam of holiness burst forth from [Francis's] wounds!" ('n Francesco fore è 'scito lo balsemo polito ch'el corpo à penetrato). See Jacopone da Todi, *Le Laude,* ed. Luigi Fallacara (Florence: Libreria Editrice Fiorentina, 1955), Laud 61; *The Lauds,* trans. Serge Hughes and Elizabeth Hughes (New York: Paulist Press, 1982), 188.

41. Marian Michalczyk, ed., *Une compilation parisienne des sources primitive franciscaines Paris: Bibliothéque nationale ms Latin 12707* (Rome: Collegio S. Bonaventura, 1983), 89.

42. Ibid., 90; "Kinship of Saint Francis," in Armstrong, Hellman, and Short, *Francis of Assisi: Early Documents,* 3:680.

of whom, like John, witnessed the crucifixion of Francis, and so on.[43] Arnald further suggested that Francis's biographies constituted a third testament, citing his four gospels as the works of Bonaventure, Julian of Speyer, Brother Leo, and Thomas of Celano. If Christ and his actions as documented in the New Testament were the fulfillment of the Old Testament, then Francis's life, as the angel of the sixth seal, also introduced a new era in church history, and the writings confirming the events of his life formed a third testament, containing the events of Christ's return.

Bartholomew of Pisa built on Arnald's nine conformities and on his vision of the mirror-reflected lives of Francis and Christ, arranging them into a tree of conformities wherein the meditant gazing upon the tree would shift back and forth, just as between the north and south walls at Padua, between the lives of Francis and Christ. Bartholomew de Rinonico of Pisa was a student of theology at Bologna, and later a master at Padua.[44] His *Book of Conformities* was considered important enough to the late medieval Franciscans to be considered for, and to win, formal approval at the General Chapter of 1399, and thereafter to be copied copiously. The *Book of Conformities* was considerably popular in the fifteenth century, if only to be ridiculed by the reformers of the following century.[45] The *Book*, which Bartholomew began compiling in 1385, contains forty biographical conformities, many of them entirely apocryphal, such as Francis's having been born in a manger. It is divided into three sections: the first on the infancy and youth of the two men, the second on their similarity in virtue, and the third on their passion, death, and glorification. The forty conformities are presented as fruits, two of each hanging on ten branches to make twenty sets of comparisons of Christ and Francis.[46] The chapter titles of Bartholomew's *Book* often follow those of Bonaventure's *Lignum vitae,* perhaps in part to affirm his own orthodox position within the order. But rather than, as Ubertino had done, superimpose Francis's life on the structure of a meditative tree of life, Bartholomew instead used the image of the tree in order to promote the side-by-side meditation

---

43. Arnald identifies John of Capella as the Judas-figure who "became angry at God and at the Order and hanged himself from a tree so that Francis would be conformed to Christ in having a perverse disciple" (Armstrong et al., 693). Arnald was not the first to distinguish a traitor among the early followers of Francis.

44. For details of Bartholomew's biography, see Carolly Louise Ericksson, "Francis Conformed to Christ: Bartholomew of Pisa's *De Conformitate* in Franciscan History" (PhD diss., Columbia University, 1969), chap. 1.

45. Twenty-two Latin manuscript copies are extant. On the circulation of the *Book,* see *De conformitate vitae beati Francisci ad vitam Domini Iesu,* in *Analecta Franciscana,* vols. 4–5, ed. B. Albizzi (Rome: Typographia Collegii S. Bonaventurae, 1912), 1.xxv–xxxii.

46. *De conformitate vitae beati Francisci ad vitam Domini Iesu,* 1.16–18.

on the lives of both men alternating between narrative parallels. Through such imaginative exercises the meditant would truly see how the two men became one. The tree helped to promote visually and imaginatively the idea of material transformation and conformity to the divine (fig. 4.3).

The purpose of the *Book of Conformities* was to demonstrate Francis's conformity to Christ by detailing the resemblances of their life narratives, their prayer, their miracles, and their virtues. In order to represent the conformity of Francis to Christ, biographical details had to be omitted or embellished. Their accuracy or modification, to Bartholomew, was of less importance than what they were chosen to depict—conformity. For example, Bartholomew asserted that Francis was like Christ in being presented as an infant, changing water into wine, and being persecuted by suffering illness, mockery, and abandonment by his family.[47] Though the majority of the *Book* was dedicated to this thick description, the exercise itself, as Bartholomew explained, served the end of proving Francis's conformity to Christ, a precept that was key to understanding of the person of Francis.

According to Bartholomew, Christ chose to transform Francis into himself, the object of his devotion, through love. "Thus that man was transformed into the semblance of Christ," he declared, denoting Francis as a *Christus typicus*.[48] Bartholomew described such transformation as *deiformis*, indicating that Francis's human body took on the form of God, infusing God with humanity in order to produce this *Christus typicus*.[49] He marveled at their acts of humility and transformation: "What a wonder it was that Christ surrendered himself to the total efficacy of the cross; and greater still was the complete surrender of blessed Francis to the stigmatization."[50] These were bold words. For Bartholomew, Francis's total conformity to Christ was a truly singular event. "Nowhere has it been written of this transformation of soul and body," he proclaimed, "but only in the testimony of the supreme pontiff, conceded in the order of his bull that was made for blessed Francis."[51]

---

47. The use of conformities can also be found in the *Actus beati Francisci et sociorum ejus,* which likened Francis to Christ in serving lepers, sending out disciples, and fasting. Although he borrowed liberally from the Spirituals in order to make his point about Francis's conformity, he vigorously denounced their position on poverty.

48. *De conformitate,* 1.10: "ea homo sic transformatus sic Christo similis reperiatur, et Christus typicus nuncupetur."

49. Erickson discusses "deiformity" as a term that Bonaventure used in his own analysis of the possibilities of human conformity to God in *Sentences* I Dist. XLVIII, art.1, quaestio 1, Concl., in *Opera omnia,* ed. Pelletier, 2:224.

50. *De conformitate,* 2.396.

51. *De conformitate,* 1.9: "De transformatione animae et corporis nullibi expresse habetur, sed solum habetur testimonio summorum pontificum in bullis suis ordini concessis, quod facta est in beate Francisco."

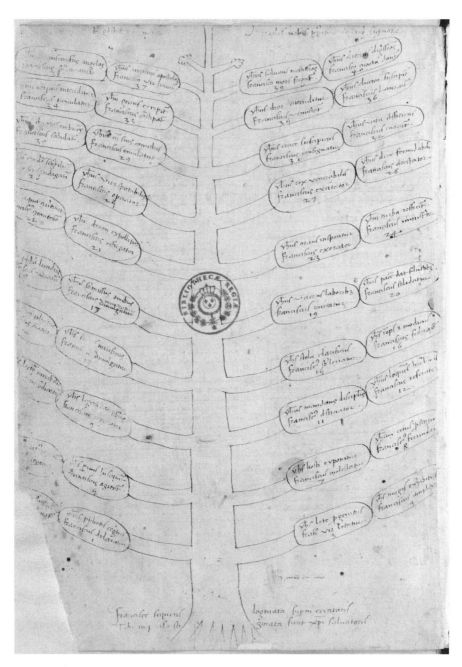

FIGURE 4.3. Bartholomew of Pisa, *Liber de conformitate vitae beati Francisci ad vitam domini Jesu.* Paris, Bibliothèque Nationale de France, MS Lat. 3328, fol. 151v.

The end result of Bartholomew's exhaustive narrative exercise of compiling biographical parallels can be found on the final folio of the Latin manuscript in the Bibliothéque Nationale de Paris. At the back of the text detailing Francis's forty conformities to Christ was a sketch of a tree with twenty fruits on branches to the left mirrored by twenty fruits on branches to the right. As in the Pacino panel, the twenty fruits on the left include scenes from the life of Christ. Here, however, those scenes are not illustrated visually, but textually with keywords referring to salient moments in Christ's life. To the right, another set of twenty fruits also contains keywords that match similar events in the life of Francis. Form conveys meaning in the *Book of Conformities*. The text was not a preacher's manual, and the arboreal diagram contained therein was not a mnemonic device designed for use in Franciscan homiletics. It was partly meditative, to be sure, the keywords releasing images on which to direct the mind's eye in contemplation. But Bartholomew's *Book* was also a dense spiritual proof text. For him, the tree's branches were proof of Francis's conformity to Christ. It confirmed that loving imitation in fact rendered his transformation, made him into holy matter like Christ. The tree for him demonstrated how Francis simultaneously could be both himself and Christ, in the same manner that Christ could be both human and divine, both body and bread. Belief in a world re-created to incarnate God and to transcend matter was a world that had opened up this possibility.

The possibility of identifying completely, bodily, with Christ was a prevailing concern shared among both branches of the quarreling late medieval Franciscans. For both branches, the tree was iconic of the promise of personal transformation and identity. Clare and Bonaventure, and their followers of both Franciscan persuasions, employed it to foster a sense of identity with Christ in imitation of his life, either imaginatively or in practice. Although they chose two different routes—for Clare, pursuit of poverty; for Bonaventure, an inflamed imagination—both of these Franciscan founders of arboreal meditation chose to emphasize the necessity of self-transformation. They each understood Francis as having founded a form of devotion that emphatically linked creator to creation and as having set a pattern for conforming creature to creator. The tree was for each of them an image through which to consider the re-creation of the person as a new entity, one that embodied God.

The tree thus operated as an image of Francis's conformity to Christ and of the promise that, in literally imitating Francis by following his Rule, all Franciscans could achieve a similar re-creation in Christ. For this reason— that Francis presented the right form of life, a form that would lead to transformation into Christ—James della Massa is said to have reported to

Angelo Clareno his vision of a tree that appeared to him while rapt for three consecutive days in impassioned contemplation:

> [I] saw a beautiful and very large tree: its root was of gold; its fruit was men, and they were all lesser brothers. Its main branches were divided according to the number of the provinces of the Order, and each branch had as many brothers as there were in the province designated for that branch.[52]

Christ himself then entered the scene, charging Francis to ascend the tree and offering a cup of the spirit of life to each of the brothers. Sure enough, some of the friars refused the cup or spat out the spirit once having sipped it. Those who declined to drink "became dark and deformed and terrifying." Then Bonaventure, receiving the chalice, consumed only half of its contents, pouring out the other half. In doing so, he "was given sharp iron fingernails like sharp-edged razors for cutting hair," which he used to claw at the trunk of the tree. According to Angelo's account of the vision, Bonaventure, the great diplomat, destroyed the spiritual offspring of Francis's plantation by attacking the trunk, which was occupied by the body of John of Parma, the fervent champion of the Spirituals and advocate of the strict observance of the Rule and of absolute poverty. Finally a storm came, uprooting Bonaventure and his followers who refused the cup. In their place grew a great golden tree, a new creation, consisting of those friars who received the cup of the spirit. The tree ushered in the body of Christ through the Franciscans' imitation of him in following Francis's life and Rule. In James's vision, the imitation of Francis's life, drinking the spirit that he offered, enabled the friars to attain the luminosity of resurrected bodies—"clothed in the brilliance of the sun"—in the sixth *status* and third age of the church.[53]

James's vision demonstrates the potency of arboreal imagery in Franciscan circles. James wished to portray a "right" interpretation of the life and legacy of Francis. And he chose to communicate—he *saw*—that life in the form of a tree. His tree was rooted in a sense that transformation occurred through practices of conformity to the life of Francis, who provided a model

---

52. *Actus beati Francisci et sociorum eius,* ed. Paul Sabatier (Paris: Fischbacher, 1902), 64.9–10; trans. in Armstrong, Hellmann, and Short, *Francis of Assisi: Early Documents,* 3:557.

53. The dating of James's account of his vision to Angelo Clareno is murky, making it difficult to speculate on his polemical use of this tree. At best, we can guess the late 1250s, so that the vision may not be a direct citation of Bonaventure's *Lignum vitae.* But Angelo's accounting of it, by which it comes to us, was composed much later, about 1323–26. Regardless of the dating of James's vision, however, it was clearly apocalyptic, drawing on the tree of life in Revelations 22 as an image of a reformed and re-created order. Burr, 33.

for imitating the life of Christ, for *being* holy matter. In the words of the Spiritual poet Jacopone da Todi (d. 1306),

> That towering palm tree you climbed Francis—
> it was with the sacrifice of Christ crucified that it bore fruit.
> you were so transfixed to him in love you never faltered,
> and the marks on your body attested to that union.
> This is the mission of love: to make two one;
> Through his prayers it transforms Francis into Christ.[54]

The object of Franciscan arboreal devotion was to "make two one," to transform the self into the beloved. Making two become one—a new creation—was what it meant to his followers for Francis to be the *alter Christus,* the Word made flesh returned to earth, setting forth a new pattern of salvation. Arboreal imagery aided the friars' imaginations in grasping how two could become one, so that the tree was an image of transformation into holy matter, for conforming the self to the substance of God.

Clare and Bonaventure had supplied a powerful image of a tree that linked Christ's incarnation to his crucifixion, and both cosmic events to a world that offered the possibility for access to divinity, for transformation into Christ. Meditation on the life of Christ via the branches of their trees led the individual to recognize this transformative potential—that material reality was destined for divinity and held the impression of God within. Through a dedicated process of training the imagination to identify with the presence of the divine in the material world, the Franciscans sought to remake themselves, to conform to the humility of their founder and possibly to his own transformation into Christ. Ubertino of Casale portrayed his own efforts at such transformation in an author portrait on the opening folio of the Assisi copy of the *Arbor vitae crucifixae Jesu Christi,* now housed in the Biblioteca del Sacro Conventa (fig. 4.4). The page depicts Ubertino ardently groping the trunk of a tree that bears the crucified body of Christ. The portrait is a guidepost, suggesting that the reader who embarked on the meditations contained in this sizable tome should posture himself in a similar fashion. On his knees, open to the divine embrace, the meditant should engage a material world that might manifest God and offer transcendence. The image speaks of the late medieval meditant's wish to achieve divine access and, through access, personal transformation. While Ubertino's goal was assimilation through poor emulation and meditation on the life and

---

54. Jacopone da Todi, *Le Laude,* Laud 61; *The Lauds:* "L'Amor è 'n quest'offizio, unir dui 'nn una forma"; Hughes and Hughes, 188–89.

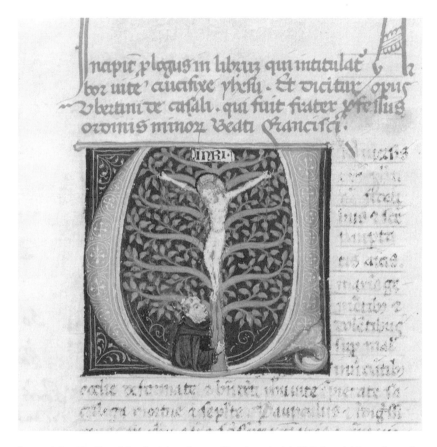

FIGURE 4.4. Ubertino of Casale, *Arbor vitae crucifixae Jesu*. Assisi, Biblioteca del Sacro Conventa, MS 328 c. 1r. Courtesy of Società internazionale di Studi francescani.

death of Christ and Francis, the ideas put forth in his treatise may have opened up avenues of interpretation that would lead to the belief in assimilation through contact.[55] For example, the visual rendition of Ubertino's imitation and his verbal testimony of assimilation are juxtaposed startlingly with a narrative description of meditation provided by Christina Ebner (d. 1355). In the Sisterbook of Engelthal, Christina reported that a young nun of the community, Alheit of Trochau, while on a contemplative stroll in

---

55. As Caroline Bynum has suggested about the thirteenth-century reverence of holy matter, "Imitation and even assimilation to Christ can come through the contact of ordinary human bodies with a carved figure hanging on a wooden cross"; one might add, with real trees, too. Caroline Bynum, *Christian Materiality: An Essay on Religion in Late Medieval Europe* (New York: Zone Books, 2011), 116.

the cloister garden one day, approached every one of its trees, threw her arms around their trunks, and proclaimed: "It seems to me that each tree is our Lord Jesus Christ!"[56] Alheit's arboreal embraces were not of metaphors—she did not hug images, visions, or illuminations of the natural world. Though her sisters may have observed her cuddling trees, Alheit imagined that she was truly wrapping her arms around Christ.[57] For both Ubertino and Alheit, the material world manifested the body of Christ, delivered its very presence, but it did so in very different ways. While Alheit's arboreal embrace was tactile, Ubertino's was meditative, a picture of the world brought within the imagination. Ubertino proposed to achieve his transformation, like Clare, by observing the material conditions of Christ in the practice of poverty and by devoting himself to contemplation of the poor lives of Francis and Christ. Alheit, on the other hand, while perhaps well trained in meditation, worked outside of the imagination. She sought God in the material of the world. She touched, grabbed hold of, and embraced holy matter.

These episodes of fourteenth-century arboreal devotion raise important questions about the relationship of metaphor and materiality in late medieval Christianity. While the image of Ubertino as a supplicant at the foot of the tree of the cross played into an established devotional tradition of portraying the life of Christ according to the branches of a tree, the illuminated tree found its referent in the very book for which it provided decoration and instruction. The painted initial referred to his text, the *Arbor vitae,* as well as the texts that it cited, Bonaventure's *Lignum vitae* and the books of Genesis and Revelation. For Ubertino, Clare, and Bonaventure, meditation on the image of a tree mediated Christ's presence, but only through a complicated process of imaginative journeying through "branches" delineating Christ's biography. Alheit's supplication, by contrast, used the tree not as an *image* for guiding contemplation of a present Christ and goading transformation into holy matter. For Alheit, the tree itself was holy matter, it bore Christ. Alheit had no need for natural images that called attention to their materiality, to

---

56. Karl Schröder, ed., *Der Nonne von Engelthal Büchlein von der Genaden Uberlast* (Tübingen: Literarischer Verein, 1871), 14. On the culture and activities of Engelthal more generally, see Leonard P. Hindsley, *The Mystics of Engelthal: Writings from a Medieval Monastery* (New York: St. Martin's Press, 1998).

57. Sisterbooks (*Schwesternbücher/Nonnenleben*) form a subgenre of *Gnadenviten,* defined by Bernard McGinn as "a form of narrative theology that present models of sanctity through accounts centered on mystical visions and unusual graces"; Bernard McGinn, *The Harvest of Mysticism in Medieval Germany* (New York: Crossroad, 2005), 350. On Sisterbooks, see Gertrud Lewis, *By Women, for Women, about Women: The Sisterbooks of Fourteenth-Century Germany* (Toronto: Pontifical Institute of Medieval Studies, 1996); Anne Winston-Allen, *Convent Chronicles: Women Writing about Women and Reform in the Late Middle Ages* (University Park: Pennsylvania State University Press, 2004).

their ability to point to and deliver Christ's presence. The natural objects to which she turned were considered as literally divine presence, holy matter. Throwing her arms around the very same material that delivered Christ's incarnation and crucifixion, Alheit's flesh embraced wood, and thereupon yielded Christ's body. She did not manipulate mental or imagistic trees, but real ones, and through them, perceived Christ's real presence.

Alheit's arboreal embraces suggest a curious relationship in the status of metaphor and its material referents in the late medieval Christian imagination. An image that was once asserted at the level of metaphor had come, in her use, to take the status of reality.[58] A God who had been pictured as re-creating the world, making matter holy, was now ascertained in matter. Painted trees and liturgical gardens, I will show in chapter 5, gave way to a sensuous verdant reality, one that manifested the presence of God while proclaiming its own essential role in the process of eternal material salvation. It was not one tree that seemed to Alheit to be Christ, but each tree, every tree. The whole world might be expected to manifest divine presence, to *be* holy matter.

---

58. For another example of the transformation from metaphor to reality during this period, see Dyan Elliott, *Fallen Bodies: Pollution, Demonology, and Sexuality in the Middle Ages* (Philadelphia: University of Pennsylvania Press, 1998).

CHAPTER 5

An Estranged Wilderness

"My sweet father," begins a letter composed by Marguerite d'Oingt (d. 1310), fourth prioress of the Carthusian monastery of Poleteins, "you should know that I heard this preached by a superior of the Franciscans, in the middle of a sermon."[1] Questioned about a writing, now lost, in which she had described the passion of Christ in a manner that did not correspond to Scripture, Marguerite deferred first to the authority of a learned male Franciscan from whom she had learned to meditate on Christ's passion and crucifixion with apparently striking imagery. We cannot know the specific terms through which she discussed the passion in this text. But we can make inferences based on Marguerite's extant writings. The *Pagina meditationum,* for example, inspired by the Septuagesima liturgy of 1286, records the meditations triggered within Marguerite's heart by thoughts of Christ's crucifixion. The meditation portrayed Jesus Christ as a mother who gave birth to a new world through his suffering. In it, she praised Christ for having created the sun, the moon, stars, rain, hours, days,

---

1. Marguerite of Oingt, *Les oeuvres de Marguerite d'Oingt,* ed. and trans. Antonin Durafour, Pierre Gardette, and Paulette Durdilly (Paris: Belles Lettres, 1965), 140–42; trans. Renate Blumenfeld-Kosinski, in *The Writings of Margaret of Oingt, Medieval Prioress and Mystic* (Woodbridge: Boydell & Brewer, 1997), 64.

even heaven and earth. The description of the creation of the world in a meditation on the life of Christ would appear incongruous until Marguerite explained her attribution of creator to Christ:

> Oh, Sweet Lord Jesus Christ, who ever saw any mother suffer such a birth! But when the hour of the birth came you were placed on the hard bed of the cross where you could not move or turn around or stretch your limbs as someone who suffers such great pain should be able to do; and seeing this, they stretched you out and fixed you with nails and you were so stretched that there was no bone left that could still have been disjointed, and your nerves and all your veins were broken. And surely it was no wonder that your veins were broken when you gave birth to the whole world in one day.[2]

Marguerite's *Pagina* was a meditation on the passion of Christ designed to glorify his death as the moment of the world's re-creation. She imagined his blood as sprinkling the earth and renewing it, altering it into a new creation that offered material transcendence and salvation. Throughout her instructional writings Marguerite addressed Christ as her "father," the "blessed Creator," "good creator," "sweet creator," who "remade [the world] better and more beautiful," and she revered Mary as the "mother of the Creator of all creatures."[3]

Her passion meditation, with its detailed narrative evocation of the passion of Christ, might be characterized as Franciscan. Although the scholarly attribution of "Franciscan" to affective passion meditation is admittedly overwrought and complicated by the presence of women's voices, nevertheless it applied here in an important way.[4] Marguerite herself regularly appealed to Franciscan authorities for her style of meditation. She deliberately affiliated her meditation with Francis and with "Franciscan" passion narrative. In addition to the anonymous Franciscan scholar through whom she justified her meditational images, Francis of Assisi appeared as the only named nonbiblical person in her *Pagina meditationum*. There, she used his example to chastise nuns and other religious who grew lazy, talkative,

---

2. Marguerite, *Pagina meditationum,* in Durafour, Gardette, and Durdilly, *Les oeuvres de Marguerite d'Oingt,* 78; Blumenfeld-Kosinski, 31.

3. Marguerite, *Pagina meditationum,* p. 74: "O beate Creator." In the *Life of Beatrice of Ornacieux* she praises the saint's invocation of Mary as "mare del creatour de tota cretura" (in Durafour, Gardette, and Durdilly, *Les oeuvres,* 136).

4. Sarah McNamer, *Affective Devotion and the Origins of Medieval Compassion* (Philadelphia: University of Pennsylvania Press, 2010), 88–95.

or malicious.[5] Marguerite thus consciously grounded her writing in an established Franciscan tradition of vivid narrative passion meditation.

Marguerite's second treatise, entitled the *Speculum,* sought to instruct the women in her community on how to engage in meditative reading of a text. The *Speculum,* written in Marguerite's native Franco-Provençal, received official approval in 1294, when Hugh, the prior of the Charterhouse of Valbonne, brought it to the Carthusian chapter general.[6] Hugh's interest in the treatise reflects Marguerite's growing reputation as a spiritual instructor.[7] He clearly saw pedagogical value in the treatise's vision sequence in which Marguerite described a woman's study of a great book that revealed God through creation.

Marguerite used the third person to relay the experiences of the female subject of the *Speculum:* "Because I desire your salvation as my own, I will tell you, as briefly as possible, of a great favor done not long ago to a person of my acquaintance."[8] The favor refers to the woman's reception, while meditating on the text, of a splendid vision of Christ's body. Marguerite's use of the third person in this instructional treatise acted to signal the reader to engage in meditation on the text itself.[9] Marguerite was therefore aware of the varied registers operating between these two texts. One was an actual Latin meditation, guiding the reader through Marguerite's process of imagining the events of Christ's passion; the other was a third-person vernacular description of a meditation, an account of the ideal experience of meditative reading, how one might approach a treatise like the *Pagina meditationum.*

Marguerite's *Speculum* introduces an unnamed woman who had so fittingly contemplated the life of Christ that it was inscribed onto her heart. In what medium she came to know so passionately the life of Christ—whether from studying the Gospels, from hearing reports from advisers, or from reading his life as outlined in the *Pagina meditationum*—is unclear. What Marguerite does make clear is that the woman's study of Christ's life made it seem to her that "he was present and that he held a closed book in his hand in order to teach from it."[10] Describing the exterior of this closed book, its

---

5. Marguerite, *Pagina meditationum,* p. 83.

6. Bernard Gaillard, "Marguerite d'Oingt," in *Dictionnaire de spiritualité: Ascétique et mystique, doctrine et histoire,* ed. Marcel Viller et al. (Paris: Beauchesne, 1980), 10:341.

7. Marguerite's letters indicate that she received questions about religious life from men and women in the region, also giving support to her growing reputation as an instructor.

8. Marguerite, *Speculum,* in Durafour, Gardette, and Durdilly, *Les oeuvres,* 90; Blumenfeld-Kosinski, 41.

9. Stephanie Paulsell, "*Scriptio divina:* Writing and the Experience of God in the Works of Marguerite d'Oingt" (PhD diss., University of Chicago, 1993), 147.

10. Marguerite, *Speculum,* p. 90; Blumenfeld-Kosinski, 42.

clasps and colors, the woman gazes at the life, humiliation, and crucifixion of Christ. Inside the book, Marguerite proceeded to describe a mirror, though she admitted that the reflection it offered was too beautiful to articulate. The opened book was literally wordless—the woman found within it no words and thus was compelled to rely on her senses to decipher what she saw within the pages' frame. On those wordless pages she observed a "delightful place" from which came all good things.[11] That "place" was the body of Christ, rendered as a stunning image of the material divine:

> He was clothed in this glorious garment which He assumed in the noble body of Our Lady. On his noble hands and feet appeared the glorious wounds that he suffered for love of us. From these glorious wounds poured forth such a great light that one was stunned by it: it was as if all the beauty of the divinity was passed on through it. This glorious body was so noble and so transparent that one could clearly see the soul inside of it. This body was so noble that one could see oneself reflected in it, more clearly than in a mirror.[12]

For Marguerite, Christ's body was a window through which one could see oneself and the whole world as it was truly created to be. Christ's body was even more reflective than a mirror. His body enabled the speculation of the re-created world. That world *was* his body.

The meditative process that Marguerite outlined in the *Speculum* frames the expressive devotion of the later medieval Carthusians. Marguerite's meditative goal was to experience the narrative of the life of Christ so intensely that her whole sensual apparatus was changed, so that she might come to read and see the world differently as a result of the act of meditation. In this chapter, I explore this desire for a changed perception of the material world. I discuss how fourteenth-century Carthusian treatises of spiritual instruction demonstrate an uneasy relationship to the real, material world and an uncertainty as to how the professed religious might properly regard it with trained meditative eyes. Although made apparent in the Carthusian treatises dedicated to meditative instruction, this uncertainty first began to glimmer in the thirteenth-century architecture of Carthusian charterhouses, where cell gardens obligated each monk to gaze upon the material world in solitary

---

11. Marguerite, *Speculum,* p. 94: "Dedenz cet livro apparisseit uns lues delicious, qui eret si tres granz que toz li monz no est que un po de chosa a regar de cen." The place described in the books seems to be the same one experienced in prayer: "Et tantot sos cuors fut si elevas que oy li fut semblanz que illi fut en un lua qui eret plus granz que toz li monz et plus reluysanz que li solouz de totes pars" (p. 98).

12. Marguerite, *Speculum,* p. 98; Blumenfeld-Kosinski, 45.

meditation. The Carthusians advised meditation, as articulated so strikingly by Marguerite, in order to perceive God's material presence in the world. They venerated the wilderness as a place of divine encounter, of divine sight, and, moreover, as a place of re-creation—in which the hands of God touched creation once again, bringing it into conformity with his image, remaking it into an object of salvation.

This chapter turns to the status of the wilderness in later medieval Carthusian devotion in order to question the relationship of natural metaphors to their literal referents in the material world. Here I examine the wilderness as a lure for the Carthusian imagination in legend, literature, and reality. Carthusians commemorated the wilderness as a valuable religious site in legends, art, and architecture. The wilderness was celebrated as a valued object of speculation—a natural terrain to be read for vestiges of God's presence in the material of creation. But as Carthusian foundations crept out of semiwilderness spaces and into the closer proximity of cities, their spiritual hermeneutics for reading God's presence in the world had to accommodate this change. How did the Carthusians continue to see Christ's presence in the wilderness when the wilderness no longer surrounded them? After an examination of the imaginative theology of speculation offered by the Dominican friar Henry Suso, among the most widely read mystical writers of the fourteenth century, I turn to Carthusian instructional treatises on speculation—specifically the *Vita Jesu Christi* of Ludolph of Saxony and the anonymously authored poem *The Desert of Religion*. Both of these texts query the status of the wilderness for Carthusian contemplatives, one insisting on the need for a real, material wilderness, and the other offering a surrogate wilderness where there was no real one present. Finally, I turn to changes in later medieval Carthusian architecture, changes that took place when the majority of the order's foundations had fled the wilderness for the more patron-friendly accessibility of cities. Outside of the phenomenological experience of the wilderness, I suggest, Carthusians promulgated a gardening mandate that resonates in the practices of the order to this day.

Carthusian architecture promoted the cell as a frame through which to speculate on the wilderness, to meditate on Christ's life via the material of the natural world. That the Carthusians were not always successful, that their "wildernesses" had to be conjured through materials other than the dense foliage of an actual wilderness, suggests their remarkable ability to blend materials through the meditating imagination. While Marguerite had appealed to Franciscan meditative innovations in the recent past in order to ground authority for her vivid written meditations, her instructions to speculate on the world as the "place" of God's body pointed in a fertile new direction. Her depiction of Christ as a codex inscribed with images of natural beauty stages the meditational work carried out in the solitary cell, work that played on ambiguity and porous boundaries between the real, the legendary, and the imagined wildernesses available to the Carthusian meditant.

The Carthusian Wilderness: A Myth of Origins

"I am living in the wilderness of Calabria," wrote Bruno of Cologne to his friend Raoul le Verd, urging the provost of Reims to adopt a life of contemplation in the Alpine forest of the Grande Chartreuse.[13] According to his followers, the Carthusian founder, Bruno of Cologne, resolved in 1084 to flee society in order to establish a solitary and devout monastic order.[14] Inflamed with "divine love" and committed to "capturing the eternal," Bruno gathered around himself six companions—four monks and two laymen—to help carry out his quest for monastic perfection in the mountainous wilderness.[15] The men solicited the aid of Bishop Hugh of Grenoble, who, coincidentally, had just received a divine vision in which seven stars in the wilderness fell to his feet. Discerning the vision to refer to his new petitioners, Hugh granted the hopeful reformers a plot of uncultivated land in the forested Dauphiné, where they built the Grande Chartreuse, the first Carthusian charterhouse.[16]

Bruno's hermetic solace in the Dauphiné was briefly interrupted in 1090 when his former pupil, Odo of Châtillon, who had since taken the title of Pope Urban II, summoned him to Rome as an adviser. After fulfilling his apostolic duties, Bruno founded yet another hermitage in the wilderness of Calabria, known as La Torre. Though his words are sparse in keeping with the adoption of hermetic silence, from there Bruno wrote of his reverence

---

13. *Lettres de premiers chartreux* (Paris: Éditions du Cerf, 1962–80), 1:68.

14. On the memory and image of Bruno as preserved and promulgated by his followers, see Alain Girard, "Les premières images de Saint Bruno," in *Saint Bruno et sa postérité spirituelle: Actes du colloque international des 8 et 9 octobre 2001 à l'Institut catholique de Paris,* ed. Alain Girard, Daniel Le Blévec, and Nathalie Nabert (Salzburg: Institut für Anglistik und Amerikanistik, 2003), 47–62; and James Hogg, "Lives of Saint Bruno," in Girard, Le Blévec, and Nabert, *Saint Bruno et sa postérité spirituelle,* 17–41.

15. See *Lettres des premiers chartreux,* 1:96. On the identity of Bruno's companions, see Raymond Boyer, "The Companions of Saint Bruno in Middle English Verses on the Foundation of the Carthusian Order," *Speculum* 53.4 (1978): 784–85.

16. On the foundation story of the Carthusian order, see Gabriel Le Bras, "Les chartreux," in *Les ordres religieux: La vie et l'art,* ed. Gabriel Le Bras (Paris: Flammarion, 1979), 1:562–653. For documents concerning the foundation, see Bernard Bligny, *Recueil des plus anciens actes de la Grande-Chartreuse, 1086–1196* (Grenoble: Imprimerie Allier, 1958); and André Wilmart, "La chronique des premiers chartreux," *Revue Mabillon* 16 (1926): 77–142.

of the wilderness and encouraged it as the most appropriate environment in which to pursue the Christian contemplative life. Addressing his friend Raoul le Verd, provost at his former school at Reims, Bruno described his wooded environs and shared his impressions of their spiritual effect. He urged his friend to adopt his lifestyle, which was "far removed from habitation." Conjuring for his correspondent an image of the lush wilderness surroundings of La Torre, Bruno praised its "agreeable plain," on which he and his monastic companions regularly luxuriated in "flourishing meadows and flowery fields" and "well-watered gardens and the useful fertility of various trees."[17] Bruno recommended the natural environment of his wilderness setting because, to him, it offered a degree of spiritual discernment not available elsewhere. He counseled his friend to retreat into the wilderness not for the scenery, but for the sight it offered. For Bruno, the solitude of the wilderness environment enabled a certain kind of spiritual seeing peculiar to wooded isolation. In the solitude and silence of the Calabrian "desert," men "could acquire that eye that with its clear look wounds the divine spouse with love, and that, because of its purity, is granted the sight of God."[18] The "desert" in eleventh-century western Europe was more properly a wilderness or a forest with associations of danger, temptation, and isolation; but it also denoted a place where, if these hindrances could be overcome, one might find tranquility and spiritual perfection in the presence of God. According to Bruno, those who followed him into wilderness solitude would see God among their surroundings.

Just before Bruno's death in 1101, the aging Landuin, superior of the Chartreuse, traveled to Calabria to petition Bruno to commit a rule for his brothers. In response, Bruno issued only a brief letter applauding their zeal and virtue. He singled out the lay brothers on whose hearts, he explained, God wrote because they could not read in books. The letter did not oblige the hermits to fulfill any binding customs and asked only that they take care of Landuin as he advanced in age. The first generation of Bruno's followers, then, had no rule and no name. They called themselves simply "Christ's poor men."[19] Their founder's only reverberating wish was that they cultivate virtue through the discernment of God in the wilderness: "For [in the wilderness]

---

17. *Lettres des premiers chartreux,* 1:68.

18. *Lettres des premiers chartreux,* 1:70.

19. In the preliminary greeting in a letter written to the monks of Cluny we find the following: "Nos indigni et humiles pauperes Christi qui in eremo Carthusiae propter amorem nominis Jesu consistimus, et caeteri praepositi nostri priores cum fratribus suis, nota facimus posteris ista quae sequuntur." PL 189:478C, supplement to the correspondence of Peter the Venerable.

it is given to the strong ones to retreat into themselves to cultivate insistently the shoots of virtues and to feed in joy on the fruits of paradise."[20]

The spiritual benefits of the wilderness to Bruno of Cologne appeared uniformly in legends and images celebrating his decision to flee society. His attempts to create an environment in which he and his companions could work to discern God in wilderness isolation proved to be the foundational act through which members of the Carthusian order would imagine their origins and fashion their self-image. The invariable presence of the wilderness in iconographic and narrative renditions of the foundation legend indicates the importance Bruno's spiritual progeny attributed to it. The wilderness was translated through the collective imagination of the Carthusians into a mandate and a defining element of the order's spiritual mission. For them, the wilderness suggested a place, a site, in which the contemplative Carthusian could see God.

Traces of such self-fashioning can be detected in various examples, both pictorial and narrative, of the Carthusian "commemoration of foundation."[21] In particular, the Bruno cycle, the pictorial legend of the foundation of the Grande Chartreuse, demonstrates the manner in which Carthusians clung to the image of their wilderness foundations, even when their houses were no longer situated in wilderness settings. In 1510, when Jean Amorbach printed the definitive collection of evolving Carthusian statutes, the *Tertia compilatio statutorum ordinis carthusiensis,* he included a woodcut depicting the Bruno cycle fashioned by the artist Urs Graf (fig. 5.1).[22] Urs Graf's image finalizes the iconography of the narrative cycle that had been evolving in Carthusian commemorations for well over a century. For example, ca. 1411 the Limbourgs began illuminating Jean de Berry's *Très riches heures,* which included a Bruno cycle in its Office of the Dead.[23] Another cycle was executed on the walls of the little cloister of the charterhouse of Saint Margaret at Basel in 1441, where, open to visitors, its imagery served the purpose of Carthusian self-promotion.[24] Between 1486 and 1489, the cycle was reproduced

20. *Lettres de premiers chartreux,* 1:68.

21. On the commemoration of foundation in the Carthusian order, see Julian Luxford, "Texts and Images of Carthusian Foundation," in *Self-Representation of Medieval Religious Communities: The British Isles in Context,* ed. Anne Müller and Karen Stöber (London: LIT, 2009), 275–305.

22. James Hogg, *Evolution of the Carthusian Statutes from the Consuetudines Guigonis to the Tertia Compilatio* (Salzburg: Institut für Anglistik und Amerikanistik, 1989). Although the finalized iconography comes from the compilation's woodcut, there are suggestions that mural paintings of the cycle were included in the decorative scheme of the little cloister at the Paris charterhouse in the mid-fourteenth century. See Luxford, "Texts and Images," 280.

23. Luxford, "Texts and Images," 281. See also Rob Drükers and P. Roelors, eds., *The Limbourg Brothers: Nijmegen Masters at the French Court 1400–1416* (Nijmegen: Ludion, 2005), 219.

24. Luxford, "Texts and Images," 282.

Figure 5.1. *Arbor pictus fundatorum Ordinis Carthusiensis*. Codex Vindobonensis Palatinus 4737, fol. 1b a. ÖNB/Wien + Image ID. Reproduction courtesy of the Hill Monastic Manuscript Library.

on canvasses in the little cloister of the charterhouse of Saint Barbara at Cologne where it too served a public function. The cycle included shields of arms and portraits of contemporary rulers, many of which were connected through benefaction with the monks of Saint Barbara's and other Carthusian foundations.[25]

Two further examples of the Bruno cycle make abundantly clear the desired connection between later medieval Carthusians and their wilderness-bound founder. A telling miniature of the cycle is contained in an unprovenanced late fifteenth-century manuscript from the Netherlands. Ten full-page miniatures portray scenes from the narrative of Bruno's conversion to solitude and foundation of the Grande Chartreuse. The artist depicts in two facing-page miniatures twelve rather than the usual seven charter monks at prayer kneeling in direct reverence of the wilderness (fig. 5.2). But what is more striking than the odd number of Bruno's companions is the subtle indication in the paired images of a tense self-awareness—the sense that only through art and prayer could they meditate in the presence of the wilderness, as their founder had recommended. In the recto image, twelve monks address a forest from which they are physically removed by the chasm of the page, in addition to the rifts of time and practice of foundation. Their reverence of this estranged wilderness is all the more curious in its context of commemoration. It suggests a certain tension between present and past, metaphorical and literal, and how the community of Carthusians might access all these wilderness forms simultaneously in their present practices.

A second example of the Bruno cycle that clearly elides past and present, real and imagined, to make a patent connection between the founder and his Carthusian progeny of the fifteenth century can be seen in the elaborately decorated English miscellany MS Additional 37049. Here the cycle is accompanied by a vernacular poem, "At þe begynyng of þe chartirhows god dyd schewe" (fol. 22r-v), explaining the details of the foundation story and emphasizing the unique devotional aspects that Carthusian life had to offer. Foremost among the foundational Carthusian principles, according to this fifty-eight-line poem, was the "lyf solytary in wildernes," because "wildernes is þe paradyse of deliciousnes to neuen."[26] According to the Carthusians, the wilderness brought *neuen,* "spiritual renewal." The Bruno cycle could be found with only slight variations in the books, churches, refectories, and cloisters of charterhouses at Paris, Basel, Florence, and Cologne and in the

---

25. Ibid.

26. James Hogg, ed., *An Illustrated Yorkshire Carthusian Religious Miscellany: British Library London Additional MS 37049* (Salzburg: Institut für Anglistik und Amerikanistik, 1997).

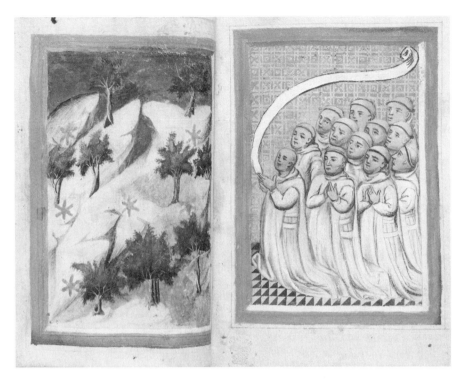

FIGURE 5.2. "Dit is dbeghin van der Certroysen ocrdenen." London, British Library, Additional MS 25042, fols. 10v.–11r. Courtesy of the British Library.

north of England.[27] In each instance, the cycle indicates that, for the purposes of self-representation, to the lay public and privately among members of the order, the wilderness was essential to Carthusian self-fashioning. A 1310 seal from the charterhouse of Žiče in present-day Slovenia once again reveals the enduring character of this wilderness self-fashioning, not only in the context of *Ordenspropaganda,* but on a much more intimate, personal level—the face (a seal) of a single charterhouse presented to the world (fig. 5.3).[28] On first

---

27. Margrit Früh, "Bilderzyklen mit dem Leben des Heiligen Bruno" in *La naissance des Chartreuses,* ed. Bernard Bligny and Gérald Chaix (Grenoble: Éditions des Cahiers de l'Alpe de la Société des Ecrivains Dauphinois, 1986), 161–78; Werner Beutler, "Die beiden Brunozyklen der Kölner Kartause St. Barbara," in *Die Kartäuser und ihre Welt: Kontakte und gegenseitige Einflüsse,* Analecta Cartusiana 62 (Salzburg: Institut für Anglistik und Amerikanistik, 1993): 3:118–212; Rudolf Riggenbach, "Die Wandbilder des Kartause," in *Kunstdenkmäler des Kantons Basel-Stadt,* ed. Casimir Hermann Baer (Basel: E. Birkhäuser & Cie., 1941), 3:577–94.

28. Ulrike Mader, "Heiligenverehrung als Ordenspropaganda," in *Die Kölner Kartause um 1500: Aufsatzband,* ed. Werner Schäfke and Rita Wagner (Cologne: Kölnisches Stadtmuseum, 1991), 275–90. On the cultural significance of seals, see Brigitte Bedos-Rezak, "Medieval Identity: A Sign and A Concept," *American Historical Review* 105 (2000): 1489–1533.

FIGURE 5.3.   Žiče charterhouse, seal, ca. 1310. Courtesy of the Archives of the Republic of Slovenia.

glance, the seal appears to depict a standard, unadorned tree of Jesse. When examined in light of other "tree of St. Bruno" images, such as those contained in the *Tertia compilatio,* however, the seal reveals itself as a reclining Bruno protecting and asserting the charterhouse's adoration of the Carthusian wilderness. These Carthusian wilderness images—the Bruno cycle and the tree of St. Bruno—suggest an enduring desire among the later medieval Carthusians to revere and promote their spiritual identity through the same natural imagery as that used by the monastic reformers whom they claimed as their founders. Estranged from the wilderness of their founders' activity, they furnished an able surrogate.

The Growth of an Order

Bruno's concern for remote solitude found official protection in the *Consuetudines* of his distant successor Guigo I, fifth prior of the Grande Chartreuse. In 1127, Guigo transformed Bruno's ideal of desert solitude into an official Rule of Carthusian life when he legislated that Carthusian monks, when making their profession, must swear an oath "in the company of the desert."[29] He further ordered that they should curtail the conventual celebrations of the Office by limiting church assemblies to matins and vespers, and by only celebrating Mass on Sundays and special feast days, because "nothing so much as solitude assists the sweetness of psalmody, pious reading, fervent prayer, the subtleties of meditation, ecstatic contemplation, and the baptism of tears" (Guigo I, *Consuetudines,* 757). Guigo believed that the Christian liturgy better promoted mystical ascent when performed in the solitary confines of the Carthusian cell. He concluded his constitutions with a paean on solitude, praising John the Baptist, the desert fathers, and Jesus, who "in the time of the apostles left for prayer in solitude, giving this especially as an example of how much solitude benefits prayer since although the apostles were his companions, he did not wish to pray among them" (Guigo I, *Consuetudines,* 757). Guigo thereby demonstrated that although Carthusians lived together in community for the purposes of stability, their individual private cells were the proper places of prayer. He cited the example of Jesus in order to explain that desert solitude was desirable not for promoting virtue, but for providing the appropriate prayer space. When Jesus prayed in the desert, he reasoned, certainly it was not because he needed to increase his virtue. Rather, Christ went into the desert in order to give humanity an example of how to pray, how to communicate with God. For Guigo, the solitude of the Carthusian wilderness enabled the monk to see God "face-to-face" (Guigo I, *Consuetudines,* 757: "facie ad faciem Deum videt"). He wrote the constitutions in order to protect the visibility of God promoted by the ideal of desert solitude.

Other Carthusians followed Guigo in praising the solitary cell as its own wilderness, in which to encounter the presence of God. When advising Carthusian novices on how best to fashion their prayers, Adam of Dryburgh, of Witham charterhouse in England, recommended that they envision the entirety of the cell as a fertile meadow, like the well-watered Calabrian meadow described by Bruno. In particular, Adam proposed that the cell was

---

29. Guigo I, *Consuetudines,* PL 153:635–757; col. 686 (hereafter cited parenthetically in text in abbreviated form).

a paradise garden, tended by the spiritual labor of its monk.[30] The labor of the Carthusian monk—"the zeal for sacred reading, the maturity of unfettered meditation, the devotion of pure prayer, and the vigor of useful activity"— transformed an ordinary cell into a heavenly garden, the garden of God's original creation.[31] Because "no one born of woman remains in the same state," each monk must transform himself and his surroundings into God's original image. The cell was the locus of such transformation—the place in which one might restore the self to God's original creation. Merely a meta-phor, the Carthusian cell as paradise garden sought to emplace the meditant in a prelapsarian context. The spiritual labor of the cell ideally served to reconstruct the self, returning the individual self to Adam's original state, humanity as God intended it before the interference of sin. In the Carthu-sian cell, creation was restored, re-created.

When Guigo issued the first set of customs of the Carthusian order, cementing Bruno's commitment to wilderness solitude, he also founded six additional desert charterhouses in which to put the regulations into prac-tice.[32] Respecting Bruno's foundational ideal of wilderness solitude, each of these houses was designed to protect the eremitic lifestyle while also provid-ing the stability of a community. The early Carthusian foundations included two houses: an "upper house" occupied by the professed monks and directed by the prior; and a "lower house" or *correrie,* in which the lay brothers lodged. Both houses had their own sparse churches, free from ornament and valuable metal vessels.[33] Within the upper house, monks lived in individual private cells radiating around a cloister.[34] Each cell included a small opening through which lay brothers could pass food, books, and other necessities, so that the cell itself was mostly self-sufficient. In these early foundations, located in remote settings free from communal ties, individual cells did not have their own gardens, though vegetable gardens were maintained by the lay brothers outside the cloister.[35] Carthusian foundations were thus chosen

---

30. The *De quadripertito exercitio cellae* is indexed under Guigo II in the Patrologia Latina; see PL 153:799–884; at col. 822: "Vere paradisus est, hortus utiquae deliciarum."

31. Adam of Dryburgh, PL 153:802: "studium sacrae lectionis, maturitas defecatae meditationis, devotio purae orationis, strenuitas utilis actionis."

32. The charterhouses of Portes in the diocese of Lyons, of Durbon in the diocese of Gap, of Sylve-Bénite in the diocese of Vienne, of Meyriat in Lyons, of Les Ecouges in Grenoble, and of Montrieux in Marseilles. All were founded between 1115 and 1117.

33. Glyn Coppack, *Christ's Poor Men: The Carthusians in England* (London: Tempus, 2002), 26.

34. Dom Augustin Devaux, *L'architecture dans l'ordre des chartreux* (Sélignac: La Grande Char-treuse, 1998); Marijan Zadnikar, "Die frühe Baukunst der Kartäuser," in *Die Kartäuser der Orden der schweigenden Mönche,* ed. Marijan Zadnikar and Adam Wienand, 51–137 (Cologne: Wienand, 1983), 51–137.

35. Coppack, *Christ's Poor Men,* 28.

with attention in the early to mid-twelfth century, valued for their isolation from land claims and peasant farmers.

By the later twelfth century, however, the typical setting of Carthusian houses underwent dramatic change—their remote wilderness location was often replaced by suburban settings in closer proximity to the town centers of Europe. Although these later Carthusian foundations continued to adhere to the founder's principle of eremitic solitude by remaining in isolated private cells, the circumstances of patronage nevertheless forced them out of the wilderness and into the proximity of other land claims and other interests. In 1257 King Louis IX founded a Carthusian house in Paris. Located on the edge of the city, the charterhouse at Paris was the first Carthusian foundation outside the European wilderness. In the course of the fourteenth century, the order would undergo a massive expansion to ninety-four new male and two new female houses, tripling in size. The presence of at least one charterhouse began to typify all the major European cities, testifying to something of a cachet for aristocratic endowments of Carthusian houses. For example, several dukes of Burgundy, attracted to Carthusian eremeticism, endowed premier houses, such as Champmol in Dijon, founded by Philip the Bold, and Pavia, founded by Gian Galeazzo Visconti (the husband of Isabelle of Valois).[36] The German and English aristocracy followed with additional endowments shortly thereafter. The earliest German charterhouse, Johannestal at Žiče was founded by the Styrian margrave Ottocar V. In 1314 Duke Frederick the Fair of Austria founded the charterhouse of Allerheiligental in Mauerbach on the occasion of his election to the throne of Germany. Other charterhouses founded in large commercial areas include Mainz in 1320, Coblenz and Trier in 1331, and Strasbourg in 1335.[37] Prince Nicola Acciaiuoli founded the Certosa of Galluzzo near Florence in 1342. Urban foundations were thus a fashionable habit that would unintentionally erode Carthusian oaths to the desert.

Particularly in England, the Carthusian order experienced a faddish spate of urban foundations. Although Henry II founded the first charterhouse at Witham in 1178, followed by those at Hinton (1227) and Beauvale (1343), the real flurry came after the 1368 establishment of the English Carthusian province, which officially created an independent English order free

---

36. Jessica Brantley, *Reading in the Wilderness: Private Devotion and Public Performance in Late Medieval England* (Chicago: University of Chicago Press, 2007), 43.

37. On the urban foundations, see Michael Aston, "The Development of the Carthusian Order in Europe and Britain: A Preliminary Survey," in *In Search of Cult: Archaeological Investigations in Honour of Philip Rahtz,* ed. M. Carver (London: University of York Archaeological Papers, 1993), 139–51.

of visitation from representatives of the Grande Chartreuse.[38] Although the early foundations, including Witham and Hinton, clung fast to the wilderness ideal, of the remaining English foundations only Hull and Mountgrace could be considered to continue in the tradition of establishing houses in wilderness settings. The proximity to cities meant that the later medieval Carthusians became enmeshed in the secular community of their surroundings. Not only could individual laypeople endow cells, in addition to founding charterhouses, but some of the foundations included schools, guesthouses, and even a public pulpit.[39] Although the Carthusians found themselves more and more exposed to public life and thus further and further removed from their foundational desert surroundings, nevertheless they managed to embrace their wilderness calling through metaphorical re-creations of their forested isolation. Later medieval Carthusians, located in cities with royal benefactors, summoned the wilderness through graphic prayers, devotional images, and narratives such as the legends and poems accompanying the Bruno cycle and the tree of St. Bruno. Their continued adoration of the wilderness—if lost in their literal setting—is found everywhere in their devotional art and literature. As we will see, city foundations compelled them to re-create even the literal wilderness as a site of monastic speculation, a means to see God in the natural world.

Speculation and Christian Hermeneutics of the Natural World

A number of later medieval Carthusian devotional treatises represent a pivotal moment in the operation of speculation of the natural world. Carthusian texts urged their readers, both lay and monastic, to *see* God in the natural world of creation. This urgency must be considered in light of the fact that much of what the sixteenth-century reformers found so detestable about lay piety was its insistent location of divinity in the stuff of quotidian material sundries. What reeked of a bastardization of the sacred to the reformers, however, was to the Christian devout of the previous century confidence in a God who entered the material world in the miracle of the incarnation and who guaranteed the redemption of matter.[40] Some of the most sophisticated

---

38. Brantley, *Reading in the Wilderness,* 44–45. The foundations include London (1370), Hull (1378), Coventry (1381), Axholme (1397), Mountgrace (1398), Sheen (1414), and Perth (1429).

39. Brantley, *Reading in the Wilderness,* 45. See also Coppack, *Christ's Poor Men,* 111–13.

40. Bynum, *Christian Materiality,* esp. 19–30 and 269–72; Jeffrey Hamburger, "Speculations on Speculation: Vision and Perception in the Theory and Practice of Mystical Devotion," in *Deutsche Mystik im abendländischen Zusammenhang,* ed. Walter Haug and Wolfram Schneider-Lastin

philosophical minds of the fourteenth century had developed a doctrine of speculation—of gazing upon the material of creation in order to penetrate the image of, to visualize, the Creator. By the fifteenth century, this doctrine had manifold devotional repercussions for the manifestation of divinity in the stuff of creation.

Speculation involved the power of seeing and comprehending God. As a Christian discipline, it had its roots in Paul, in Romans 1:20: "For the invisible things of him, from the creation of the world, are clearly seen, being understood by the things that are made." Twelfth-century Christian Neoplatonists found inspiration in Paul's ideas about creation's mirroring capacity, and the potential of the human sensory apparatus to detect God's *invisibilia* in the things that are made—that is, in the created world. Speculation is related, of course, to *speculum,* or mirror. It was premised on the notion that the material world, or creation, reflected or mediated God, the Creator.[41]

The practice of Christian speculation changed in the later Middle Ages, largely in response to the pressure of devotional practices. Commentaries on Romans 1:20, such as those of Pseudo-Hugh of St. Victor and Bernard of Clairvaux, agreed that the natural world was indeed a visible form of the divine hand, though these writers tended to construe the world as merely a rough vestige, not an actual presence.[42] An emerging Victorine anthropology, however, allowed for further sanctioning of the physical world and the role it could play in knowledge of God. Richard of St. Victor, for example, granted the physical world powerful corresponding or mirroring characteristics, which might enable the senses to perceive beyond the physical terrain. The physical world was a jumping off point that, if regarded properly, could lead the meditant up into the contemplation of God. In Richard's configuration, the imagination played the key role in transitioning the meditant from the world to its greatest referent. The imagination was a ladder taking the meditant from sensory perception of the world to contemplative heights, or in Peter Lombard's formulation, it was the *imago Dei,* the matrix linking the correspondences between corporeal and incorporeal, humanity and divinity, creation and the Creator.[43]

The Rhenish mystic and Dominican friar Henry Suso represents a further shift in the role of speculation in the Christian hermeneutics of the natural

---

(Tübingen: Max Niemeyer Verlag, 2000), 353–408; Eamon Duffy, *Stripping of the Altars: Traditional Religion in England, 1400–1580* (New Haven, CT: Yale University Press, 1992), 377–423.

41. Hamburger, "Speculations on Speculation," 359.

42. Ibid., 371–76; for Pseudo-Hugh of St. Victor, see *Quaestiones in Epistolas Pauli ad Romanos,* q. 32–34, PL 175:438–40.

43. Hamburger, "Speculations on Speculation," 377.

world, one that would prove tremendously influential in Carthusian, indeed in much later medieval Christian, hermeneutics of the physical world. Suso's 1330 *Büchlein der ewigen Weisheit* (Little Book of Eternal Wisdom), as well as its later revised and translated Latin edition, the 1334 *Horologium sapientiae* (Clock of Wisdom), documents the stunning revelry with which the self-styled Exemplar greeted the created world as a direct reflection of the perfection of the Creator. In the *Horologium,* Suso's young protagonist fell in love with "the divine bride," by chancing on her gaze while strolling through a blossoming meadow. While admiring the springtime flowers he was jolted into recognition of their true identity:

> Suddenly from the region of the highest and loftiest peaks, there appeared a stunning flower of the field, delightful to see, and it seemed incomparably more beautiful than all the flowers I had seen before. As I hastened to gaze on it, behold! Suddenly it changed and appeared no more. But one like the goddess of all beauty stood before me, blushing like a rose and gleaming with snowy brightness; and she shone more brightly than the sun and uttered words of beauty. This lady presented in herself the sum of all that could be desired, and with the sweetest fragrance, diffused far and wide in all directions like the scent of the panther, she drew all people to her love, and said in the most dulcet voice, "Come unto me, all you who desire me, and take your fill of my produce. I am the mother of fair love and of fear, of knowledge and of holy hope."[44]

Here, Suso's protagonist reveals his reaction to a world transformed before his very eyes. The world—the flower—attracted him by its natural beauty. Once appreciated, it was re-created, becoming something else, something greater. The flower identified herself as the fair goddess, Eternal Wisdom, and inducted the protagonist into the ways of speculation, instructing him on seeing the Creator in the surface of creation.[45]

For Suso, the whole created world was a mirror of divinity, so that the contemplation of God began with such springtime meanderings as the one described in the *Horologium*. In this way, the immaterial creator was the exemplar of material creation. Suso's concern with creator/created exemplarism was carried over into his own authorship, through which he forged

---

44. *Horologium Sapientiae,* ed. Pius Künzle (Freiburg: Universitätsverlag, 1977), 1.6, pp. 418–19; trans. Edmund College, *Wisdom's Watch upon the Hours* (Washington, DC: Catholic University Press, 1994), 321.

45. On Suso's gendered treatment of Eternal Wisdom, see Barbara Newman, "Henry Suso and Medieval Devotion to Christ," *Spiritus: A Journal of Christian Spirituality* 2.1 (Spring 2002): 1–14.

an exemplary spiritual identity in his *Exemplar,* a compilation of four books of spiritual instruction written in Middle High German for a predominantly enclosed female readership.[46] One of those books was the *Little Book of Truth,* in which the disciple of "eternal truth" learned that all creatures existed in the Creator as an "eternal exemplar."[47] The exemplar was the Creator's "eternal being according to how it gives itself universally to all creatures so that they might come to be." According to this teaching, the Creator existed within creation. Continuing to instruct on the correspondence between creatures and Creator, the treatise explained how creatures might know the Creator through creation:

> All creatures eternally in God *are* God and have there no basic difference.... They are the same life, being and power insofar as they are in God and are this same One and nothing less. But after their issuing forth, when they take on their own being, each has its own special being distinguished by its own form which gives it its natural being. (*Büchlein der Wahrheit,* p. 336; Tobin, 311)

In this passage, Suso is intensely concerned with the relationship between Creator and creation, with the implications of a world in which natural being and divine being exist in a continuum. If all of creation had its "natural being" in God, and only its form varied from the prototype, then humanity, indeed all of creation, would know God's being in knowing the stuff of creation. Each elemental being in creation had its own form, but its essence by degree participated in its original being, from which it came, so that "when a creature finds itself to be a creature, it acknowledges its Creator and God" (*Büchlein der Wahrheit,* p. 336; Tobin, 311). Speculation, for Suso, involved this reckoning of creature and Creator.

Suso's *Exemplar* outlined for his female audience the ideal model for speculation. Speculation on earthly creation was exemplary of the activity of God—specialized sight mimicked God's mode of action in creation. According to Suso, speculation was God's own mode of being, taking joy in creation, marveling at his reflection in the mirror of his creation. By means

---

46. As Hamburger notes, the title that Suso chose for this compilation, *The Exemplar,* demonstrates his belief that his own life and experiences should act as examples to be imitated. See Jeffrey Hamburger, "Medieval Self-Fashioning: Authorship, Authority, and Autobiography in Suso's *Exemplar,*" in *The Visual and the Visionary: Art and Female Spirituality in Late Medieval Germany* (New York: Zone Books, 1998), 233–78.

47. *Büchlein der Wahrheit,* in *Deutsche mystische Schriften,* ed. Georg Hofmann (Düsseldorf: Patmos Verlag, 1966), 336; trans. Frank Tobin, in *Henry Suso: The Exemplar with Two German Sermons* (New York: Paulist Press, 1989), 311 (hereafter cited parenthetically in the text in abbreviated form).

of the discipline of speculation, "nature transformed into supernature."[48] Just as God saw his reflection in creation, so also should creation discern God's image in itself. Suso counseled his disciples always to behold the beauty of creation, seeing in it the Creator and recognizing that by such means nature was transformed into the supernatural. "When I look at attractive living forms or see pleasing creatures," Suso wrote, "they say to my heart 'Oh look how very pleasing he is from whom we flowed forth, from whom all beauty comes'" (*Büchlein der Wahrheit,* p. 308; Tobin, 286). Suso taught that God's mode of being was to gaze upon his own reflection in creation. The meditative gaze recommended by Suso imitated God's pleasure—the act of speculation was itself the exemplar.

Although in theory Suso proclaimed a speculative worldview in which all of creation mirrored the radiant face of the Creator, in practice Suso appears to have mediated through images his own appreciation of material creation. Suso's treatises are rife with enthusiastic, descriptive praise of natural phenomena and his visionary experiences among all manner of trees, flowers, thorns, and meadows. He relates in great detail his journeys through meadow and forest, mountain and valley.[49] But Suso's reported experience of natural creation always remained at the level of the imaginary, the visionary. Rather than gazing directly at naked creation, like the blindness and confusion caused by vision of the sun, Suso proposed the use of images.[50]

The most superior image for prayer, according to Suso, was the person of Christ himself. "And the best thing for [meditation] that I know," he exclaimed, "is the dear image of Jesus Christ." [51] In the *Little Book of Eternal Wisdom,* Suso fashioned just such a dear image of Jesus, whereby he instructed his disciples to pray. The *Little Book* was a meditation on Christ's passion, and it demonstrated the critical role of the incarnation in re-creating the world. For Suso, the incarnation of Christ in Mary's womb rendered

48. *Büchlein der ewigen Weisheit,* p. 314: "Natur in Übernatur gewandelt." Robert Bartlett has shown that this word "supernatural" was rare in Latin, first emerging in the mid-thirteenth century in the climate of mendicancy and Scholasticism. In the vernacular, the term emerged even later (1375 in French, according to Bartlett). See Robert Bartlett, *The Natural and the Supernatural in the Middle Ages* (Cambridge: Cambridge University Press, 2008), 14–16.

49. Ernst Robert, *European Literature and the Latin Middle Ages,* trans. Willard Trask (Princeton, NJ: Princeton University Press, 1973), 193–202.

50. Many of these images are reproduced in Hamburger, *The Visual and the Visionary,* 197–278.

51. *Briefbüchlein,* in Karl Bihlmeyer, *Heinrich Seuse: Deutsche Schriften* (Frankfurt: Minerva, 1961), 391; trans. Bernard McGinn, in *The Harvest of Mysticism in Medieval Germany* (New York: Crossroad, 2005), 211. See also Heinrich Stirnimann, "Mystik und Metaphorik: Zu Seuses Dialog," in *Das "einig Ein": Studien zu Theorie und Sprache der deutsche Mystik,* ed. Alois M. Haas and Heinrich Stirnimann (Freiburg: Universitätsverlag, 1980), 249–53. He is said to have decorated his private chapel with pictures, notably of the desert fathers. See Hamburger, *The Visual and the Visionary,* chaps. 4 and 5.

the world so that God could once more touch creation, inhabiting it. In the person of Christ, God entered creation in order to become a "pure bright mirror of divine majesty."[52] Before God's incarnation, nature would have been utterly incomprehensible, a result of humanity's fallen state and utter estrangement both from God and from the delicate workings of the natural world. But God was now manifest in the world, according to Suso, because of the incarnation, forever linking divinity with creation. God's incarnation implanted a mirror of divinity through which to see God in creation. The world was re-created for creatures to see the Creator.

Suso's understanding of the incarnation as a divine act that interlaced the world with a mirror explains his expressive devotion. Take, for example, his annual practice of erecting a maypole to celebrate the coming of spring, the renewal of the fruitful abundance and colorful beauty of the earth after its long hibernation underneath the icy blanket of winter. The *Exemplar* reports that Suso annually erected a "spiritual maypole." His maypole was no ordinary arbor; it was the cross of Christ. Instead of decorating it with flowers in the manner typical of secular spring revelers, Suso decorated his maypole with spiritual graces, honing his own virtues in celebration of Christ's springtime resurrection: "Instead of red roses I offer you today for your eternal adornment my heartfelt love."[53] One wonders how, exactly, he displayed his virtues on the cross. It is likely that this was an image he conjured in meditation, though numerous illuminations of Suso kneeling in prayer before a roseate crucifix suggest that there may have been some visual dimension to the practice he recommended.

It is not without significance that Suso's writings were among the most often copied at the Carthusian charterhouses of England.[54] There was an important developmental link between Suso's speculative hermeneutics of the natural world and later Carthusian devotional practices. What Suso posited at the level of vision and image, many Carthusians actualized in practice. The physical created world was the image through which they prayed; in creation they claimed to encounter and indeed to see God. While Suso's roseate tree may have hung on the wall of his private chapel, those found in Carthusian records suggest that speculation was an outdoor activity.

---

52. *Büchlein der ewigen Weisheit,* p. 282: "klarer Spiegel der göttlichen Hoheit"; trans. Tobin, 266.

53. *Das Leben,* in Hofmann, *Deutsche mystische Schriften,* 43; trans. Tobin, 83.

54. Other than the Benedictines, the Carthusians crafted and housed the greatest number of the 223 manuscripts; see Pius Künzle, ed., *Heinrich Seuses Horologium sapientiae* (Freiburg: Universitäts-verlag, 1977), 215–28 and 250–89.

The Wilderness of the Cell

The speculative hermeneutics of the Carthusian wilderness found its most able spokesperson in Ludolph of Saxony. Ludolph entered the Carthusian order at Strasbourg in 1340. Before professing his vow to the desert, he was a member of the Dominican order, which in part explains his adaptation and expansion of Suso's ideas. Ludolph's *Vita Jesu Christi,* written in the 1350s, is one of the only later medieval spiritual texts to rival the popularity of Suso's *Horologium* and greatly depends on it.[55] Another contribution to Ludolph's work is the *Meditationes vitae Christi,* which has been estimated to constitute 5 percent of Ludolph's text.[56] Ludolph combined and thereby transformed the traditions of speculation and passion meditation in his subtle recommendation that the ideal monastic environment in which to witness Christ's presence on earth was actually the Carthusian wilderness.

Like his Carthusian forefather, Guigo I, Ludolph praised the desert for conjuring Christ's presence in meditation. He illustrated the spiritual effects of desert meditation by citing numerous examples of biblical worthies who saw divine traces while surrounded in the wilderness in retreat from the world. John the Baptist, for example, "remained in the desert where the air is more pure, the sky more open, and God more intimate."[57] The desert air was unsullied, free from the stains placed on nature by human sin. There, according to Ludolph, God was closer, more present to humanity. By praising the desert in this manner, Ludolph drew on the Carthusian wilderness tradition and recommended that the kind of meditative history he offered was suited primarily for the solitude of the Carthusian cell. The earthly desert was the most appropriate space, following the model of Christ, for Carthusian prayer. That desert, we will see, was the monastic cell.

Ludolph began his meditation on the life of Jesus by considering creation itself. He began with an examination of God's role as artisan, as maker of the physical universe and father of Christ, and pondered the implications of the original act of creation. For God to create suggested to him that God

---

55. The charterhouse of Mainz, where Ludolph composed the *Vita Christi,* housed nine copies of the *Horologium.* On the influential nature of Ludolphus's work, see Heinrich Boehmer, *Loyola und die deutsche Mystik* (Leipzig: B. G. Teubner, 1921), 17; and Elizabeth Salter, "Ludolph of Saxony and His English Translators," *Medium Aevum* 33 (1964): 26–35. See Mary Immaculate Bodenstedt, *The Vita Christi of Ludolphus the Carthusian* (Washington, DC: Catholic University of America Press, 1944), 35–37, on the textual borrowings from the *Horologium.*

56. Bodenstedt, *The Vita Christi,* 30–31.

57. Ludolphus de Saxonia, *Vita Jesu Christi ex Evangelio et approbatis Ecclesia Catholica doctoris sedule collecta,* ed. L. M. Rigollot (Paris: Palmé, 1865), I.14 (hereafter cited parenthetically in the text in abbreviated form by part and chapter).

was an artist, and one who took a distinct pleasure in looking upon his own masterwork. God's relationship to the physical created world was much like that of an artist to a favorite piece:

> For creatures are produced by God just as works of art are through an artist. For he is the artist of all things, acting through his understanding. Now that which is produced through art, or in the understanding, is produced through the concept of the art of the understanding. Just as a house in exterior fact is brought forth from a house which is in the soul, so in divine matters the Word is the same concept as in the divine mind.... Therefore everything that was made was made through him, whether spiritual or bodily creatures. (*VJC* I.1)

Just as the artist first imagines, and then materially fashions, a product, so God imagined the world before its creation: "All things which are made or have been made, he arranged to make, and before they came into being he knew them as made, and they lived and flourished in his mind and presence" (*VJC* I.1). The physical world of creation—the *ordo creationis*—offered itself as a blueprint of God's imagination. God's imagination provided the unformed stuff of creation. Ludolph began with a basic Christian Platonism. But in this meditation, the visible, material world and its invisible, perfect form would inch closer and closer to one another until they were scarcely distinguishable.

Ludolph's meditation was an instruction book for how to look upon the material world to see God. The material world was like a mirror if regarded properly:

> The light shines even in the shadows of this world because the creator appears in creation. Just as in heaven God is the mirror of created things in whom created things shine and in whom we see all things that pertain to our joy, thus, in this life, conversely, created things are the mirror of the creator in which we can speculate upon our creator. (*VJC* I.1)

The material world reflected God's image because it was God's creation, God's imagination materialized. But human sight of God in this world was hampered by sin, a physical impairment for speculation. Owing to the history of humanity, its fall from grace, the world was not immediately *evident* as a matrix for God. He explained: "In [humanity's] fall all the elements suffered harm. For formerly, the earth did not bring forth thorns and thistles, nor was the air then as dense as it is now, but it was purer" (*VJC* II.87). Owing to the sin of humanity, God's presence was no longer immediate in the created world. Ludolph prayed that God continue to extend his hands into his work, continue to remake his own creation to refine it according to the blueprint of his imagination:

> You created all things visible and invisible, and, as part of that creation, also this miserable sinner of yours. I adore you, I praise you, I glorify you. Be propitious to me a sinner and do not despise the work of your hands, but save and aid me by your holy name. Extend your right hand to the work of your hands, succor fleshy weakness. You who made me, remake (*refice*) me for I am stained with vices; you who formed me, reform (*reforma*) me for I am corrupted by sins. (*VJC* I.1)

Ludolph's plea was for God's continued restoration of humanity, and thus of creation. A reformed humanity could more clearly see God in the world, could regain the immediacy of God's presence through material forms. According to Ludolph, God's image did not merely linger passively within the material world. The meditant had to actively coax out his *vestigia*. This process of active discernment required self-awareness, conforming the self to God's original intended human nature, to the *imago Dei* originally implanted in creation. This task of self-conformity was eased, according to Ludolph, by the fact that Christ was ever incarnate, ever re-implanting the divine presence in the material world. For Ludolph, the significance of the incarnation was to bring humans into the knowledge and ability to perceive God in the created world. The Son proceeded from the Father, according to Ludolph, "through eternal nativity" (*VJC* I.1: "Per aeternam nativitatem"). Therefore the incarnation was not a past event, one that was completed in history. Rather, the incarnation was ever recurring, ever present. Christ's generation was "divine and eternal," and, Ludolph asserted, humans must train their minds to imagine the world as eternally generating God's presence (*VJC* I.1: "De divina et aeterna Christi generatione"). According to Ludolph, the incarnation as a reiterative event should guide human perception of the natural world. It was this sense of the world as repeatedly recapitulating God's physical presence that Ludolph evoked when he described his strict religious observance in the solitude of the cell as a "manger," where he acted as daily witness to the incarnation.[58] The eternality of God's generation in matter guaranteed that the matter of re-creation, all that was in it, might be holy.

God's material incarnation was always *in act* through the process of proper meditation on the life of Christ. Ludolph offered his readers guidance in

---

58. *Vita Jesu Christi*, I.9: "et in praesipio reclinari voluisti, da mihi elementissime Domine, per tuam inenarrabilem nativitatem renasci in me novae vitae sanctitatem."

how to imagine the world, how to speculate on the material of this world that manifested Christ's presence. He took as his subject the life of Christ but made that history a present one. For Ludolph, meditation was a process of historical imagining. Events of the past were integral to imagining the present in a proper sense, to perceiving the present world in its conditions as a vehicle for seeing God. Ludolph explained in his prolegomena that the forthcoming meditation was a historical narrative, but one that must be recognized for its present recapitulation:

> Although many of these things are narrated as if in the past, nevertheless you should meditate on all of them as if they were being performed in the present; because without doubt you will taste a greater pleasantness from this. Therefore, read about what was done as if it were being done. Place before your eyes past actions as if they were present. (*VJC* I.proemium)

Meditation as a historical mode of imagining required the individual to transport past events into the present to act as witness to them firsthand. The ever-recurring process of the incarnation, of making God present in the material of creation, according to Ludolph, took place through the imaginative faculty of individual meditants:

> Descending of course from the bosom of the Father into the womb of the virgin, like another witness with the angel of holy conception, you may exist in pure faith; and congratulate the Virgin Mother who is thus made fertile because of you. (*VJC* I.proemium)

The meditant re-created the incarnation—acted as witness to it—in the imagination. Mary reconceived through meditation. She was God's point of contact with creation, the earth in which God planted himself as a seed to grow forever in the stuff of creation. Therefore, her renewal of the elements was continuing, propelled through Ludolph's speculative meditation. In order for that seed of Christ continually to blossom forth the devotee must properly cultivate it. Speculation on the natural world was the discipline proper to such cultivation. If perceived properly, the natural world became a sacred space for meeting God.

It was unclear to what, precisely, Ludolph referred when he encouraged Carthusian meditants to take to the desert, like Christ, to pray, and to discover the image of God in the material world. A real wilderness? A metaphorical desert? An image of these natural spaces? A fifteenth-century French translation of the *Vita Jesu Christi* provides a provisional answer. Created for Charles VIII of France, the manuscript occupies four volumes, in which

140 illuminations beautifully depict scenes based on the gospel life of Christ that Ludolph presented in his text. One nongospel image, however, is of particular importance. Located on the opening folio, it portrays the author in his cell writing the *Vita* (fig. 5.4). Christ crucified appears before his eyes as Ludolph writes the meditations. Instruments of his passion, the lance, the whip, and the column, surround him as Ludolph gazes at the suffering Christ eye to eye. Directly behind the person of Christ hanging from the cross is an opening to the cell garden. Christ has materialized before the garden of the cell.[59] Speculation out into the verdant world made Christ present. His cell was thus the vessel for Christ's incarnation.

A coeval Carthusian devotional text, the poem *The Desert of Religion,* provides a further opportunity to consider the relationship of literal encounters with the natural world to the imagistic, metaphorical, and visionary ones recommended by Suso and his spiritual ancestors.[60] *The Desert of Religion* is a poetic paean to and instruction in monastic wilderness speculation. Although its author is unknown, it was most likely written for a Benedictine or Carthusian house.[61] It was one of very few Middle English texts to have been invariably illustrated, suggesting its use as a premodern "imagetext."[62] *The Desert* exists in three extant manuscripts, all of which bear the same complex and interdependent program of images and explanatory captions accompanying the text of the poem itself.[63] Based largely on the lengthy, didactic *Speculum*

---

59. A later folio (vol. 3, fol. 47v) depicts another Carthusian at his desk copying manuscripts. He is directly in front of the cell garden as he writes.

60. The poem is located in British Library MS Additional 37049, fols. 46r–67r; BL MS Cotton Faustina B VI, part II, fols. 1r–23r; and Stowe 39, fols. 11r–32r. Each manuscript is described in W. Hübner, "The Desert of Religion," in *Archiv für das Studium der neueren Sprachen und Literaturen* 126 (1911): 56–74. It was most likely produced between 1460 and 1470 in the north of England, in a Carthusian setting. On dating, see Brantley, *Reading in the Wilderness,* 46–57; and A. I. Doyle, "English Carthusian Books Not Yet Linked with a Charterhouse," in *"A Miracle of Learning": Studies in Manuscripts and Irish Learning, Essays in Honour of William O'Sullivan,* ed. Toby Barnard, Dáibhí Ó Cróinín, and Katharine Simms (Aldershot, UK: Ashgate, 1998), 128. On the scribal origins of the poem, see James Hogg, "Unpublished Texts in the Carthusian Northern Middle English Religious Miscellany British Library MS Additional 37049," in *Essays in Honor of Erwin Stürzl on His Sixtieth Birthday,* ed. James Hogg (Salzburg: Institut für Englische Sprache und Literatur, 1980), 1:241–84.

61. See Brantley, *Reading in the Wilderness,* 112, on its intended audience. Though the original author of the poem is unknown, the scribe of Additional 37049 was Carthusian.

62. On illustrations among the three manuscript copies, see Anne McGovern-Mouron, "The Desert of Religion in British Library Cotton Faustina B VI, pars II," in *The Mystical Tradition and the Carthusians,* ed. James Hogg (Salzburg: Institut für Anglistik und Amerikanistik, 1995), 9:149–52; and Brantley, *Reading in the Wilderness,* chap. 3, pp. 79–120. Brantley borrows the term "imagetext" from W. J. T. Mitchell, which means a combined medium of image and texts, each inseparable from, and incomprehensible without, the other.

63. Brantley, *Reading in the Wilderness,* 23. For an earlier interpretation of *The Desert,* see Hope Emily Allen, "*The Desert of Religion:* Addendum," *Archiv für das Studium der neueren Sprachen über Literaturen* 127 (1911): 388–90.

FIGURE 5.4. Ludolph of Saxony, *Vita Christi*. MSS Hunter 36, fol. 1r. By permission of University of Glasgow Library, Special Collections.

vitae, putatively authored by William of Nassington in the fourteenth century, *The Desert* transformed the moralized couplets of its prototype into a visual and performative spiritual experience.[64] *The Desert,* however, artfully altered the text of the *Speculum vitae,* emphasizing the highly visual experience of meditation by rendering it into imagistic diagrams based wholly on trees and wilderness settings. In doing so, it suggested that the act of meditation required a proper relationship to the image of the natural world.

A poem designed explicitly to instruct Carthusians on the meditative life of the cell, *The Desert* took for its subject trees in the wilderness but also offered itself as a surrogate wilderness or wilderness training ground.[65] In the absence of actual wilderness isolation in later medieval England, *The Desert* provided through text and image an imaginary forest on which the Carthusian could meditatively gaze.[66] *The Desert* was a substitute for the desert of the wilderness. Although the real wilderness on which to set one's sights was absent from Carthusian life in fifteenth-century England, it was replicated in meditational texts and practice.

The author of *The Desert* sought to instruct meditants in the practice of speculation. "In þat entent—als men may loke," the author proposed, "als wildernes is wroght in þis boke."[67] Through such instruction, the poem promised to deliver the wilderness in a double series of illustrations that accompanies each section (fig. 5.5). The reader first encountered a line of verse on the recto of each folio, each poetic section taking up the praise of wilderness eremitic life. Adjacent to the line of text was an illustrative image—in the Additional and Cotton MSS, the text of the poem aligned with the left-hand margin and the illustrations in the right; in the Stowe MS, the text is presented in paragraph form in the upper half of the folio, while the illustrations occupy the bottommost space. The second series of image-texts appeared on the verso. Invariably, it featured a tree that represented in diagrammatic fashion a spiritual theme considered in the previous text, so that every other page of the poem was an arboreal diagram illustrating figuratively what the poem sought to convey. *The Desert of Religion* took the compendium of allegorical virtues and vices from the *Speculum vitae,* attached them to the Scholastic mnemonic of tree diagrams, and through such means transformed them into a lesson in how to perceive the material world as carrying God's presence.

---

64. On the *Speculum vitae,* see Hope Emily Allen, "The *Speculum vitae:* Addendum," *PMLA* 32.2 (1917): 133–62.

65. Hübner, "The Desert of Religion," 921–22.

66. Brantley, *Reading in the Wilderness,* 83.

67. Hübner, "The Desert of Religion," 73.

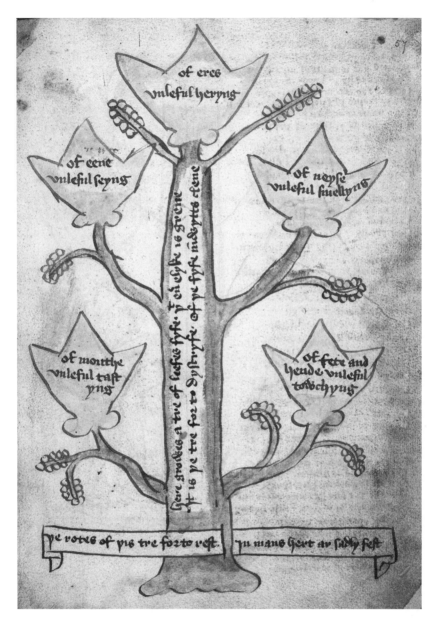

Figure 5.5. *The Desert of Religion.* London, British Library, MS Additional 37049, fol. 57. Courtesy of the British Library.

The *Desert of Religion* sought to conjure for Carthusian monks the experience of the wilderness to which Bruno's letters testified. It opens and closes with injunctions to locate the self in the presence of the wilderness. "Elongavi fugiens et manis in solitudine," begins the poem, citing Psalm 54.[68] It then proceeds to introduce the poem with that constant biblical allusion in Carthusian writing, the story of Jesus's flight into the desert for solitude and prayer: "He went in-to deserte to dwell,/ Als itt is wryten in þe gospell:/ Ductus est Jesus in desertum a spiritu."[69] In between, the poem's didactic trees instructed the reader on the proper religious life: "Bath þu may study and see/ vertus to folow and vices to flee." Because the Carthusian reader inhabited the wilderness of the cell, his job was to act as "gode gardynere" in cultivating this forest of virtues. If sin remained well weeded, uprooted from the forest, then God's presence would grow in the trees planted therein. The place of religion, therefore, according to *The Desert,* was the wilderness of the Carthusian cell: "[F]le in to þis wyldernes. If þu will be perfite:/ And hald þe þare in halynes. Als falles to gode hermet."[70] All good Carthusians who seek perfection, it taught, must flee into the wilderness in order to enact holiness.

At the time of the poem's creation and circulation, however, nary a wilderness was to be found in England, which had undergone the process of deforestation centuries before, and what dense wooded realms remained were strictly patrolled under royal right.[71] The *Desert* therefore posited a number of veritable proxy wildernesses. There were first the pictures and allusions to the legendary wilderness of the first Carthusian foundations, those that provided such spiritual awakening as decried by Bruno and Guigo. Then there was the wilderness of the later medieval Carthusian cell, a metaphorical wilderness meant to indicate the charter monk's solitude and isolation. There was also the wilderness of *The Desert,* that series of trees through which the solitary monk should meditatively wander as he perused the poem. According to the poem, all three wildernesses were conflated in the experience of reading and seeing the arboreal illustrations it offered. The poem re-created the experience of one such as Bruno for those monks bereft of an actual wilderness to inhabit—*The Desert* promised to deliver the wilderness to the suburban-dwelling charter monk. It sought to instruct real monks on the art of wilderness prayer by presenting them with images of hermits at

---

68. Ibid., 59.

69. Ibid.

70. James Hogg, An Illustrated Yorkshire Carthusian Religious Miscellany, fol. 46r.

71. On deforestation, see Michael Williams, *Deforesting the Earth: From Prehistory to Global Crisis* (Chicago: University of Chicago Press, 2002); on English forests, see Joan Thirsk and H. P. R. Finberg, *The Agrarian History of England and Wales* (Cambridge: Cambridge University Press, 2011).

prayer in the wilderness. *The Desert* thereby played on the ontological status of images and their referents by emphasizing its own structure and construction. The poem forced its reader to question the relationship of the wilderness images on the page to the wilderness of the Carthusian foundation legends. Through prayer and careful cultivation of virtue and avoidance of vice, the solitary cell itself became the wilderness where God could be found.

The trees of *The Desert* helped the Carthusian to see the world. "In þis wod here may yu se,/Sprygand full fayr a-nother tre" are the words directing the reader to yet another tree diagram. In the wilderness of the book readers saw another tree, a visual cue. And by this tree they should understand that "Þis suld men sett in þair ortȝarde."[72] Just as the speculative principle espoused by Suso had recommended viewing the world of creation as a mirror reflecting God's image, so *The Desert* offered itself—the experience of the wilderness—as a mirror. As the Carthusian monk looked into the pictures of the book, he saw over and over again illustrations of silent white-robed Carthusian monks like himself and hermits such as Richard Rolle and Mary Magdalene praying in the desert. His own image was reflected back to him in the wilderness pictures.

The Desert offered to the Carthusian something that, in fifteenth-century England, was patently not available to the inhabitant of the cell—the spiritual experience of the wilderness that the order's founders had recommended. In its stead, *The Desert* instructed speculation on the natural world, while also lamenting the loss of available sights on which the Carthusian might practice his training. In closing, the poem insisted that its reader "Take gude keep to þis tretis,/ Þat here is writen on englis;/ For itt is taken of bokes sere/ And made groveand in treys here."[73] Only three known copies of the poem survive, suggesting that the author may have recognized its scarcity—that is, the scarcity of the wilderness to which it referred, and so asked his readers to take good care of it. But more important, it was "made groveand" in its trees. The trees, which throughout the illustration of the poem represented the wilderness, made religion *groveand*. The author asks the poem's readers to make *groveand* through *treys* as a form of recapitulation, a continuing process. Continually to replicate the processes it discusses, to speculate on the fabricated wilderness. For the author of this poem, the very act of re-creating, imaginatively and in reality by duplicating this treatise and practicing its instruction, was a participation in God's original act of re-creating the world in the incarnation and crucifixion of Christ.

---

72. Hübner, "The Desert of Religion," 61.
73. Ibid., 72.

A Wilderness Re-created: The Architecture of the Late Medieval Charterhouse

Because they so rarely departed from their cells, the later medieval Carthusians lived their lives defined by cloister architecture. When the European aristocracy began to found accessible charterhouses in urban environs in the thirteenth century, a notable architectural adaptation accompanied their move out of the desert. Archaeological excavations of Hinton Charterhouse, for example, have revealed what became the consistent Carthusian layout (fig. 5.6). Each of Hinton's fifteen cells, placed squarely along the periphery of the great cloister, contained its own private, walled garden, most totaling three times the size of the cell, some equaling a full five times the square footage allotted to the cell. Plans of Mount Grace charterhouse reveal the same Carthusian valuation of the physical exterior environment (fig. 5.7). Each of these modern reproductions is confirmed by one of the earliest extant plans, that of the waterworks at London charterhouse (ca. 1430–40), which reveals individual cells equipped with private garden enclosures.[74]

Excavations of individual cell gardens of Mount Grace have shown that these spaces were not used for food cultivation. In fact, most of the cell gardens investigated showed minimal signs of any cultivation whatsoever. Rather, these outdoor spaces, which surrounded and enclosed the cell, were private wildernesses intended for the speculation of individual Carthusian meditants. Exiting the garden threshold of the cell, the Carthusian did not gaze upon a small, prim *hortus conclusus* equipped with pert cabbages or red roses. In fact, the term "cell garden" is misleading, as it suggests a great degree of human cultivation. These were miniwildernesses where the solitary Carthusian experienced the "desert of religion," a grand wilderness space containing the presence of God.

Guigo's *Customs* provided the most complete information on what the twelfth-century cells would have included. The *Customs* legislated that all cells be equipped with straw, a felt cloth, a cushion, a covering of coarse sheepskin, and a coverlet of rustic cloth. Each cell should be outfitted with such utensils as thread, two needles, scissors, and a razor with a grindstone and throng for sharpening. For the preparation of solitary meals, the cells must contain all the necessary pots, pans, and platters for cooking, wood for the fire, and an axe for cutting firewood. And so that the monk could exercise his pastoral labor of "preaching with [his] hands," the cell included a desk, chalk, two pumices, two inkhorns, two knives for scratching parchment,

---

74. One can see a reproduction of this plan in Brantley, *Reading in the Wilderness,* 37.

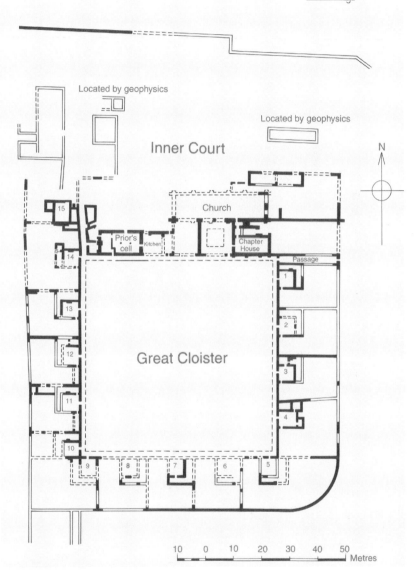

FIGURE 5.6. Plan of Hinton Charterhouse. Glyn Coppack and Simon Hayfield after Philip Fletcher.
© English Heritage.

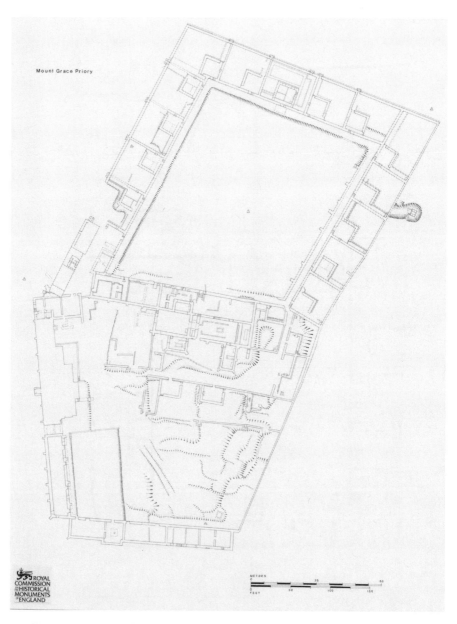

Mount Grace Priory

METRES
0   25   50
FEET
0   50   100   150

FIGURE 5.7. Plan of Mount Grace Charterhouse. Glyn Coppack and Simon Hayfield after RCHM(E). © English Heritage.

a parchment pricker, and lead drypoints, a ruler, and a pencil. By the twelfth-century development of the legislation of the Carthusian order, there is no indication that the tools to cultivate cell gardens were included in the architecture of the charterhouse or the supplies of the cell. No shovels or pots of any sort are mentioned in the *Customs* among the materials for the outfitting of the cell.

There is a problem here, one that has irked scholars for quite some time. As Dennis Martin has noticed, "Everyone who knows anything at all about Carthusians knows that each Carthusian monk has his own individual garden walled off from his neighbor's, a garden that is his to tend or not tend as he chooses."[75] And yet, there is virtually no commentary, no legislation, no Carthusian directive, explaining *why* these gardens emerged, or how the charter monks should use them. Even the later medieval *Customs* unfortunately does not mention these evasive cell gardens. Nor does the *Statutes.* Nor the *Chartae.* Indeed the private Carthusian cell gardens appear nowhere in the legislation or otherwise documented history of the order.[76]

In the absence of written material, one can gain some information on Carthusian cell gardens from archaeological excavations. Excavations of English charterhouses founded in the thirteenth and fourteenth centuries suggest that cell gardens may have been a later addition to the architecture of the cell. Locus Dei, the charterhouse of Hinton in Somerset, was originally founded by William Longespée, the Earl of Salisbury. He planned for the location of the house in the somewhat more populous and accessible Hatherop in 1222. When the earl died in 1226, the monks petitioned his wife, Ela, for a more remote and isolated site, as the bustling Hatherop seemed antagonistic to the Carthusian vow regarding wilderness solitude. In 1227, Ela instigated the building of permanent structures on her manor lands at Hinton.[77] While her estate may have offered equitable removal from the offending crowds, it was hardly a wilderness. And it was perhaps for this reason that the layout of the new monastic plan at Hinton included

---

75. The *Customs* does mention the large vegetable garden, chapter 63, col. 743: "Ortus et quae ad eum pertinent, uni deputantur e fratribus, qui de omnibus ad procuratorem recurrit, eique de cunctis rationem." For the quotation, see Dennis Martin, "Cultivating Cult: A Down-to-Earth View of Carthusian Gardening," in *Liber amicorum James Hogg, Kartäuserforschung 1970–2006,* (Salzburg: Institut für Anglistik und Amerikanistik, 2008), 71.

76. Martin has made a study of the statutes, narratives, and *ordinationes* of the order and found nothing other than a few unremarkable comments in the 1680 statutes.

77. James Hogg, *The Architecture of Hinton Charterhouse* (Salzburg: Institut für Englische Sprache und Literatur, 1975).

the addition of private gardens attached to each individual cell, where, in order to promote or lay claim to some sense of Bruno's original plan, they might enjoy the experience of the wilderness among the "well-watered gardens [and] fruitful and diverse trees."

Excavations of Mount Grace charterhouse reveal that monks tended their cell gardens according to a variety of plans, which would be expected among a community that shared no official guidelines for garden maintenance. L-shaped gardens, for example, were divided into three square beds edged with stones.[78] Some garden plots also included raised beds along the west and back walls of the garden and the west wall of the cell. Archaeologist Glyn Coppack has concluded that there are no traces of planting within the beds, supporting the idea that these gardens were truly wilderness spaces.[79] A second garden excavated by Coppack contained an outline for a square plot to the north of the cell and two rectangular beds to the west. In the north plot, a number of pits were filled with compost, marking the location of deeper-rooted plants.[80]

Faced with the great conundrum of the Carthusian gardens, I add the following argument to the chorus of scholarly speculation. When, owing to the circumstances of patronage, Carthusian monks found themselves surrounded not by desert wilderness, but amid the hustle and imposition of city life and patron requests, they outfitted their cells with the surrogate wilderness of their private gardens, a physical place in which to see God's presence in the material of the world. The circumstances of late medieval urban foundations led to the Carthusian architecture that invariably included private gardens annexed to each individual cell. These gardens provided the wilderness in which late medieval Carthusians could seek their requisite *neuen*. That is, according to a fifteenth-century Carthusian poem on the origins of the order, the wilderness effected spiritual intimacy: "wildernes is

---

78. Coppack, *Christ's Poor Men;* see also Glyn Coppack, *Mount Grace Priory: North Yorkshire* (London: English Heritage, 1991).

79. Coppack, *Christ's Poor Men,* 88.

80. In fact much of the Carthusian reputation for cultivating private gardens comes from the highly decorative nature of their postmedieval continental gardens. By the mid-sixteenth century the charterhouses of Pavia and Dijon, in particular, drew attention because of their lush gardens. See Devaux, *L'architecture,* 1:128–70. The most famous Carthusian pleasure garden was located at the Paris charterhouse; noted especially for its trees and shrubs, it was located precisely where the Jardin du Luxembourg now blooms. See Bernard Montgolfier, J. P. Willesme, Isabelle Charles, and Christian Lambert, eds., *La Chartreuse de Paris: Museé Carnavalet, 12 mai-9 août 1987* (Paris: Musée Carnavalet, 1987). James Hogg has published photo documentation of the resplendent gardens of Italian, Spanish, and French charterhouses; see James Hogg, Ingeborg Hogg, Francisco Zubillaga, *Las cartujas de Las Cuevas, Cazalla de la Sierra y Grenada; The Charterhouses of Las Cuevas, Cazalla de la Sierra, and Grenada* (Salzburg: Institut für Englische Sprache und Literatur, Universität Salzburg, 1979).

þe paradyse of deliciousnes to neuen."[81] The Carthusians thus brought the spiritual hermeneutics of speculation of the natural world to its greatest iteration in suggesting that in the real physical natural world might one truly encounter the presence of God. When the Carthusians moved out of the wilderness and into the city they took with them a respectful adherence to Guigo's words about the effectiveness of prayer in solitude. They had to re-create both imaginatively and literally the desert conditions on which their forefathers had relied for spiritual intimacy, for seeing God in clarity as praised by Bruno. Their monastic work was to make *flourshyand* by purveying the world of the cell.

The place of the wilderness in later medieval Carthusian spirituality poses vexing questions for medieval prayer more generally, questions about the ontological status of metaphor, and of the material world from which metaphor is spun. At the beginning of this study, a twelfth-century treatise for the instruction of enclosed women, the *Speculum virginum,* taught virgins to see and perceive God in their own bodies and communities. In order to do so, the *Speculum* author turned to imagery drawn from the natural world, making the body of the virgin an emblem of re-creation. He cultivated a sense of virginal responsibility in religious life, a possibility of incarnating God within the virgin body, linking her liturgical work in community to that of Mary as a renewer of the world's elements, the vessel of incarnation. At this study's close, Ludolph of Saxony's early fifteenth-century meditational treatise taught charter monks to perceive God through meditative acts of speculation on the material forms of the real world. The later medieval Carthusians grasped at the authority of the world itself as the site of God's presence. Each movement sprang from a quest to understand the world as riddled with new possibilities owing to its re-creation in the incarnation and crucifixion of Christ. Each strove for access to a present God and sought to train the self to apprehend that God.

---

81. The poem takes its title from its incipit, "at þe begynyng of þe chartirhows God dyd schewe." It is reproduced at fol. 22r-22v in Hogg, *An Illustrated Yorkshire Carthusian Religious Miscellany,* 25–26.

Conclusion

I have sought to illuminate the devotional origins and development of the medieval doctrine of the world's re-creation. To posit that the material world was re-created by the incarnation and crucifixion of Christ was to insist on a new manner of perception. It was to regard the whole world as capable of manifesting divine presence, in bodies, in earth, in things. Both the learned and the less so shared a regard for matter as capable of such presence, of such transformation. This comprehension of matter as potentially holy emerged in religious communities that were undergoing rigorous self-evaluation, thinking deeply about what it would mean to live in community. A dedicated religious life, it seems, required faith in the possibility that one could genuinely experience the presence of God in the world. It required the will to live by a set of instructions that might enhance that experience. And it required a great deal of practice to prepare the self to discern God in matter. Thus I have given particular attention to treatises designed to train the imagination properly to see God in this manner.

Imaginative, meditative re-creations of God's intersection with matter often gave way to physical, performative re-creations, such as Hildegard's liturgical drama or Francis's eucharistic celebration at Greccio. All were attempts to see, to feel, to sense, God in creation. And thus I have argued that the purpose of some of the more literal expressions of later medieval devotion was to achieve access to a God who was fully present in the material world, while simultaneously materially transcendent. My argument emphasizes devotional rejoicing in the possibility that a re-created world offered for later medieval *religiosi* of living a fully spiritual life on earth. As other scholars have shown, however, the re-created world also inspired fear and new mechanisms of control to limit and contain God's presence and human access.[1]

The twelfth century saw the nascence of a profound devotional and liturgical observance of matter's potential to manifest God, and of matter's promise of divine redemption. Beginning in the twelfth century, within several different religious communities one begins to notice expressions, both in theory and praxis, of rejoicing in the potential for divine access offered by objects in the material world. The narrative I have constructed traces Christian perceptions of natural matter as potentially holy and suggests that matter's re-creation was celebrated through lush verdant imagery emphasizing initially the incarnation, and recognizing all the elements of the natural world as revelatory of God owing to Mary's part in re-creating the world. From this recognition came a new spiritual ideal of virginity in which enclosed women attained a fresh identity. Like Mary, they might give birth to Christ's presence through their practice of virtue. And thus they made their communities God-bearing. Through liturgy and devotion, they remade their communities into a reflection of the divine image. By the thirteenth century, fresh spiritual ideals emerged from new institutional structures in religious life. But a desire to make God visible in the material of the world remained. Enclosed by necessity owing to her sex, Clare sought to share Christ's material condition, his poor life, by adopting poverty. Her way of giving meaning and explaining the absolute necessity of this life for communities of virgins was to meditate on a tree that reflected in its branches Christ's impoverished material condition, a condition they shared as his virgin brides. Bonaventure, too, and even those in the order who disagreed with his policies, found meaning for this life by meditating on the branches of a tree. Transformation was possible. Matter could be made holy, made to reflect and mediate the divine, though the Franciscans disagreed on how this was so. The final phase in my reconstruction of this belief moved from meditational models to the material world itself as a site for speculation, for glimpsing God's presence. The Carthusians saw the material world—trees, gardens, rocks, flowers—as potentially manifesting God and thus attracting the meditative gaze. Casting one's eyes upon that world, one might find God manifested in its sundry objects.

---

1. Caroline Bynum, *Christian Materiality: An Essay on Religion in Late Medieval Europe* (New York: Zone Books, 2011); Dyan Elliott, *Proving Woman: Female Spirituality and Inquisitional Culture in the Later Middle Ages* (Princeton, NJ: Princeton University Press, 2004).

Although I have discussed only the incipience of this development among the Carthusians, by the later fifteenth century this final flowering would inspire the proliferation of praise for manifold material objects as the locus of the divine, including blood relics, animated statues, and sacramentals.[2]

Scholars of the religious life of the later Middle Ages have worked within two models of interpretation explaining the religious behavior of the period. One model sees the interiority of Christian women and men, the world denial of Marguerite Porete, for example, as a rejection of the material world as sinful and a source of suffering and distraction.[3] The other model interprets the interest in a suffering God as a cultivation of compassion and desire for imitation.[4] The emergence of a reverence for the re-created world as a central feature of Christian cult in the later Middle Ages challenges both of these models. My interest in the imaginative theology of re-creation offers an alternative understanding of later medieval devotion as embracing the material world as potentially holy matter, matter through which God was made visible. The material thrust of later medieval devotion and doctrine was the intellectual and emotional culmination of the cultural poetics I have described, a poetics that struggled and rejoiced in the problem and potential of God's having created, entered, and re-created the world. Later medieval Christian object-love should be regarded as a desire for access to a God whose presence had been promised, in material on earth and through the salvation of material in heaven.

Although I have limited my discussion to techniques and instructions developed by those who took religious vows, the theology of the world's re-creation wrought changes in the perception of the world, devotional changes in the lives of the laity and semireligious as well. Catherine of Siena, with whom I introduced this study, offers a powerful example of how a re-created world may have appeared outside of the cloister and chapter house. Throughout the *Dialogue,* Catherine described the work of God in the world, the marks of God's presence in the world, through natural manifestations. In their conversations, God explained divine presence in the world in terms of speculating on a tree, a river, or a garden. And though it was Christ's blood that watered the garden of the world, that fertilized the

---

2. Bynum, *Christian Materiality,* esp. 125–76.

3. See Joanne McGuire Robinson, *Nobility and Annihilation in Marguerite Porete's Mirror of Simple Souls* (Albany: SUNY Press, 2001); Caroline Walker Bynum, *The Resurrection of the Body in Western Christianity, 200–1336* (New York: Columbia University Press, 1995), 214–20.

4. See Gail McMurray Gibson, *Theater of Devotion: East Anglian Drama and Society* (Chicago: University of Chicago Press, 1989); Rachel Fulton, *From Judgment to Passion: Devotion to Christ and the Virgin Mary, 800–1200* (New York: Columbia University Press, 2005).

mantellate's vision of a great tree that connected humanity and divinity, she did not recommend an imitative suffering. Instead, she advised loving the material. God repeatedly acted in the *Dialogue* to instruct Catherine on perception, showing, revealing, illuminating, for her his presence in the world: "I have shown you, dearest daughter, that in this life guilt is not atoned for by any suffering simply as suffering, but rather by suffering borne with desire, love and contrition of heart. The value is not in the suffering but in the soul's desire."[5] Continuing to discuss the mechanics of proper love, God explained to her that divine understanding begins with knowledge of the self. Through self-examination, one came to understand the world as a new creation: "I willed to create you anew (*ricreare*) in grace. So I washed you and made you a new creation (*ricreati*) in the blood that my only-begotten son poured out with such burning love" (Catherine of Siena, *Il dialogo*, 4, p. 7; Noffke, 29). The crucifixion of Christ acted on the world, so that "God became human and [humanity was] made divine" (*Il dialogo*, 13, p. 37; Noffke, 50.).

Suffusing her imagination with images of trees, gardens, rivers, thorns, and flowers, God repeatedly showed Catherine his presence in the material of the world, asking: "Can you see?" (Catherine of Siena, *Il dialogo*, 15, p. 42; Noffke, 53). *Manifestare*—the word recurs throughout Catherine's works.[6] For Catherine, God manifested himself in the world's matter through his blood, but also through more ordinary objects like trees and rivers. For her, blood manifested God's love in the material world, and that divine love of the material, that divine being in material, must be returned in kind.[7] Catherine thus instructed her disciples not in suffering but in seeing, in sensing, God's presence in the physical world. "The love God had for his creature," she taught, "was so strong that he was moved to draw us to himself, and to give our very selves his own image and likeness so that we might enjoy him and taste him, and thus participate in his eternal beauty." The whole world was God's creature, to whom he showed such affectionate love that he drew it to himself, enveloping and transforming the whole through love,

---

5. Catherine of Siena, *Il dialogo della divina provvidenza ovvero libro della divina dottrina*, ed. Giuliana Cavallini (Rome: Edizioni Cateriniane, 1968), 4, p. 6; *Catherine of Siena, The Dialogue*, trans. Suzanne Noffke (Mahwah, NJ: Paulist Press, 1980), 29 (hereafter cited parenthetically in the text in abbreviated form).

6. Four hundred times, to be exact. See Jane Tylus, *Reclaiming Catherine of Siena: Literacy, Literature and the Signs of Others* (Chicago: University of Chicago Press, 2009), 174–79.

7. On Catherine's blood devotion, see Caroline Bynum, *Wonderful Blood* (Philadelphia: University of Pennsylvania Press, 2007); her reading of the depiction in Paris, Bibliothèque Nationale, MS All. 34 of Catherine flagellating herself before a bleeding crucifix, with blood splashing into the air in drips and streams (fol. 4v) suggests multivalence in meanings of blood piety (Bynum, *Wonderful Blood*, 154).

so that "God is not hidden from us; or rather, at first he was hidden from our coarse natures, before the Word, only Son of God became incarnate, but when he wanted to become our brother, he dressed himself in the coarseness of our humanity, and so made himself manifest to us."[8] Catherine understood the incarnation as an act of love that re-created the world so that God was manifest—in trees, in blood, in love. It was a world shared by another unschooled visionary, Margery Kempe, who was compelled to weep at the manifestations of God's presence she so routinely encountered:

> And sumtyme, whan sche saw the crucyfyx, er yf sche sey a man had a wownde er a best whethyr it wer, er yyf a man bett a childe befor hir, er smet an hors er another best wyth a whippe, yyf sche myth sen it er heryn it, hir thowt sche saw owyr Lord be betyn er wowndyd, lyk als sche saw in the man er in the best.[9]

Properly seen and loved, each and every fragment of creation contained the whole story of the incarnation of divinity and the salvation of materiality. Close attention to the doctrine of God's re-creation of the world suggests that the material thrust of the period's characteristic forms of devotion were far more considered than previous accounts have allowed.

Each tiny fragment of creation, when perceived according to the theology of re-creation, contained a potential mode of divine becoming, of transformation, of hope. The thousands of shards of ordinary wood circulating throughout Europe and purporting to be relics of the true cross truly were, when seen with believing eyes, manifestations of divinity, so that not only did these wooden splinters contain the whole tree of the cross, but so did each tree, every tree. They were fragments of a wood that continued to send out shoots in the created world, unsevered from the Creator who had implanted his divinity there through crucifixion. The magnificent gold and jewel-encrusted reliquaries that displayed the tiny splinters speak of the willingness, the desire, to see the whole world as manifesting God's presence. For example, at the Benedictine abbey of Zwiefalten a reliquary designed by a local goldsmith named Ulrich took the shape of a book at the center

---

8. *Le lettere di S. Caterina da Siena, ridotte a miglior lezione,* ed. Niccolò Tommaseo (Florence: G. Bargera, 1860); trans. Suzanne Noffke, in *The Letters of Catherine of Siena* (Tempe: Arizona Center for Medieval and Renaissance Studies, 2008), Letter 108, pp. 211–12.

9. *The Book of Margery Kempe,* ed. Lynne Staley (Kalamazoo, MI: Medieval Institute Publication, 1996), 1.28.1585–87; trans. Liz Herbert McAvoy, in *The Book of Margery Kempe: An Abridged Translation* (Cambridge: Brewer, 2003), 37: "And sometimes if she saw the crucifix, or if she saw a man or animal had a wound, whichever it were, or if a man beat a child in front of her or whipped a horse or any other animal, if she were to see or hear it, she thought she saw our Lord being beaten or wounded, just as she witnessed it in the man or the animal."

of which was a small double-armed cross housing a shard of the true cross (fig. conclusion 1). The *Zwiefalten Chronicle* explained that although only the most precious wood of the cross could be seen on display in this reliquary, within it lay an additional relic from Christ's manger, thus increasing its potency by connecting material remains from Christ's nativity with those from his crucifixion.[10] Four enamel medallions on the periphery of the oblong rectangular reliquary depict Christ's head, two hands, and feet.[11] At the center, where his body would be expected, was the window that displayed the wood of the cross, so that Ulrich, and all the pilgrims who flocked to view the relics, equated the body of Christ in its earthly presence with the fragments of wood contained on the exterior and hidden in the interior of the gilded box. The material world manifested the body of God for those trained to see it that way.

The possibilities of the re-created world threatened, just as they comforted. The world as God's body was a tremulous place. Not every object in the natural world manifested God's presence; but speculation unleashed the possibility that every object *might* do so. Denial of God's natural presence thus came in many forms. Marguerite Porete and Nicholas of Cusa sought to encounter a wholly other God who could be attained only through the rejection of material, of words, of representations. Lollards and Hussites adamantly opposed the use of devotional images other than the Eucharist and unembellished crosses. The papal chancery increasingly policed miracle procedure, while theologians limited, through physiological theory and Aristotelian terminology, rationale for material change. Matter that might at any moment body forth an eternal God was suspect. And yet the defining principle of Christian theology was God's sometime intersection with created matter. That theology licensed the desire to experience God in material forms, to identify God in the things of creation.[12]

For this reason, because of the insistence and desire to experience God in the world, divinity would continue to materialize, making matter holy in spite of episcopal attempts to control such transformations. Writing in 1670, a Carthusian lay brother, François Gentil, provided a dim memorial of late

10. On the Chronicle, see Luitpold Wallach et al., Die Zwiefalter Chroniken Ortleibs und Bertholds, 2nd ed. (Sigmaringen: Schwäbische Chroniken der Stauferzeit, 1978); Herrad Spilling, Sanctarum reliquiarum pignera gloriosa: Quellen zur Geschichte des Reliquienschatzes der Benediktinerabtei Zwiefalten (Bad Buchau: Federsee Verlag, 1992). On the visibility of relics contained in cross reliquaries, see Cynthia Hahn, Strange Beauty: Issues in the Making and Meaning of Reliquaries, 400–circa 1204 (University Park: Pennsylvania State University Press, 2012), 87–89.

11. For a description, see the catalog *Treasures of Heaven: Saints, Relics, and Devotion in Medieval Europe* (London: British Museum Press, 2010), 46.

12. On these efforts, see Bynum, *Christian Materiality.*

Figure C.1. Reliquary of the True Cross. Zwiefalten, Germany. Photograph courtesy of Rose Hajdu.

medieval efforts to see, and to make, matter holy. Gentil had begun collecting the wisdom he had gathered from his experiences cultivating the gardens of the Paris charterhouse of Vauvert. Compiling it in a treatise published in 1704 under the title *Le jardinier solitaire,* the Carthusian's instructions for cultivation demonstrate a very different valuation of the material world than the one I have characterized as belonging to a later medieval perception of holy matter.[13] The extensive gardening tract records in exhaustive detail the technical wisdom amassed in centuries of Carthusian gardening practices, ranging from the most basic planting and grafting procedures to highly scientific accounts of soil acidity and regional climactic variations. Gentil recommends gardening not for the spiritual insight it offers, or for the experience of salvation in the material world. Although he reflects favorably on the "religious sentiments" that gardening inspires, he notes that it is most worthwhile as a meditational break, a means of resting the mind from its contemplative work, and he frames his treatise as knowledge imparting, as a compendium of facts that he has learned about the plants of the physical world.[14]

As the Carthusians were well known internationally for their gardening practices, Gentil's treatise received instant acclaim in Europe and America. Reprinted dozens of times in France, and considerably expanded to include advice on other European soils, the work appeared in two different English translations in London in 1706. Contained in them, and buried among the specialized horticultural minutiae, is a solitary trace of the speculatory practice of later medieval Christianity. After discussing dozens of flowers, when and where best to plant each, how properly to cultivate them for longevity, beauty, diet, shade, and whatever other characteristics the gardener fancies, the author paused at the passion flower whereupon he launched into an entirely uncharacteristic digression on Christ's passion:

> This plant cannot be thought other than a miracle, seeing as it bears a flower on which God has been pleased to imprint the chief mysteries of the Passion and Death of our Blessed Savior. All that behold cannot but be astonished to consider how't was possible that torments should be represented to us on a flower.[15]

---

13. François Gentil and Louis Liger, *Le jardinier solitaire: The Solitary Carthusian Gard'ner* (London: B. Tooke, 1706).

14. Dennis Martin, "Cultivating Cult: A Down-to-Earth View of Carthusian Gardening," in *Liber amicorum James Hogg, Kartäuserforschung 1970–2006,* ed. James Hogg, and Meta Niederkorn-Bruck (Salzburg: Institut für Anglistik und Amerikanistik, 2008), 83.

15. Gentil and Liger, *Le jardinier solitaire,* 374.

All who gaze upon the flower, the treatise insisted, were swept into a divine moment of contemplation, for the flower itself, growing up from the very soil of the earth, bore the imprint of the mysteries of the passion and death of Christ. The spiky leaves conveyed the lance that pierced his side; its thorns were the crown worn by the Savior; its stamen, the very nails that bound his flesh to wood. The whole flower was a material manifestation of a world rendered anew by Christ's passion, of a world redesigned to reflect and contain the continuing presence of Christ. And after his brief paragraph of impassioned paean to the flower's analogical resemblances, to this burst of divine presence on the surface of the material earth, the author returned immediately to his steady prose wherein soil saturation has meaning only with regard to leaf-to-stalk ratio: "The passion flower will thrive well enough in all sorts of earth but better in moist than in light."[16]

By the seventeenth century, the Paris Carthusians at Vauvert had become one of the largest suppliers of fruit trees in Europe, exporting their plants to Poland, Germany, England, and Scandinavia.[17] Indeed, the vegetable matter outlived the charterhouse, the last cells of which were destroyed by revolutionaries in 1792. While two trees of each variety were transplanted to the Jardin des Plantes, the verdant lands of the former charterhouse were confiscated for use by the Jardin du Luxembourg. The architect Jean Chalgrin repurposed the nursery and vineyard of the charterhouse as a formal garden, one offering a broad perspective.[18] Perspective: he shaped the grounds to offer sight. But sight of what? From the palace at Luxembourg one could look out across the prim gardens to the Paris observatory, where one might train one's eyes skyward to count the stars, to decipher patterns, to predict weather. There was a great deal of speculation in these acts, observing in order to see certainties, to find pleasure, and to profit—all acts of knowing the world correctly as a fixed place, unyielding to God or the human imagination.

---

16. Ibid., 374–75.

17. Barbara Trimmel, "Der einsiedlerische Gärtner: Das Lehrbuch der Gartenbaukunst des Dom François le Gentil aus der Kartause Vauvert," in *Liber Amicorum James Hogg, Kartäuserforschung 1970–2006,* ed. James Hogg and Meta Niederkorn-Bruck (Salzburg: Institut für Anglistik und Amerikanistik, 2008), 175.

18. Pauline Delafon, *Mémoire du Luxembourg: Du jardin des chartreux au jardin du Sénat* (Paris: Beau Livre, 2004).

BIBLIOGRAPHY

Primary Sources

Adam of Dryburgh. *De quadripertito exercitio cellae.* PL 153:799–884.

Anselm of Canterbury. *The Prayers and Meditations of Saint Anselm, with the Proslogion.* Trans. Benedicta Ward. Harmondsworth, UK: Penguin, 1973.

———. *S. Anselmi Cantuariensis archepiscopi opera omnia.* Ed. F. S. Schmitt. 6 vols. Edinburgh: Thomas Nelson and Sons, 1946–61.

Armstrong, Regis J., ed. and trans. *The Lady: Clare of Assisi: Early Documents.* Rev. ed. Hyde Park, NY: New City Press, 2005.

Armstrong, Regis J., Wayne Hellman, and William J. Short, eds. *Francis of Assisi: Early Documents.* 4 vols. Hyde Park, NY: New City Press, 1999–2002.

Bartholomew of Pisa. *De conformitate vitae beati Francisci ad vitam Domini Iesu.* In *Analecta Franciscana,* vols. 4–5, ed. B. Albizzi. Rome: Typographia Collegii S. Bonaventurae, 1912.

Bernard of Clairvaux. *On the Song of Songs.* Trans. Killian Walsh. 4 vols. Kalamazoo, MI: Cistercian Publications, 1983.

———. *Sancti Bernardi opera.* Ed. Jean Leclercq. Rome: Editiones Cistercienses, 1957–77.

Bernard Silvester. *The Cosmographia of Bernardus Silvestris.* Trans. Winthrop Wetherbee. New York: Columbia University Press, 1990.

Bonaventure. *Bonaventure: The Soul's Journey into God, The Tree of Life, The Life of Saint Francis.* Trans. Ewert Cousins. Mahwah, NJ: Paulist Press, 1978.

———. *The Disciple and the Master: St. Bonaventure's Sermons on St. Francis of Assisi.* Ed. and trans. Eric Doyle. Chicago: Franciscan Herald Press, 1983.

———. *Legenda maior S. Francisci.* In *Analecta Franciscana,* 10:555–652. Quaracchi: Collegium S. Bonaventurae, 1926–41.

———. "A Letter to the Abbess and Sisters of Saint Clare in Assisi." In *Simply Bonaventure: An Introduction to His Life, Thought, and Writings,* trans. Ilia Delio, 185–86. Hyde Park, NY: New City Press, 2001.

———. *Lignum vitae.* In *S. Bonaventurae opera omnia,* ed. R. P. Bernardini et al., 8:68–86. Quaracchi: Collegium S. Bonaventurae, 1882–1902.

Catherine of Siena. *Catherine of Siena, The Dialogue.* Trans. Suzanne Noffke. Mahwah, NJ: Paulist Press, 1980.

———. *Il dialogo della divina provvidenza ovvero libro della divina dottrina.* Ed. Giuliana Cavallini. Rome: Edizioni Cateriniane, 1968.

De fructibus carnis et spiritus. PL 176:997–1006.

Exordium magnum ordinis Cisterciensis. PL 185:995–1198C.

Gilbert of Holland. *Sermones in canticum II.* PL 184:17C–22B.

——. *Tractatus VII ad Rogerum abbatem.* PL 184:276–81.

Guigo I. *Consuetudines.* PL 153:639–757.

Haimo of Hirsau. *Vita Willihelmi abbatis Hirsaugiensis.* Ed. Wilhelm Wattenbach. MGH SS 12:209–25.

Herrad of Hohenbourg. *Hortus deliciarum.* Ed. Rosalie Green, Thomas Julian Brown, and Kenneth Levy. 2 vols. London: Warburg Institute, 1979.

Hildegard of Bingen. "Epistola XXIII." In *Hildegardis Bingensis epistolarium,* 61–66. CCCM 91. Turnhout: Brepols, 1966.

——. *The Letters of Hildegard of Bingen.* Trans. Joseph Baird and Radd Ehrman. 3 vols. New York: Oxford University Press, 1994.

——. *"Ordo virtutum:* The Play of Virtues." In *Nine Medieval Latin Plays,* ed. and trans. Peter Dronke. Cambridge Medieval Classics 1. Cambridge: Cambridge University Press, 1994.

——. *Symphonia: A Critical Edition of the "Symphonia armoniae celestium revelationum."* Ed. and trans. Barbara Newman. 2nd ed. Ithaca, NY: Cornell University Press, 1998.

Honorius Augustodunensis. *Gemma animae.* PL 172:541–738.

——. *Speculum ecclesiae.* PL 172:807–1107.

Hübner, W. "The Desert of Religion." *Archiv für das Studium der neueren Sprachen und Literaturen* 126 (1911): 57–74.

Isidore of Seville. *Etymologia.* PL 82:73–728.

Jacopone da Todi. *The Lauds.* Trans. Serge Hughes and Elizabeth Hughes. New York: Paulist Press, 1982.

——. *Le laude.* Ed. Luigi Fallacara. Florence: Libreria Editrice Fiorentina, 1955.

Lettres des premiers chartreux. 2 vols. Paris: Éditions du Cerf, 1962–80.

Ludolphus de Saxonia. *Vita Jesu Christi e quatuor evangeliis et scriptoribus orthodoxis concinnata.* Ed. L. M. Rigollot, A. C. Bolard, and J. Carnandet. Paris: Palmé, 1865.

Marguerite of Oingt. *Les oeuvres de Marguerite d'Oingt.* Ed. and trans. Antonin Durafour, Pierre Gardette, and Paulette Durdilly. Paris: Belles Lettres, 1965.

——. *The Writings of Margaret of Oingt, Medieval Prioress and Mystic.* Trans. Renate Blumenfeld-Kosinski. Woodbridge, UK: Boydell & Brewer, 1997.

Osbert of Clare. *The Letters of Osbert of Clare.* Ed. E. W. Williamson. London: Oxford, 1929.

——. "Osbert of Clare, Prior of Westminster, to Adelidis, Abbess of Barking." In *Guidance for Women in Twelfth-Century Convents,* ed. Jocelyn Wogan-Browne and trans. Vera Morton, 15–49. Cambridge: D. S. Brewer, 2003.

Otloh of St. Emmeram. *Dialogus de tribus quaestionibus.* PL 146:59–134.

Sabatier, Paul, ed. *Actus Beati Francisci et sociorum ejus.* Paris: Fischbacher, 1902.

Seyfarth, Jutta, ed. *Speculum virginum.* CCCM 5. Turnhout: Brepols, 1995.

Suso, Henry. *Deutsche mystische Schriften.* Ed. Georg Hofmann. Düsseldorf: Patmos Verlag, 1966.

——. *Heinrich Seuses Horologium sapientiae.* Ed. Pius Künzle. Freiburg: Universitätsverlag, 1977.

——. *Henry Suso: The Exemplar with Two German Sermons.* Trans. Frank Tobin. New York: Paulist Press, 1989.

——. *Wisdom's Watch upon the Hours.* Trans. Edmund College. Washington, DC: Catholic University of America Press, 1994.

Thomas of Celano. *Vita prima S. Francisci.* In *Analecta Franciscana,* vol. 10, ed. Michael Bihl. Florence: Quaracchi, 1941.

Ubertinus de Casali. *Arbor vitae crucifixae Jesu.* Ed. Charles T. David. Turin: Bottega d'Erasmo, 1961.

——. "Tree of the Crucified Life of Jesus." In *Francis of Assisi: Early Documents: The Prophet,* ed. and trans. Regis Armstrong, Wayne Hellmann, and William Short, 146–203. New York: New City Press, 2001.

William of St. Thierry. *Cantici Canticorum priora duo capita brevis commentatio ex. S. Bernardi sermonibus contexta, ubi de triplici statu amoris.* PL 184:407–36.

Secondary Sources

Aers, David, ed. *The Powers of the Holy: Religion, Politics, and Gender in Late Medieval English Culture.* University Park: Pennsylvania State University Press, 1996.

Alberzoni, Maria Pia. *Chiara e il papato.* Milan: Edizioni Biblioteca Francescana, 1995.

——. *Clare of Assisi and the Poor Sisters in the Thirteenth Century.* St. Bonaventure, NY: Franciscan Institute Publications, 2004.

——. "Clare of Assisi and Women's Franciscanism." *Greyfriars Review* 17.1 (2003): 5–38.

——. "San Damiano nel 1228: Contributo alla 'questione clariana.'" *Collectanea Franciscana* 67 (1997): 459–76.

Allen, Hope Emily. "*The Desert of Religion:* Addendum." *Archiv für das Studium der neueren Sprachen über Literaturen* 127 (1911): 388–90.

Andenna, Cristina. "Chiara d'Assisi: Alcune riflessioni su un problema ancora aperto." *Rivista di Storia e Letteratura Religiosa* 34 (1998): 547–79.

——. "Chiara d'Assisi: La questione dell'autenticità del 'Privilegium paupertatis' e del Testamento." *Rivista di Storia della Chiesa in Italia* 51 (1997): 595–97.

Aniel, Jean Pierre. *Les maisons des chartreux: Des origines à la chartreuse de Pavie.* Geneva: Droz, 1983.

Armstrong, Edward. *Saint Francis, Nature Mystic: The Derivation and Significance of the Nature Stories in the Franciscan Legend.* Berkeley: University of California Press, 1973.

Armstrong, Regis J. "Starting Points: Images of Women in the Letters of Clare." *Collectanea Franciscana* 62 (1992): 63–100.

Arnold, Ellen. *Negotiating the Landscape: Environment and Monastic Identity in the Medieval Ardennes.* Philadelphia: University of Pennsylvania Press, 2013.

Asseldonk, Optatus Van. *Maria, Francesco e Chiara: Una spiritualità per domani.* Rome: Collegio San Lorenzo da Brandisi, 1989.

——. "'Sorores Minores': Una nuova impostazione del problema." *Collectanea Franciscana* 62 (1992): 595–634.

——. "Sorores Minores e Chiara d'Assisi a San Damiano: Una scelta tra clausura e lebbrosi?" *Collectanea Franciscana* 63 (1993): 399–421.

Astell, Ann. *Eating Beauty: The Eucharist and the Spiritual Arts of the Middle Ages.* Ithaca, NY: Cornell University Press, 2006.

——. *The Song of Songs in the Middle Ages.* Ithaca, NY: Cornell University Press, 1990.

Aston, Michael. "The Development of the Carthusian Order in Europe and Britain: A Preliminary Survey." In *In Search of Cult: Archaeological Investigations in Honour of Philip Rahtz,* ed. M. Carver, 139–51. London: University of York Archaeological Papers, 1993.

Baert, Barbara. *A Heritage of Holy Wood: The Legend of the True Cross in Text and Image.* Boston: Brill, 2004.

Baier, Walter. *Untersuchungen zu den Passionsbetrachtungen in der "Vita Christi" des Ludolf von Sachsen: Ein quellenkritischer Beitrag zu Leben und Werk Ludolfs und zur Geschichte der Passionstheologie.* Analecta Cartusiana 44. Salzburg: Institut für Englische Sprache und Literatur, 1977.

Bartlett, Robert. *The Natural and the Supernatural in the Middle Ages: The Wiles Lecture Given at Queens University Belfast, 2006.* Cambridge: Cambridge University Press, 2008.

Bartoli, Marco. "Chiara d'Assisi: Donna del secolo XIII." In *Chiara d'Assisi e il movimento clariano in Puglia: Atti del convegno di studi per l'VIII centenario della nascita di S. Chiara d'Assisi organizzato dal Centro di studi francescani della Biblioteca provinciale dei Cappuccini di Puglia,* ed. Pasquale Corsi and Ferdinando Maggiore, 15–32. Cassano delle Murge: Messaggi, 1996.

———. *Clare of Assisi.* Trans. Sister Frances Teresa. Quincy, IL: Franciscan Press, 1993.

———. "Gregorio IX, Chiara d'Assisi e le prime dispute all'interno del movimento francescano." *Rendiconti della Accademia Nazionale dei Lincei: Classe di Scienze Morali, Storiche e Filologiche* 35 (1980): 97–108.

———. "La povertà e il movimento francescano femminile." In *Dalla "sequela Christi" di Francesco d'Assisi all'apologia della povertà: Atti del XVIII Convegno internazionale, Assisi, 18–20 ottobre 1990,* ed. Enrico Menestò, 221–48. Spoleto: Centro Italiano di studi sull'Alto Medioevo, 1992.

Bauerreiss, Romuald. *Arbor vitae: Der "Lebensbaum" und seine Verwendung in Liturgie, Kunst und Brauchtum des Abendlandes.* Munich: Neuer Filser Verlag, 1938.

Beach, Alison. *Women as Scribes: Book Production and Monastic Reform in Twelfth-Century Bavaria.* Cambridge: Cambridge University Press, 2004.

Beckwith, Sarah. *Christ's Body: Identity, Culture, and Society in Late Medieval Writings.* New York: Routledge, 1993.

Bedos-Rezak, Brigitte. "Medieval Identity: A Sign and a Concept." *American Historical Review* 105 (2000): 1489–1533.

Bell, David. *What Nuns Read: Books and Libraries in Medieval English Nunneries.* Kalamazoo, MI: Cistercian Publications, 1995.

Belting, Hans. *Likeness and Presence: A History of the Image before the Era of Art.* Trans. Edmund Jepcott. Chicago: University of Chicago Press, 1994.

Bennett, Jane. *Vibrant Matter: A Political Ecology of Things.* Durham, NC: Duke University Press, 2010.

Bériou, Nicole. "De la lecture aux epousailles: Les images dans la communication de la Parle de Dieu au XIIIe siècle." *Christianesimo nella Storia* 14 (1993): 535–68.

Berman, Constance. *The Cistercian Evolution: The Invention of a Religious Order in Twelfth-Century Europe.* Philadelphia: University of Pennsylvania Press, 2000.

Bernau, Anke, Ruth Evans, and Sarah Salih, eds. *Medieval Virginities.* Toronto: University of Toronto Press, 2003.

Bestul, Thomas. *Texts of the Passion: Latin Devotional Literature and Medieval Society.* Philadelphia: University of Pennsylvania Press, 1996.

Beutler, Werner. "Die beiden Brunozyklen der Kölner Kartause St. Barbara." In *Die Kartäuser und ihre Welt: Kontakte und gegenseitige Einflüsse,* 3:118–212. Analecta Cartusiana 62. Salzburg: Institut für Anglistik und Amerikanistik, 1993.

Biernoff, Suzannah. *Sight and Embodiment in the Middle Ages.* New York: Palgrave, 2002.

Bihel, S. "S. Franciscus fuitne Angellis Sexti Sigilli?" *Antonianum* 2 (1927): 57–90.

Biller, Peter, and Alistair Minnis, eds. *Medieval Theology and the Natural Body.* York: York Studies in Medieval Theology, 1998.

Binns, Alison. *Dedications of Monastic Houses in England and Wales, 1066–1216.* Woodbridge, UK: Boydell, 1989.

Bligny, Bernard. *Recueil des plus anciens actes de la Grande-Chartreuse, 1086–1196.* Grenoble: Imprimerie Allier, 1958.

———. *Saint Bruno: Le premier chartreux.* Rennes: Ouest-France, 1984.

Bodenstedt, Mary Immaculate. *The Vita Christi of Ludolphus the Carthusian.* Washington, DC: Catholic University of America Press, 1944.

Bolton, Brenda. "Mulieres Sanctae." In *Women in Medieval Society,* ed. Susan Mosher Stuard, 141–58. Philadelphia: University of Pennsylvania Press, 1976.

Boswell, John. *Christianity, Social Tolerance, and Homosexuality: Gay People in Western Europe from the Beginning of the Christian Era to the Fourteenth Century.* Chicago: University of Chicago Press, 2005.

Bouchard, Constance. "The Cistercians and the *Glossa Ordinaria.*" *Catholic Historical Review* 86.2 (April 2006): 183–92.

———. *Holy Entrepreneurs: Cistercians, Knights, and Economic Exchange in Twelfth-Century Burgundy.* Ithaca, NY: Cornell University Press, 1991.

Bourke, P. M. "The Treatment of Myth and Legend in the Windows of St. Neot's, Cornwall." *Folklore* 97.1 (1986): 63–69.

Boyer, Raymond. "The Companions of Saint Bruno in Middle English Verses on the Foundation of the Carthusian Order." *Speculum* 53.4 (1978): 784–85.

Bradley, Ritamary. "Backgrounds of the Title *Speculum* in Medieval Literature." *Speculum* 29 (1954): 100–115.

Brantley, Jessica. *Reading in the Wilderness: Private Devotion and Public Performance in Late Medieval England.* Chicago: University of Chicago Press, 2007.

Brooke, Rosalind. *Early Franciscan Government: Elias to Bonaventure.* Cambridge: Cambridge University Press, 1959.

Brown, Peter. *The Body and Society: Men, Women, and Sexual Renunciation in Early Christianity.* New York: Columbia University Press, 1988.

Brundage, James, and Elizabeth Makowski. "Enclosure of Nuns: The Decretal *Periculoso* and Its Commentators." *Journal of Medieval History* 20 (1994): 143–55.

Bücher, Karl. *Die Frauenfrage im Mittelalter.* 2nd ed. Tübingen: Laupp, 1910.

Bugge, John. *Virginitas: An Essay in the History of a Medieval Ideal.* The Hague: Martinus Nijhoff, 1975.

Burr, David. "Eucharistic Presence and Conversion in Late Thirteenth-Century Franciscan Thought." *Transactions of the American Philosophical Society* 74 (1984): 1–113.

——. *The Spiritual Franciscans: From Protest to Persecution in the Century after Francis.* University Park: Pennsylvania State University Press, 1999.

Burton-Christie, Douglas. *Word in the Desert: Scripture and the Quest for Holiness in Early Christian Monasticism.* Oxford: Oxford University Press, 1993.

Bynum, Caroline. *Christian Materiality: An Essay on Religion in Late Medieval Europe.* New York: Zone Books, 2011.

——. *Fragmentation and Redemption: Essays on Gender and the Human Body in Medieval Religion.* New York: Zone Books, 1991.

——. *Holy Feast and Holy Fast: The Religious Significance of Food to Medieval Women.* Berkeley: University of California Press, 1988.

——. *Jesus as Mother: Studies in the Spirituality of the High Middle Ages.* Los Angeles: University of California Press, 1988.

——. *The Resurrection of the Body in Western Christianity, 200–1336.* New York: Columbia University Press, 1995.

——. *Wonderful Blood: Theology and Practice in Late Medieval Northern Germany and Beyond.* Philadelphia: University of Pennsylvania Press, 2007.

Cadden, Joan. *Meanings of Sex Difference in the Middle Ages: Medicine, Science, and Culture.* Cambridge: Cambridge University Press, 1993.

Callaey, Frédégand. *L'idéalisme franciscain spirituel au XIVe siècle: Étude sur Ubertin de Casale.* Louvain: Bureau du Recueil, 1911.

——. "L'influence et diffusion de l'*Arbor vitae* de Ubertin de Casale." *Revue d'Histoire Ecclésiastique* 17 (1921): 533–46.

Cames, Gérard. *Allegories et symboles dans l'Hortus deliciarum.* Leiden: Brill, 1971.

Camille, Michael. "Seeing and Reading: Some Visual Implications of Medieval Literacy and Illiteracy." *Art History* 8 (1985): 26–49.

Campagnola, Stanislao da. *L'angelo del sesto sigillo e l' "Alter Christus": Genesi e sviluppo di due temi francescani nei secoli XIII-XIV.* Rome: Laurentianum-Antonianum, 1971.

Carruthers, Mary. *The Craft of Thought: Meditation, Rhetoric, and the Making of Images, 400–1200.* Cambridge: Cambridge University Press, 2000.

Casagrande, Giovanna. "Presenza di Chiara in Umbria nei secoli XIII-XIV: Spunti e appunti." *Collectanea Franciscana* 62 (1992): 481–505.

Caviness, Madeline. "Anchoress, Abbess, and Queen: Donor and Patrons or Intercessors and Matrons?" In *The Cultural Patronage of Medieval Women,* ed. June McCash, 105–54. Athens: University of Georgia Press, 1996.

——. "Another Dispersed Window from Soissons: A Tree of Jesse in the Sainte-Chapelle Style." *Gesta* 20 (1981): 191–98.

——. *Visualizing Women in the Middle Ages.* Philadelphia: University of Pennsylvania Press, 2002.

Chapman, James. *Saint Francis of Assisi and Giotto, His Interpreter.* Chicago: Faithorn, 1916.

Chazelle, Celia. *The Crucified God in the Carolingian Era: Theology and Art of Christ's Passion.* Cambridge: Cambridge University Press, 2001.

——. "Pictures, Books, and the Illiterate: Pope Gregory I's Letters to Serenus of Marseilles." *Word and Image* 6 (1990): 138–53.

Chenu, M.-D. "Nature and Man—The Renaissance of the Twelfth Century." In *Nature, Man, and Society in the Twelfth Century: Essays on New Theological Perspectives in the*

Latin West, ed. and trans. Jerome Taylor and Lester Little, 1–48. Chicago: University of Chicago Press, 1968.

Clough, Patricia. *The Affective Turn: Theorizing the Social.* Durham, NC: Duke University Press, 2007.

Coakley, John. "Gender and the Authority of the Friars: The Significance of Holy Women for the Thirteenth-Century Franciscans and Dominicans." *Church History* 60.4 (1991): 445–60.

Cohen, Adam. "The Art of Reform in a Bavarian Nunnery around 1000." *Speculum* 74.4 (1999): 992–1020.

Cohen, Jeffrey Jerome, ed. *Animal, Vegetable, Mineral: Ethics and Objects.* Washington, DC: Oliphaunt Books, 2012.

Collingwood, R. E. *The Idea of Nature.* Oxford: Clarendon Press, 1945.

Constable, Giles. *The Reformation of the Twelfth Century.* Cambridge: Cambridge University Press, 1998.

——. "Renewal and Reform in Religious Life." In *Renaissance and Renewal in the Twelfth Century,* ed. Robert Benson, Giles Constable, and Dana Lanham, 37–67. Toronto: PIMS, 1982.

Conway, Charles Abbot. *The Vita Christi of Ludolph of Saxony and Late Medieval Devotion Centered on the Incarnation: A Descriptive Analysis.* Salzburg: Institut für Englische Sprache und Literatur, 1975.

Cook, William. *Images of Francis of Assisi in Painting, Stone, and Glass from the Earliest Images to circa 1320 in Italy.* Florence: Leo S. Olschki, 1999.

Cooke, Kathleen. "Donors and Daughters: Shaftesbury Abbey's Benefactors, Endowments, and Nuns c. 1086–1130." *Anglo-Norman Studies* 12 (1989): 29–45.

Coppack, Glyn. *Christ's Poor Men: The Carthusians in England.* London: Tempus, 2002.

——. *Mount Grace Priory: North Yorkshire.* London: English Heritage, 1991.

Corrie, Rebecca. "The Antiphonaries of the Conradin Bible Atelier and the History of the Franciscan and Augustinian Liturgies." *Journal of the Walters Art Gallery* 55 (1993): 65–88.

Cousins, Ewert. "On the Humanity and Passion of Christ." In *Christian Spirituality: High Middle Ages and Reformation,* ed. Jill Raitt, Bernard McGinn, and John Meyendorf, 375–91. New York: Crossroad, 1987.

Cronon, William. "The Trouble with Wilderness; or, Getting Back to the Wrong Nature." In *Uncommon Ground: Toward Reinventing Nature,* ed. William Cronon, 69–90. New York: Norton, 1995.

Curschmann, Michael. "*Pictura laicorum litteratura?* Überlegungen zum Verhältnis von Bild und volkssprachlicher Schriftlichkeit im Hoch- und Spätmittelalter bis zum Codex Manesse." In *Pragmatische Schriftlichkeit im Mittelalter,* ed. Hagen Keller et al., 211–29. Munich: Fink, 1992.

Damiata, Mariano. *Pietà e storia nell'"Arbor vitae" di Ubertino da Casale.* Florence: Edizioni Studi Francescani, 1988.

Daston, Lorraine, and Fernando Vidal, eds. *The Moral Authority of Nature.* Chicago: University of Chicago Press, 2004.

Delafon, Pauline. *Mémoire du Luxembourg: Du jardin des chartreux au jardin du Sénat.* Paris: Beau Livre, 2004.

Delarun, Jacques. *Francis of Assisi and the Feminine.* St. Bonaventure, NY: Franciscan Institute, 2006.

Derbes, Anne. *Picturing the Passion in Late Medieval Italy: Narrative Painting, Franciscan Ideologies, and the Levant.* Cambridge: Cambridge University Press, 1996.

Devaux, Augustin. *L'architecture dans l'ordre des Chartreux.* Sélignac: La Grande Chartreuse, 1998.

Dinzelbacher, Peter, and Dieter Bauer, eds. *Frauenmystik im Mitttelalter.* Ostfildern: Schwabenverlag, 1985.

Douglass, Rebecca. "Ecocriticism and Middle English Literature." *Studies in Medievalism* 10 (1998): 136–63.

Doyle, A. I. "English Carthusian Books Not Yet Linked with a Charterhouse." In *"A Miracle of Learning": Studies in Manuscripts and Irish Learning; Essays in Honour of William O'Sullivan,* ed. Toby Barnard, Dáibhí Ó Crónín, and Katharine Simms, 122–36. Aldershot, UK: Ashgate, 1998.

Dreyer, Elizabeth. *Holy Power, Holy Presence: Rediscovering Medieval Metaphors for the Holy Spirit.* New York: Paulist Press, 2007.

Dronke, Peter. "The Composition of Hildegard of Bingen's *Symphonia.*" *Sacris Erudiri* 29 (1969–70): 381–93.

Duby, Georges. *Saint Bernard: L'art cistercien.* Paris: Arts et métiers graphiques, 1994.

Duffy, Eamon. *Stripping of the Altars: Traditional Religion in England, 1400–1580.* New Haven, CT: Yale University Press, 1992.

Duggan, L. "Was Art Really a Book of the Illiterate?" *Word and Image* 5 (1989): 227–51.

Dupriez, Flore. *La condition féminine et les pères de l'Église latine.* Montreal: Éditions Paulines, 1982.

Economou, George. *The Goddess Natura in Medieval Literature.* Notre Dame, IN: University of Notre Dame Press, 2002.

Ehrenschwendtner, Marie-Luise. "Creating the Sacred Space Within: Enclosure as a Defining Feature in the Convent Life of Medieval Dominican Sisters (13th–15th c.)." *Viator* 41 (2010): 301–16.

Elkins, Sharon. *Holy Women of Twelfth-Century England.* Chapel Hill: University of North Carolina Press, 1988.

Elliott, Dyan. *The Bride of Christ Goes to Hell: Metaphor and Embodiment in the Lives of Pious Women, 200–1500.* Philadelphia: University of Pennsylvania Press, 2012.

———. *Fallen Bodies: Pollution, Sexuality, and Demonology in the Middle Ages.* Philadelphia: University of Pennsylvania Press, 1999.

———. *Proving Woman: Female Spirituality and Inquisitional Culture in the Later Middle Ages.* Princeton, NJ: Princeton University Press, 2004.

Epstein, Steven. *The Medieval Discovery of Nature.* Cambridge: Cambridge University Press, 2012.

Ericksson, Carolly Louise. "Francis Conformed to Christ: Bartholomew of Pisa's *De Conformitate* in Franciscan History." PhD diss., Columbia University, 1969.

Esmeijer, Anna. *Divina Quaternitas: A Preliminary Study in the Method and Application of Visual Exegesis.* Assen: Gorcum, 1978.

Evans, Roger. *Sex and Salvation: Virginity as Soteriological Paradigm in Ancient Christianity.* Lanham, MD: University Press of America, 2003.

Fassler, Margot. "Mary's Nativity, Fulbert of Chartres, and the *Stirps Jesse:* Liturgical Innovation circa 1000 and Its Afterlife." *Speculum* 75 (2000): 389–434.

——. *The Virgin of Chartres: Making History through Liturgy and the Arts.* New Haven, CT: Yale University Press, 2010.

Felten, Franz J. "Frauenklöster und -sifte im Rheinland: Ein Beitrag zur Geschichte der Frauen in der religiösen Bewegung des hohen Mittelalters." In *Reformidee und Reformpolitik im Spätsalisch-Frühstaufischen Reich: Vorträge der Tagung der Gesellschaft für Mittelrheinische Kirchengeschichte vom 11. bis 13. September 1991 in Trier,* ed. Stefan Weinfurter, 189–300. Mainz: Selbstverlag, 1992.

——. "Verbandsbildung von Frauenklostern: Le Paraclet, Prémy, Fontevraud mit einem Ausblick auf Cluny, Sempringham und Tart." In *Vom Kloster zum Klosterverband: Das Werkzeug der Schriftlichkeit,* ed. Hagen Keller and Franz Neiske, 277–341. Munich: Fink 1997.

Fleming, John. *An Introduction to the Franciscan Literature of the Middle Ages.* Chicago: Franciscan Herald Press, 1977.

Frassetto, Michael, ed. *Medieval Purity and Piety: Essays on Medieval Clerical Celibacy and Religious Reform.* New York: Garland, 1998.

Frugoni, Chiara. *Francesco e l'invenzione delle stimmate: Una storia per parole e immagini fino a Bonaventura e Giotto.* Turin: G. Einaudi, 1993.

Früh, Margrit. "Bilderzyklen mit dem Leben des Heiligen Bruno." In *La naissance des Chartreuses,* ed. Bernard Bligny and Gérald Chaix, 161–78. Grenoble: Éditions des Cahiers de l'Alpe de la Société des Écrivains Dauphinois, 1986.

Fulton, Rachel. *From Judgment to Passion: Devotion to Christ and the Virgin Mary, 800–1200.* New York: Columbia University Press, 2005.

——. "Mary." In *Christianity in Western Europe, c. 1000–c. 1500,* ed. Miri Rubin and Walter Simons, 283–96. Cambridge: Cambridge University Press, 2009.

——. "Mimetic Devotion, Marian Exegesis, and the Historical Sense of the Song of Songs." *Viator* 27 (1996): 86–116.

——. "The Virgin in the Garden: or, Why Flowers Make Better Prayers." *Spiritus* 4.1 (2004): 1–23.

Gaillard, Bernard. "Marguerite d'Oingt." In *Dictionnaire de spiritualité: Ascétique et mystique, doctrine et histoire,* ed. Marcel Viller et al., 10:341. Paris: Beauchesne, 1980.

Gennaro, Clara. "Chiara, Agnese e le prime consorelle: Dalle 'Pauperes dominae' di S. Damiano alle Clarisse." In *Movimento religioso femminile e francescanesimo nel secolo XIII,* ed. Roberto Rusconi, La Società Internazionale di Studi Francescani, 167–91. Assisi: La Societa, 1980.

Gentil, François, and Louis Liger. *Le jardinier solitaire: The Solitary Carthusian Gard'ner.* London: B. Tooke, 1706.

Gibson, Gail McMurray. *The Theater of Devotion: East Anglian Drama and Society in the Late Middle Ages.* Chicago: University of Chicago Press, 1989.

Gilchrist, Roberta. "Unsexing the Body." In *Archaeologies of Sexuality,* ed. Robert Schmidt and Barbara Voss, 89–104. New York: Routledge: 2000.

Girard, Alain. "Les premières images de Saint Bruno." In *Saint Bruno et sa postérité spirituelle: Actes du colloque international des 8 et 9 octobre 2001 à l'Institut catholique de Paris,* ed. Alain Girard, Daniel Le Blévec, and Nathalie Nabert, 47–62. Salzburg: Institut für Anglistik und Amerikanistik, 2003.

Gougaud, Louis. "Muta praedicatio." *Revue Benedictine* 42 (1930): 168–71.

Grau, Engelbert. "Das Privilegium paupertatis der hl. Klare: Geschichte und Bedeutung." *Wissenschaft und Weisheit* 38 (1975): 17–25.

——. "Das Privilegium paupertatis Innocenz III." *Franziskanische Studien* 21 (1949): 337–49.

——. "Die Schriften der heiligen Klara und die Werke ihrer Biographen." In *Movimento religioso femminile e francescanesimo nel secolo XIII,* ed. Roberto Rusconi, La Società Internazionale di Studi Francescani, 195–238. Assisi: La Societa, 1980.

——. "St. Clare's *Privilegium paupertatis:* Its History and Significance." *Greyfriars Review* 6 (1992): 327–36.

Green, Monica. "The *De genecia* Attributed to Constantine the African." *Speculum* 62 (1987): 299–323.

Green, Rosalie. "The Adam and Eve Cycle in the *Hortus deliciarum.*" In *Late Classical and Medieval Studies in Honor of Albert Mathias Friend, Jr.,* ed. Kurt Weitzmann, 340–47. Princeton, NJ: Princeton University Press, 1995.

Gregg, Melissa, and Gregory Seigworth, eds. *The Affect Theory Reader.* Durham, NC: Duke University Press, 2010.

Griffiths, Fiona. *The Garden of Delights: Reform and Renaissance for Religious Women in the Twelfth Century.* Philadelphia: University of Pennsylvania Press, 2007.

Grundmann, Herbert. *Religious Movements in the Middle Ages.* Trans. Steven Rowan. London: University of Notre Dame Press, 1995.

Hahn, Cynthia. *Strange Beauty: Issues in the Making and Meaning of Reliquaries, 400– circa 1204.* University Park: Pennsylvania State University Press, 2012.

Hale, Rosemary. "*Imitatio Mariae:* Motherhood Motifs in Devotional Memoirs." *Mystics Quarterly* 16 (1990): 193–203.

Hamburger, Jeffrey. "Am Anfang war das Bild: Kunst und Frauenspiritualität im Spätmittelalter." In *Studien und Texte zur literarischen und materiellen Kultur der Frauenklöster im späten Mittelalter: Ergebnisse eines Arbeitsgesprächs in der Herzog August Bibliothek Wolfenbüttel, 24–26 Febr. 1999,* ed. Falk Eisermann, Eva Schlotheuber, and Volker Honemann, 1–44. Leiden: Brill, 2004.

——. *Saint John the Divine: Deified Evangelist in Medieval Art and Theology.* Berkeley: University of California Press, 2002.

——. "Speculations on Speculation: Vision and Perception in the Theory and Practice of Mystical Devotion." In *Deutsche Mystik im abendländischen Zusammenhang: Neu erschlossene Texte, neue methodische Ansätze und theoretische Konzepte,* ed. Walter Haug and Wolfram Schneider-Lastin, 353–408. Tübingen: Max Niemeyer Verlag, 2000.

——. *The Visual and the Visionary: Art and Female Spirituality in Late Medieval Germany.* New York: Zone Books, 1998.

Hamburger, Jeffrey, and Anne-Marie Bouché, eds. *The Mind's Eye: Art and Theological Argument in the Middle Ages.* Princeton, NJ: Princeton University Press, 2006.

Hamburger, Jeffrey, and Susan Marti. *Crown and Veil: Female Monasticism from the Fifth to Fifteenth Centuries.* Trans. Dietlinde Hamburger. New York: Columbia University Press, 2008.

Hammond, Jay. "Clare's Influence on Bonaventure." *Franciscan Studies* 62 (2004): 101- 18.

Harrison, Robert Pogue. *Forests: The Shadow of Civilization.* Chicago: University of Chicago Press, 1992.

Henderson, George. "*Abraham Genuit Isaac:* Transitions from the Old Testament to the New Testament in the Prefatory Illustrations of Some Twelfth-Century English Psalters." *Gesta* 26 (1987): 127–39.

Hindsley, Leonard P. *The Mystics of Engelthal: Writings from a Medieval Monastery.* New York: St. Martin's Press, 1998.

Hogg, James. *The Architecture of Hinton Charterhouse.* Salzburg: Institut für Englische Sprache und Literatur, 1975.

———. *Evolution of the Carthusian Statutes from the Consuetudines Guigonis to the Tertia Compilatio.* Salzburg: Institut für Anglistik und Amerikanistik, 1989.

———. *An Illustrated Yorkshire Carthusian Religious Miscellany: British Library London Additional MS 37049.* Salzburg: Institut für Anglistik und Amerikanistik, 1997.

———. "Unpublished Texts in the Carthusian Northern Middle English Religious Miscellany British Library MS Additional 37049." In *Essays in Honor of Erwin Stürzl on His Sixtieth Birthday,* ed. James Hogg, 1:241–84. Salzburg: Institut für Englische Sprache und Literatur, 1980.

Hogg, James, Ingeborg Hogg, and Francisco Zubillaga. *Las cartujas de Las Cuevas, Cazalla de la Sierra y Grenada; The Charterhouses of Las Cuevas, Cazalla de la Sierra, and Grenada.* Salzburg: Institut für Englische Sprache und Literatur, 1979.

Holdsworth, Christopher. "The Blessing of Work: The Cistercian View." In *Sanctity and Secularity,* ed. D. Baker, 59–76. Oxford: Oxford University Press, 1973.

Hollywood, Amy. *The Soul as Virgin Wife: Mechtild of Magdeburg, Marguerite Porete, and Meister Eckhart.* Notre Dame, IN: University of Notre Dame Press, 1995.

Holsinger, Bruce. *Music, Body, and Desire in Medieval Culture: Hildegard of Bingen to Chaucer.* Stanford, CA: Stanford University Press, 2001.

Hooke, Della. *Trees in Anglo-Saxon England: Literature, Lore, and Landscape.* Rochester, NY: Boydell, 2010.

Horner, Shari. *The Discourse of Enclosure: Representing Women in Old English Literature.* Albany: SUNY Press, 2001.

Hotchin, Julie. "Abbot as Guardian and Cultivator of Virtues: Two Perspectives on the *Cura monialium* in Practice." In *Our Medieval Heritage: Essays in Honour of John Tillotson for His 60th Birthday,* ed. Linda Rasmussen, Valerie Spear, and Diane Tillotson, 50–64. Cardiff: Merton Priory Press, 2002.

———. "Enclosure and Containment: Jutta and Hildegard at the Abbey of St. Disibod." *Magistra* 2 (1996): 103–23.

———. "Female Religious Life and the *cura monialium* in Hirsau Monasticism, 1080–1150." In *Listen, Daughter: The "Speculum virginum" and the Formation of Religious Women in the Middle Ages,* ed. Constant Mews, 59–83. New York: Palgrave, 2001.

———. "Images and Their Places: Hildegard of Bingen and Her Communities." *Tjurunga* 49 (1996): 23–38.

———. "Women's Reading and Monastic Reform in Twelfth-Century Germany: The Library of the Nuns of Lippoldsberg." In *Manuscripts and Monastic Culture: The Twelfth-Century Renaissance in Germany,* ed. Alison Beach, 139–89. Turnhout: Brepols, 2007.

Hourihane, Colum. *Looking Beyond: Visions, Dreams, and Insights in Medieval Art and History.* Princeton, NJ: Princeton University Press, 2010.

Howie, Cary. *Claustrophilia: The Erotics of Enclosure in Medieval Literature.* New York: Palgrave, 2007.

Iriarte, Lazaro. *Franciscan History: The Three Orders of St. Francis of Assisi.* Chicago: Franciscan Herald Press, 1982.

Jehl, Rainer. "Die Geschichte des Lasterschemas unde seiner Funktion." *Franziskanische Studien* 64 (1982): 261–359.

Johnson, Elizabeth. "Marian Devotion in the Western Church." In *Christian Spirituality: High Middle Ages and Reformation,* ed. Jill Raitt, 392–414. New York: Crossroad, 1988.

Johnson, Mark. *The Body in the Mind: The Bodily Basis of Meaning, Imagination, and Reason.* Chicago: University of Chicago Press, 1987.

Johnson, Penelope. "The Cloistering of Medieval Nuns: Release or Repression, Reality or Fantasy?" In *Gendered Domains: Rethinking Public and Private in Women's History,* ed. Dorothy Helly and Susan Reverby, 27–39. Ithaca, NY: Cornell University Press, 1992.

——. *Equal in Monastic Profession: Religious Women in Medieval France.* Chicago: University of Chicago Press, 1991.

Jónsson, Einar Már. *Le miroir: Naissance d'un genre littéraire.* Paris: Belles Lettres, 1989.

Jordan, Mark. *The Invention of Sodomy in Christian Theology.* Chicago: University of Chicago Press, 1997.

Jordan, William. "The Last Tormentors of Christ: An Image of the Jew in Ancient and Medieval Exegesis, Art, and Drama." *Jewish Quarterly Review* 78 (1987): 21–47.

Joyner, Danielle. "A Timely History: Images and Texts in the *Hortus Deliciarum.*" PhD diss., Harvard University, 2007.

Kampers, Franz. *Mittelalterliche Sagen vom Paradiese und vom Holze des kreuzes Christi in ihren vornehmsten Quellen und in ihren hervorstechendsten Typen.* Cologne: J. P. Bachem, 1897.

Karnes, Michelle. *Imagination, Meditation, and Cognition in the Middle Ages.* Chicago: University of Chicago Press, 2011.

Katzenellenbogen, Adolph. *Allegories of the Virtues and Vices in Medieval Art: From Early Christian Times to the Thirteenth Century.* Toronto: University of Toronto Press, 1989.

Kay, Sarah. *The Place of Thought: The Complexity of One in Late Medieval French Didactic Poetry.* Philadelphia: University of Pennsylvania Press, 2007.

Kelly, Kathleen Coyne. *Performing Virginity and Testing Chastity in the Middle Ages.* London: Routledge, 2000.

Kessler, Herbert. *Neither God nor Man: Words, Images, and the Medieval Anxiety about Art.* Freiburg im Breisgau: Rombach, 2007.

——. *Spiritual Seeing: Picturing God's Invisibility in Medieval Art.* Philadelphia: University of Pennsylvania Press, 2000.

Kieckhefer, Richard. *Unquiet Souls: Fourteenth-Century Saints and Their Religious Milieu.* Chicago: University of Chicago Press, 1984.

Kienzle, Beverly. *Hildegard of Bingen and Her Gospel Homilies.* Turnhout: Brepols, 2009.

——. "Hildegard of Bingen's Teaching in Her *Expositiones evangeliorum* and *Ordo virtutum.*" In *Medieval Monastic Education,* ed. George Ferzoco and Carolyn Meussig, 72–86. New York: Leicester University Press, 2000.

Kiser, Lisa. "The Garden of St. Francis: Plants, Landscape, and Economy in Thirteenth-Century Italy." *Environmental History* 8.2 (April 2003): 229–45.

Kiser, Lisa, and Barbara Hanawalt, eds. *Engaging with Nature: Essays on the Natural World in Medieval and Early Modern Europe.* Notre Dame, IN: University of Notre Dame Press, 2008.

Klapisch-Zuber, Christiane. *L'ombre des ancêtres: Essai sur l'imaginaire médiéval de la parenté.* Paris: Fayard, 2000.

Klein, Peter, ed. *Der mittelalterliche Kreuzgang: Architektur, Funktion und Programm.* Regensburg: Schnell & Steiner, 2004.

Knowlton, Edgar C. "The Goddess Nature in Early Periods." *Journal of English and Germanic Philology* 19 (1920): 224–53.

Knox, Lezlie. "Audacious Nuns: Institutionalizing the Franciscan Order of Saint Clare." *Church History* 69 (2000): 41–62.

——. *Creating Clare of Assisi: Female Franciscan Identities in Later Medieval Italy.* Leiden: Brill, 2008.

Kurmann-Schwartz, Brigitte. "Gender in Medieval Art." In *A Companion to Medieval Art,* ed. Conrad Rudolph, 128–50. London: Blackwell, 2006.

Kuster, Niklaus. "Clare's Testament and Innocent III's Privilege of Poverty: Genuine or Clever Forgeries?" *Greyfriars Review* 15 (2001): 171–252.

Ladner, Gerhard. "Medieval and Modern Understanding of Symbolism." *Speculum* 54.2 (1979): 223–56.

Lambert, Malcolm. *Franciscan Poverty: The Doctrine of Absolute Poverty of Christ and the Apostles in the Franciscan Order, 1210–1323.* St. Bonaventure, NY: Franciscan Institute Publications, 1998.

Lane, Belden. *The Solace of Fierce Landscapes: Exploring Desert and Mountain Spirituality.* New York: Oxford University Press, 1998.

Lastique, Esther, and Helen Rodnite. "A Medieval Physician's Guide to Virginity." In *Sex in the Middle Ages: A Book of Essays,* ed. Joyce Salisbury, 56–82. New York: Garland, 1991.

Latour, Bruno. *Reassembling the Social: An Introduction to Actor-Network Theory.* Oxford: Oxford University Press, 2005.

Lautenschläger, Gabrielle. "*Viriditas:* Ein Begriff und seine Bedeutung." In *Hildegard von Bingen: Prophetin durch die Zeiten; Zum 900. Geburtstag,* ed. Edeltraud Forster, 224–37. Freiburg: Herder, 1997.

Lazzeri, Zeffirino "Il 'Privilegium paupertatis' concesso da Innocenzo III e che cosa fosse in origine." *Archivum Franciscanum Historicum* 11 (1918): 270–76.

Le Bras, Gabriel. "Les chartreux." In *Les ordres religieux: La vie et l'art,* ed. Gabriel Le Bras, 562–653. Paris: Flammarion, 1979.

Leclercq, Jean. *The Love of Learning and the Desire for God: A Study of Monastic Culture.* Trans. Catherine Misrahi. New York: Fordham University Press, 1961.

Lefebvre, Henri. *The Production of Space.* Trans. Donald Nicholson-Smith. Oxford: Oxford University Press, 1991.

Le Goff, Jacques. "Wilderness in the Medieval West." In *The Medieval Imagination,* trans. Arthur Goldhammer, 47–59. Chicago: University of Chicago Press, 1988.

Leoncini, Giovanni. "Considerazioni sull'iconografia di san Bruno 'prototipo' del Certosino: Un'indagine sulle stampe dal XV al XVII secolo." In *San Bruno et la*

Certosa di Calabria: Atti del Convegno Internazionale di Studi per il IX Centenario della Certosa di Serra S. Bruno (Squillace, Serra S. Bruno 15–18 settembre 1991), ed. Pietro De Leo, 167–72. Catanzaro: Rubbettino, 1995.

Lester, Anne E. *Creating Cistercian Nuns: The Women's Religious Movement and Its Reform in Thirteenth-Century Champagne.* Ithaca, NY: Cornell University Press, 2011.

Lewis, C. S. *Studies in Words.* Cambridge: Cambridge University Press, 1960.

Lewis, Gertrud. *By Women, for Women, about Women: The Sisterbooks of Fourteenth-Century Germany.* Toronto: Pontifical Institute of Medieval Studies, 1996.

Leys, Ruth. "The Turn to Affect: A Critique." *Critical Inquiry* 37 (2011): 434–72.

Luongo, Thomas. *The Saintly Politics of Catherine of Siena.* Ithaca, NY: Cornell University Press, 2006.

Luxford, Julian. "Texts and Images of Carthusian Foundation." In *Self-Representation of Medieval Religious Communities: The British Isles in Context,* ed. Anne Müller and Karen Stöber, 275–305. London: LIT, 2009.

MacCormack, Carol. "Nature, Culture, and Gender: A Critique." In *Nature, Culture, and Gender,* ed. Carol MacCormack, 1–24. Cambridge: Cambridge University Press, 1980.

MacDonald, Alasdair, Bernhard Ridderbos, and R. M. Schlusemann. *The Broken Body: Passion Devotion in Late Medieval Culture.* Groningen: Egbert Forsten, 1998.

Mader, Ulrike. "Heiligenverehrung als Ordenspropaganda." In *Die Kölner Kartause um 1500: Aufsatzband,* ed. Werner Schäfke and Rita Wagner, 275–90. Cologne: Kölnisches Stadtmuseum, 1991.

Maleczek, Werner. "Das 'Privilegium Paupertatis' Innocenz III und das Testament der Klara von Assisi: Überlegungen sur Frage ihrer Echtheit." *Collectanea Franciscana* 65 (1995): 5–82.

Martin, Dennis. "Cultivating Cult: A Down-to-Earth View of Carthusian Gardening." In *Liber amicorum James Hogg, Kartäuserforschung 1970–2006,* ed. James Hogg, Alain Girard, and Daniel Le Blévec, 71–86. Salzburg: Institut für Anglistik und Amerikanistik, 2008.

Matter, Ann. *The Voice of My Beloved: The Song of Songs in Western Medieval Christianity.* Philadelphia: University of Pennsylvania Press, 1990.

McGinn, Bernard. *The Flowering of Mysticism: Men and Women in the New Mysticism, 1200–1350.* New York: Crossroad, 1998.

——. *The Harvest of Mysticism in Medieval Germany.* New York: Crossroad, 2005.

——. "Ocean and Desert as Symbols of Mystical Absorption in the Christian Tradition." *Journal of Religion* 74.2 (April 1994): 155–81.

McGovern-Mouron, Anne. "The Desert of Religion in British Library Cotton Faustina B VI, pars II." In *The Mystical Tradition and the Carthusians,* ed. James Hogg, 149–52. Salzburg: Institut für Anglistik und Amerikanistik, 1995.

McLaughlin, Megan. *Sex, Gender, and Episcopal Authority in an Age of Reform, 1000–1122.* Cambridge: Cambridge University Press, 2010.

McNamara, JoAnn. *Sisters in Arms: Catholic Nuns through Two Millennia.* Cambridge, MA: Harvard University Press, 1996.

McNamer, Sarah. *Affective Devotion and the Origins of Medieval Compassion.* Philadelphia: University of Pennsylvania Press, 2010.

Meier, Christel. "Zum Verhältnis von Text und Illustration im überlieferten Werk Hildegards von Bingen." In *Hildegard von Bingen, 1179–1979: Festschrift zum*

800. Todestag der heiligen, ed. Anton Brück, 159–70. Mainz: Selbstverlag der Gesellschaft für Mittelrheinische Kirchengeschichte, 1979.

Melville, Gert, and Anne Müller, eds. *Female "vita religiosa" between Late Antiquity and the High Middle Ages: Structures, Developments, and Spatial Contexts.* Berlin: LIT Verlag, 2011.

Mews, Constant, ed. "Hildegard, the *Speculum virginum* and Religious Reform." In *Hildegard von Bingen in ihrem historischen Umfeld: Internationaler wissenschaftlicher Kongress zum 900. Jährigen Jubiläum, 13–19. September 1998 Bingen am Rhein,* ed. Alfred Haverkamp and Alexander Reverchon, 237–70. Mainz: P. von Zabern, 2000.

——. *Listen, Daughter: The "Speculum virginum" and the Formation of Religious Women in the Middle Ages.* New York: Palgrave, 2001.

Meyer, Wilhelm. *Die Geschichte des Kreuzholzes vor Christus.* Munich: Verlag der k. Akademie, 1881.

Miller, Andrew Robert. "German and Dutch Versions of the Legend of the Wood of the Cross." PhD thesis, Oxford University, 1992.

Montgolfier, Bernard, J. P. Willesme, Isabelle Charles, and Christian Lambert, eds. *La Chartreuse de Paris: Museé Carnavalet, 12 mai-9 août 1987.* Paris: Musée Carnavalet, 1987.

Mooney, Catherine. "*Imitatio Christi* or *Imitatio Mariae:* Clare of Assisi and Her Interpreters." In *Gendered Voices: Medieval Saints and Their Interpreters,* ed. Catherine Mooney, 52–77. Philadelphia: University of Pennsylvania Press, 1999.

Moorman, John. *A History of the Franciscan Order: From Its Origins to the Year 1517.* Oxford: Clarendon Press, 1968.

Morrison, Karl. *I Am You: The Hermeneutics of Empathy in Western Literature, Theology, and Art.* Princeton, NJ: Princeton University Press, 1988.

Moulinier, Laurence. "Abbesse et agronome: Hildegarde et le savoir botanique de son temps." In *Hildegard of Bingen: The Context of Her Thought and Art,* ed. Charles Burnett and Peter Dronke, 135–56. London: Warburg Institute, 1998.

Mueller, Joan. *Clare of Assisi: The Letters to Agnes.* St. Bonaventure, NY: Michael Glazier, 2004.

——. *The Privilege of Poverty: Clare of Assisi, Agnes of Prague, and the Struggle for a Franciscan Rule for Women.* University Park: Pennsylvania State University Press, 2006.

Mussafia, Adolfo. "Sulla leggenda del legno della Croce.*" Sitzungsberichte der kaiserlichen Akademie der Wissenschaften* 63 (1860): 165–216.

Newman, Barbara. *God and the Goddesses: Vision, Poetry, and Belief in the Middle Ages.* Philadelphia: University of Pennsylvania Press, 2003.

——. *Sister of Wisdom: St. Hildegard of Bingen's Theology of the Feminine.* Berkeley: University of California Press, 1987.

——, ed. *Voice of the Living Light.* Berkeley: University of California Press, 1998.

——. "What Did It Mean to Say 'I Saw'? The Clash between Theory and Practice in Medieval Visionary Culture." *Speculum* 80 (2005): 1–43.

Newman, Martha. *The Boundaries of Charity: Cistercian Culture and Ecclesiastical Reform.* Stanford, CA: Stanford University Press, 1996.

——. "Labor: Insights from a Medieval Monastery." In *Why the Middle Ages Matter,* ed Celia Chazelle, Simon Doubleday, Felice Lifshitz, and Amy Remensnyder, 106–20. New York: Routledge, 2012.

Nimmo, Duncan. *Reform and Division in the Medieval Franciscan Order: From St. Francis to the Foundation of the Capuchins.* Rome: Capuchin Historical Institute, 1987.

O'Connell, Patrick. "The *Lignum vitae* of Saint Bonaventure and the Medieval Devotional Tradition." PhD diss., Fordham University, 1985.

Oliver, Judith. "A Bundle of Myrrh': Passion Meditation in French Vernacular Poems and Images in Some Liège Psalters." In *Tributes in Honor of James H. Marrow: Studies in Painting and Manuscript Illumination of the Late Middle Ages and Northern Renaissance,* ed. Jeffrey Hamburger and Anne S. Korteweg, 361–73. London: Harvey Miller, 2006.

Olson, Linda, and Katherine Kerby-Fulton, eds. *Voices in Dialogue: Reading Women in the Middle Ages.* Notre Dame, IN: University of Notre Dame Press, 2005.

O'Reilly, Jennifer. *Studies in the Iconography of the Virtues and Vices in the Middle Ages.* New York: Garland, 1988.

Ortner, Sherry. "Is Female to Male as Nature Is to Culture?" In *Woman, Culture and Society,* ed. Michelle Rosaldo and Louise Lamphere, 67–87. Stanford, CA: Stanford University Press, 1974.

Parisse, Michel. "Les chanoinesses dans l'Empire germanique." *Francia* 6 (1978): 107–27.

Pastan, Elizabeth Carson. "'And He Shall Gather Together the Dispersed': The Tree of Jesse at Troyes Cathedral." *Gesta* 37 (1998): 232–39.

Paulsell, Stephanie. "*Scriptio divina:* Writing and the Experience of God in the Works of Marguerite d'Oingt." PhD diss., University of Chicago, 1993.

Peterson, Ingrid. *Clare of Assisi: A Biographical Study.* Quincy, IL: Franciscan Press, 1993.

Pfau, Marianne Richert. "*Armonia* in the Songs of Hildegard von Bingen: Manifestations of Compositional Order." *Acta* 15 (1988): 69–84.

Potestà, Gian-Luca. *Storia ed escatologia in Ubertino da Casale.* Milan: Vita e pensiero, 1980.

Potter, Robert. "The *Ordo virtutum:* Ancestor of the English Moralities?" *Comparative Drama* 20 (1986): 201–10.

Powell, Morgan. "The Mirror and the Woman: Instruction for Religious Women and the Emergence of Vernacular Poetics." PhD diss., Princeton University, 1997.

——. "The *Speculum virginum* and the Audio-Visual Poetics of Women's Religious Instruction." In *Listen, Daughter: The "Speculum virginum" and the Formation of Religious Women in the Middle Ages,* ed. Constant Mews, 111–36. New York: Palgrave, 2001.

Prangsma-Hajenius, Angélique. *Le légende du Bois de la Croix dans la littérature française médiévale.* Assen: Van Gorcum, 1995.

Quinn, Esther. *The Quest of Seth for the Oil of Life.* Chicago: University of Chicago Press, 1962.

Rackham, Oliver. *Ancient Woodland: Its History, Vegetation, and Uses in England.* London: Castlepoint Press, 2003.

Raurell, Frederic. "La Lettura del Cantico dei Cantici al tempo di Chiara e la IV Lettera ad Agnese di Praga." In *Chiara: Francescanesimo al femminile,* ed. Davide Covi and Dino Dozzi, 188–289. Rome: Edizione Dehoniane, 1992.

Reeves, Marjorie. "The *arbores* of Joachim of Fiore." *Papers of the British School at Rome* 24 (1956): 124–36.

———. "The Originality and Influence of Joachim of Fiore." *Traditio* 36 (1980): 269–316.

Rice, Nicole. "Temples to Christ's Indwelling: Forms of Chastity in a Barking Abbey Manuscript." *Journal of the History of Sexuality* 19 (2010): 115–32.

Riggenbach, Rudolf. "Die Wandbilder des Kartause." In *Kunstdenkmäler des Kantons Basel-Stadt,* ed. Casimir Hermann Baer, 3:577–94. Basel: E. Birkhäuser & Cie., 1941.

Ringler, Siegfried. *Viten- und Offenbarungsliteratur in Frauenklöstern des Mittelalters: Quellen und Studien.* Munich: Artemis, 1980.

Ritchey, Sara. "The Place of Nature in Twelfth-Century Spirituality." *Religion Compass* 4 (June 2009): 595–607.

———. "Rethinking the Twelfth-Century Discovery of Nature." *Journal of Medieval and Early Modern Studies* 39.2 (2009): 225–55.

———. "Spiritual Arborescence: Trees in the Medieval Christian Imagination." *Spiritus* 8.1 (2008): 64–82.

Ritscher, M. Immaculata. "Zur Musik der hl. Hildegard von Bingen." In *Hildegard von Bingen 1179–1979: Festschrift zum 800. Todestag der heiligen,* ed. Anton Brück, 189–210. Mainz: Selbstverlag der Gesellschaft für mittelrheinische Kirchengeschichte, 1979.

Robinson, Joanne McGuire. *Nobility and Annihilation in Marguerite Porete's Mirror of Simple Souls.* Albany: SUNY Press, 2001.

Robinson, J. W. "The Late Medieval Cult of Jesus and the Mystery Plays." *Publications of the Modern Language Association* 80 (1965): 508–14.

Roest, Bert. *Order and Disorder: The Poor Clares between Foundation and Reform.* Leiden: Brill, 2013.

Rohrbacher, S. "The Charge of Deicide: An Anti-Jewish Motif in Medieval Christian Art." *Journal of Medieval History* 17 (1991): 297–321.

Rubin, Miri. *Corpus Christi: The Eucharist in Late Medieval Culture.* Cambridge: Cambridge University Press, 1991.

Rudd, Gillian. *Greenery: Ecocritical Readings of Late Medieval English Literature.* Manchester: Manchester University Press, 2007.

Rudolph, Conrad. *The Things of Greater Importance: Bernard of Clairvaux's "Apologia" and the Medieval Attitude toward Art.* Philadelphia: University of Pennsylvania Press, 1990.

Ruether, Rosemary Radford. *Sexism and God-Talk: Toward a Feminist Theology.* Boston: Beacon Press, 1983.

Ruh, Kurt. *Geschichte der abendländischen Mystik.* Munich: Beck, 1990.

Rusconi, Roberto. "The Spread of Women's Franciscanism in the Thirteenth Century." *Greyfriars Review* 12.1 (1998): 35–75.

Sabatier, Paul. "Le privilège de la pauvreté." *Revue d'Histoire Franciscaine* 1 (1924): 1–54.

Salih, Sarah. "Performing Virginity: Sex and Violence in the Katherine Group." In *Constructions of Widowhood and Virginity in the Middle Ages,* ed. Cindy L. Carson and Angela Jane Weisl, 95–112. Basingstoke, UK: Macmillan, 1999.

———. *Versions of Virginity in Late Medieval England.* Cambridge: Brewer, 2001.

Salter, Elizabeth. "Ludolph of Saxony and His English Translators." *Medium Aevum* 33 (1964): 26–35.

Sauer, Joseph. *Symbolik des Kirchengebäudes und seiner Ausstattung in der Auffassung des Mittelalters.* Freiburg: Herder, 1924.

Scarry, Elaine. *The Body in Pain: The Making and Unmaking of the World.* New York: Oxford University Press, 1985.

——. *Dreaming by the Book.* Princeton, NJ: Princeton University Press, 2001.

Schama, Simon. *Landscape and Memory.* New York: Knopf, 1996.

Sheingorn, Pamela. "The Virtues of Hildegard's *Ordo virtutum:* or, It Was a Woman's World." In *The "Ordo virtutum" of Hildegard of Bingen: Critical Studies,* ed. Audrey Davidson, 43–61. Kalamazoo, MI: Medieval Institute Publications, 1992.

Schipperges, Heinrich. *Healing Nature of the Cosmos.* Trans. John Broadwin. Princeton, NJ: Markus Weiner, 1997.

Schmidt, Margot. "Miroir." In *Dictionnaire de spiritualité: Ascétique et mystique, doctrine et histoire,* ed. Marcel Viller et al., 10:1290–1303. Paris: Beauchesne, 1980.

Schmidt-Görg, Joseph. "Zur Musikanschauung in den Schriften der hl. Hildegard von Bingen." In *Der Mensch und die Künste: Festschrift für Heinrich Lützeler zum 60 Geburtstage,* ed. Heinrich Lützeler, 230–37. Düsseldorf: Verlag L. Schwann, 1962.

Schmitt, Jean-Claude. "Écriture et image: Les avatars médiévaux du modèle grégorien." In *Théories et pratiques de l'écriture au Moyen Age: Actes du Colloque, Palais du Luxembourg-Senat, 5 et 6 mars 1987,* ed. Emmanuèle Baumgartner and Christiane Marchello-Nizia, 119–53. Paris and Nanterre: Centre de Recherches du Department de Français de Paris X, 1988.

——. *Femmes, art et religion au Moyen Age: Colloque international, Colmar, Musée d'Unterlinden, 3–5 mai.* Strasbourg: Presses universitaires Strasbourg, 2004.

——. "La culture de l'imago." *Annales: ESC* 51 (1996): 3–36.

——. *Le corps des images: Essais sur la culture visuelle au Moyen Age.* Paris: Gallimard, 2002.

Schmitt, Miriam. "Hildegard of Bingen: *Viriditas,* Web of Greening Life-Energy I." *American Benedictine Review* 50 (1999): 253–76.

——. "Hildegard of Bingen: *Viriditas,* Web of Greening Life-Energy II." *American Benedictine Review* 50 (1999): 353–80.

Schmitz, Philibert. *Historie de l'ordre de saint Benoit.* Maredsous: Éditions de Maredsous, 1942–56.

Schmucki, Octavian. *The Stigmata of Saint Francis of Assisi: A Critical Investigation in the Light of Thirteenth-Century Sources.* Trans. Canisius Connors. St. Bonaventure, NY: The Franciscan Institute, 1991.

Schreiner, Klaus. "Hirsau und die Hirsauer Reform: Spiritualität, Lebensform und Sozialprofil einer benediktinischen Erneuerungsbewegung im 11. und 12. Jahrhundert." In *Hirsau, St. Peter und Paul 1091–1991,* ed. Klaus Schreiner, 59–84. Stuttgart: Forschungen und Berichte der Archäologie des Mittelalters in Baden-Württemberg, 1991.

Schröder, Karl, ed. *Der Nonne von Engelthal Büchlein von der Genaden Überlast.* Tübingen: Literarische Verein, 1871.

Schulenburg, Jane Tibbets. "Strict Active Enclosure and Its Effect on Female Monastic Experience." In *Medieval Religious Women: Distant Echoes,* ed. John Nichols and Lillian Shank, 51–86. Kalamazoo, MI: Cistercian Friends, 1984.

——. "Women's Monastic Communities, 500–1100: Patterns of Expansion and Decline." *Signs* 14 (1989): 261–92.

Scillia, Charles. "Abbess Herrad of Landsberg and the Arbor Patriarcharum." *Proceedings of the Patristic, Medieval, and Renaissance Conference* 8 (1984): 35–42.

Sheldrake, Philip. *Spaces for the Sacred: Place, Memory, and Identity.* Baltimore: Johns Hopkins University Press, 2001.

Siewers, Alfred. *Strange Beauty: Ecocritical Approaches to Early Medieval Landscape.* New York: Palgrave, 2009.

Signori, Gabriela. *Maria zwischen Kathedrale, Kloster und Welt: Hagiographische und historiographische Annäherungen an eine hochmittelalterliche Wunderpredigt.* Sigmaringen: Thorbecke, 1995.

Simbeni, Alessandro. "Il *Lignum vitae Sancti Francisci* in due dipinti di primo trecento a Padova e Verona." *Il Santo* 46 (2006): 185–214.

——. "L'iconografia del *Lignum vitae* in Umbria nel XIV secolo e un'ipotesi su un perduto prototipo di Giotto ad Assisi." *Franciscana: Bollettino della Società Internazionale di Studi Francescani* 9 (2007): 149–83.

Sorrell, Roger. *St. Francis Assisi and Nature: Tradition and Innovation in Western Christian Attitudes toward the Environment.* New York: Oxford University Press, 1988.

Southern, Richard. *The Making of the Middle Ages.* New Haven, CT: Yale University Press, 1953.

Spilling, Herrad. *Sanctarum reliquiarum pignera gloriosa: Quellen zur Geschichte des Reliquienschatzes der Benediktinerabtei Zwiefalten.* Bad Buchau: Federsee Verlag, 1992.

Stahuljak, Zrinka. *Bloodless Genealogies of the French Middle Ages: Translatio, Kinship, and Metaphor.* Gainesville: University of Florida Press, 2005.

Stock, Brian. *The Implications of Literacy: Written Language and Models of Interpretation in the Eleventh and Twelfth Centuries.* Princeton, NJ: Princeton University Press, 1983.

——. *Myth and Science in the Twelfth Century: A Study of Bernard Silvester.* Princeton, NJ: Princeton University Press, 1972.

Stubblebine, James. *Assisi and the Rise of Vernacular Art.* New York: Harper & Row, 1985.

Sullivan, Lisa. "Workers, Policy-Makers, and Labor Ideals in Cistercian Legislation, 1134–1237." *Cîteaux: Commentarii Cistercienses* 40 (1989): 175–99.

Sweet, Victoria. *Rooted in the Earth, Rooted in the Sky: Hildegard of Bingen and Premodern Medicine.* New York: Routledge, 2006.

Taborroni, Andrea. *Paupertas Christi et apostolorum: L'ideale francescano in discussione (1322–1324).* Rome: Instituto Storico Italiano per il Medio Evo, 1990.

Tazi, Nadi, ed. *Keywords: Nature.* New York: Other Press, 2005.

Tellenbach, Gerd. *The Church in Western Europe from the Tenth to the Early Twelfth Century.* Cambridge: Cambridge University Press, 1993.

Thirsk, Joan, and H. P. R. Finberg. *The Agrarian History of England and Wales.* Cambridge: Cambridge University Press, 2011.

Thomas, Keith. *Man and the Natural World.* New York: Pantheon, 1983.

Thompson, Augustine. *Francis of Assisi: A New Biography.* Ithaca, NY: Cornell University Press, 2012.

Thompson, Margaret. *The Carthusian Order in England.* New York: Macmillan, 1930.

Thompson, Sally. *Women Religious: The Founding of English Nunneries after the Norman Conquest.* Oxford: Oxford University Press, 1991.

Trimmel, Barbara. "Der einsiedlerische Gärtner: Das Lehrbuch der Gartenbaukunst des Dom François le Gentil aus der Kartause Vauvert." In *Liber amicorum James Hogg: Kartäuserforschung 1970–2006,* ed. James Hogg and Meta Niederkorn-Bruck, 175–85. Salzburg: Institut für Anglistik und Amerikanistik, 2008.

Turner, Denys. *Eros and Allegory: Medieval Exegesis of the Song of Songs.* Kalamazoo, MI: Cistercian Publications, 1995.

Tylus, Jane. *Reclaiming Catherine of Siena: literacy, literature and the signs of others.* Chicago: University of Chicago Press, 2009.

Uebel, Michael. *Ecstatic Transformation: On the Uses of Alterity in the Middle Ages.* New York: Palgrave, 2005.

Vanderputten, Steven. *Monastic Reform as Process: Realities and Representations in Medieval Flanders.* Ithaca, NY: Cornell University Press, 2013.

Van Os, Henk. "St. Francis of Assisi as a Second Christ in Early Italian Painting." *Simiolus: Netherlands Quarterly for the History of Art* 7.3 (1974): 115–32.

Van Tongeren, Louis. *Exaltation of the Cross: Toward the Origins of the Feast of the Cross and the Meaning of the Cross in Early Medieval Liturgy.* Leuven: Peeters, 2000.

Vernarde, Bruce. *Women's Monasticism and Medieval Society: Nunneries in France and England, 890–1215.* Ithaca, NY: Cornell University Press, 1997.

Wallach, Luitpold, et. al. *Die Zwiefalter Chroniken Ortliebs und Bertholds.* 2nd ed. Sigmaringen: Thorbecke, 1978.

Watson, Arthur. *Early Iconography of the Tree of Jesse.* Oxford: Oxford University Press, 1934.

Watson, Robert. *Back to Nature: The Green and the Real in the Late Renaissance.* Philadelphia: University of Pennsylvania Press, 2006.

White, Hugh. *Nature, Sex, and Goodness in the Medieval Literary Tradition.* New York: Oxford University Press, 2000.

Wickham, Chris. *Land and Power: Studies in Italian and European Social History, 400–1200.* London: British School at Rome, 1994.

Williams, George. *Wilderness and Paradise in Christian Thought.* New York: Harper, 1962.

Williams, Michael. *Deforesting the Earth: From Prehistory to Global Crisis.* Chicago: University of Chicago Press, 2006.

Williams, Raymond. *Keywords: A Vocabulary of Culture and Society.* New York: Oxford University Press, 1983.

Wilmart, André. "La chronique des premiers chartreux." *Revue Mabillon* 16 (1926): 77–142.

Winston-Allen, Anne. *Convent Chronicles: Women Writing about Women and Reform in the Late Middle Ages.* University Park: Pennsylvania State University Press, 2004.

Wogan-Browne, Jocelyn. *Saints' Lives and Women's Literary Culture, 1150–1300: Virginity and Its Authorizations.* Oxford: Oxford University Press, 2001.

Wood, Jeryldene. *Women, Art, and Spirituality: The Poor Clares of Early Modern Italy.* Cambridge: Cambridge University Press, 1996.

Zadnikar, Marijan. "Die frühe Baukunst der Kartäuser." In *Die Kartäuser: der Orden der schweigenden Mönche,* ed. Marijan Zadnikar and Adam Wienand, 51–137. Cologne: Wienand, 1983.

Zimmerman, Albert, and Andreas Spear, eds. *Mensch und Natur im Mittelalter.* Berlin: Walter de Gruyter, 1991.

Zimmerman, Béatrice Aklin. "Die Nonnenviten als Modell einer narrativen Theologie." In *Deutsche Mystik im abendländischen Zusammenhang: Neu erschlossene Texte, neue methodische Ansätze, neue theoretische Konzepte,* ed. Walter Haug, 563–80. Tübingen: Niemeyer, 2000.

Ziolkowski, Jan. *Alan of Lille's Grammar of Sex: The Meaning of Grammar to a Twelfth-Century Intellectual.* Cambridge: Medieval Academy of America, 1985.

INDEX

Page numbers followed by letter *f* indicate figures.

actor-network perspective, 7n15
Adam (biblical character): dying, legends of, 20n48, 21; Hildegard on, 60–61, 71
Adam of Dryburgh, 36, 171–72
Adelidis (abbess of Barking), 32–33
Advent, liturgy of, 14
Aelred of Rievaulx, 15, 36, 117
affective devotion: Bonaventure and, 123–24, 125; Franciscans and, 160; women and, 7–8, 69, 70, 115, 117
Agnes of Prague, 92, 101, 101n36; Clare of Assisi's letters to, 93, 96–97, 100–111, 118; monastery of, Gregory IX and, 102–3, 105
agricultural labor: monastic ideal of, 15, 16, 25, 37–40; vs. women's labor, 34n42
Alan of Lille, 4, 42, 66–67
Alberzoni, Maria Pia, 91
Alexander IV, Pope, 118
Alheit of Trochau, 3, 10, 156–58
allegorical reading: Hildegard's liturgies and, 62, 64; *Speculum virginum* and, 43, 47
Amadeus of Lausanne, 14
Ambroise of Milan, 20
Amorbach, Jean, 166
analogical reading, *Speculum virginum*'s instruction in, 48, 52, 53
Andernach, abbey at, 29, 55
Angelo Clareno, 139, 154
Anselm of Canterbury, 13–14, 15, 69
architecture, Carthusian, 163, 190–95, 191*f*, 192*f*
Arnald of Sarrant, 149–50, 150n43
art: Bonaventure's *Lignum vitae* and, 112–14, 113*f*, 115, 125, 145, 147; Carthusian, wilderness images in, 166–70, 167*f*, 169*f*, 170*f*; created world as work of, Carthusians on, 181
Assisi: Basilica of Saint Francis in, 135n17, 143–44, 147. *See also* Clare of Assisi; Francis of Assisi

Augustine, St., 13, 17
Augustinian communities: manuscripts of *Speculum virginum* in, 29; women in, 26, 27

Baert, Barbara, 20
Barking, Benedictine house of, 32–33
Bartholomew of Pisa, *Book of Conformities,* 149, 150–53, 151*f*
Bartlett, Robert, 178n48
Basilica of Saint Francis in Assisi, 135n17, 143–44, 147
Basilica of Santa Maria Maggiore in Bergamo, 114n49
Benedictines: Clare of Assisi and, 94–95; monastic reform and, 26, 27, 56; women's communities of, 26, 33
Benedict XI, Pope, 141
Bergamo, Basilica of Santa Maria Maggiore in, 114n49
Bernard of Clairvaux, 14, 15, 52, 69, 70; admonitions against use of images, 36; on natural world, 39, 175; reading of *Song of Songs* by, 97, 98
Bernard of Silvestris, 4, 66
Bernards, Matthäus, 48n74
body: in doctrine of re-creation, 9; and female religious experience, 7–8, 54; of Francis of Assisi, 133, 134–36; God's, in images of natural world, 22; incarnation resonating in, 70. *See also* body of Christ; body of Mary; body of virgin(s)
body of Christ: in affective devotion, 8, 9; Bonaventure on, 121, 124; Clare of Assisi on, 103–4, 110, 118; efforts to visualize in images of natural world, 22; in Eucharist, 13; Francis of Assisi's incarnation in, 125, 126, 133, 143–44, 151; in Hildegard's liturgies, 64, 68, 73; *Lignum vitae* paintings depicting, 113*f*, 114, 147; Marguerite d'Oingt on, 161, 162; trees identified with, 20, 68, 121, 154, 158, 201; Ubertino on, 142, 144, 157

body of Mary: Clare of Assisi on, 104; in doctrine of re-creation, 10, 14, 43; as garden, 42, 71–72, 74; Hildegard on, 71–72, 75, 76, 104; natural images associated with, 14–15; *Speculum virginum* on, 42, 43; veneration of, 15

body of virgin(s): Clare of Assisi on, 96; as emblem of re-creation, 195; image of God in, 40, 41, 54, 73; as paradise garden, 33–34, 44–46; *Speculum virginum* on, 31–34, 40, 41, 42, 44–47, 51, 53–54, 89; wilderness compared to, 42

Bonaventure of Bagnoregio, 118–19; Angelo Clareno on, 154; Clare of Assisi and, 115, 116–17, 117n60, 118, 120, 122, 125; influence of, 127, 137, 141, 150; *Legenda maior,* 128, 130, 131, 132–33, 135n18, 137, 139; *Lignum vitae,* 23, 91, 93, 115, 118, 119–25, 137; on mental images, 115–16, 120; paintings based on, 112–14, 113*f,* 115, 125, 145, 147; philosophy of imagination, 133; tree images used by, 115, 116, 118, 119–21, 124, 137, 153, 155, 197

Boniface VIII, Pope, 141

book: of nature, 17; in tree of Jesse image, 49–50

Book of Conformities (Bartholomew of Pisa), 149, 150–53, 151*f*

Bouchard, Constance, 96n16

Bruno of Cologne, 16, 36, 38, 164–66, 172, 188

Bruno cycle, 166–69, 167*f,* 169*f*

Butler, Judith, 31n34

Bynum, Caroline, 3, 7, 8n21, 156n55

Cames, Gérard, 82

Carruthers, Mary, 10, 34

Carthusians: cell gardens of, 162, 184, 188, 190–95, 191*f,* 192*f;* cloister architecture of, 163, 190–95, 191*f,* 192*f;* and doctrine of speculation, 175–79, 181, 195, 197–98; early foundations of, 172–73; expressive devotion of, 162; founder of, 164–66; gardening practices of, 203–4; later (urban) foundations of, 173–74; monastic cells of, 163, 164, 171–72, 180, 182, 190; solitary meditations of, 162–63, 164, 171, 172–73, 188; wilderness ideal of, 16, 23, 163, 164–74, 180, 186–88, 190–95

Casagrande, Giovanna, 126n80

Catherine of Siena, *Dialogue,* 1–2, 198–200

Caviness, Madeline, 63

Celano, 129–31, 134–36

cell. *See* monastic cell

Chalgrin, Jean, 204

Charles VIII (king of France), 183

Chartres Cathedral: relics at, 15; *stirps Jesse* iconography at, 63

Chenu, Marie-Dominique, 4

Christ: life of, Francis of Assisi's life compared to, 143, 149–53, 151*f. See also* body of Christ; crucifixion; incarnation; material world, God's presence in; poverty of Christ

Cistercians: and Clare of Assisi, 96; and imageless devotion, ideal of, 35–36; monastic estates of, perception of the divine in, 37–38; readings of *Song of Songs,* 96, 96n16, 97–98; and sacred land tenure, 15, 16; *Speculum virginum* manuscripts in houses of, 29; veneration of Mary by, 15

Clare of Assisi, 91–112; Benedictines and, 94–95; and Bonaventure, 115, 116–17, 117n60, 118, 120, 122, 125; Cistercians and, 96; crucifixion as theological focus of, 93, 100, 106, 107, 108–9, 110; epistolary vs. hagiographical, 114, 125–26; factors shaping spirituality of, 93–94; Hildegard of Bingen compared to, 103–4; innovative meditation of, 92–93, 107–8, 115, 120; legacy of, 23, 91–92, 111, 114, 116, 125–26, 128, 139–40; letters to Agnes of Prague, 93, 96–97, 100–111; in *Lignum vitae* paintings, 113*f,* 114; mirroring trope used by, 92, 93, 100, 102, 106–9, 112; natural imagery used by, 93, 96, 106, 110; nuptial imagery used by, 98–100, 102, 105, 109–10; on poverty of Christ, 107–8, 111, 112; pursuit of poverty by, 23, 93–96, 99, 105, 110, 112, 197; *Song of Songs* and, 96–100; tree images used by, 100, 106, 107, 108–9, 110, 118, 153, 155; on virginity, 96, 100–105, 101n35

cloister, female: Hildegard's notion of, 57, 62, 64–66, 72, 73, 77; Mary's womb compared to, 72, 73, 77, 104–5; and new conceptions of incarnation, 10; as paradise garden, 45–46, 50, 62, 64–66, 78, 85; rules governing, 27–28

Comsographia, 66

Conrad of Hirsau, 37

Constance (queen of Hungary), 101

Constitutiones Hirsaugienses, 27

Coppack, Glyn, 194

cross: relics of, 20, 21, 200–201, 202*f. See also* tree of the cross crucifixion: Bonaventure on, 121, 122–23; Clare of Assisi on, 93, 100, 106, 107, 108–9, 110; devotional shift from incarnation to, 93; Franciscans' understanding of, 132; and incarnation, tree image linking, 155; Marguerite d'Oingt on, 160; and re-creation, 1, 3, 12, 93, 100, 107, 115, 160, 196; tree image in, 19–21; Ubertino on, 140. *See also* cross; tree of the cross

cura monialium (care of nuns), 26–27, 29, 30

Customs (Guigo), 190–93

desert: biblical references to, 171, 180; Carthusian monastic cell as, 180; use of term, 38n62, 165. *See also* wilderness

The Desert of Religion (poem), 18, 163, 184–89, 187f

Dialogue (Catherine of Siena), 1–2, 198–200

Dionysius, *Divine Names,* 141

Disibodenberg, monastery of, 56, 58

double monasteries, 26, 26n7, 27

The Dream of the Rood (poem), 20

Eberbach, abbey of, 29

Ebner, Christina, 156

Eckbert of Schönau, 117

Economou, George, 5–6

Elias, Brother, 92

Elizabeth of Hungary, 101n36

Ember week, 14

enclosure: Clare of Assisi on, 96; consecrated women and ideal of, 25, 27–28; Hildegard's ideal of, 59–60; as locus of daily incarnation, 9, 51; in Mary's womb, 72; *Speculum virginum* on, 22, 29, 51; and virginity, 28, 32, 51, 59–60. *See also* cloister, female; women, enclosed

Engelthal: community at, 3; Sisterbook of, 156

England, Carthusian foundations in, 173–74

Eucharist: doctrine of re-creation and, 9, 12–13; in Francis of Assisi's celebration at Greccio, 131, 196

Exaltation of the Cross, feast of, 20

Exemplar (Suso), 177

Fassler, Margot, 57n5, 60

Feast of Mary's Nativity, 14, 19

Florence, Santa Croce, tree of life fresco at, 146, 147

Florence, Santa Maria dei Monticelli, tree of life panel at, 112–14, 113f, 125, 146

Fourth Lateran Council of 1215, 12, 94

Franciscans: arrival in Germany, 101n36; Bonaventure and, 118–19, 137; Clare of Assisi's legacy and, 23, 91–92, 111, 114, 125–26, 128, 139–40; on crucifixion, 132; and doctrine of re-creation, 128, 144, 197; on God's presence in material world, 135–36, 197; on incarnation, 131; on love as transformative agent, 132, 133, 134, 141, 142; and Marguerite d'Oingt's style of meditation, 160–61; pursuit of poverty by, 131, 137; Second Order of, 114; Spiritual vs. Conventional, 137, 154; trees in devotional expressions of, 92–93, 127–28, 137, 138n23, 153–55; and tripartite division of world history, 138. *See also* Spiritual Franciscans

Francis of Assisi, 91; as *alter Christus,* 119, 131, 132–36, 139, 141, 143–44, 145, 155; as *alter Christus,* tree imagery and, 127, 128, 147, 149; Bonaventure on, 119, 125, 128, 130, 131, 132–33; as *Christus typicus,* 151; Clare of Assisi's exegesis compared to, 100; and female devotional communities, 94, 95; frescoes depicting life of, 145–49, 146f, 148f; Jesus envisioned as mother of, 143–44; life of, comparison with life of Christ, 143, 149–53, 151f; in *Lignum vitae* paintings, 113f, 114; on material world, God's presence in, 10, 129–30, 136; practice of poverty, 93; staging of nativity at Greccio, 130–31, 134n16, 196; stigmata of, 132–36, 143, 145; and tripartite division of world history, 138, 139, 141

Frederick II (Holy Roman Emperor), 101

Frederick the Fair of Austria, 173

Fulbert of Chartres, 14, 19

Fulton, Rachel, 69, 70

garden(s): of Carthusian monastic cells, 162, 184, 188, 190–95, 191f, 192f; in *Hortus deliciarum,* 80, 81, 88. *See also* paradise garden

gardening practices, Carthusian, 203–4

Gentil, François, 201–4

German lands: Franciscans in, 101n36; monastic reform efforts in 12th century, 25–27, 57

Gian Galezzo Visconti, 173

Gilbert of Foliot, 36

Gilbert of Holland, 15, 36, 38–39, 98

Gilbert of Swineshead, 36

Godfrey of Admont, 52

Grande Chartreuse, 164; pictorial legend of
foundation of, 166–69, 167*f*, 169*f*

Greenhill, Eleanor, 48n74

Gregory IX, Pope, 95–96, 99, 102–3, 105,
114, 125. *See also* Ugolino, Cardinal

Gregory the Great, 35n47

Guerric of Igny, 14

Guigo I, 171, 172, 180, 188; *Customs*,
190–93

Hamburger, Jeffrey, 177n46

Hammond, Jay, 117n60

Harding, Stephen, 15

Henry II (king of England), 173

Herrad of Hohenbourg, 37, 79; Hildegard of Bingen compared to, 78, 79, 81,
85–88; *Hortus deliciarum,* 57, 78–89, 83*f*,
86*f*–87*f*

Hildegard of Bingen: Clare of Assisi compared to, 103–4; at Disibodenberg, 56, 58;
doctrine of re-creation and, 56, 60, 62,
66; Herrad of Hohenbourg compared to,
78, 79, 81, 85–88; ideals of virginity and
enclosure, 59–60; imaginative theology
of, 73, 77–78; interpretation of salvation history by, 60–61, 63–64, 77, 81,
90; liturgical performances scripted by,
22, 56, 57, 60, 61–78, 89–90; on Mary's
eternal predestination, 53; merry band of
virgins of, 55; natural images in liturgies
of, 56, 62–64, 70–71, 72, 73, 77–78, 79,
89; *Ordo virtutum,* 61, 62–69, 70–71, 89;
public persona of, 58; rhetoric of reform
and, 89; at Rupertsberg, 58, 59; *Scivias,* 18;
Speculum virginum and, 55–57, 63, 70, 73,
78; *stirps Jesse* in liturgies of, 63–64, 71,
74–75; *Symphonia armoniae celestium revelationum,* 62, 70–78; theology of music,
60–62, 71–72; theology of re-creation,
56, 60, 62, 66, 67–68, 70, 71, 73–74,
76–77; theology of virginity, 56, 59–60,
61, 66–67, 77–78, 81

Hinton Charterhouse, 190, 191*f*

Hirsau, abbey of: and monastic reform, 27,
56; and *Speculum virginum,* 29–30, 56

Hohenbourg monastery, women at, 82, 83*f*,
84–85, 86*f*–87*f*

Hollywood, Amy, 7–8

Holsinger, Bruce, 72, 75

holy matter, 3, 23; Carthusians on, 182;
Clare of Assisi on, 105, 112; emergence
of concept of, 196–97; Francis of Assisi

and, 129–30, 136, 153, 155; Spiritual
Franciscans on, 128, 134, 141; tree as,
157–58; tree as image of transformation
into, 155; world as, medieval perception
of, 3, 11, 57, 158, 198, 201–4

Honorius Augustodunensis, 20–21, 37, 42;
Speculum ecclesiae, 80, 82

Honorius III, Pope, 95

Horologium (Suso), 176, 180

Hortus deliciarum, 57, 78–89; Hildegard's
liturgies compared to, 78, 79, 81; natural
images in, 78–81, 85; *Speculum virginum*
compared to, 78–79, 80–81, 85, 88–89;
trees in, 81, 82–83, 83*f*

Hugh of Grenoble, 164

Hugh of St. Victor, 75

Hugh of Valbonne, 161

Hussites, 201

images, devotional use of, 34–36, 35n47;
Bonaventure on, 115–16; monastic estates and, 36–39; women and, 35. *See also*
natural images

imagetext, premodern, 184–89, 187*f*

imagination: Bonaventure's philosophy of,
133; God's, created world as blueprint
of, 181; in monastic memory work, 34;
in process of knowing God, 116, 155,
175, 196; and re-creation of incarnation,
Ludolph of Saxony on, 182–83

imaginative theology, 8n20; of access to
God within material world, 8; of Hildegard of Bingen, 73, 77–78; on natural
phenomena, 23; of re-creation, 10. *See
also* re-creation, doctrine of

incarnation: Bonaventure on, 121–22;
Catherine of Siena on, 200; Clare of Assisi on, 107–8; and crucifixion, tree image linking, 155; enclosed women's work
as act of, 9, 34, 51, 63–64, 66, 67–68,
70, 73, 77; Eucharist and, 13; as ever-
recurring process, Ludolph of Saxony on,
182–83; female cloisters and new conceptions of, 10; Franciscans' understanding of, 131; of Francis in body of Christ,
125, 126, 133, 143–44, 151; Herrad's interpretation of, 81; Hildegard's interpretation of, 60–61, 63–64, 77, 81, 90; Mary
and, 14–15, 61, 195; monastic cell as vessel of, 184; music and, 60, 61–62, 71–72;
natural imagery associated with, 197; and
re-creation, 1, 3, 10, 12, 17, 57, 70, 71, 75,
78, 89, 144, 178–79, 195, 196; Renaissance and emphasis on, 11–12; *Speculum*

virginum and new theology of, 31–32, 41; Suso on, 178–79; virginity and, 31–32, 46, 47, 57, 60, 63–64, 73, 74, 77, 195
Innocent IV, Pope, 105, 114
Irenaeus, 20
Irimbert (abbot of Admont), 59
Isaac of Stella, 15
Isabelle of Valois, 173
Isaiah 11, 15, 19, 63. *See also* tree of Jesse
Isidore of Seville, 21–22

Jacopone da Todi, 149n40, 155
James della Massa, 153–54
Jean de Berry, *Très riches heures,* 166
Joachim of Fiore, 138, 138n23
Johannes Parsimonius, 30
Johannes Trithemius, 30, 48n74
John the Baptist, 180
John of Capella, 150n43
John of Fecamp, 69
John of Parma, 119, 154
Johnson, Timothy, 129n5
John Trittenheim, 62n26
Juniper, Brother, 92
Jutta (nun at Disibodenberg), 58

Karnes, Michelle, 134
Kempe, Margery, 200
Kienzle, Beverly Mayne, 60n17
Knox, Lezlie, 101

labor of the land: monastic ideal of, 15–16, 25, 37–40; vs. women's labor, 34n42
land. *See* labor of the land; monastic estates
Landuin (superior of Chartreuse), 165
Legenda maior (Bonaventure), 128, 130, 131, 132–33, 135n18, 137, 139
Leo, Brother, 92, 116, 117
Libellus de Nativitate Sanctae Mariae, 19
ligna: Franciscan use of imagery of, 112–14, 113f; shift from *virga* to, 93
Lignum vitae (Bonaventure), 23, 91, 93, 115, 118, 119–25, 137; influence of, 127, 137, 141, 150; paintings based on, 112–14, 113f, 115, 125, 145, 147
Little, Lester, 134n15
Little Book of Eternal Wisdom (Suso), 178
The Little Flowers of Saint Francis, 128
Lollards, 201
London Charterhouse, 190
Louis IX (king of France), 173
love: Catherine of Siena's *Dialogue* and, 199; as transforming agent, Franciscans on, 132, 133, 134, 141, 142

Ludolph of Saxony, 180, 195; *Vita Jesu Christi,* 163, 180–84, 185f

magistra, 27
Maleczek, Werner, 92n1
Marguerite d'Oingt: and Carthusian meditation, 163–64; *Pagina meditationum,* 159–61; *Speculum,* 161–62
Marguerite Porete, 198, 201
Marian commentaries on *Song of Songs,* 42–43, 97
Martin, Dennis, 193
Mary (Virgin Mother): in Bonaventure's meditation, 123; in Clare of Assisi's meditation, 104–5, 123; eternal predestination of, 19, 52–53; Herrad of Hohenbourg on, 84; Hildegard's liturgies on, 71–72, 73, 75–77, 104; and incarnation, role in, 14–15, 61, 195; Ludolph of Saxony on, 183; as mirror, 50–51, 77; natural images in descriptions of, 14–15, 52, 71–72, 74; and re-creation, doctrine of, 10, 13–15, 50, 53, 74; reliquaries of, 15; Renaissance and intense devotion to, 12; *Song of Songs* on, 42–43; *Speculum virginum* on, 42, 48–54; in tree of Jesse, 48, 49f, 50; and virtue of virginity, 31, 33; womb of, cloister compared to, 72, 73, 77, 104–5. *See also* body of Mary
material world, God's presence in: Carthusians on, 174–79, 181, 195, 197–98; Catherine of Siena on, 1–2, 199–200; Clare of Assisi on, 111; development of concept of, 12, 16–18, 22, 196–98; doctrine of re-creation and, 3–4, 8–9, 198–200; Franciscans on, 135–36, 197; Francis of Assisi on, 10, 129–30, 136; Hildegard's liturgical performances on, 89–90; Ludolph of Saxony on, 181; monastic land tenure as hermeneutics for, 15–16; monastic reformers on, 37; relics of the true cross and, 201; *Speculum virginum* on, 25, 35, 40–41, 46–47, 89; texts inviting exploration of, 34; training of imagination to recognize, 155; trees as emblems of, 3, 10, 21–22, 157–58; virgins' bodies as hermeneutics for, 31–32, 40, 41, 46–47, 53–54, 89; women's communities and theology of, 69–70. *See also* holy matter; re-created world
maypole, Suso's, 179
McGinn, Bernard, 157n57
McNamer, Sarah, 8, 32n35, 43n72, 69, 70, 110

meditation(s): Bonaventure's, 115–16, 119–25, 147; Clare of Assisi's, 92–93, 107–8, 115, 120; monastic, goal of, 34; solitary, Carthusians and, 162–63, 164, 171, 172; *Speculum virginum* on, 34–35; Ubertino's, 141–42; use of images in, 34–36, 35n47; use of trees in, 18, 119–21, 157; women and, 8, 35

Meditationes vitae Christi, 180

men, pastoral care of women *(cura monialium),* 26–27, 29, 30

Mews, Constant, 55

mirror, of the divine: Bonaventure on, 124; Carthusians on, 175, 179; Clare of Assisi on, 92, 93, 100, 102, 106–9, 112; Ludolph of Saxony on, 181; Marguerite d'Oingt on, 162; Mary as, 50–51, 77; natural world as, 16–17, 31, 35, 181; *speculum* texts and, 24, 40–41, 44; virgins as, 46–47

monastic cell, Carthusian, 163, 164, 171–72, 180, 182, 190; as desert, 180; equipment of, 190–93; gardens of, 162, 184, 188, 190–95, 191*f,* 192*f;* as manger, 182

monastic estates: labor of the land on, 15–16, 25, 37–40; as material image of paradise, 36–39. *See also* cloister

monastic reform, 12th-century, 25–27; and doctrine of re-creation, 89; natural imagery associated with, 57, 89, 93; and *Speculum virginum,* 25–28, 30; and use of images in meditation, 36

Monticelli altar panel, 112–14, 113*f,* 125, 146

Moulinier, Laurence, 66n40

Mount Grace Charterhouse, 190, 192*f,* 194

MS Additional 25042, Bruno cycle in, 168, 169*f*

MS Additional 37049, Bruno cycle in, 168

Mulvaney, Beth, 135n17

music, Hildegard's theology of, 60–62, 71–72

natura: as continuator of God's creation, 12th-century poets on, 66–67; vs. modern concept of nature, 9; in *Speculum virginum,* 30–31

natural images: Bonaventure's use of, 125; Catherine of Siena's use of, 199; Clare of Assisi's use of, 93, 96, 106, 110; in descriptions of Mary, 15, 52, 71–72, 74; in *The Desert of Religion,* 186, 187*f;* doctrine of re-creation and, 10; in Hildegard's liturgies, 56, 57, 62–64, 70–71,

72, 73, 77–78, 79, 89; in *Hortus deliciarum,* 78–81, 85; incarnation associated with, 197; monastic estates and, 36–39; rhetoric of reform and, 57, 89, 93; in *Song of Songs,* 39, 57; in *Speculum virginum,* 35, 42, 43–44, 110, 195; in Suso's meditations, 178; use in religious instruction of women, 88

natural world: doctrine of re-creation and new understanding of, 17–18, 22–23; as mirror of the divine, 16–17, 31, 35, 181; theology of, 12th-century interest in, 66–67

nature, medieval perceptions of: as immaterial, 4, 6, 9; vs. material world, 3, 9–10; vs. modern concept, 9; vs. re-created world, 6–7, 9–10; scholarship on, 4–6, 7

Neoplatonists, 175

Newman, Barbara, 8n20

Newman, Martha, 34n42

Nicholas of Cusa, 201

Nicola Acciaiuoli, 173

nuptial imagery: Clare of Assisi's use of, 98–100, 102, 105, 109–10; in *Song of Songs,* Cistercian interpretations of, 97–98

Odile, Saint, 84, 85

Odo of Châtillon, 164

On the Fruits of the Flesh and of the Spirit, 37

Order of Saint Clare, 111

ordo recreationis. See re-created world

Ordo virtutum (Hildegard of Bingen), 61, 62–69, 70–71, 89

Osbert of Clare, 32–33

Otloh of St. Emmeram, 37

Ottocar V (Styrian margrave), 173

Pacino di Bonaguida, altar panel by, 112–14, 113*f,* 125, 146, 147, 153

Padua, friary of, arboreal frescoes in, 147–49, 148*f*

Pagina meditationum (Marguerite d'Oingt), 159–61

paradise garden: Carthusian cell as, 172; female cloister as, 45–46, 50, 62, 64–66, 78, 85; Mary's body as, 42, 71–72, 74; monastic estate as image of, 36–39; virgin body as, 33–34, 44–46

Paris charterhouse at Vauvert, 203–4

Paul (apostle): and doctrine of speculation, 175; on natural world as mirror of the divine, 17, 31

performance: Francis of Assisi's celebration at Greccio as, 130–31, 134n16, 196;

Hildegard's liturgies as, 56, 60, 62, 64–65, 76, 88, 89, 196; of *Speculum virginum,* 30, 31, 32n35, 51; virginity as, 31n34, 32, 43n72

Peter Lombard, 18, 18n41, 175

Peter Olivi, 138

Peter the Chanter, 13

Philip of Harvengt, 42

Philip the Bold, 173

Pinder, Janice, 51n77

poverty: Clare of Assisi's pursuit of, 23, 93–96, 99, 105, 110, 112, 197; communities dedicated to, 23, 95, 111–12; Franciscans' understanding of, 131, 137, 140, 144, 145; practice of, as incarnation, 145; and transformation, 144; Ubertino's vision of, 140, 143, 144–45; and virginity, Clare of Assisi's understanding of, 100–105, 110

poverty of Christ: Bonaventure on, 122; Clare of Assisi on, 107–8, 111, 112; Ubertino on, 140

Powell, Morgan, 48n74

Premsyl Otokar I (king of Bohemia), 101

Pseudo-Hugh of St. Victor, 175

Rainaldo of Ostia, 96, 105

Raoul (provost of Reims), 38

Raoul le Verd, 164, 165

Raurell, Frederic, 96n16

re-created world *(ordo recreationis):* as blueprint of God's imagination, 181; vs. nature, medieval perceptions of, 6–7, 9–10; reverence for, emergence in later Middle Ages, 198. *See also* material world

re-creation, doctrine of, 1–4, 10, 12, 198; and Carthusian cell, 172, 174; and changes in perception of material world, 3–4, 8–9, 198–200; crucifixion in, 1, 3, 12, 93, 100, 107, 115, 160, 196; and Eucharist, 9, 12–13; Franciscans and, 128, 144, 197; and Hildegard's liturgical performances, 56, 60, 62, 66, 67–68, 70, 71, 73–74, 76–77; importance of, 2–3, 10, 23; incarnation in, 1, 3, 10, 12, 17, 57, 70, 71, 75, 78, 89, 144, 178–79, 195, 196; in Marguerite d'Oingt's *Pagina,* 159–60; Mary in, 10, 13–15, 50, 53, 74; and monastic land tenure, 15–16; monastic reform of 12th century and, 89; and natural world, new understanding of, 17–18, 22–23; origins of, 9, 12, 13, 22, 196; in *Speculum virginum,* 31–32, 40, 41–54; tree images and, 18, 19, 153, 155;

virginity in, 40, 57, 67, 195; women and, 8–9, 40, 41–54, 67–68

reform. *See* monastic reform

relics: of Mary, 15; of true cross, 20, 21, 200–201, 202*f*

Renaissance, theological innovation of, 11–12

Rheinbrohl, church of, 57

Rhineland, monastic reform efforts in 12th century, 25–27, 57

Richard of Springiersbach, 29

Richard of St. Victor, 175

Robert of Molesme, 15

Ruffino, Brother, 92

Rupert of Deutz, 42, 52, 70, 80

Rupertsberg, monastery of, 58, 59. *See also* Hildegard of Bingen

Saint Denis, abbey of, 63

Salih, Sarah, 31n34

San Damiano, community of, 91, 92, 94, 95; Bonaventure and, 116–17

Scivias (Hildegard of Bingen), 18

Selby, historian of, 36

Sergius I, Pope, 20

Siewers, Alfred, 7n15

Simbeni, Alessandro, 147n39

sisterbook(s), 157n57; of Engelthal, 156

solitude, Carthusian ideal of, 162–63, 164, 171, 172–73, 188

song, as incarnational act, Hildegard of Bingen's liturgies and, 60, 61–62, 71–72, 78

Song of Songs: Cistercian readings of, 96, 96n16, 97–98; influence on Clare of Assisi, 96–100; Marian commentaries on, 42–43, 97; natural imagery in, 39, 57; in *Speculum virginum,* 42–43, 44, 45; Ubertino's use of imagery from, 141

speculation, doctrine of, 175–79, 181, 195, 197–98; Carthusian instructional treatises on, 163, 180–89; *The Desert of Religion* on, 186; Ludolph of Saxony and, 183; Peter Lombard and, 18n41

Speculum (Marguerite d'Oingt), 161–62

Speculum ecclesiae (Honorius Augustodunensis), 80, 82

Speculum virginum, 22, 24, 25, 40–54; and analogical reading, instruction in, 48, 52, 53; circulation of, 100; Clare of Assisi's theology compared with, 93, 108, 110; dialogue between *magister* and *discipula* in, 35, 43–44; doctrine of re-creation and, 31–32, 40, 41–54; early manuscripts of, 48n74; function of, 40–41; on God's

Speculum virginum (Continued)
  presence in material world, 25, 35, 40–41, 46–47, 89; and Hildegard of Bingen, 55–57, 63, 70, 73, 78; *Hortus deliciarum* compared to, 78–79, 80–81, 85, 88–89; ideals presented in, 29; material world reflected in, 40, 89; on meditation practices, 34–35; monastic reform context of, 25–28, 30; natural imagery in, 35, 42, 43–44, 110, 195; and new theology of incarnation, 31–32; origins of, 29–30; *Song of Songs* in, 42–43, 44, 45; structure of, 30–31; tree of Jesse in, 48–50, 49*f*, 57; virgins of, Hildergard's virgins compared to, 55–56

Speculum vitae, 184–86

Spiritual Franciscans: Bonaventure's *Lignum vitae* and, 137; Clare of Assisi's legacy and, 111, 139–40; on holy matter, 128; and potential for human transformation, 132

stirps Jesse. See tree of Jesse

Suger (abbot of St. Denis), 63

Suso, Henry, 10, 163, 175–79, 184; *Exemplar,* 177; *Horologium,* 176, 180; *Little Book of Eternal Wisdom,* 178

Swineshead, abbey of, 36

Symphonia armoniae celestium revelationum (Hildegard of Bingen), 62, 70–78

Taddeo Gaddi, *Tree of Life,* 146

Tenxwind (*magistra* at Andernach), 29, 55, 56

Tertulian, *Treatise on the Incarnation,* 19

Theobald (archbishop of Canterbury), 33

Thomas Aquinas, 18

Thomas of Celano, 129–31, 134–36

Thorney, abbey of, 39

transubstantiation, doctrine of, 12–13

Treatise on the Incarnation (Tertulian), 19

tree(s): body of Christ identified with, 20, 68, 121, 154, 158, 201; in Bonaventure's meditations, 115, 116, 118, 119–21, 124, 137, 197; in Carthusian wilderness images, 167*f*, 169*f*, 170, 170*f*; in comparison of lives of Christ and Francis, 150–53, 151*f*; in *The Desert of Religion,* 186, 187*f*; as emblematic of re-creation, 18, 19, 153, 155; of the fall, 19, 20, 20n48, 21; in Franciscan devotional expressions, 92–93, 127–28, 137, 138n23, 153–55; in frescoes depicting life of Francis, 146–47, 146*f*; as holy matter, 157–58; in *Hortus deliciarum,* 81, 82–83, 83*f*; importance

in Christianity, 18–19; maypole, Suso and, 179; mirror suspended on, Clare of Assisi on, 92; in Pacino di Bonaguida's altar panel, 112–14, 113*f*; and personal transformation, promise of, 153; pervasive imagery of, 18; presence of God in, 3, 10, 21–22, 157–58; in Revelations 22, 154n53; in Ubertino's *Arbor vitae,* 139, 139n27, 140, 155–56, 156*f*, 157. *See also* tree of Jesse; tree of the cross

tree of Jesse *(stirps Jesse),* 15, 19; appeal to women, 63; Bonaventure on, 121; Francis of Assisi and, 129, 130; Hildegard's liturgies and, 63–64, 71, 74–75; iconography of, 19, 63; in *Speculum virginum,* 48–50, 49*f*, 57

Tree of Life (Taddeo Gaddi), 146

tree of the cross, 19–21; Clare of Assisi's focus on, 100, 106, 107, 108–9, 110, 118; in *Lignum vitae* paintings, 112–14, 113*f*

Très riches heures (Jean de Berry), 166

Ubertino of Casale, 150; *Arbor vitae crucifixae Jesu Christi,* 137–45, 155–56, 156*f*, 157; visual depictions of Francis's life based on, 145–49, 146*f*, 148*f*

Ugolino, Cardinal, 94n7, 95–96

Urban II, Pope, 164

Urban IV, Pope, 111

Urs Graf, Bruno cycle by, 166, 167*f*

Ursula, Saint, 72

Vauvert, Paris charterhouse at, 203–4

Verona, San Fermo Maggiore, fresco depicting life of Francis in, 145–47, 146*f*

virga: Hildegard's allusions to, 63, 75–78; musical connotation of, 75; shift to *ligna* from, 93, 118; *virgo* associated with, 19, 75–77

virginity: Clare of Assisi on, 96, 100–105, 101n35; collective, reformed monastic life and, 46; enclosure and, 28, 51, 59–60; Herrad of Hohenbourg on, 79, 84; Hildegard's theology of, 56, 59–60, 61, 66–67, 77–78, 81; as ideal for consecrated women, 25, 32, 33; and incarnation, 31–32, 46, 47, 57, 60, 63–64, 73, 74, 77, 195; Mary as mirror and guide for, 50–51; medieval conceptions of, 31n34; as performance, 43n72; and procreation, 33, 72; and re-creation, 40, 57, 67, 195; *Speculum virginum* on, 22, 30, 31, 50–51; spiritual ideal of, 32, 51, 77, 197. *See also* body of virgin(s); women, enclosed

Virgin Mary. *See* Mary

viriditas, Hildegard of Bingen on, 56, 68n47, 71, 72, 73, 77–78, 89

Vita Jesu Christi (Ludolph of Saxony), 163, 180–84, 185*f*

White, Hugh, 6

wilderness: in Carthusian art, 166–70, 167*f,* 169*f,* 170*f*; in Carthusian devotion, 16, 23, 163, 164–74, 180, 186–88, 190–95; Cistercians' claims regarding, 37; in *The Desert of Religion,* 186–88, 187*f*; Ludolph of Saxony on, 180; Mary's body compared to, 42; monastic ideals and, 15, 16, 38n62; private, cell gardens as, 190–95

William Longespée, 193

William of Conches, 4

William of Hirsau, 27, 39

William of Malmesbury, 39

William of Nassington, 186

William of Newburgh, 42

William of Saint Thierry, 96n16, 97–98

women: and affective devotion, 7–8, 69, 70, 115, 117; and doctrine of re-creation, 8–9, 10; meditation practices of, use of images in, 35; monastic communities of, growth in 12th century, 24–26; pastoral care of *(cura monialium),* 26–27, 29, 30; pauperistic movement among, 95, 111–12; *stirps Jesse*'s appeal to, 63. *See also* cloister, female; women, enclosed

women, enclosed/consecrated: Clare of Assisi on role of, 100, 104–7, 109–10, 115; Herrad of Hohenbourg on role of, 82, 83*f,* 84–85, 86*f*–87*f*; incarnational work of, 9, 34, 51, 63–64, 66, 67–68, 70, 73, 77; role in re-creation, 32n35, 41–54, 67–68; as vessels of the divine, 23; virginity as ideal for, 25, 32, 33. *See also* cloister, female

Wood, Jeryldene, 114n50

world. *See* material world; natural world; re-created world

Žiče, charterhouse of, 173; seal from, 169–70, 170*f*

Zwiefalten, abbey of, reliquary of true cross at, 200–201, 202*f*